What if God Wrote the Bible?

by Scott E. Lane

TRILOGY

What if God Wrote the Bible?

Trilogy Christian Publishers A Wholly Owned Subsidiary of Trinity Broadcasting Network

2442 Michelle Drive Tustin, CA 92780

Rights Department, 2442 Michelle Drive, Tustin, CA 92780.

Trilogy Christian Publishing/TBN and colophon are trademarks of Trinity Broadcasting Network.

Cover design by: Natalee Dunning

10 9 8 7 6 5 4 3 2 1

Library of Congress Cataloging-in-Publication Data is available.

ISBN: 978-1-63769-880-8

E-ISBN: 978-1-63769-881-5

Acknowledgments

I owe a lot too many people in terms of the concepts, writing, editing, and structure of this book. First on that list is Dr. Bill Tierney. Dr. Tierney gave me the idea for this book and the title. He did that at an FCA conference I attended with him in 1986. The questions examined have expanded since I saw his two presentations, and the research has been greatly expanded and updated since those introductory talks. But his concept underpins this work since it was his presentations that led me to do 15-months of study and research and moved me from being a theistic evolutionist to a biblical creationist. For that, I am eternally grateful.

No less grateful am I to the late Dr. Duane Gish, who served as a mentor for me in the field of creation science and edited and vetted my first set of creation presentation notes.

Thanks to the members of the board of the San Antonio Bible Based Science Association, who each contributed in some way by contributing research, critiquing, and helping me edit the multimedia presentations from which this book was originally conceived and structured. Of special note is Dr. Carl Williams, who did some of the initial editing and contributed great ideas on how to structure this book. Dr. Daniel Harris is thanked for his extensive editing and contributions to the Prescience sections of this book.

Thanks as well to the Rev. Jeff Roman, who edited the Philoical and Logical Coherence chapter from a theological poir

I also give thanks to Katelyn Wilkinson, who lent her writing skills to do some of the editing, and to the editors at TBN, who helped finish this work.

Finally, of course, I must give credit to God the Father, Jesus the Son, and the Holy Spirit for guiding me in doing this work and for God's Holy words.

TABLE OF CONTENTS

INTRODUCTION

There were several times in my youth and young adulthood in which I doubted the Bible and my faith due to the apparently rampant incongruities between the "Bible stories" and what science, history, and society say is true today. Further, I was haunted by the wealth of religions across the world and the mathematical improbability that the one religion I was brought up in was the only right one. Research shows that I am not alone.

Our society is more secularized today than ever before and becoming more so each day. The current trends toward acceptance of homosexual behavior, attacks on Christians as being bigoted, and the marginalizing of the Christian faith in America, which has occurred in the last fifty years, underscore this phenomenon. In the 1970s and 1980s, I, like the rest of our society, was on the verge of judging Christianity to be unsubstantiated and passé. Fortunately, someone pointed me to the historical and scientific information I needed to verify my faith in the light of what seems an avalanche of societal beliefs today that the Bible is mythical.

This book was written to answer these questions of faith I had in my youth, and I believe most people have at some time in life. We all have a need to know what "the secret of life" is, or if there is one? We all, at some point in our life, decide what to do with God. Some of us trust him blindly; some reject that he exists. Many make their own version of God, which they tuck away into a corner of their psyche.

I had a dear English teacher in high school who did just that. She thought of God as "daddy," and daddy would never send anyone to hell. That was what she believed, in spite of the fact that the version of God she had invented in her mind was in conflict with the one revealed in the Bible. Unfortunately, our quaint ideas about God and the nature of reality do not become right simply because we want them to be or because they comfort us. Whichever reality is true; there is a God, there is not one, he is the God of the Bible, or the one of the Koran, or anyone of the other myriad of beliefs out there which claim to be the ultimate truth, whatever it is true will not be altered by our comfortable constructs we make in our own mind.

Either there is a God, or there is not one. If there is a God, then he may be the one of the Bible, or the Hindus, or the Koran, but he probably will not be all of these due to the massive differences in these faiths and their descriptions of the Almighty. Truth is truth, and it is not variable nor often comfortable. This book was written to help many to ferret out this deep investigation of truth, which all people go through in their lives. The "big questions" of what is true, is there a God and, who is He? And with this, who and what am I? That is what we are after here.

WHAT IF?

In the Bible, 2 Timothy 3:16-17 (NIV) says, **"All Scripture is God-breathed and is useful for teaching, rebuking, correcting and training in righteousness, so that the servant of God may be thoroughly equipped for every good work."**

This indicates the Bible believes in itself, but is it really truthful and dependable. Is the Bible God's Holy Word? Or is it just the writing of men?

In the summer of 1986, Dr. Bill Tierney, then head of the Biology Department at the U.S. Air Force Academy, presented the concept for this book to me and several other participants in a lecture at Granby, Colorado. The title and concept of this book are the same as what Dr. Tierney showed us that day. The evidence has been refined and expanded over the more than three decades since that talk, and the core assumptions have also been expanded, but the core question is the same.

What If God Wrote the Bible? If God wrote the Bible, what kind of evidence would he leave? What kind of evidence would be left if God was the Creator of all things and the writer/inspirer of scripture? If God wrote the Bible, we would expect to find the following evidence:

1. If the Bible in Genesis relates the original creation account known by man before all other religions and creation accounts, we would expect most origin stories of other cultures to reflect and **borrow elements of the original**;

2. **Historical**—We would expect Geology and History to support the Bible;
3. GOD writing *history* **in advance** in the Bible;
4. GOD would **protect his word**;
5. **Philosophical and logical coherence**—The Bible should hang together as if written by one author with central themes running throughout; and
6. We should find **prescience** in the Bible.

Is the Bible the Original Creation Story in Our World?

We will investigate whether there is evidence the Biblical Creation account was the original creation story predating all others. We will see if most other religions and culture's creation stories "borrow elements" from Genesis as we would predict they would if it were the original. Further, we will see if there is other evidence for the Genesis Creation account being taken as the original creation account preceding all others.

Do Geology and History support the Bible?

It is charged by some that the Bible is full of errors and is not supported by archaeology and historical records. We will examine whether these charges are true. If the Bible was written by God, then the history recorded in its original texts must have been 100 percent factual and without error. The Bible is not purely a history book, but where it does talk of historical events, we would expect to find it error-free in the recording of those events.

Does GOD write History in advance?

If the Bible was written by God, and he is the omniscient (all-knowing) God described therein, then it will reveal his advanced knowledge of what will happen in history. If the Bible is God's Word, it should contain far more verifiable predictions about history than the works of Nostradamus and be free of errors in those predictions. A trick that Nostradamus could not pull off, as his predictions of the future have often been wrong. We will compare what the Bible says with historical occurrences and see if this foreknowledge is in evidence.

Has God protected His Words?

Has God protected his words in the Bible over the centuries, or has it gradually or not so gradually been altered over the centuries? We will examine evidence of whether the Bible has changed over time, been rewritten, or added to by men. Or is there evidence that its message has been miraculously preserved over thousands of years of time?

Philosophical and Logical Coherence

Does the Bible read and "hang together" as if it were written by one author and one mind, or does it appear to be just the writings of about forty men over almost 2000 years? We will look at evidence for the Bible's authorship and whether it seems to have an overall message and purpose. Likewise, we will investigate whether the Bible is full of contradictions within itself (a frequent charge), which would mean it did not have one omniscient writer.

Prescience

The Bible is not primarily a science book. But, since it is supposed to have been written by the Creator of all things, he would have understood the science for that creation thousands of years before we could ever hope to. We will examine if the Bible mentions or alludes to and shows an understanding of science that the men of 2000 and 3000 years ago could, in no way, have known.

Is the Bible the Original Creation Story in Our World?

If the Bible is the work of God, and his creation account is the one original and true account, how on earth would we seek to prove such a thing? We will start by examining creation stories from varied cultures and religions from all over the world and from times past and present. If Genesis is the original creation account, we should find a considerable number of elements that have been *borrowed* from the Genesis account contained in the creation stories of all of these other cultures. Before we start looking at the creation stories of other cultures, however, we need to remember what the Bible says happened at the creation.

In Genesis, Chapter 1 of the Judeo-Christian Old Testament, the Bible says:

> **In the beginning, God created the heavens and the earth. Now the earth was formless and empty, darkness was over the surface of the deep, and the Spirit of God was hovering over the waters.**

It also says God created: light, dry land, vegetation, sun, moon, stars, birds, fish, insects, animals, and finally a first man (**in that order**), each reproducing according to its **kind**. And all of this was supposedly done in **six literal 24-hour days!**

What do we see in other culture's origin stories?

Eastern Creation Stories

Buddhism: *According to Buddhist writings and theology, creation occurs repeatedly throughout time in cycles. At the beginning of each cycle,* **land forms, in darkness, on the surface of the water. Spiritual beings** *who populated the universe in the previous cycle are reborn; one of them takes the form of* **a man and starts the human race. Unhappiness and misery reign.** *(This is today.) Eventually, the* **universe dissolves; all living creatures return to the soul life,** *and the cycle repeats.*[1]

In this chapter, each creation story from the various cultures will be in *italics*. Note the bold portions of this passage on Buddhist creation beliefs, as they look to have elements that are either borrowed from or closely parallel the Genesis account. The order of those similar elements is the same in this Buddhist account as in the Genesis account. Notice that "land forms in darkness, on the surface of the water, Spiritual beings…takes the form of a man and starts the human race, Unhappiness and misery reigns…Eventually, the universe dissolves" is all in the same order in both the Bible as well as this Buddhist creation account. It is interesting that both accounts mention forming the earth or land from water, as creation out of water is a central theme of the biblical creation account.

Chinese Were Monotheistic

Contrary to common knowledge, the Chinese prior to 500 BC were monotheistic (one God). Polytheism (multiple gods) only comes to China with the advent of Taoism and Confucianism around 500 BC. Buddhism would be introduced to Chinese culture around 100 BC, giving them the three major belief systems they have today.

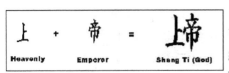

The diagram to the left shows the formation of the Chinese ideographs for their God "Shang Ti," which was formed out of the characters (radicals) of heavenly and emperor.

Note the **bold** passages of this Chinese writing from 2250 BC—Emperor Sun sacrificed to Shang Ti. *"...**in the beginning, there was great chaos, without form and dark. The five elements (planets) had not begun to revolve, nor the sun or moon shine.** Thou, O spiritual Sovereign Shang Ti...**didst divide the grosser part from the purer. Thou madest heaven; Thou madest earth; Thou madest man. All things with reproducing power got their being."*[2]

It should be pointed out that the sacrifices of Emperor Sun were close to those of the Hebrews and included **blood sacrifices of unblemished first-born sheep for forgiveness of sins.** For more than 4000 years (till the emperor was deposed in 1911), the Chinese emperor would sacrifice an unblemished bull to their monotheistic God in a ceremony with prayers, praise, and hymns. This sacrifice was called the "border sacrifice," as it was originally performed on the eastern border of China on top of Mount Tai in Shang Dong and later at Xian at the "Alter of Heaven." In the 15th century, this ceremony was moved to Beijing, and the "Temple of Heaven" complex was built for this purpose. Today this complex is a prime tourist attraction, but few people concern themselves or can find its ancient origins and meanings. In fact, the practices here parallel those of the ancient Hebrews.[3]

As with the Buddhist account, there is a partial restating of Genesis 1:2 when they say, *"in the beginning, there was great chaos, without form and dark."*

The *planets not revolving, nor the sun or moon shining,* is in the correct biblical order because these things did not happen in the Genesis account till Day 4. The correct Genesis order is paralleled when they say, *"Thou madest heaven; Thou madest earth; Thou madest man."* Finally, this Chinese writing refers to the Genesis concept of every animal reproducing according to its **kind** (restated ten times in Genesis 1 for emphasis) and **biogenesis** (life only comes from life) when it said, *"All things with reproducing power got their being."*

It should be noted that an inspection of the early Chinese radicals (picture characters representing words or phrases) includes more than

118 "words," which show a deep understanding of Genesis chapters one through eleven. And this in-depth knowledge of the Bible and Genesis is reflected in a language formed about 1000 years before the first five books of the Bible were put into written form by Moses.

Hence, what we find repeated in the early Chinese language is a repetition of either what the early Chinese brought by "word of mouth" from the Middle East as they migrated eastward, or they had scrolls, tablets, or other "hard writings" which they carried with them of the events of the creation through to the flood.

We will detail more of these radical characters in the next chapter. Because of these, Chinese can be seen as the "smoking gun" of creation accounts which both mirrors and shows an in-depth knowledge of the original Genesis creation account in their own creation story, as well as in their symbolic language.

Pan Gu and Nü Wa (China)

This story is a synthesis of three stories from classical Chinese mythology around 100 BC. It exhibits considerable polytheistic additions in the 2400 years since that of "Shang Ti," which we talked about earlier.

*"Long, long ago, when heaven and earth were still one, the entire universe was contained in an egg-shaped cloud. All the matter of the universe swirled **chaotically** in that egg. Deep within the swirling matter was **Pan Gu**, a huge giant, who grew in the chaos.*

*Many centuries later, there was a goddess named Nü Wa, who roamed this wild world that Pan Gu had left behind, and she became lonely in **her solitude**. Stopping by a pond to rest, she saw her **reflection** and realized that there was nothing like herself in the world. She resolved to **make something like herself for company**. From the edge of the pond, she took **some mud and shaped it in the form of a human being**."[4]*

In this story, everything is originally chaotic, very reminiscent of the Bible, which said that in the beginning the earth was formless and void (chaotic). Pan Gu comes out of the chaos (God). The first goddess in the world is lonely after Pan Gu leaves, as man was in

Eden before Eve. This goddess makes a man in her own image for companionship, just as the "God of the Bible" made a man in his own image. She made this first human being from the mud (dust of the ground in the Bible). All of this resonates with the biblical account, with only the reverse of the creator of man being a woman (although she is a goddess). But like the Bible, this goddess forms the first human being.

It is very instructive to see how very much this creation story deviates from the original creation account revealed by the Chinese language formed some 2400 years before this tale. It had amazing details in perfect harmony with Genesis chapters 1-11. With time, word-of-mouth transmission, and man's tendency to embellish and add to stories, we find creation stories vary over time. People change them to their own liking, and with the infusion of other religions and cultures, we see how much a story we know was in one form originally (which was very close to the Bible), can be transformed into something almost unrecognizably different in a little more than two millennia.

Boshongo, Africa

The Boshongo creation story says, *"In the beginning only darkness, water and the great god Bumba existed. One day, in pain, Bumba vomited up the sun, which dried up some of the water and revealed land. He then vomited up the moon, stars, then animals and finally man."*[5]

In the beginning only darkness, water, and...god. This part of the Boshongo creation account is analogous to Genesis 1:1-2, which interestingly is often the case with creation stories from all over the world. Also, if you get past the "vomiting," you will note that the order of what is created **"darkness-water-god, then sun (or light), dry land, then the moon, then stars, then animals, and then man"** with one partial deviation is analogous to the Genesis order of creation. The land "revealed" out of water is especially parallel to the Genesis account.

Mayans (Central America)

We have now changed continents and hemispheres, but we still find biblical parallels. The Mayan account of creation says, *"In the beginning were the sea, sky and the Maker. The Maker ...created the* **Earth, mountains, trees and animals, but they could not speak. So he created humans first from the mud**_of the Earth (perfected with corn)."*[6]

Note that the bold portions are not only parallel to what Genesis says but in the exact same order. I find it particularly interesting to find the origin story of the Mayans, who were an ocean removed from the creation and thousands of years removed from the biblical account, paralleled the Bible's claim that man was formed from the *dust of the ground* when they say the "mud of the earth!" The cultural infusion of corn into the tale (a nonbiblical element) makes great sense when you know how important that crop was to their livelihood.

Gaia

Much of this account of the origin of the Earth and its divinities comes from the *Theogony* **written by Hesiod, a Greek poet estimated to have lived around 700 BC.**

"In the beginning, there was Chaos, the abyss. Out of it *first emerged Gaia, the* **earth,** *which is the foundation of all. Next came Tartaros, the* **depth in the Earth, where condemned dead souls go to their punishment,** *and Eros…Gaia and Uranus went on to* **have twelve children…** *Prometheus, one of the Titans, made the first* **humans from clay,** *and he brought them fire from Mt. Olympus. However,* **Zeus, as king of the gods** *and no friend of Prometheus,* **became disgusted with the behavior of humans. He and his brother, Poseidon, caused rains to fall and rivers to flood, so that all of the humans would be drowned. However, Zeus finally saw one blameless couple huddled in a boat, trying to ride out the flood, and eventually he decided that they could survive…**

These two survivors were Deucalion, a son of Prometheus, and Pyrrha, a daughter of Epimetheus and Pandora. When the little boat bearing

Deucalion and Pyrrha came to rest in the muddy and mossy landscape, they decided that they must consult the oracle of the Titan goddess Themis to see what they should do, alone in this strange world....[7]

This is an important creation myth in a lot of ways. It starts out as many do with there being nothing but "chaos and the abyss" (nothing) parallel to scripture. It alludes to the creation of the earth as the Bible does but gives it mystical worth as the progenitor of all. It makes mention of the twelve children, which is reminiscent of the twelve sons of Abraham and the twelve tribes of Israel. Prometheus, one of the Titans, *makes humans out of clay* as in the Bible (dust of the ground).

There is a separate special place for the gods (Mount Olympus), just as the Bible has a special home of God being in heaven. Created after god in this story is an evil protagonist, just as the Serpent (Satan) comes along in the Bible after God is introduced.

The head god, Zeus, becomes disgusted with the behavior of humans, just as God in the Bible did, and sent a flood to wipe them out just as the Bible accounts. However, just as in the Bible, this god saw a blameless couple in a boat and allowed them to be saved. When they find dry land, they first consult the Oracle, much as Noah built a place to worship and worshiped the God who had saved him and his family. From this couple, the world is repopulated, just as in the biblical account.

This is an important creation story in that it still resonates with us today in modern society. It is the root of most of the "mother earth" and "mother nature" ideas we have heard of. It gave us the concept of the eternal earth, which so resonates through most eastern religions. Still, with all these differences, we see many parallels with the Hebrew biblical accounts.

The Epic of Gilgamesh and the Enuma Elish (Middle East)

Modernists have posited that the Bible is actually not the original creation story, but that the Epic of Gilgamesh and the Babylonian

Enuma Elish predated the Bible, and thus it is the Bible which borrowed from them.

The reasoning for their position is that the writings of Moses have been dated to around 1450 to 1200 BC (many date its writing circa 1250 BC). The Gilgamesh saga and the Enuma Elish have both been dated to around 1800 BC. Since both of these writings contain elements of the Bible's creation account, it stands to reason they say that the Bible borrowed elements of its creation account from them and not vice versa, and thus the Bible is not the original creation account.

You will read later in this book how the accepted chronology which places the writing of the Bible around 1250 BC is not necessarily true, and the Epic of Gilgamesh and the Enuma Elish may not have preceded the Bible by many years, but for the moment, let us assume this may be true as most Egyptologists and archaeologists agree. Below I have summarized the content of these two ancient writings and how they compare with the biblical account.

Epic of Gilgamesh

The Gilgamesh Saga is an epic poem from Mesopotamia and is amongst the earliest surviving works of literature (dated to around 1800 BC). It parallels the story of Cain and Abel. It also contains nine elements of the story of Noah's Ark and the Flood, as well as heroic battle tales. It is an exceptionally long and detailed story that parallels the Bible in many places.[8]

Enuma Elish

The Enuma Elish is a Babylonian "Creation" Account written in Cuneiform script also around 1800 B.C. It was recorded on seven tablets, each of which corresponds to one of the seven days of the biblical creation week. According to this account, *in the beginning the Earth was without form and empty* (just as the Bible says). Both the Enuma Elish and the Bible suggest that order came out of this formless state. Both records tell of the creation of the plant life, the moon, stars, animals, and man in that order.[9]

Among the similarities in the Bible and the Enuma Elish accounts have remarkably similar order. I have summarized the order of the creation as told in the Enuma Elish below.

Biblical Order in the Enuma Elish

Primeval unorganized matter on first tablet (just as the Genesis account, it says that all the matter in the universe was created on the first day).

Tablet 1—Coming of light (God said, "let there be light" on day 1).

Tablet 2—Creation of the firmament (sky and heavens) (Genesis refers to the creation of the firmament using the Hebrew word *raqia*, which means "expanse" or "spread out thinness" on day 2).

Tablet 3—Appearance of dry land (On day 3 in Genesis, God "separated the waters together into one place and the dry land appeared").

Tablet 4—Creation of luminaries (On day 4 in Genesis, God "placed" the sun, moon, and stars in the sky).

Tablet 6—Creation of man on the sixth tablet (just as God in the Bible created man on the sixth day of creation).

Deity rests (this occurs on the seventh tablet, which is consistent with the biblical account of God resting on the seventh day).

It is clear from all these similarities that it is highly likely one of these accounts borrowed from the other(s). By a pure reckoning of the assigned dates (the Enuma Elish and Gilgamesh written around 1800 BC, Bible written 1450 to 1250 BC) for the writing of these three documents, the modernist claim that the Bible borrowed from the two earlier accounts would seem reasonable. However, there are two "details tests" which linguists and archaeologists use to confirm whether one writing borrowed from another.

The first detail to note is that in a survey of 300 some odd creation accounts from around the world, it is the details of the biblical account which are consistently borrowed and not the details particular to the Gilgamesh saga or the Enuma Elish. This fact could be suggestive of the Bible account having predated these other two writings in some form, and they borrowed from it; or it simply could mean that the Bible, when written about 1400 BC, was far more distributed around the world than the other two. This infers that this "details test" shows a better sense of the Bible's popularity and exposure to other cultures, but not so much attests to it not being borrowed from the other two texts. However, that is one inference that could be made.

The one mitigation to this thought is the fact that the particular details of the Bible are contained in the creation accounts of the Mayans and Delaware Indians, showing that this story was known for centuries before the writing of either the Enuma Elish or Gilgamesh since these cultures would have had to acquire this influence of their accounts before they left the Asian continent, which was well before 2000 BC.

The more telling details test is the linguistic analysis of each text. It has been found by linguistic anthropologists that when one text borrows from another and tells a story based on another source, the second text invariably *embellishes* on the details of the first text.[10] When we examine all three texts, we find that that the *Epic of Gilgamesh* and *the Enuma Elish* are far more embellished stories than the account in Genesis.

This has led many noted scholars to conclude that contrary to the modernist interpretation, the biblical account *does indeed predate* that of the Enuma Elish or Gilgamesh either by word of mouth or in some other written form which we do not now have.[11] (There is mention in the Bible of earlier writings which may be the source of much of what Moses and Joshua edited around 1450 BC. We do not know if this is true since the Bible does not explicitly state this, nor do we have these ancient writings to evaluate today).

As we will find out later, there are far older writings than any of these three, which confirm the biblical account predates not only the Enuma Elish and Gilgamesh but all other contenders.

Before exploring those ancient writings, let us continue our perusal of creation accounts from across the world. More than a billion people across the world claim the Muslim faith. Below I have summarized what we find in Islam's holy book, the Koran (Qur'an), about the creation.

Examples of the Wide Breadth of Sumerian Creation Stories

The Sumerians, as far back as 4500 years ago, would imprint pottery and many other items with stories, contracts, receipts, documents, and much more. They would imprint these cuneiform writings on items by constructing cylinder seals which could be rolled across the wet clay of pottery or any other such item of choice, imprinting on these items the story or images to be transmitted or retained. On these varied items, which have been excavated, we have found a record of many different creation accounts. Here is one good example of what has been found on clay tablets and pottery.

The Sumerians believed that *"their ancestors had **created the ground they lived on by separating it from the water**. According to their creation myth, **the world was once watery chaos**. The **mother of Chaos was Tiamat, an immense dragon**. When **the gods appeared to bring order out of Chaos, Tiamat created an army of dragons**. Enlil called the winds to his aid. Tiamat came forward, her mouth wide open. Enlil pushed the winds inside her and she swelled up so that she could not move. Then Enlil split her body open. He laid half of the body flat to form the Earth, with the other half arched over it to form the sky. The gods then beheaded Tiamat's husband and **created mankind from his blood, mixed with clay**."*[12]

Note the striking similarities with the biblical account here. Land first appears as it is separated from water, just as in the Bible. The world began in watery chaos, just as it is stated in Genesis 1:2. "The mother of Chaos…an immense dragon…" is clearly consistent with biblical stories of Satan as the dragon (or snake) and his creating an army of dragons (fallen angels). Also, as happens so many times, mankind is made from clay (the "dust of the ground").

One of the oldest Sumerian seals shows a seated woman reaching for one of *two fruits hanging from a tree*. A man also reaches for fruit opposite her, and behind her, a *serpent* slithers. This cylinder from ancient Samaria shows every key element from Genesis chapter 3.[13]

Islamic Stories About Creation

Islam shares with Judaism and Christianity the story of a world-creating divine act spaced out over six periods. The Islamic creation account, like the Hebrew one, involves Adam and Eve as the first parents living in paradise. As in the Hebrew account, in the Qur'an, God warns Adam and Eve not to eat fruit from a certain tree, but they do anyway, earning expulsion from Paradise.

The creation narrative of Islam is further developed in many verses in the Qur'an. According to the Qur'an, the skies and the earth were joined together as one "unit of creation," after which they were "cloven asunder." After the parting of both, they simultaneously came into their present shape, after going through a phase when they were smoke-like.

Some parts of the Qur'an state that the process of creation took six days. While other parts claim that the process took eight days: two days to create the Earth, four days to create the mountains, to bless the earth and to measure its sustenance, and then two more days to create the heavens and the stars.

However, the consensus among Muslim scholars is that the process of creation took six days, not eight; they claim that the four days for creating the mountains, blessing the earth, and measuring its sustenance implicitly include the two days for creating the earth.[14]

It is clear from its reading and almost identical details (of which there are many) that this account was derived from the biblical account written about 700 years earlier.

The Qur'an

Thus the Qur'an says *the universe, this world, and all that is in it were created in six days. The Qur'an talks of Adam and Eve as the first humans created by God. It tells of their eating the forbidden fruit and being expelled from Eden. The Qur'an even includes the flood and its coming to rest on a mountain* (although not Mount Ararat).

Note, like so many of the creation accounts of the 300 we studied, the Qur'an uses uniquely biblical details. This book is just another to reflect a variety of recurring themes seen in creation accounts from around the world. While these recurrent themes are not contained in all of the 300 creation accounts cited, they do recur in most of them. A list of these recurrent themes found in the Qur'an and most other creation stories are recorded below.

Recurrent Themes

Beginning—darkness and water
A single God or Creator
Biblical order—heavens, land, vegetation, animals, and man
Sacrifice of a God/man
Pain and suffering come into the world
Human race comes from a first man (often made from mud/dirt)
Spiritual beings
Earth is dissolved in the end

The Worldwide Flood

One of the most striking of these recurrent themes, which are repeated in 270 creation accounts from around the world, is the recurrence of flood legends.

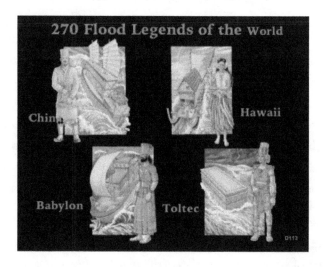

The details differ in some ways from one story hereto the other, but again there are recurrent themes that are striking. All tell of a *great flood which killed off all life*. All tell of a *giant boat being built and that man and animals were saved from the flood on this boat*. Some details attest to how closely they were to the original in the Bible and that they are tied to the biblical account. Such minute details as Noah's name are repeated or only slightly skewed. For example, in the Hawaiian tale, the boat builder's name is either "No" or "Nuu" in their language, and in the Delaware Indian's account, his name is "Nenabush."

Let's look at a small sample of these flood legends from across the world.

Hawaii

According to the Hawaiian flood account, *long after the first man, Kuniuhonna, the world became a wicked and terrible place to live* (congruent to the biblical account). *There was only one good man left in the world, and his name was Nuu* (again consistent with the biblical account).[15] *Nuu built a large boat or house raft to save his family from a flood. When the boat landed safely at Mauna Kea in the Hawaiian Islands (the highest point in the Hawaiian Islands), Nuu offered pigs and coconuts to the moon in thanks. In response, the Creator descended on a rainbow to reveal to men that he saved mankind.*[16]

The story is obviously skewed from the original, as any generationally retold story is. But, many main themes of the world getting very wicked, only one good man left, Noah's family being saved by the patriarch building a boat, a huge flood destroying all life but that in the boat, offering sacrifices and worship to God after their deliverance and the association of the rainbow with the flood all make it clear that this flood story was a residual of the original biblical account. The similarities are just too close and numerous.

American Plains Indians

One American Indian tribe (the Pawnee) has a flood legend that tells of how *giants on the earth offended the creator, which they* called *"Ti-ra-wa." Because of this, God drowned them in a flood. Then he made the first man and woman, who became the ancestors of the Pawnee people.*[17]

One attribute of these flood accounts, which we will expound upon later, is that the farther you get from the Middle East, where we believe the flood account was originally recorded and taught, the more the stories seem to be changed and corrupted from the original. Due to the distance traveled by these peoples, they are becoming isolated from the original cultures of the mid-East, and the inaccuracies of retelling these stories over generations by individuals without the support of the original culture, such huge variances are to be expected in these accounts.

In this case, these Indians have morphed the biblical accounts of giants from the Bible such as Goliath, the Nephilim, the flood account destroying all life on earth, and the creation account so that their flood account is embedded in their creation or recreation account. But the similarities of a flood brought by God to destroy all life on earth because of our offenses and an original man and woman being provided by God at the creation all forcefully point to this account being a residual of the original biblical account. Remember also that earlier in this chapter, we showed you multiple examples of other occasions like this where over time and distance by the inefficient transmission of "word of mouth," we saw some very morphed accounts combining the worldwide flood and the creation. Both, however, point back to the original biblical accounts.

The Maidu Creation Legend

The Maidu are a Native American people of northern California. In the Maiduan language, Maidu means "man."[18] The following is a capsulation of the Maiduan Creation Legend.

"In the beginning there was no sun, no moon, and no stars. All was dark and everywhere only water existed. A raft with two persons floated on the water. From the sky the "Earth Initiate"

came down on a rope to the raft. **His face was covered and never seen**, nor could be seen by man. **His body shone like the sun.**

Turtle was one of the two beings in the raft. He dove into the water to get earth. After **six years** he returned, covered in slime and with **dirt under his fingernails. Earth Initiate took this dirt, formed it into a ball and with it emerged the land.** Earth Initiate called on his sister to come up and there was **the light of the first sunrise.**

Earth Initiate then called on his brother to rise and the **moon arose for the first time. He called the stars by name and the stars appeared. He then made a tree which grew and shaded them. Coyote and rattlesnake** were then formed **out of the ground.** Coyote could see the Earth Initiate's face.

Earth Initiate then made birds of the air, more trees then animals. Out of mud he made first the deer then all other animals.

In the middle of the afternoon he began to make people. He took dark red earth, mixed it with water and formed the first man and woman. He laid them together in his house which no one else could enter. He laid man on his right side and woman on his left. In the early morning the woman began to tickle his side, but he did not react. **These two first people shone of white like no one since.** The Coyote does laugh at her tickles.

The cunning Coyote tells the first lie.

All fruits are easy to obtain and people do not have to work. No one ever gets sick and dies. When one grows old they may always venture to a special lake of water and regenerate as young.

Coyote talks them out of this easy existence by not following Earth Initiate's rules and gave into their burning desires and sets to compete amongst one another in races. The Coyote's son is killed in the first race.

A year after this everything has changed. **Al people had spoken the same language. But, people had a burning and everyone began to speak different languages and we thus separated into different tribes who went off to live in different directions.**

Everyone will now have all kinds of troubles and accidents.
They will have to work to get food and will die and be buried.
This will continue till the Earth Initiate returns and at that time
everything will be made over into its original perfect state. Coyote
in the end sees his son and he is not dead! Coyote then kills himself
in his burning for food."[19]

This is, of course, a strikingly parallel legend with respect to the biblical account. There is absolutely nothing in the beginning except water. There are originally two people or persons, as in the Bible. God, known as "Earth Initiate," comes from the sky (heaven) and interacts with his creation as God did in the beginning in the Bible and in Eden. God's face cannot be seen by men, and his body shines like the sun, as is many times described in the Bible.

Earth is formed from the water, as in the Bible. The turtle dives to get the mud to form the earth and is under water for six years, very reminiscent of the six days of creation in the Bible. The sun, moon, and stars (even calling each star by name as the Bible says God can) are called on to appear as God did in scripture. He first formed a single tree that shaded them, reminiscent of the "Tree of Life" in the Garden of Eden. All animals and man will be made from the ground or mud (biblical dust of the Earth). The first animals to appear are the rattlesnake and coyote. The snake is frequently the first animal to be mentioned in creation accounts as it refers to the biblical reference of the serpent in the Garden of Eden. In this account, the coyote is mentioned with the snake, and the coyote is given the role of Satan, the liar. It is of note that the coyote is also in the role of Satan in Navajo creation legends, showing a borrowing of these accounts.[20]

The first pair of man and woman are formed by God, and he lays them in His house (Eden). The man on his right (favored side) and the woman on his left. She tickles His side (reminiscent of a woman being taken out of man's side in the Bible), but God does not react. Satan (the Coyote), however, does and shows knowledge of the woman giving into Satan. These first two people had a bright white sheen to them. This is an observation prevalent in a lot of creation accounts, which may allude to their state of grace as sinless people in line with God's original created intentions as described in the Bible.

They begin in an Eden-like environment with easy-to-get food and designed to live forever. However, the Coyote (Satan=serpent) gets them burning with desires and sets them against one another in competitions. In the first competition, the coyote's son is killed, very reminiscent of the killing of Abel, son of Adam and Eve, and the perceived competition between the brothers, as perceived by Cain, in the Bible.

As in the Bible, all people originally spoke just one language, and the biblical Babel account is retold here with their languages confused and their separation into different lands.

After the "fall of man," everything, it says, has changed. They have to work for food, they have many troubles, and will eventually all die and be buried. These are all recounted in the Bible as effects of the curse brought about by man's fall from God's grace in Eden and their expulsion from Eden.

Just as in the Bible, it is promised that God will return at the end of the world and remake this world back into its original perfect state. The son is not dead, who was thought to be, perhaps a reference to the Messiah. The coyote (Satan) dies in the end, as he does in scripture. It is both amazing, and I think revealing, to see an origin story so paralleling the biblical account from a people, who lived on a different continent and hemisphere from the Hebrews, and which was obviously separated from the original account for thousands of years. Anyone who says that this creation legend was not heavily influenced and based on the biblical account is not being honest with themselves.

Toltec (Mexico)

The Toltec Indians of Mexico have a flood legend that tells of a *"first world" that lasted for 1716 years* (this is amazingly close to the biblical total of 1656 years listed in the Masoretic text of the Bible) before *a great flood covered even the highest mountains. It tells that a few men escaped the flood in a "closed chest," which they called a "toptlipetlocali."*

Following the flood, the men built a great tower to provide safety. However, during the construction of the tower, their languages were confused, and they wandered to other parts of the world. This Toltec legend says that seven friends and their wives "who spoke the same language" crossed "great waters," lived in caves, and journeyed for 104 years till they came to the "Hue Hue Tiapalan." Also known as southern Mexico.[21]

Again, the biblical parallels are striking, with the idea of a pre-flood world being quite different from today, just as it is related in the Bible. They built a boat and survived a great flood. This account even parallels the biblical account of Babel, the confusion of the languages, and the dispersal of all humankind. Anyone, who would dispute that this legend, written in a different hemisphere than the Hebrews and thousands of years later, was not patterned after the biblical account, and these people informed of the biblical account, is lying to themselves.

Peru

Peruvian Indians have an account of *how the creator, which they called "Viracocha," sent a flood to destroy all the unruly giants on the Earth which he had made. Only two giants survived this flood, on a boat, which they say landed at Tiahuanaco."* The creator then made animals to fill the earth, and he made people from clay.[22]

Again, due to time, distance, and bad transmission, this story is highly skewed and morphed from the creation account, but the original biblical details of God bringing flood destruction because of his creation's sins, salvation from the flood was on a boat, that at the creation God started with two beings and he also made animals to fill the Earth and made us all from clay (the dust of the ground as the Bible states it), makes it unmistakable where these details came from, the original biblical account. It also has mixed into it the retelling of giants among us before the flood as told in the Bible. This infusion of the giants with this detail also being in the Toltec legends shows that one of these stories influenced the other.

Hudson Bay, North America

According to the flood legend of Indians in America's Hudson Bay region, *"one of the gods" became angry at the giants and decided to drown them in a flood. But, this one god warned a man to build a large canoe. The man sent out an otter (in the Bible it was a dove), who retrieved dirt from which the man remade the earth.*[23]

In this case, again, the flood story is severely skewed by time, distance, and faulty transmission, but it still has enough marks of the original to make it clear where at least one of its sources was from.

Scandinavia (Far Northern Europe)

"When Odin (their primary god) killed the first frost giant, Ymir, his blood deluged the earth. The frost giant Bergeimer and his wife survived in a hollowed out tree."[24]

This is only a brief excerpt of how this story begins. This story, like the last, is highly corrupted with infusions of the heavy winter climate they existed in and their resultant culture. But, the mentions of giants, God angry with them, saving a man and his wife in a makeshift boat all make it clear they are reminiscent of the original biblical account. Let's see what the flood legends look like when we get closer to the Middle East.

Inca Creation Story (Western South America)

This story is as recorded by Incan priests, from the iconography on Incan pottery and architecture, and the myths and legends which survived amongst the native peoples. According to these accounts, in the most ancient of times, *"the earth was covered in darkness."*

"Then, out of a lake called Collasuyu (modern Titicaca), the god Con Tiqui Viracocha emerged, bringing some human beings with him. Then Con Tiqui created the sun (Inti), the moon, and the stars to light the world. It is from Inti that the Sapa Inca, emperor of Tawantin

Suyu, is descended. **Out of great rocks, Con Tiqui fashioned more human beings, including women, who** *were already pregnant.*

Then **he sent these people off into every corner of the world. He kept a male and female with him** *at Cusco, the "navel of the world."*

Con, the Creator, *was in the form of a man without bones.* **He filled the earth with good things to supply the needs of the first humans. The people, however, forgot Con's goodness to them, and rebelled. So, he punished them by stopping the rainfall. The miserable people were forced to work hard, drawing what little water they could find from stinking, drying riverbeds."** [25]

The earth covered in darkness sounds familiar. A god then emerges from a lake (water). How often does water play a part in these stories?! The creation of the sun, moon, and stars to light the world could be lifted right out of the Bible. Humans are fashioned out of rocks (dirt). This story includes the dispersion of mankind like the dispersion at Babel but also keeps the first couple back in a special place living with God, like the Garden of Eden in the Bible. The first humans were given everything they needed, just like Adam and Eve, but again like Adam and Eve, it is said they "rebelled." In turn, their god punished them with a hard life. The parallels with the Bible in this story are easy to see.

Akkadia (Mesopotamia—Middle East)

*"***Angry over human** *noise, the* **gods decide to flood the earth.** *But, the kind* **goddess Ea warned Utnapishtim to build a cube shaped ark** *to save his family and animals from the worldwide flood."* [26]

In spite of the mention of multiple gods in their religion, note how much closer and with firm biblical details added this account comes to the biblical account of the flood. As we get closer, in regards to time and distance to the Middle East, the lands of the account in the Hebrew culture (Genesis), and source of the flood account, we find the accounts grow ever closer to the original. This is what we would expect if the Hebrew account was the original creation account.

Babylonia (Middle East)

Babylonian records list *ten "great kings" who lived before a great flood came to destroy the Earth. One man survived this flood, and all of the people of the Earth descended from this one man.*[27]

This fable again alludes to a pre-flood world, a great flood, and the repopulating of the world via one man or family. As was the custom in Middle Eastern cultures of the time, only the man and not his family or especially wives or daughters would be mentioned, as only men were spoken of in records. Also, it should be noted the list of ten "great kings" amazingly coincides exactly with the ten generations of man listed in the Bible from Adam to Noah prior to the flood.

Tanzania (Southern Africa)

According to their flood legend, *God told two men to take seeds and animals onto a boat so they could survive a mountain covering flood. These men sent out a dove and then a hawk to see if the earth had dried up.*[28]

Again, we see details such as seeds and animals from the biblical account preserved in this flood legend closer to the Middle East origin point. The inclusion of a dove being sent out to find dry land is another close detail.

China (circa 100 BC)

According to one Chinese legend, *a sky god flooded the earth. A brother and a sister survived on a boat. They had a deformed child which the brother cut into pieces. The earth was repopulated from the pieces.*[29]

Gross, but illuminating. This account gives the echo of the flood account of the Bible we find all over the world, but again, as we move away from the Middle East, we see time, distance, and faulty human word of mouth transmission seriously corrupting the details.

Another Chinese flood legend is far closer to the original. It relates that *Fuhi was the "father of their civilization." It says that Fuhi and his wife, their three sons, and three daughters escaped a great flood. He and his family were the only people left alive on the Earth. After the great flood, this family repopulated the Earth.*[30] If you do not see the biblical references here, you are not conscious!

Western Australia

According to their flood account, *a man named Gajara and **his family survived a worldwide flood** on **a raft that he had built. He sent out birds to see if the waters had receded.*** Pleased by the smell of cooking kangaroo, the **god Ngadja placed a rainbow in the sky to stop the rain clouds**.[31]

Although this story is heavily skewed from the original by time, distance, and poor transmission, it has unmistakable elements which are reflective of where this story came from.

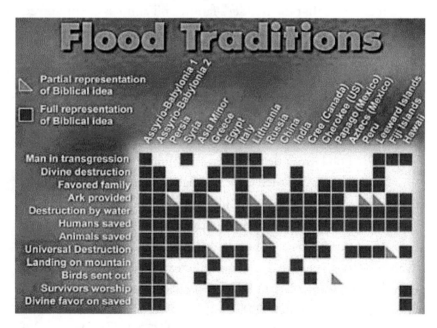

This table shows how many of these details are distributed in creation accounts from across the world. Of special note, please recognize how close the Assyrian, Babylonian, and Persian accounts are to the original biblical text. Also, note how these accounts seem to become more skewed and more varied from the original as those cultures are farther from the Middle East. This is exactly the pattern we would expect to see if the Bible was the original source of these accounts, and details are lost and embellished upon as these peoples moved farther and farther away from the Middle East and the original source.

Nippur Tablet c. 2100 BC

These fragments of stone, with writing in a language very akin to ancient Hebrew, give evidence of the biblical creation account 300 years before either the Epic of Gilgamesh or the Enuma Elsih were written. These writings were found in a library excavation in the Babylonian City of Nippur.

The text of these fragments tells of a deluge that destroys all life on Earth. It says that God commanded the building of a great ship. It also says that the builder's family and animals are preserved on this ship.[32]

These tablet fragments excavated in the 1890s include broken lines of text saying, "It shall sweep away all men together... before the deluge coming forth... Build a great ship... It shall be a houseboat carrying what has been saved... [br]ing the beasts of the field, the birds of heaven." The references here are clearly referring to the worldwide flood event described in the Bible.[33]

This is just the first such evidence that says we have far more than details tests to tell us that the biblical creation account was composed and widely known far before the Enuma Elish or Gilgamesh epic. The next two pieces of evidence, Chinese ideographs, and The Wallam Olum, show that the biblical creation account was known to man as far back as 2500 BC and predates the Enuma Elish and Gilgamesh by more than 700 years!

This evidence is an inconvenient truth for skeptics but is well documented. This evidence not only gives details in lock step with the biblical account, but it also verifies the biblical claim and view of biblical archaeologists that the biblical creation account predated Gilgamesh and the Enuma Elish. This also makes it very likely that Genesis was the account from which both of these Babylonian creation accounts were copied or drawn from. Again, this is counter to the claims by many Bible skeptics, which claim the Bible was written much later and, in fact, borrowed from these other two works.

Chinese Ideographs

The Chinese language was first encoded into a written text circa 2500 BC in the form of word/concept pictures or ideographs. These ideographs are composed of simple base pictures called "radicals," which stand for simple concepts or words. These radicals can be combined to form other words or more complex concepts. An example of this is shown with formation of the word "boat" in Chinese. To form the word boat, the ancient Chinese chose to put together the radicals of "vessel," "eight," and "mouths" (the symbol translated "mouth" here could also mean "persons").[34]

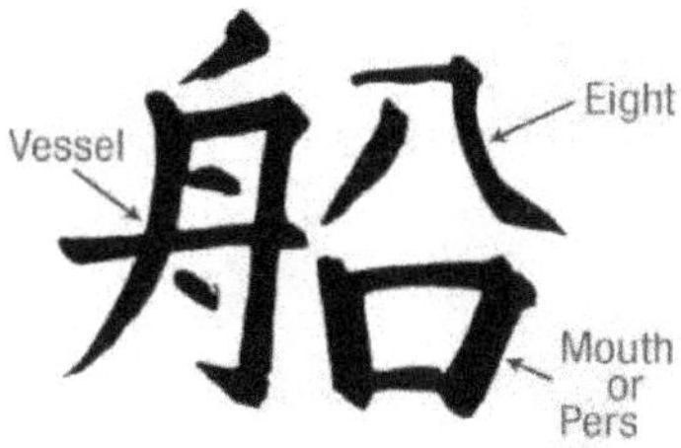

Chinese symbol for "boat" c. 2500 BC (diagram from www.ocf.berkeley.com)

Now, this example is not only instructive in showing you how the Chinese written language is structured, but it also shows you our first hint of the secret of Genesis hidden in the Chinese language. I understand why someone would use the concept of "vessel" to define a "boat," but why would the Chinese choose to use "eight" and "mouths or persons" to define a boat? The answer that the Reverend C. H. Kang came to over fifty years ago was that they were referring to the Genesis flood account and the Bible's statement that there were "eight people" on the ark.

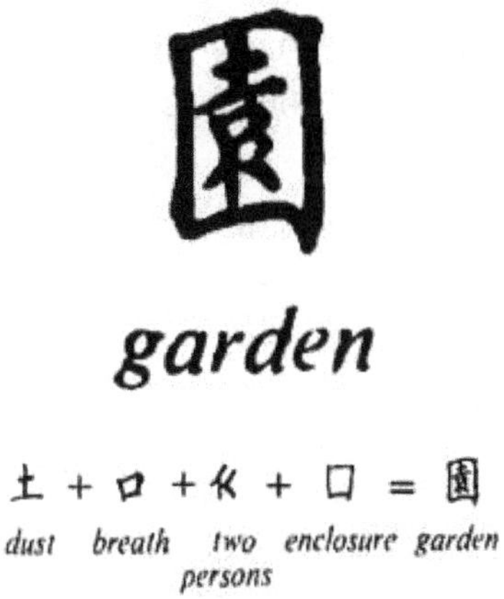

The Discovery of Genesis, C.H. Kang and Ethel Nelson, p. 54

The case for this connection between Genesis and the Chinese language becomes more and more evident as you examine other Chinese ideographs. Another excellent example is the Chinese symbol for garden. The symbol is composed of the radicals for "dust" + "breath" + "two persons"

+ "enclosure" = "garden." What other garden could these ancient Chinese have been thinking of when they formed this word than the Garden of Eden where man was first formed from the "dust of the ground," first given the "breath of life," where "two people" first lived together?[35]

If a person without a biblical insight were forming this word, they would likely have used symbols for flowers or trees to form the word "garden," but their use of these biblical concepts shows that they were exposed to the Genesis account prior to 2500 BC when the Chinese written language was formed.

More examples are found in the formation of the words for "devil and tempter."

To form "devil," the ancient Chinese put together the radicals for "secret" + "man" + "garden" + "alive." This could easily allude to the devil's suggestion to Eve in the garden that the secret to knowledge and life was in the fruit.

Further, the word symbol for "tempter" is composed of all for these radicals for "devil" + "trees" + "cover," for it was in the *trees* that man first sinned by eating the fruit of the tree they were forbidden to eat of. After this, they tried to "cover" themselves to hide their shame.[36]

It is apparent from these examples that the ancient Chinese were well acquainted with the story of Adam and Eve, the garden, Satan, and even Noah.

I do a presentation that features 115 more examples of this knowledge of the Bible in Chinese, making it crystal clear that the ancient Chinese knew of the Genesis account more than a thousand years before Moses wrote it down and more than 700 years before the Enuma Elish or the Gilgamesh saga. In fact, these symbols reveal an intimate knowledge of not only Adam and Eve and Noah but also of Babel, the dispersion, "the curse," and biblical theology. You already saw in a previous example the concept of the *Trinity* revealed in the Chinese language. There is no reason whatsoever for the "God Spirit" to be described in such a clear way of "three persons hovering over the waters" unless they had been exposed to God's Word.

What is so very striking when I go over these ideographs is how clear the intent and theology are. Moreover, how it does not waiver in the slightest from the Genesis account we see in the Bible today. Indeed, this is a "God thing" we will talk about later, illustrating how God has protected His word for more than 4500 years in a miraculous way.

But what this evidence says about the Bible, being the first origin account, is clear. This is just another of the 300 origin accounts from around the world which contains elements of the Genesis account, but it predates the Bible by a thousand years, indicating as we would expect (if it's God's words) the Genesis account was known to man from the beginning of our existence. Thus, this account existed in man's memory long before Moses wrote down the first five books around 1400 BC.

"Wallam Olum" (Red Record)

Another great example of this truth is the "Red Record," which is the history of the "Lenni Lenape" (meaning "original people") which appear to be our oldest Indian records (these are the Delaware Indians). Their "Wallam Olum" (translated "Red Record") tells the creation account and history of the Indians crossing of Asia and the Bering land bridge into North America. Such details place the origins of the document to more than 4000 years ago.

Their history was recorded in their own ideographs or picture symbols, as shown to the right. Each picture symbol is related to a word or concept, just as in the Chinese language and in Egyptian Hieroglyphics.

This record was given to Dr. Ward by a Delaware Indian in return for medical help given by him in 1820. The record was on sticks or tablets made from wood bark. Dr. Ward gave the "bark sticks" to botanist and antiquarian Constantine

Samuel Rafinesque. Rafinesque purportedly translated this record and published a translation in 1836.

Although this record has been questioned today, intense studies of its authenticity in the 19th century seem to verify it quite nicely. While there was controversy about the *Wallam Olum*, it was treated as a genuine account by historians, anthropologists, and archaeologists for more than 100 years. Ephraim G. Squier, widely regarded as an influential figure of American 19th-century archaeology, republished the text in 1849. He accepted it as genuine, partially on internal evidence, but also because the educated Indian chief (*Kah-ge-ga-gah-bowh*) (aka George Copway), to whom he showed the manuscript, "unhesitatingly pronounced it authentic, in respect not only to the original signs and accompanying explanations in the Delaware dialect, but also in the general ideas and conceptions which it embodies as what had been taught to him as a boy in their culture. He also bore testimony to the fidelity of the translation." It should be noted that many elements of this account are shared by the Hurons and Ottawa Indians, which the Delaware were akin to giving further credence to this creation story being reflective of their original account. The French circa 1600 were amazed how close their creation accounts were to the Bible[37]

More recently, in the 1990s, linguists have questioned the translation techniques of Rafinesque. They claim the account was anglicized (made to conform to the Bible) in the mid-19th century. As a result of their work, the council of the Delaware Indians has withdrawn their support for this record as being theirs. It looks, however, as if this was a political move to make the Delaware Indians a more legitimate modern player and not be seen as only a stem of the Judeo-Christian account and to avoid becoming a part of the creation controversy. Today, many scholars and many Delaware Indians still believe this record is authentic and testify that it relates to the creation account they have been taught from birth.[38]

While this record is controversial, I also side with the scholars who believe it is genuine and its contents are in striking agreement with the Genesis account. In this account, it says that the "Great Spirit" created everything from water, just as the Bible contends. It further agrees with the Bible that land was separated from the waters, and different kinds of creatures were formed next. Both accounts say the last to be created was a man... followed by a woman (correct biblical order). Both say people originally lived in harmony with each other and were created immortal, meant to live forever.

The *Wallam Olum* says evil and turmoil entered this world only after a *snake* brought corruption into creation, which is amazingly close to a summary of the biblical account of the *serpent*. The picture (at right) shows a Delaware Indian pictograph of the snake's interaction with humans and conflict.

After this, the Red Record says things deteriorated until a great flood came, which coincides with the Bible. The record says "Nenabush" built a vessel and brought humanity through the great flood (just as Noah did in the Bible). Fascinating how in so many of these stories, the Noah character has a different name, but that name frequently starts with an "N" (or that dialects equivalent)! After this, the record tells of *the trek through great fields of ice* to North America.[39]

These records show that the Genesis account predates the Enuma Elish and Gilgamesh and all other accounts by many hundreds of years!

It is also interesting to note the resemblances between many Chinese and Delaware Indian Ideographs. Both the Chinese and Delaware Indian glyphs for "fruit" show a flower sprouting from the ground. Glyphs in both languages are very similar. The Chinese glyph for misery is very reminiscent of the Delaware glyph for sorrow. The symbols in each language for prayer, garden, and many other concepts are similar to each other. This may indicate these ideographs not only came from a shared experience and knowledge of the Bible, but also that these two groups may have diverged from each other along the trek of their two cultures across Asia. Such a scenario is very consistent with the biblical account of the dispersion after Babel.

Recurrent Themes From
Creation Stories From Across the World

Many of these stories begin in darkness, and the generation of light is part of the creation itself. In many stories, humans and other beings are made from clay, mud, or the dust of the ground. Creation from clay has often been cited as evidence of a primitive culture, at least by people from cultures with stories of creation "*ex nihilo*" (from nothing), but both are biblical.

One story from a seemingly primitive culture nonetheless has elements that accord well with modern science. The *Jicarilla Apache* story, in which a human is made from a variety of mineral and organic materials, is comparable with our modern view that the human body physically consists of many chemical substances and that our intake of "minerals" is critical to our health (but it also says we were made from the dirt as in the Bible).

It should be noted that of the more than three hundred creation stories reviewed for this study across the world and throughout history, the twenty-nine presented in this book are very representative of the whole. Most of these stories were picked randomly to represent the wealth of creation myths and stories from across the world. The only filter for their inclusion was to make sure that we had a good representation of accounts from all six continents and all major cultures.

Only five of these creation accounts were specifically selected for themselves to be included in this sampling. Those include the *Genesis account*, which of course, was included to show what all other accounts were to be compared to. Also deliberately included were the *Gilgamesh Saga* and the *Enuma Elish*, which we felt had to be included for their antiquity, as well as to examine the charge that the Bible was somehow sourced from them. We also intentionally included the *Chinese Ideographs* and the *Wallam Olum* account to show how the full and intact Genesis account can be traced to a period almost a thousand years before Moses was to have written it all down just after 1450 BC. None were included just because they showed more tendencies toward the Genesis account. Thus, from this chapter, you can know that you got a pretty good feeling for how creation accounts from across the world compare to the biblical account.

The chart on the next page shows how many biblical elements can be identified in creation stories from across the world. Note that as you go to the right on the chart, you get ever further away from the Middle East and are moving away from where the Bible was written. The Sumerian and Egyptian texts (close to the Genesis origin point) have most of the biblical creation elements, but that fades as we move away from the Middle East. As we get away from where the Bible was written, the tales become more skewed from the original, as we would expect if our thesis is correct of the Bible being the original creation account that fed most others.

But distance is not the only factor in how story elements are lost or skewed. Time and stability of culture seem to be even more of a factor.

Notice how the Qur'an, written in the Middle East but more than 2100 years after the Bible, varies from the Bible more than the older Sumerian and Egyptian stories written closer to when the Bible was put down. Also, notice the similarities to the Bible in what is revealed in the Chinese Writings circa 2500 BC and the vast differences in the Chinese Creation account from 100 BC. This reveals that time, retelling by word of mouth, and copying errors play massive roles in the skewing of stories from the original.

The Wallam Olum (Delaware Indians) is an outlier to this rule and points to the possibility of its being preserved since it was held in an early symbolic language and not by word of mouth. Another difference between the Chinese and the Delaware Indians is the stasis of the Delaware Indian culture as opposed to the Chinese culture, which morphed from monotheism to polytheism a few hundred years before the 100 BC account.

However, it is also possible that this is evidence that the skeptics are right, and Wallam Olum was artificially injected with biblical tenants in the 19th century. If this is true, however, and the Wallam Olum was eliminated from this data set, it would make the data on this chart an even stronger data sample. In that case, time and distance from where and when the Bible was written would be in an almost perfect correlation for our thesis of retained or lost biblical elements.

Creation Stories from across the World / Biblical Elements	Enuma Elish / Sumerian	Egypt	Koran (Middle East)	Greek / Roman	Yoruba of Nigeria	Wakaranga Zimbabwe,	Brahmanas Upanishad	Naba Zid-Wendé (West	Chinese Writing (2500 BC)	Pan Gu/ Nü Wa China (100	Korean	Norse / Scandinavia	Cherokee	Hopi Indians	Wolum Olum (Delaware)	Mayans	Aztecs	Peru	Aborigines	Kono people of Guinea	Japan	Maori (New Zealand)
Nothing / chaos	x	x				x	x					x	x	x					x	x	x	x
Man 1st Immortal	x	x													x				x			
2 Original Humans	x	x	x	x		x	x		x	x	x	x			x			x		x	x	x
Dirt, dust, clay	x	x	x		x				x	x					x			x	x	x	x	
Day and Night	x	x	x					x														
Tree of Life	x		x	x						x												
Snake or Serpent	x	x	x	x		x			x		x			x	x	x			x			
Single Creator	x	x	x	x	x		x		x					x	x			x	x			
Create Light	x	x				x	x													x		x
Start with Water	x	x	x			x	x	x				x	x	x	x	x						
Biblical order	x	x			x				x					x		x	x	x		x		
Eden Environment		x	x	x	x	x			x					x		x			x	x		
Six or Seven days	x		x								x			x						x		
Land Appearing	x				x	x	x						x	x		x	x				x	
Create Luminaries	x			x				x														x
Evil enters World	x	x	x	x	x	x			x				x	x		x			x	x	x	
Babel - Dispersion	x			x					x					x	x							
One Language to many				x					x					x	x					x		
Deity Rests	x		x			x																
Flood / Boat	x		x	x					x	x	x	x		x	x			x				
Fighting Brothers	x	x		x									x							x		x
Trinity	x					x			x												x	

There are some elements of the more than three hundred creation stories from across the world and throughout history which do recur but are not totally in accord with the idea that almost all creation stories reflect that they were initially derived from previous knowledge of the Genesis account. For example, some stories tell of a "primordial egg" from which the earth, a god, or all life came from.

Another recurrent theme in some stories is that of birth from a primordial mother god, previous existence, or an undefined cosmos. These themes do not predominate, as you have seen from the wide variety of samples we have shown you. However, they are easily explained as not being a part of the original Genesis account, but instead as very reasonable inclusions over the centuries for cultures to inject into their creation stories, since these nonbiblical elements are tightly aligned with our human concepts of how we see things **begin** or come into being today in nature.

It Was the Original!

Did we find evidence for the Bible's creation account in the book of Genesis to be the original creation account? A perusal of more than 300 creation stories from all over the world showed what we expected to find if Genesis is the original creation account. The vast majority of these stories contained threads, if not large portions, which either were very reminiscent of the Genesis account or were clearly copied from that account. The logical conclusion to be drawn from everything we have covered so far is these borrowed elements and themes reflected in creation stories from cultures all over the world and, for thousands of years, indicate they all came from or were influenced by this original work, the Bible. This transmission may have been from people who were handing down stories by word of mouth or via other writings with the same creation account and the same theological tenants copied from the Bible!

This evidence is so clear that such noted anthropologists as PhDs. Kenneth Kitchen, D. J. Wiseman, Garry Brantley, and Charles Pfeiffer have all declared the Bible to be the original source of the creation accounts we see around the world. Thus, Genesis is the original creation account as we expected to find if God wrote the Bible![40]

Now, if we had not found ample evidence for the Bible's creation account in hundreds of creation accounts and stories from all over the world, it would have put our premise of God's authorship of the Bible into serious doubt. The fact that we do find such evidence all across the world fulfills our premise for this evidence, but it only starts to make a circumstantial case for God writing or inspiring others to write the Bible. While we have good evidence for the biblical account of creation being the first and most widely spread account of the world's creation, it is still possible that that is all it is; the first, the most widely repeated, and borrowed from story of creation, but not necessarily the truth of creation, nor God's Word.

Skeptics will also point out that since all of these stories concern creation and there are limited ideas as to how "we came to be," such that there were bound to be similarities between these tales whether they came from one original story or not. Such a charge could be true, but the question on the similarity of origin stories is only the first in our set of several questions we will examine to determine if God is actually the author of the Bible.

Skeptics aside, the answer to the question of whether the Genesis account was the world's first creation account seems to be yes. Thus, the evidence we have so far examined makes a good case for searching further to see whether there is more evidence of God's authorship of the Bible.

What about Historical Records?

It is rumored that the Bible and historical accounts are sometimes in conflict, showing that the Bible is in error and thus not inerrant and thereby not God's word. **What's the truth? If the Bible is God's word, then we would expect it to be completely truthful and that we can confirm its accuracy via historical and anthropological records and discoveries.**

Dr. Robert Dick Wilson (1856–1930)

One of many people to take up this investigation of the Bible's accuracy and authority as God's word was the brilliant 19th and 20th-century scholar, Dr. Robert Dick Wilson. His exceptional intellect is shown in the fact that he graduated from Princeton at age 20!

Wilson was a deep believer in Christ and the God of the Bible. He devoted his life to the investigation of biblical translations and interpretations to understand the original meanings of God's word. He spent 45 years of his life studying the Old Testament.

To make his investigations possible, competent, and exhaustive, he spent years becoming fluent in Hebrew and all related languages. He also learned and became fluent in all of the languages the Bible was translated in up to 600 AD so that he was not dependent on others' work in evaluating translations from one language to another.

Dr. Wilson rejected the "Higher Criticism" by many scholars over the past several centuries that the Bible is full of errors and thus not inspired by God. His intent was to make Old Testament criticism and evaluation of the Bible an absolutely objective science, based on evidence rather than on opinions, as is so often the case. He made a detailed analysis of the Old Testament, showing the bulk of it to be archaeologically supportable. His work featured a close inspection of the book of Daniel, in which he found archaeological support for most of it as real history, as he did with most of the rest of the Old Testament.

One of many research efforts he worked on was of twenty-nine kings of Israel, Egypt, Moab, Damascus, Tyre, Babylon, Syria, and Persia as found in the Bible and on historical monuments found by archaeologists. His research found that of the twenty-nine selected kings, which were both mentioned in the Bible and for which we have archaeological evidence detailing their lives, the Bible in its account of them was found to be 100 percent accurate! This is a miraculous achievement for the Bible due to the very limited libraries and ability to exchange information three thousand years ago!

After studying documents and artifacts that were up to 4000 years old, Wilson found that the Bible correctly named every one of the ancient kings, placed them in the correct country, and listed them in correct chronological order. No other document even comes close to the accuracy of the biblical account on this subject.[41]

By comparison, Ptolemy's (the great Greek historian, scientist, and philosopher) writings list only nineteen of the twenty-nine kings researched by Wilson. **Ptolemy misspelled them all.** That is not surprising with respect to the extremely limited resources available to Ptolemy, as previously discussed. The God-like miracle is that the Bible arguably got all twenty-nine of the king's names spelled correctly. (The biblical spellings of three of these kings' names are debated. An impressive feat in itself, considering the antiquity of the writings being drawn from and the fact there are 195 Hebrew consonants with no vowels. Therefore, it is many times debatable how Hebrew terms, words, or names should be translated into the spelling of other languages which do have vowel constructs.) Thus, the case can be made that there are essentially no errors anywhere in the biblical record of these accounts as verified in other historical writings.

We are deeply indebted to the scholarship, devotion, sacrifice, and faith of men such as Dr. Wilson, who have given us such unequivocal proof of the inerrancy of scripture right down to the spelling of ancient names![42]

Sir William Ramsay (1851–1939)

Educated in the "Tubingen School of Thought" at Oxford, Sir William Ramsay was taught and believed in the "Higher Criticism," which said the Bible was only very error-filled writing of men and not inspired by God. He was the son of two atheists and an atheist himself.

As a scholar, archaeologist, and committed atheist, he found the biblical New Testament book of Acts to be ripe for proving biblical inaccuracies. Luke, a medical doctor, wrote the book of Acts and the Gospel of Luke. In the book of Acts, Luke mentions 32 countries, 54 cities, 9 Mediterranean Islands, and 95 people groups (65 of these people groups are not mentioned elsewhere in the New Testament). That's 190 historical facts that can be verified or found in error. Sir Ramsey believed this would be an easy book to prove error-prone as he believed the entire Bible to be.

In the late 1800's Ramsay spent twenty-five years in Asia Minor (Turkey, among other countries) trying to disprove Luke's careful documentation in the book of Acts. He investigated over one hundred of these historical facts cited in the book of Acts. Every reference from the Bible which could be verified via archaeological evidence was found, to his astonishment, to be 100 percent correct.[43]

How could Luke have been so accurate? Luke was not one of the original disciples. All of his sources were secondhand observers. His writings were based on his conversations with disciples and relatives of original disciples about seventy years after Christ's birth. He had no access to modern libraries, information technology, and the matters he was investigating were not supported by the governments of the time, and thus, getting this information was made even more difficult. Even modern journalists make errors. But, Luke, about forty years after the fact, with few eyewitnesses and fewer information resources, compiled a book with 100 percent historical accuracy. It seems impossible for him to have done that without divine help!

In Ramsay's book, "*The Bearing of Recent Discovery*," he concluded: "Further study… showed that the book (Acts) could bear the most minute scrutiny as an authority for the facts of the Aegean world, and that it was written with such judgment, skill, art and perception of truth as to be a model of historical statement."[44]

On page 89 of the same book, Ramsay said, "I set out to look for truth on the borderland where Greece and Asia meet, and found it… [in Acts]. You may press the words of Luke in a degree beyond any other historian's and they stand the keenest scrutiny and the hardest treatment…"

When Ramsay turned his attention to Paul's letters, most of which the critics dismissed as forgeries, he concluded that all thirteen New Testament letters that claimed to have been written by Paul were authentic.

Sir William Ramsey's twenty-five years of archaeological excavations and investigations turned him from being an atheist into being a firm believer in the Bible and our Savior Jesus Christ. Amazingly, the Bible converted a skeptic and atheist, who was bent on disproving the Bible into a believer! What he found in twenty-five years of scholarly research was that the Bible was not only true, but that God existed and had a plan for his life!

The Trail of Skeptics, Who Have Been Converted by the Bible

Actually, there is a long list of people throughout history, and some very recently, who have set out to prove the Bible wrong and, after painstaking research, came to the opposite conclusion. Their research proved to themselves that the Bible was not only valid but the work of God. Thus, these previous skeptics were converted to faith in God by the evidence compiled during their research, like Ramsey.

Four of the more recent examples of this phenomenon are Frank Morison, Lee Strobel, Josh McDowell, and Andre Kole.

The book "*Who Moved the Stone?*" by Albert Henry Ross (written under the pen name of **Frank Morison**) was to be a treatise on Christianity as a fraud. It turned out instead to be a great defense of the resurrection of Christ as a historical fact. The author started out to write a book debunking the "myth" of the resurrection and ended up becoming a Christian and writing one of the best-known defenses of the resurrection as a result of his research into the resurrection. It was written in 1930 and continues to be printed and circulated today.[45]

Lee Patrick Strobel (born January 25, 1952) is an American Christian apologetic author and an investigative journalist. He originally set out to disprove the Bible and the Christian faith when his wife was converted to the faith and intended to teach it to their kids. He was an unbeliever and horrified of this. It made him set out to prove to her that the Bible was false and Christianity had no validity.[46]

As in the cases before, however, his research led him to the inescapable conclusion that the Bible and Christianity were valid, and he has converted to the faith. He has written several books, including four which received ECPA Christian Book Awards (1994, 1999, 2001, 2005) and a series that addresses challenges to a biblically inerrant view of Christianity. His classic book is the *Case for Christ*. Strobel also hosted a television program called "Faith Under Fire" on PAX TV and runs a video apologetics website. Strobel has been interviewed on numerous national television programs, including ABC's 20/20, Fox News, and CNN.

Josh McDowell considered himself an agnostic as a young man. He honestly believed that Christianity was worthless. In college, however, he did a research paper in which he truthfully tried to examine the evidence for the faith and the Bible in an effort to disprove them and support his agnostic position. "However, when challenged to intellectually examine the claims of Christianity, Josh discovered compelling, overwhelming evidence for the reliability of the Christian faith ... After his conversion, his plans for law school turned instead to plans to tell a doubting world about the truth of Jesus Christ. After studying at Kellogg College, Josh completed his college degree at Wheaton College and then attended Talbot Theological Seminary, where he graduated Magna Cum Laude with a Master of Divinity degree."[47]

Andre Kole, one of the most well-known illusionists in the world, was challenged, as he was a skeptic, to investigate the validity of the miracles of Jesus from a magician's point of view. That investigation eventually convinced him that Jesus was really his Savior. Kole has been quite prolific in his field since he has been named "Inventor of the Decade" by the International Magicians Society and has been awarded by The Academy of Magical Arts in Hollywood (from "Inside Magic." 2004. Andre Kole's Mission of Magic)…

In one of his informative essays, *"Magic and the Bible,"* Kole says that he was about 25 years old when he "was challenged as a magician and as a skeptic to examine the miracles of Christ from a magician's point of view." However, "In making this investigation," explains Kole, "I not only discovered that Jesus Christ had to be, who He claimed to be the Son of God and the Savior of the world; but I also discovered that He is the "magic" ingredient, who really makes life worth living."[48]

Don't "Rubbish" the Bible

More than a hundred years ago, a venerable college professor in England was putting up with a young student, who was complaining about, tearing down, and generally trashing the Bible as an error filled writing of men. His professor eventually told him that it was not wise, as he put it, to "rubbish the Bible" because that book had an amazing way of coming back to haunt any claim made against it when researched.

Dr. Robert Wilson (1856-1930 reliable Hebrew Bible) found this to be evident in his research. Sir William Ramsey (1851-1939

NT scholar) was converted to Christianity by his research, which had been intended to disprove the faith. Frank Morrison (journalist/lawyer 1900) also was converted by research of the Bible. Josh McDowell set out to do a college paper disproving the Bible and instead proved the existence of the God of the Bible to himself and millions of others through his writings, speaking, and ministry with "Campus Crusade for Christ." Lee Strobel used his journalistic training to investigate the faith of Christianity and the Bible to disprove it to his family. In the course of his research, he was converted by the evidence he found. Andre Kole researched skeptically the miracles of Christ from a professional magician's perspective and was converted to the faith by the evidence of these being true miracles and not man-made illusions.

All of these unbelievers and many more did years of research to disprove the Bible and became believers as a result of their research.

Quirinius, Governor of Syria

A favorite way to discredit the Bible in the 1800s was to point out what the Bible said about Quirinius, the governor of Syria. The book of Luke says that Quirinius was governor of Syria when Jesus Christ was born. Other passages in the Bible and research of extra-biblical sources have convinced us that the standard calendar used today is off and that Christ was actually born in around 4 BC. Nonreligious records known in the nineteenth century showed that Quirinius was made governor of Syria after 6 AD. This discrepancy was used by Bible critics, and those who believed in the "higher criticism" to show the Bible was not inerrant and thus could not be written by God!

This is one of the things which first drew Sir William Ramsey to do his research on the book of Luke, convinced that it was full of such errors which would prove that the Bible was not inspired by God. This puzzle was solved, however, in 1912 when further archaeological evidence was uncovered. In 1912, an ancient inscription, dated to have been written around 10 BC, was found saying that

Quirinius was governor in Syria and Cilicia. Apparently, Quirinius ruled in Syria during two different periods of time, as do so many of our governors today. After more than a century of belief that historical records verified that the Bible was in error, it was found that Quirinius could have been governor of Syria at the time of Christ's birth, just as the Bible recorded.

This one supposed Bible contradiction, which was untrue, had been used for more than a century to mislead people to believe the Bible had been disproven. The damage done in the lives of so many people over this falsehood pushed by so many in the "*intelligencia*" who wished to believe in this lie and thought they had the evidence to prove it, makes me shake my head at the damage we inflict on ourselves and the self-delusion we enforce upon ourselves as a species.[49]

The Wall of Jericho Fell Out!

We have found and excavated the biblical city of Jericho. The walls had fallen out as the Bible describes, rather than been pushed in by an attacker, as might be logical otherwise.

It could not have been the strategy of the Israelites to use grappling hooks to pull down the walls, as the outer and inner walls contained an earthen berm more than 30 feet across (so wide dwellings were built atop it), and the outer wall was more than 20 feet high. Thus, grappling hooks would serve only to pull a few rocks off of the outer wall without giving access to the city.

It is clear that the Israelites could not have accomplished what we see at the excavation. Indeed, it would have taken an enormous event such as tornadic activity or earthquake to get the effects we see. However, the focused effect we see at the site of the inner and outer walls being collapsed out at spaced intervals around the city seems clearly intentional. The collapses form ramps allowing the Israelites easy and surrounding access to the city and its inhabitants. This is exactly the scenario they would need to affect an invasion of the city (and this scenario agrees with the biblical account). Such regular intervals and perfect ramps attest not to random seismic or weather activity, but to direct intervention by force beyond the abilities of man at that time. An inspection of these ramps shows they were certainly not made by grappling hooks nor (aside from one main entrance) were they natural entrances into the city as designed by the cities residents. They are unmistakable evidence of the truth of God's Word![50]

Ebla Tablets

This collection of 1800 complete tablets, and 4700 fragments, discovered in the 1970s in northern Syria, were written in Sumerian and Cuneiform script. They are Babylonian / Syrian writings that talks about Sodom and Gomorrah and life in the biblical land of Ur. The Ebla talks of cities which at the time of tablet's discovery were otherwise unknown in archaeology, and skeptics had said that they did not exist except in the error-prone Bible. These finds confirmed the existence of these ancient cities mentioned in the Bible. They further talk about Abraham and other biblical characters dating to a time between 2250 and 2500 BC.[51]

These tablets are very consistent with the Bible when they said, "Lord of Heaven and Earth...The Earth was not, you created it.... The light of Day was not, you created it."[52]

Thus, these are not only archaeological finds which confirm biblical accounts, but these stand as another cultural set of artifacts that show a creation story very consistent with the biblical account.[53]

Further confirmation of the Abraham accounts was found when Abraham's home and the city of Ur were excavated by Sir Leonard Woolley in the 1920s and 1930s. Woolley from this dig also discovered that as much as 500 years before Abraham's time, fully 20 percent of all homes unearthed had writing materials showing how widespread writing was. And the writings were diverse, ranging from books to records, receipts, and more. This is evidence against the skeptics' claims, which hold that Abraham and even Moses, who would live several hundred years later, could not write, and therefore,

Moses could not be the author or editor of the first five books of the Bible, as he is credited with being.

These writings, found both in the Ebla tablets and the excavations of Woolley, verify that writing was widely used 1000 years before Moses, falsifying the biblical error claim that Moses could not have written the first five books of the Bible since writing was not taught, nor practiced yet. We also have the "Black Stele of Hammurabi" find, which has writing on it dated 300-400 years before Moses, which gives further evidence of writing predating Moses and verifying that the Bible could have been written as described.

Wooley further uncovered evidence from Abraham's time that people were skilled in Algebra, Geometry, and Quadratic Equations. This information fits in well with the biblical worldview that man started out very smart (perfect in the Garden of Eden) but degenerated over time. Rather than the secular worldview that we were first cavemen and gradually developed upwardly.[54]

Slings and Stones Verified as Major Weapons in History

The Bible mentions slings and stones being used as deadly weapons by individuals such as the young King David and by whole armies. David is said to have used the sling and stones to kill Goliath, according to 1 Samuel chapter 17. The Bible also describes 700 Benjamites (members of one of the twelve houses of Israel) who it says used slings and stones and were so practiced and skilled with them that they never missed! (Judges 20:16) Incidentally, the Bible also says that all of these 700 men chosen by God were left-handed. That should put to rest some people's misconceptions of the Bible being the source of now properly discarded myth of left-handedness being the "devil's paw" and forcing kids to write right-handed.

Archaeological finds have now verified that "slingers" played an important part in the Persian, Greek, Roman, and various Mesopotamian armies and were considered to be equal to or better than bowmen. Although used most extensively in Europe and the Near East, evidence of its usage can be found throughout the world, with the notable exception of Australia.[55] This evidence not only gives credence to the biblical accounts but shows that the Bible is relating factual accounts of that day.

Joseph in Egypt

One scholar commented that "the clustering of Egyptian loan-words in Genesis chapter 41 (The Joseph account) and Exodus 2:3 (the description of Moses basket), suggest that the writer knew the cultural setting that he was writing about, and was not making it up in another land, centuries after the event... The author's comment about Egypt in Genesis 13:10 and his statement about Zoan in Numbers 13:22 also suggest a firsthand knowledge of Egypt. Moses fits such a writer well."[56]

Further Egyptian records, as well as the Mari and Hammurabi texts of the period of Joseph, reveal how accurate the biblical details are.[57]

The price Joseph was sold into slavery for in the Bible, 20 shekels (Genesis 37:28), is exactly the slave price in the Mari, Hammurabi, and Brooklyn Papyrus, all from the Joseph time period. By the time of the 5th century BC, during the Persian exile (when some critics think the Joseph account was invented and inserted), the price of a slave had risen to over 90 shekels. You see, we are not the only persons who ever had to deal with inflation! That is a tenant of currency systems throughout time. A fifth-century writer inserting the Joseph account would have to have known the correct price of a slave 1000 years earlier, and that is highly unlikely with the lack of records, archaeology, and libraries in that time.[58]

The texts of the time show that the biblical names such as Potiphar, Zaphenath-paneah, Asenath (the name of Joseph's wife in Genesis 41:45), and Potiphera found in Genesis 39:1 and 41:45 are authentic to the period.

Until the time of Rameses II in the 13th century BC, it was common for the title of Pharaoh to stand alone with no name added, as occurred in the biblical Joseph account. We will explore more of the meaning of this cultural detail in our Exodus section, but for now, it is another consistency with the biblical account and the culture of the time.

The phrase "overseer of the house" used in Genesis 39:4 is exactly the phrase used in Egyptian texts early in the second millennium BC. Taskmasters, brick quotas, and straw for brick making described in Exodus 5:6-8, as well as the holidays for religious festivals described in Exodus 5:1, and foreigners working as slaves talked of in Exodus 1:14 are all attested to in the concurrent Egyptian writings of the time.

According to Genesis 50:2 and 26, Jacob and Joseph were mummified and placed in coffins. But, neither mummification nor coffins were known in Canaan during the Bronze Age (3000 to 1200 BC). This points to an Egyptian context for these accounts[59]

The writings of Moses in the Bible make a very specific claim that the people of Israel were in Egypt for exactly 430 years, according to Exodus 12:40-41. Question—could the ancients tell time this well, to be so exact? Excavations of Mesopotamian sexagesimal timekeeping (using base sixty) and finds of ancient Egyptian base ten calendars, as well as the previous invention of water clocks, all show that this type of time and calendar keeping was possible in ancient times.[60]

The Supposed Numbers Contradiction

By one reading of Exodus 12:37, there were some 600,000 fighting men who left in the Exodus from Egypt, which would have made the entire traveling party about 3 million. This would be a huge logistical problem in all respects for Moses and the Israelites.

Six hundred thousand fighting men would have dwarfed the Egyptian army of the time, which archaeology has shown to be about 24,000 men. Also, archaeological estimates of the population of Canaan at the time (15th century BC) put the total population of just 140,000 total, meaning that a force of 600,000 Israelites would have overwhelmed the Canaanites, even if there were "giants."[61]

According to Exodus 23:30, God promised to drive out the Canaanites "little by little" until Israel's numbers were large enough to occupy the land. Deuteronomy 7:1, 9:1, 11:23, and 20:1 all warn that the Canaanites are more numerous than the Israelites are. This would not have been true if the Israeli army was at a strength of over half a million men.[62]

The Hebrew word for thousand (*eleph*) can refer to a thousand, as it seems to in Genesis 20:16, a clan or family as it does in Joshua 22:14, Judges 6:15, and Micah 5:2, or a "unit" as it does in the context of 1 Samuel 17:18. The context must decide the meaning, and the meaning can change even in the same context. This means the problem here is not with the accuracy of the text but with contextual translation.

This means that Exodus 12:37, rather than being read as 600 thousand men, could be read as 600 units of men. A military unit at the time was approximately ten men.[63]

This would give the Israelites at the time an army of about 6000 men and a total traveling population of about 30,000, plus the Levites and the "many other people," who accompanied Israel according to the book of Exodus. This number is not only logistically more tenable for this trip and Moses' leadership, but it fits all the rest of the biblical statements of the Israeli army throughout the books of Exodus and Joshua.[64]

Interpreted in this way, Exodus 12:37 does not pose a contradiction or biblical error, which contradicts what we have found through archaeology, but rather supports what other documents and archaeological finds have uncovered.

Three Hypothesis of The Pentateuch Apart From Moses as Single Author

The Torah (or Pentateuch) is the collective name for the first five books of the Bible: Genesis, Exodus, Leviticus, Numbers, and Deuteronomy. According to Hebrew tradition, they were dictated by God to Moses or written by Moses under the inspiration of God. Moses used either word of mouth accounts handed down to him, or possibly he partially copied from other writings handed down by the Hebrews. But when modern critical scholarship (by modernists) began to be applied to the Bible, it was frequently theorized that the Pentateuch did not appear to be the unified text of a single author. Thus, the Mosaic authorship of the Torah had been largely rejected by secular scholars since the 17th century, and the modernist consensus is that it is the product of a long evolutionary process of multiple authors over a period of as much as a thousand years.[65]

The documentary hypothesis, supplementary hypothesis, and fragmentary hypothesis are three models used to explain the origins and composition of the first five books of the Bible via such fragmentary and evolutionary concepts. All three agree that the Torah is not a unified work from a single author (traditionally Moses) but is made up of sources combined over many centuries by many authors and editors. They differ on the nature of these sources and how they were combined. According to the documentary hypothesis, there were four sources, each originally a separate and independent book or document, joined together at various points in time by a series of editors (also called "redactors").[66] The Fragmentary hypotheses see the Torah as a collection of small fragments, and supplementary hypotheses suggest a single core document was supplemented by fragments taken from many sources.[67] This would make the first five books of the Bible the product of multiple sources far exceeding the four-source documentary hypothesis theory.

A version of the documentary hypothesis, frequently identified with the German scholar Julius Wellhausen, was almost universally accepted for most of the 20th century, but that consensus has now collapsed. As a result, there has been a revival of interest in fragmentary and supplementary approaches, frequently in combination with each other and with a documentary model, making it difficult to classify contemporary theories as strictly one or another. Modern scholars increasingly see the completed Torah as a product of the time of the Achaemenid Empire (probably 450-350 BC), although some would place its production in the Hellenistic period (333-164 BC) or even the Hasmonean dynasty (140-37 BC).[68] Of its constituent sources, Deuteronomy is generally dated between the 7th and 5th centuries

BC; there is much discussion of the unity, extent, nature, and date of the Priestly source material (one of the four unidentified sources for the documentary hypothesis). Deuteronomy continues to be seen as having had a history separate from the first four books, and there is a growing consensus by modernists that Genesis developed apart from the Exodus stories until joined to it by what they call "the Priestly writer."[69]

Please note, however, that in spite of all of this secular criticism over the last three hundred years, no consensus has emerged, with varying theories coming to the forefront and then falling out of favor. It is just as probable that the Pentateuch is a collection of accounts handed down to Moses via word of mouth and lost books of antiquity. Secularists noting that the Bible is the product of several sources might, in fact, be true, but not in the way modernists frequently try to steer the interpretation of the linguistic data. Most biblical scholars believe that the Pentateuch was edited and put together from multiple sources, including completion of the work by Joshua in the last book. But most biblical scholars also agree that it is perfectly possible for all of this to have occurred in the fifteenth century BC when Moses lived and does not have to be moved to the fifth century BC, which would tend to delegitimize the Pentateuch as being the inerrant word of God as written by Moses.

The Jewish Talmud, however, holds that Moses was the major, if not only author of the first five books of the Bible.[70] This statement is not falsified if it turns out that he was both the author of much of it, as well as the editor, who included much outside information.

Reasons to Reject the Documentary Hypothesis

There are many reasons to reject this skeptical attack on the Bible. First, consider what the Bible itself says about the authorship of the Pentateuch.

The Pentateuch states that Moses wrote these books in Exodus 17:14; 24:4; 34:27; Numbers 33:1–2; Deuteronomy 31:9–11. In his rejection of Mosaic authorship, Wellhausen nowhere discussed this biblical evidence. It is easy to deny Mosaic authorship if one ignores the evidence for it. But that is not an honest scholarship.

We also have the witness of the rest of the Old Testament in Joshua 1:8; 8:31–32; 1 Kings 2:3; 2 Kings 14:6; 21:8; Ezra 6:18; Nehemiah 13:1; Daniel 9:11–13; Malachi 4:4. Each of these writers, from Joshua to Malachi, testify to their belief that Moses was the author of the Torah. The testimony of Joshua is particularly persuasive since he would have been an eyewitness to this.

The New Testament is also clear in its testimony: Matthew 19:8; John 5:45–47; 7:19; Acts 3:22; Romans 10:5; Mark 12:26. The divisions of the Old Testament were clearly in place in the Jewish mind long before the time of Christ, namely, the Law of Moses (first five books of the Old Testament), the Prophets (the historical and prophetic books), and the Writings (the poetic books of Job, Psalms, Proverbs, etc.). So, when Jesus referred to the Law of Moses, His Jewish listeners knew exactly what He was referring to.[71]

Moses' qualifications to Write

Dr. Terry Mortenson and Bodie Hodge of Answers in Genesis said in their article, "Not only is there abundant biblical witness that Moses wrote the Pentateuch, Moses was fully qualified to write the Pentateuch. He received an Egyptian royal education (Acts 7:22) and was an eyewitness to the events recorded in Exodus to Deuteronomy, which contain many references or allusions to Egyptian names of places, people, and gods, as well as Egyptian words, idioms, and cultural factors. He also consistently demonstrated an outsider's view of Canaan (from the perspective of Egypt or Sinai). And as a prophet of God, he was the appropriate recipient of the written records or oral traditions of the patriarchs from Adam to his own day, which the Holy Spirit could use to guide Moses to write the inerrant text of Genesis. There is no other ancient Hebrew, who was more qualified than Moses to write the Pentateuch."[72]

Some modernists have suggested that in spite of his Egyptian education, writing was not that developed for almost all of the general public in the fifteenth century BC, so no one, including Moses, could have written all this. That idea has been "put to bed" by multiple evidence that complex writing not only existed at the time of Moses but for many centuries before him. There is also good evidence that it was commonplace among the general populace, not just the elite, to use writing frequently (we documented evidence for this in the Ebla section of this chapter).

Fallacious Reasoning of the Skeptics

Another reason for rejecting the documentary hypothesis and accepting the biblical testimony to the Mosaic authorship of the Pentateuch is the erroneous assumptions and reasoning of the skeptics.

They assume their conclusion. They assumed that the Bible is not a supernatural revelation from God and then manipulated the biblical text to arrive at that conclusion. They were implicitly Deistic or atheistic in their thinking. They assumed that Israel's religion was simply the invention of man, a product of evolution, as they believe all religions are.

Based on evolutionary ideas, they assumed that "the art of writing was virtually unknown in Israel prior to the establishment of the Davidic monarchy (around 1000 AD); therefore, there could have been no written records going back to the time of Moses." This claim not only attacks the intelligence of the ancient Israelites but also the Egyptians, who trained Moses. Were the Egyptians incapable of teaching Moses how to read and write? Since the time the documentary hypothesis was first proposed, archaeologists have discovered scores of written records pre-dating the time of Moses. It is hard to believe that Israel's ancient neighbors knew how to write, but the Jews could not.

Liberal Bible scholars allegedly based their theories on evidence from the biblical text, and yet they evaded the biblical evidence that refutes their theories. Theirs was a "pick and choose" approach to studying the Bible, which is hardly honest scholarship in pursuit of truth.

Further, they arbitrarily assumed that the Hebrew authors were different from all other writers in history. They made the very biased assumption that the Hebrews were incapable of using more than one name for God or more than one writing style regardless of the subject matter. They even denied that they could use more than one of several possible synonyms for a single idea.

Their subjective bias led them to illegitimately assume that any biblical statement was unreliable until proven reliable (though they would not do this with any other ancient or modern text), and when they found any disagreement between the Bible and ancient pagan literature, the extra-biblical text was automatically given preference and trusted as a historical witness. This practice violates the well-accepted concept known as "Aristotle's dictum," which advises that the benefit of the doubt should be given to the document being analyzed rather than the critic. In other words, the Bible (or any other book) should be considered innocent until proven guilty or reliable until its unreliability is convincingly demonstrated.[73]

Although many examples have been found of ancient Semitic authors using repetition and duplication in his narrative technique as Moses did, skeptics assume that when Hebrew authors did this, that this was compelling evidence of multiple authorship of the biblical text.[74] Again, this is a claim not made with other texts.

The skeptics erroneously assumed, without any other ancient Hebrew literature to compare with the biblical text, that they could, with scientific reliability, establish the date of the composition of each book of the Bible.[75] In fact, they give little or no weight to the biblical dating clues.

To date, no manuscript evidence of the J-document, E-document, P-document, D-document (the supposed four unknown sources for the documentary hypothesis), or any of the other supposed fragments have ever been discovered. And there are no ancient Jewish commentaries that mention any of these imaginary documents or their alleged unnamed authors. All the manuscript evidence we have is for the first five books of the Bible attest to the Pentateuch existing just as we have it today. This is confirmed by the Jewish testimony (until the last few centuries) that these books are the writings of Moses.

Is the Documentary Hypothesis the Same Thing as the Tablet Model of Genesis?

These two ways of dividing Genesis are not similar at all. The Tablet Model is based on the Hebrew word "*toledoth*," which appears eleven times in Genesis (Genesis 2:4; 5:1; 6:9; 10:1; 11:10; 11:27; 25:12; 25:19; 36:1; 36:9; 37:2) and helps to tie the whole book together as a single history. Our English Bibles translate "toledoth" variously as "this is the account" or "these are the generations" of Adam, Noah, Shem, etc. Scholars disagree about whether each toledoth follows or precedes the text with which it is associated. In this case, the name associated with the toledoth is either the author or custodian of that section. Regardless, the eleven uses of toledoth unite the book as a history of the key events and people from the Creation to the time of Moses.

Unlike the JEDP model, the Tablet model shows a reverence for the text of Genesis and attention to these explicit divisions provided by the book itself. These divisions represent either oral traditions or written texts passed down by the Genesis patriarchs to their descendants, which Moses then used to put Genesis into its final form under the inspiration of the Holy Spirit.

We think it very likely that Moses was working with written documents because the second toledoth (Genesis 5:1) reads, "this is the book of the generations of Adam," where "book" is a translation of the normal Hebrew word meaning a written document. Also, the account of the Flood after the third toledoth (Genesis 6:9) reads like a ship's log. Only evolutionary thinking would lead us to conclude that Adam and his descendants could not write. Early man was highly intelligent: Cain built a city (Genesis 4:17), six generations later, people were making musical instruments and had figured out how to mine ores and make metals (Genesis 4:21-22), Noah built a huge boat for his family and thousands of animals to survive a year-long flood, etc.[76]

Answering a Few Objections

A number of objections have been raised by the proponents of the documentary hypothesis. We will respond to only a few of the most common ones. But the other objections are just as flawed in terms of logic and a failure to pay careful attention to the biblical text.

Skeptic's claim: "Moses couldn't have written about his own death, which shows that he didn't write Deuteronomy."

The death of Moses is recorded in Deuteronomy 34:5-12. These are the last few verses of the book. Like other literature, past and present, it is not uncommon for an obituary to be added at the end of someone's work after he dies, especially if he died very soon after writing the book. The obituary in no way nullifies the claim that the author wrote the book.

In the case of Deuteronomy, the author of the obituary of Moses was probably Joshua, a close associate of Moses, who was chosen by God to lead the people of Israel into the Promised Land (for Moses was not allowed to because of his disobedience), and who was inspired by God to write the next book in the Old Testament. A similar obituary for Joshua was added by an inspired editor to the end of Joshua's book (Joshua 24:29-33).

Skeptic's claim: "The author of Genesis 12:6 seems to imply that the Canaanites were removed from the land, which took place well after Moses died?"

Genesis 12:6: "Abram passed through the land to the place of Shechem, as far as the terebinth tree of Moreh. And the Canaanites were then in the land."

So the argument is that an author, after Moses, had to have written this statement to know that the Canaanites were removed in the days Joshua, who began judging the Canaanites for their sin after Moses died.

To this claim, there are two clear responses. First, Moses could have easily written this without knowing that the Canaanites would be removed after his death because due to warring kingdoms or other factors, people groups did get removed from territories. So, it was just a statement of fact about who was living in the land at the time of Abraham. But secondly, it could also be a comment added by a later editor working under divine inspiration. The editorial comment would in no way deny the Mosaic authorship of the book of Genesis. Editors sometimes add to books by deceased authors, and no one then denies that the deceased wrote the book.

Skeptic's claim, "Genesis 14:14 mentions the Israelite region of Dan, which was assigned to that tribe during the conquest led by Joshua after Moses died. So Moses could not have written this verse."

Genesis 14:14–15 (NKJV):

Now when Abram heard that his brother was taken captive, he armed his three hundred and eighteen trained servants who were born in his own house, and went in pursuit as far as Dan. He divided his forces against them by night, and he and his servants attacked them and pursued them as far as Hobah, which is north of Damascus.

Genesis 14:14 mentions Dan. However, Dan in this context is not the region of Dan, that Israelite tribe's inheritance given when the Jews took the Promised Land, but a specific ancient town of Dan, north of the Sea of Galilee that was in existence long before the Israelites entered the land. Jewish historian Josephus, just after the time of Christ, says:

"When Abram heard of their calamity, he was at once afraid for Lot his kinsman, and pitied the Sodomites, his friends and neighbors; and thinking it proper to afford them assistance, he did not delay it, but marched hastily, and the fifth night attacked the Assyrians, near Dan, for that is the name of the other spring of Jordan; and before they could arm themselves, he slew some as they were in their beds, before they could suspect any harm; and others, who were not yet gone to sleep, but were so drunk they could not fight, ran away."[77]

This specific place (Dan) was known to Abraham (long before Moses) as one of the springs of Jordan. It is possible that Rachel was already aware of that name (Dan), as it meant "judge," and used it for the son of her handmaiden (Genesis 30:6). It seems Rachel viewed this as the Lord finally turning the tide in judgment and permitting her a son. In the same way, this was where the Lord judged his enemies through Abraham. All this history shows that it is possible for Moses to have known this name for this area.

But again, even if "near Dan, for that is the name of the other spring of Jordan," was added by a later inspired editor, this would not mean that it was inaccurate to say Moses wrote Genesis.

Skeptic's claim: "The author of Genesis 36:31 obviously knew about kings in Israel which took place well after Moses, so Moses could not have written this."

Such a claim is without a warrant. Moses was clearly aware that this had been prophesied about the nation of Israel when Lord told Abraham (Genesis 17:6) and Jacob (Genesis 35:11) that Israel would have kings. Also, Moses himself prophesied in Deuteronomy 17:14–20 that Israel would have kings. So knowing that kings were coming was already a common knowledge prophecy to Moses. Skeptics claim this only because their biased worldview denies the existence of prophecy as a reality.

It Was Moses

There is abundant biblical and extra-biblical evidence that Moses wrote the Pentateuch during the wilderness sojourn after the Jews left their slavery in Egypt and before they entered the Promised Land (during the second half of the fifteenth century BC). Contrary to the modernists and other skeptics, it was not written after the Jews returned from exile in Babylon (around 500 BC or later). Christians who believe Moses wrote the Pentateuch do not need to feel intellectually intimidated. It is the enemies of the Bible and skeptics of the idea of God that are failing to think carefully and face the facts honestly.

These writings were endorsed by Jesus, the New Testament apostles and Old Testament prophets, and Joshua, who witnessed Moses writing at least most of it. We now find that Mosaic authorship is supported via linguistic and archaeological evidence. The attack on the Mosaic authorship of the Pentateuch is nothing less than an attack on the veracity, reliability, and authority of the Bible. We find no substantiation for it unless its proponents have other agendas, which we suspect they do.[78]

Evidence the Pentateuch
Was Written Long Before the Fifth Century BC

Two small amulets were found in 1979 in the Hinnom Valley in Jerusalem and deciphered in 1989. They show quotations from the first five books of the Bible. These silver scrolls positioned by the nature of their early Hebrew script date them **before 587 BC**. Since many skeptics have charged the first five books of the Bible were either completely written or edited during the fifth century BC or later, which allowed them to write in fulfilled prophecies after they happened, this evidence shows the Old Testament Bible had been written before this supposed critical date.[79]

Hammurabi Black Stele

This shining black diorite pillar called the **Hammurabi Stele** was discovered in 1901 at the Acropolis of ancient Susa by a French archaeological expedition under M. J. de Morgan. The stele (also called a stela, which is an upright stone slab or column, typically bearing a commemorative inscription) is decorated with a bas-relief (sculptural relief in which the projection from the surrounding surface is slight) of Hammurabi being commissioned by the sun god Shamash to inscribe the laws. The code contains nearly 4,000 lines of text containing around 282 laws, a historical prologue, and a literary and religious epilogue.

Hammurabi was the king of Babylon around 2000 BC and a *contemporary of Abraham*, the first Hebrew. Hammurabi is identified by scholars as the "Amraphel" of the Bible (Genesis 14), who was one of the kings who captured Abraham's nephew Lot.

The discovery of the Hammurabi Stele was one of the most important discoveries in Biblical Archaeology. It is an original document from the time of Abraham, bearing testimony of a highly advanced system of law and a remarkably advanced time period. This shows again how man is degenerating over time, as biblical accounts would attest to, not getting more organized as secular evolutionary archaeology supposes.[80]

The Black Obelisk

In the 1840s, a British man named *Austen Henry Layard* had a desire to travel to the Middle East and dig around some of the strange-looking mounds near the City of Mosul (not my idea of a good time, but it takes all kinds). He had heard many tales about things being found in these mounds. He was looking for any trace of evidence that would lead him to the lost city of Nineveh mentioned in the Bible, where Jonah, after much divine coercion, reluctantly went to witness the capital of the ancient Assyrian Empire. Little did he know that one of his discoveries would turn Europe upside down with excitement!

At this site, he discovered a black limestone monument which is known today as **The Black Obelisk of Shalmaneser III.** This discovery brought a new authenticity and historicity to some of the accounts in the Bible, including Jonah. It also gained him the support of the British Museum and all the finances he needed to continue his excavations and become known as "The Father of Assyriology."[81]

The Pilate Inscription

It wasn't long ago when many scholars were questioning the actual existence of a Roman Governor with the name of Pontius Pilate, the procurator, who ordered Jesus' crucifixion according to the New Testament. In June 1961, Italian archaeologists led by Dr. Antonio Frova were excavating an ancient Roman amphitheater near Caesarea-on-the-Sea (Maritima) and uncovered this interesting limestone block. On the worn face is a monumental inscription which is part of a larger dedication to the Roman leader Tiberius Caesar which clearly says that it was from *"Pontius Pilate, Prefect of Judea."* This established not only Pontius Pilate's existence but confirmed his position as governor of Judea as detailed in the Bible.[82]

Another artifact, a stamp found with Pontius Pilate's name on it found in 2016, further establishes this critical biblical character as a true fixture in history.

Caiaphas Ossuary

Workers building a water park two miles south of the Temple Mount in Jerusalem in 1990 inadvertently broke through the ceiling of a hidden burial chamber dating to the first century A.D. In it, they found the *Caiaphas Ossuary.* This is one of twelve bone boxes discovered in a burial cave in south Jerusalem in November 1990, two of which featured the name "Caiaphas."[83] The especially beautiful ossuary bore the inscription "Yehosef bar Qayafa" which means "Joseph, son of Caiaphas," and held the bones of a sixty-year-old male. The limestone ossuary measures about 37 cm high by 75 cm long and are housed in the Israel Museum, Jerusalem.[84]

It has been suggested that this belonged to Joseph, son of Caiaphas, known as the High Priest Caiaphas in the New Testament. According to the Canonical gospels, Caiaphas was the major antagonist of Jesus, presided over the Sanhedrin during his trials, interrogated him, and handed him over to Pilate for execution. Caiaphas is a historic personality, known and named as such by Flavius Josephus and others.

This ossuary should be distinguished from the less ornate Miriam ossuary, which came to light in June 2011. The latter is a looted, though authenticated artifact from the Valley of Elah, bearing the inscription: "Miriam, daughter of Yeshua, son of Caiaphas, priest of Ma'azya from Beit Imri."[85]

These artifacts and the writings of contemporary historians verify the existence and position of Caiap has as detailed in the Bible.

The Megiddo Seal Bearing King Jeroboam's Name

It is very interesting that the "*Jasper Seal*," found at Tel Megiddo bearing the name of King Jeroboam, who ruled in the Northern Kingdom of Israel, would contain the symbol for their rival, the Southern Kingdom of Judah. But in examining all of the circumstances involved and seeing what the Bible says, it is no wonder that the prosperous and victorious Northern Kingdom of Israel would boast with a symbol of their enemy.

The inscription actually proclaims the name and rank of its owner, one of the ministers of King Jeroboam II, who reigned from 787-747 BC. The word "servant" is the Hebrew word "*ebed*" and is mentioned in the Bible as one of high dignity in the government. Many seals have been discovered with similar inscriptions like "the servant of the king."

This artifact gives credence and verifies what the Bible says in 2 Kings 14:23-25 "*In the fifteenth year of Amaziah the son of Joash, king of Judah, Jeroboam the son of Joash, king of Israel, became king in Samaria, and reigned forty-one years. And he did evil in the sight of the LORD; he did not depart from all the sins of Jeroboam, the son of Nebat, who had made Israel sin.*" The inscription and dating of this seal both correspond to this biblical quote substantiating this biblical account's historicity.[86]

Hezekiah Versus Idol Worship Evidenced

In southern Judah, a few miles from Beer-Sheba has been found the ruins of the ancient fortress city of Arad. Arad is mentioned as an important frontier town and defense fortress for southern Judah after the conquest time of Joshua, as described in Joshua 12:14. It was destroyed and rebuilt many times, in many battles, with many different foes.

As described in the Old Testament and found throughout ancient Israeli ruins, the Israelites frequently built altars away from Jerusalem, which were modeled after the "altar of burnt offerings" in Jerusalem. A temple sanctuary discovered in Arad in the 1960s shows all the indications of a full sanctuary area. It included a large courtyard and sacrificial altar in the center with evidence in it of burnt offerings. The altar's dimensions conform to that described in the Jewish temple in Exodus 20:25 and 27:1. At the west end of the courtyard was a semblance of the holy place enclosing their version of the "holy of holies."[87]

The discoveries at Arad substantiate two pieces of Jewish history. First, it gives more evidence for the Exodus accounts regarding the dimensions of the altar in Jerusalem being followed in Israel. However, that was already well established. But, more importantly, it gives evidence for the frequent complaints by the Old Testament prophets against the Israelites for building altars and holy places outside of Jerusalem, which would also be outside of God's directions. This charge was made against the people of Israel in Isaiah 17:8 and 65:3. Although this has been debated by some modernists and revisionists, the consensus among archeologists is that these burnt remains at Arad gave good evidence of the reforms by Hezekiah in 2 Kings 18:3-6 when he had destroyed many of the forbidden altars across Israel, fully substantiating as real history this portion of 2 Kings.[88]

Another historical verification of these biblical accounts is found in Beer-Sheba. In 1973 the remains of a broken altar used in the 8th century BC was discovered. Its size, dimensions, and the four-horned design show that it was clearly a copy of the "altar of burnt offerings" in Jerusalem since they followed the construction instructions from Exodus 27:1-2. Its broken remains, when found, again substantiate the biblical account of Hezekiah's reforms to do away with the forbidden altars and the Israelites defying the prohibition against such altars. Again, while some modernists will date these remains to 587 BC, most scholars believe this site dates to the time of Hezekiah's reforms in the early part of the 8th century BC.[89]

Sennacherib's Hexagonal Prism

This amazing discovery, excavated in Nineveh in the 1830s, records the Assyrian king Sennacherib's (son of the Assyrian King Sargon) campaign near the end of 8th Century BC, which includes his siege of Jerusalem during the reign of "Hezekiah the Judahite" in 701 BC. There are 500 lines of writing in the Akkadian language on this magnificent clay prism.

Sennacherib, in 703 BC, captured Babylon, then under the control of King Merodach-baladan. The prism boasts of how Sennacherib and his forces entered Babylon jubilantly. It also states that he "plundered 75 strong walled cities and 420 small cities."[90]

For a while, the deposed King of Babylon, Merodach-baladan, ruled in southern Babylonia and attempted to ally himself with King Hezekiah of Judah. The prophet Isaiah warned in 2 Kings 20:12-18 that any alliance with Babylon would be a foolish move.

The Assyrian Sennacherib's invasion of Judah in 701 BC is one of the most dramatic events in Jewish history and in the Bible. It has been intensively studied by both biblical scholars and secular archaeologists.[91]

On the death of his father, King Sargon, Sennacherib moved his capital to Nineveh (just outside of present-day Mosul in Iraq) and decorated his palace with some two miles of wall panel sculptures detailing his exploits.

Hezekiah became a target due to his dalliances with Merodach-baladan and his refusal to pay tribute. Hezekiah also made overtures of alliance with Egypt, as he saw a conflict brewing and Israel in need of support. These facts are alluded to in the Bible and verified in Egyptian and Assyrian records.

Sennacherib's own records tell of his first taking Phoenicia, then Philistia along the coast, before turning inland to Judah and Israel.

His style of war and occupation was brutal, as he would plunder a defeated territory, burn it, and lay it to waste.

Sennacherib says in his records, "As to Hezekiah, the Jew, he did not submit to my yoke, I laid siege to 46 of his strong cities, walled forts and countless small villages in the vicinity, and conquered by means of well-stamped ramps and battering rams brought near (to walls, along with) the attack of foot soldiers, (using) mines, breeches, as well as sapper work."

Finally, Sennacherib reached the major fort city of Lachish, 40 miles southwest of Jerusalem. Sennacherib's wall inscriptions made no mention of the siege of Lachish, but they give a vivid description of the battle. The record of this invasion is told graphically in the Bible in 2 Kings Chapter 18, 2 Chronicles chapter 32 and in Isaiah chapters 36 and 37, and these details match the Assyrian accounts.[92]

After Lachish, Hezekiah knew the next target would be Jerusalem. Hezekiah also knew that their best chance was to withstand a long siege since his forces were inadequate to go up against the Assyrians, and he would stake his hopes on waiting until help arrived from Egypt, from whom he had requested help. To endure a long siege, Jerusalem needed large stores of food and water. He moved to ensure that Jerusalem would have adequate water supplies and to deny access to water to the Assyrians.

Engineering to Save the Day!

So how did Hezekiah ensure that Jerusalem would have the water needed to endure a siege from Sennacherib? It says in 2 Chronicles 32:2-3 that Hezekiah's engineers blocked off "all of the springs and the streams that flowed through the land." But they did even more. According to 2 Chronicles 32:30 and 2 Kings 20:20, "they blocked the upper outlet of the Gihon spring and channeled the water down to the west of the City of David."

To achieve this, they dug an underground channel deep in the limestone rock on which the city of Jerusalem is built. This tunnel ran for 1748 feet from the Gihon spring near the floor of the Kidron

Valley outside the eastern wall of the city and wound it underground to the Siloam Pool, which was safely within the city walls.[93]

Archaeologists still debate how this miraculous tunnel, with only a 0.6 percent rise and fall gradient, could have started from opposite ends, followed a course underground, going as deep as 160 feet below the surface, and met at halfway point with the technology of the day? These tunnels were discovered by Edward Robinson in 1838, which led not only to this verification of the accounts in the biblical books of 2 Kings and 2 Chronicles but also fostered more than a century of investigation into how it was all accomplished. Some theorize that they followed an underground water source known as the Karstic Channel. Others have thought that they were directed in their digging by acoustic hammering on the rocks above the surface. There are no vertical shafts along the main lines of the tunnel, which could have checked and guided their progress.[94]

In 1880 a boy playing in the tunnel found an inscription chiseled into the rock at the halfway point left by Hezekiah's engineers in 701 BC. In part, the inscription reads, "While (stone cutters were swinging their) ax, each man toward the fellow, and while there were still three cubits to be cut through, (there was heard) the voice calling of a man calling to his fellow, for there was overlap (perhaps a crevice) of rock on the right… And when the tunnel was driven through, the quarry men hewed (the rock) each man toward his fellow, ax against ax, and the water flowed from the spring toward the reservoir for 1200 cubits, and the height of the rock above the heads was 100 cubits."[95] This inscription and the tunnel itself verifies the biblical account of Hezekiah directing the channeling of the water into Jerusalem and away from the Assyrians.

What is in agreement is that most of it was achieved by Hezekiah's engineers.[96] Assyrian records show that Hezekiah had four years to prepare for Sennacherib's attack and siege. This was adequate time for the engineers to complete their work.[97]

Another fascinating thing is how the Assyrian records are so silent on what happened in the siege of Jerusalem. The siege of

Jerusalem is mentioned in Sennacherib's Stele, and that is all. Interestingly, Jerusalem was the only city mentioned as being besieged on Sennacherib's Stele, of which the capture is not mentioned. That is consistent with the biblical account that the siege did occur, but the city was not captured. Why there is nothing more in the Assyrian records is explained when you follow the end of the siege as told from the Bible.

The Bible tells us that some time into the siege, an angel of the Lord struck down 185,000 of the Assyrians in one night (Isaiah 37:36). Not surprisingly, Sennacherib left this defeat and his retreat from Jerusalem out of his propagandist history.

Sennacherib returned to his capital of Nineveh, where his sons Adrammelech and Sharezer murdered him (Isaiah 37:38 and verified in the Babylonian Chronicles), and his already installed heir, Esarhaddon, took his throne. What a great welcome home by the family! But again, this fate for Sennacherib and his family is both recorded in the Bible and verified on the walls of Sennacherib's palace.

Domesticated Camels

One of many charges of historical inaccuracy about the Bible is the writings from Abraham's, the Patriarchs, and Moses' times saying that they used domesticated camels for transportation. Some scholars have disputed this because of a find of camels just before 1000 BC, but no other finds of camels with humans buried before that, indicating to them that our domestication of camels did not occur until just before 1000 BC. If true, his would invalidate biblical accounts from 1450 to 2000 BC, which mentioned the domesticated use of camels.

However, a cylinder seal found by Manfred Bietek (the University of Vienna and one of the foremost archaeologists of our time) shows a picture of a two-hump camel with a couple riding on top of it. This seal has been dated to between 1800 and 1650 BC. Showing that camels were domesticated for transportation far earlier than the 1100 to 1400 BC date secular archaeologists assign to domesticated camels. This gives clear evidence that the mentions of camel use during Abram's and other times prior to Moses are archaeologically plausible and gives credence to such biblical references to them in ancient times.

Further, the reference to domesticated camels in the Bible has been shown consistent with a few other figurines of camels with loads on their backs dating to the second millennium BC.[98]

Qur'an and Jewish Writings

The Qur'an contains references to more than fifty people and events also mentioned in the Bible. The Qur'an talks of Christ and of many Old Testament figures, adding to the long list of historical writings verifying their existence. Among that list are the writings of Josephus and other famous Jewish writers, who give vivid details to most Old Testament figures and historical accounts.[99]

One example of these events and people is the story of Joseph interpreting Pharaoh's dream while imprisoned. The Bible says this:

> Then Pharaoh said to Joseph, "In my dream I was standing on the bank of the Nile, when out of the river there came up seven cows, fat and sleek, and they grazed among the reeds. After them, seven other cows came up—scrawny and very ugly and lean. I had never seen such ugly cows in all the Land of Egypt. The lean, ugly cows ate up the seven fat cows that came up first. But even after they ate them, no one could tell that they had done so; they looked just as ugly as before. Then I woke up." "In my dreams I also saw seven heads of grain, full and good, growing on a single stalk. After them, seven other heads sprouted—withered and thin and scorched by the east wind. The thin heads of grain swallowed up the seven good heads. I told this to the magicians, but none could explain it to me."
>
> Genesis 41:17-24 (ESV)

The Qur'an says: (Quran: Yusuf|12.43) The king (of Egypt) said: "I do see (in a vision) seven fat kine, whom seven lean ones devour, and seven green ears of corn, and seven (others) withered. O ye chiefs! Expound to me my vision if it be that ye can interpret visions."

Pharaoh's cupbearer, who had been previously imprisoned with Joseph, suddenly remembers his promise in both accounts and tells Pharaoh about the man who foretold his own restoration to favor. Pharaoh sent for Joseph from prison, asking Joseph to interpret his dream.

In the Qur'anic account, Joseph insists that the Vizier's wife vindicate him before the king before Joseph agrees to do so (this is not mentioned in the Bible); Pharaoh summons the Vizier's wife, who admits her lies about Joseph and proclaims his innocence. Notice this embellishment on the biblical account, which is often indicative of the detailed embellishment we described earlier, which is so often indicative of an account copied from and embellishing on a previous account.

The Qur'an now rejoins the biblical narrative, where Joseph reveals the meaning of the king's dream: Egypt will have seven years of good crops, followed by seven years of famine, and the famine will be worse than the abundance. The king rewarded Joseph by giving him charge over the storehouses over the entire land of Egypt.[100] Thus, this section of the Qur'an validates the account of Joseph as an interpreter of dreams in Egypt.

Moabites Did Attack Israel

The Bible tells of the Israelites being attacked by the Moabites in 2 Kings 3:4–8. Well, guess what was dug up in 1868? If you're an archaeologist, you may have guessed it was what is called the **Moabite Stone** (also called the "Mesha Stele"), which records the Moabites attacking Israel, and it is accredited to King Mesha of Moab. The stone, dated to about 840 BC, tells of the Moabites being under Hebrew rule of many years until they revolted, attacked Israel, and regained their lands.[101]

The stone was discovered intact by the Anglican missionary Frederick Augustus Klein at the site of ancient Dibon (presently Dhiban, Jordan) in August 1868. Klein was led to it by a local Bedouin, although neither of them could read the text. Before it could be seen by another European, the next year, it was smashed by local villagers during a dispute over its ownership. A papier-mâché impression (technically called a "squeeze") had been obtained by a local Arab on behalf of Charles Simon Clermont-Ganneau, and fragments containing most of the inscription (613 letters out of about a thousand) were later recovered and pieced together. The squeeze and the reassembled stele are now in the Louvre in Paris, France.[102]

The Moabite Stone is the longest Iron Age inscription ever found in the region, and constitutes the major evidence for the Moabite language, and is a "cornerstone of Semitic epigraphy" (the study of ancient inscriptions and their meanings) and history.[103] The stone, whose story parallels, with some differences, an episode in the Bible's Books of Kings, provides invaluable information on the Moabite language and the political relationship between Moab and Israel at one moment in the 9th century BC. It is the most extensive inscription ever recovered that refers to the kingdom of Israel (the "House of Omri"); it bears the earliest verifiable and certain extra-biblical reference to the Israelite God, Yahweh, and the earliest mention of the "House of David" (i.e., the kingdom of Judah).[104]

It is also one of four known contemporary inscriptions containing the name of Israel, the others being the Merneptah Stele, the Tel Dan Stele, and the Kurkh Monolith.[105] Its authenticity has been disputed over the years, and some biblical skeptics suggest the text was not historical but a biblical allegory. In fact, the conduct of the military operations and the ritual slaughter of captives described is so remarkably similar to the style and ideology of biblical accounts of "holy war" that many interpreters were at first inclined to regard the Mesha stele as a forgery, but on paleographic grounds, its authenticity is now undisputed. Today the stele is regarded as genuine and historical by the vast majority of biblical archaeologists today.[106]

A portion of the Mesha Stele has come under some dispute recently in 2019 as some archaeologists have suggested the section which refers to the "House of David" instead refers to "King Balak" (also a biblical figure). There are several missing letters in this part of the inscription, so it could be interpreted either way on this. Either way, however, the Mesha Stele still verifies Israel as a nation-state in the 9th century BC, and even if it is correctly reinterpreted as referring to King Balak, then this also gives credence to another biblical account.

Sodom and Gomorrah

Much has been made of the biblical account of the "five cities on the plain" and the destruction of Sodom and Gomorrah as fiction. However, as reported in the archaeological magazine "Bible and Spade," biblical archaeologist *Dr. Bryant Wood of Associates for Biblical Research* located the city gates, crushed graves, towers, a temple, the water supply, and thick city walls on the plain. Uninhabitable since the destruction, the remains were identified by Dr. Wood as Sodom and Gomorrah. Geologist Dr. Steve Austin studied the geological evidence, including the fault zone, the burn layer, the bitumen that erupted, and the city's calamitous fall to its ruin. Together, they have confirmed the truthfulness of the Genesis account.[107]

As written in the Bible in Genesis 14:8, all five "cities of the plain" were located on the Jordanian shore of the Red Sea. The most prominent and northerly of these cities in ancient times was called Bab edh-Dhra, which seems to be the Arabic rendering of Sodom. Next in line was Numeira (Gomorrah), then the modern city of Safi (Zoar or Bela, to which Lot fled according to the Bible and which was not destroyed), then Admah and Zeboiim. The key was finding Zoar. Mentioned in other Scriptures and ancient maps, it led to the discovery of the other nearby ruins.[108]

These five cities had all been situated along the Dead Sea Rift, a major tectonic plate boundary. At God's command, the rift ruptured, spewing great quantities of liquid and gaseous hydrocarbons high into the atmosphere. These ignited, setting the whole region ablaze and covering it with "fire and brimstone." Abraham saw the firestorm from Mamre, about 20 miles away. The fiery mixture almost certainly didn't come from a point source, such as a volcano, but destroyed the whole area along the linear fault. The cities were crushed and burned, just as the Bible describes. The city of Sodom actually straddled a fault, causing half of it to fall about 100 meters into the fault crevasse. No one survived. Today, numerous bodies remain trapped in the rubble.[109]

When Lot made his choice of the best land, he was between Bethel and Ai according to Genesis 13:3. The Hebrew word for "plain" used in the Bible is "*kikkar*" or "disk-shaped." A disk-shaped alluvial plain in this area meets the Genesis 13:10 criteria of "Well watered like the garden of the Lord." The area is richly fertile even today.

Scorched walls and floors were buried beneath a fortified city unearthed in the area dating to the Middle Bronze Age—the time, according to the Bible, of Abraham and Lot. These walls and floors were buried beneath three feet of "dark grey ash" and pottery shards which had been subjected to temperatures exceeding 2000 degrees Fahrenheit. Archaeology shows this whole area was left abandoned for seven hundred years, which one would expect between the total destruction of the peoples and cities on this plain, as well as the resultant fear to return to such an area where such a calamity had occurred.[110]

The Case of the Missing Kings

For years the Bible was challenged by critics, who said there was no archaeological evidence for the existence of Kings Sargon and Nebuchadnezzar, both mentioned in the Bible.

King Sargon

The Bible said in Isaiah 20:1 (NASB), "In the year that the supreme commander, sent by **Sargon king of Assyria**, came to **Ashdod** and attacked and captured it." This text was challenged by critics for decades because they knew of no king named Sargon in the lists of Assyrian kings in any other archaeological finds. Now Sargon's palace has been recovered at Khorsabad, including a wall inscription and a library record endorsing the battle against the Philistine city of *Ashdod*.[111]

Nebuchadnezzar

Likewise, Bible critics said, 'There was no such king as Nebuchadnezzar' since at that time in the 19th century, there had been no archaeological evidence for his existence outside of the Bible. The Bible tells of Jerusalem being attacked by King Nebuchadnezzar in 586 BC (2 Kings 24:10). But Nebuchadnezzar's palace and library were uncovered, proving the Biblical account. In fact, Nebuchadnezzar was unknown to modern historians until it was confirmed by the German professor Koldewey, who excavated in Babylon approximately 100 years ago.

In the 1930s, in Southern Israel, further verification was uncovered as the "Lachish Letters" were uncovered and deciphered, describing how Nebuchadnezzar did attack Jerusalem.[112]

The Dispersion After Babel

Ancient historical records of multiple regions around the world verify the "Table of Nations" from Genesis chapter 10 as a true account and listing of family heads dispersed after the confusion at Babel.

A few examples of this historical verification will illuminate how good this evidence is and how well it corresponds to the biblical account.

The famous **Tower of Babel stele** (a stone or wooden slab, generally taller than it is wide, erected as a monument, very often for funerary or commemorative purposes) shows Nebuchadnezzar II, who destroyed Jerusalem in 586 BC, and his plans to finish building the infamous tower that had been abandoned many hundreds of years earlier.[113]

The first of Noah's grandsons to be mentioned in the Bible in Genesis chapter 10 is **Gomer** (not to be confused with the more well-known Gomer, wife of Hosea), the first son of Japheth. He is identified in Genesis chapter 10 as a grandson of Noah, who first goes to the Turkish regions of today and lives in the area of Galatia. Josephus writes that Galatians were previously called "Gomerites," a name transposed to "Galatia" over time.

Gomer then went north into the Baltic regions after Babel. In examining records of the Baltic States, we find accounts of Gomer (found in many Germanic forms) as being credited as the first inhabitant of these areas. Gomer's existence and his inhabiting these states are further attested to by his names (in various forms) being included in the historical lore of many Germanic and northern European states. His descendants migrated westward to what are now called *France and Spain*. For many centuries, France was called "Gaul," after the descendants of Gomer. Northwest Spain is called "Galicia" to this day, named for this biblical grandson of Noah. All of these European, Baltic, and Turkish records verify what the Bible says of where Gomer went to after the dispersion.

Some of the Gomerites migrated further to what is now called *Wales*. The Welsh historian, Davis, records a traditional Welsh belief that the descendants of Gomer 'landed on the Isle of Britain from France, about three hundred years after the flood'. He also records that the Welsh language is called Gomeraeg (after their ancestor Gomer).

Other members of the Gomer clan settled along the way, including in *Armenia*. The sons of Gomer were 'Ashkenaz, and Riphath, and Togarmah' (according to Genesis 10:3). *Encyclopedia Britannica* says that the Armenians traditionally claim to be descended from Togarmah and Ashkenaz. Ancient Armenia reached *Turkey*. The name "Turkey" probably comes from Togarmah. Others of them migrated to *Germany*. *Ashkenaz* is the Hebrew word for "Germany."[114]

According to the Bible, **Javan** was the fourth son of Noah's son Japheth. According to the Roman-Jewish historian Flavius Josephus, Javan traveled to Greece after the dispersion. This opinion was shared by most writers of the Middle Ages. Not only is the biblical character of Javan's existence and travel to Greece verified in Greek historical records and mythology, but even today, the Jews refer to Greece as Javan due to the reality of this truth to them through history.[115]

Cush, according to Genesis, was the eldest son of Ham, grandson of Noah, and father of the oft-debated Nimrod. Regional records show that Cush ventured to western Africa and southern Asia as the Bible says he did in the dispersion. In western Africa, he settled in the current area of Ethiopia. The fact that inhabitants of that region still call themselves "Cushites" attests to this account.[116] Ethiopians' origins from Cush are also confirmed in the writings of Josephus.

There is some debate among scholars as to the identification of where "the land of Cush" was. While many identify Ethiopia, some say southern Asia or the southern portion of the Arabian Peninsula is more likely.[117] This debate may be one in which both parties are correct, and a difference in ancient geography may show why there is confusion and a debate. Creation scientists believe the world was composed of one supercontinent (Pangaea) prior to the worldwide flood. They believe that the movement of the continents to their present-day positions took not billions of years as conventional geology assumes but occurred in a very short period of time of a few hundred years or less. If this is true, then referring to Cush as southern Asia, southern Arabia, or eastern Africa makes more sense in light of the fact that these areas would be essentially connected prior to continental drift.

The Tower of Babel and the dispersion are written outside of the Bible in the writings of Sumerian tablets (a Babylonian account) as well as by Chinese and Egyptian writings and in the writings of many other cultures.

Another thing that fits into the Babel account is the genetic relatedness of Australian Aborigines and the people of India. Recent DNA testing has found strong DNA similarities between these people groups. The large number of similar genetic markers across both of their genomes gives us clear evidence that the people of India and

Australia intermarried 4000-5000 years ago. This also helps explain the many linguistic similarities between the peoples of Southern India and many Aboriginal tribes.[118]

This genetic and linguistic evidence fits in well with the biblical account of the dispersion from Babel. This dispersion would have occurred a few hundred years after the flood, which by a biblical timeline would have been more than 4000 years ago. As a result, some of the groups dispersed from Babel would have settled in India, and others traveled further to Australia.[119] This expansion to the Southeast and relations between the groups may have been helped by a land bridge between Asia and Australia since one product of the worldwide flood would have been an ice age, locking up huge amounts of water in ice on the continents and lowering sea levels, allowing direct land travel between Asia and Australia, as well as Asia and North America via the Bering Strait.

More Sons of Japheth

In the Bible, **Japheth** is ascribed to have had seven sons: Gomer, Magog, Tiras, Javan, Meshech, Tubal, and Madai. According to the historian Josephus, this is confirmed in his "Antiquities of the Jews I.6" which says: "Japheth, the son of Noah, had seven sons: they inhabited so, that, beginning at the mountains Taurus and Amanus, they proceeded along Asia, as far as the river Tanais (Don), and along Europe to Cadiz; and settling themselves on the lands which they light upon, which none had inhabited before, they called the nations by their own names."[120] Josephus subsequently detailed the nations supposed to have descended from the seven sons of Japheth.

Tubal is mentioned in the Old Testament book of Eze-kiel. Ezekiel mentions him along with Gog and Meshech. Ti-glath-pileser I, king of Assyria in about 1100 BC, refers to the descendants of Tubal as the Tabali. *Josephus* recorded their name as the Thobelites, who were later known as "*Iberes*"(Iberia). They also came to Georgia (Tbilisi, the capital, is named after Tubal.) These families later moved north, crossed the Caucasus to the river

Tobol and hence to the famous city of Tobolsk, north of the (central) Black Sea, and finally went to Russia and built the city of Tobolsk.[121]

Noah's grandson Meshech also traveled into Russia and gave his name to what is now Moscow. This is a very interesting historical background where in Hippolytus of Rome's chronicle (234 AD), the "Illyrians" were identified as Meshech's offspring. In addition, Georgians have traditions that they, and other Caucasus people as well as Armenians, share descent from Meshech (Who the Georgian's called Meskheti). Moreover, according to a legend first appearing in the Kievan Synopsis (1674), Moscow (Moskva) was founded by King Mosokh, son of Japheth (i.e., Meshech), and was named for him and his wife, Kva. In this legend, they are also said to have had a son, Ya, and daughter, Vuza, who gave their names to the nearby Yauza river.[122]

Mizraim

The Bible says **Mizraim** was a son of Ham and father of various African races (Genesis 10:6), but particularly father of the Egyptians, to whom his name was given. "Mizraim" is also the Hebrew word for Egypt in the Bible, and this country is still called "Misr" in Arabic.[123]

Manetho was an ancient Egyptian historian and priest who lived and wrote his histories around 270 BC. His chronology of the Kings and Pharaohs of Egypt is one of the most important texts for the current chronology of the history of Egypt.

In his history of Egypt, he wrote that "after the Flood," Ham the son of Noah begat "**Aegyptus or Mestraim**" (very reminiscent of Mizraim), who was the first to establish himself in the area now known as Egypt at the time when the tribes began to disperse."

The Bible says that Ham "begat" (bore as a son) Mizraim. Egypt today is known as *Mizraim* or *mitsrayim* in Hebrew. Manetho wrote that the "dispersion of the tribes" was five years after Noah's descendant Peleg was born. This agrees with Genesis 10:25, which says of Peleg that "in his days the earth was divided."[124]

Further, Egyptologist Patrick Clark says that from the earliest times, the ancient Egyptians "called themselves and their land a throaty name of Kham or Cham (close to the biblical Ham)."[125] It is thus clear that ancient Egyptians knew full well that they came from the descendants of Noah, just as the Bible describes.

Finally, we have found evidence even beyond historical records. Science has now been found that verifies this account. The first full DNA sequencing of ancient Egyptian mummies has found that the Egyptian people of the pharaonic times were more closely related to modern and ancient Europeans and near-eastern inhabitants than to present-day Egyptians. These mummies "have the closest genetic links to the Fertile Crescent and eastern populations of what is now *Israel*," said research leader Johannes Krause.[126] Modern Egyptians have a sub-Saharan African component to their genome, from a cultural mixture in more recent times. But this was not found in the ancient mummies.

This is consistent with the biblical account, which says that the early Egyptians came from the line of Mizraim, Noah's grandson. This African component in recent years has been touted by evolutionists as showing the Egyptians were most likely descended from African people and in line with the secular and evolutionary "Out of Africa" theory of human origins. This secular theory is not supported by this latest DNA evidence. Instead, the biblical account of early Egyptians coming from the Middle East is supported by this evidence.[127]

Further Sons of Ham

Phut (how would you like to have that name?) and **Canaan,** according to the Bible, were sons of Ham. Ancient authorities outside of the Bible are fairly universal in identifying Phut with the Libyans (*Lebu* and *Pitu*), the earliest neighbors of Egypt to the west. This is consistent with the biblical account.

Canaan is known to be the name of a nation and people who settled the Eastern shore of the Mediterranean in what is now called Israel, Lebanon, and Syria. The name "Canaan" is mentioned in the "Mari letters" around 1800 BC (and possibly in the earlier "Ebla tablets," although this is disputed) as well as in Egyptian records.[128]

Shem

Shem (in Hebrew means "Name") was Noah's oldest son and part of Noah's family of eight, who survived the great flood according to the Bible. He was father to five sons (Genesis 10:22), who became the fathers of the five Semitic nations, as shown below. Shem was actually the father of the nations of the ancient Near East, including the Israelites and the Jewish religion, and therefore Judaism, Islam, and Christianity sprang from the line of Shem. These sons' names and the regions which they inhabited are verified in the writings of Josephus.

The Five Semitic Nations:

1. **Elam** (The Persians) settled northeast of the Persian Gulf. Elam is the ancient name for "Persia," which is itself the ancient name for Iran. Until the time of Cyrus, these people here were called *Elamites*, and they were still often called that even in New Testament times. In Acts 2:9, the Jews from Persia, who were present at Pentecost, were called Elamites. The Persians are thus descended from both Elam, the son of Shem, and from Madai, the son of Japheth. Since the 1930s, they have called their country Iran. Local genealogies contained in ancestral records outside of the Bible verify these two ancestors.

2. **Asshur** (The Assyrians) was the Biblical name for Assyria, settled between the Euphrates and Tigris Rivers. Asshur is also the Hebrew word for "Assyria." Assyria was one of the great ancient empires. Every time you see the words Assyria or Assyrian appear in an English translation of the Old Testament, they are translated from the word "Asshur." He was worshipped by his descendants.

Historian Bill Cooper has said of his research, 'Indeed, as long as Assyria lasted, that is until 612 BC, accounts of battles, diplomatic affairs, and foreign bulletins were daily read out to Asshur's image; and every Assyrian king held that he wore the crown only with the express permission of Asshur's deified ghost.'[129]

3. **Arphaxad** (The Babylonians) settled in Chaldea. Arphaxad was the progenitor of the Chaldeans. This "is confirmed by the Hurrian (Nuzi) tablets, which render the name as Arip-hurra—the founder of Chaldea."[130] His descendant, Eber, gave his name to the Hebrew people via the line of Eber-Peleg-Reu-Serug-Nahor-Terah-Abram (Genesis 11:16–26). Eber's other son, Joktan, had 13 sons (Genesis 10:26–30), all of whom appear to have settled in Arabia.[131]

4. **Lud** (The Lydians) settled in Asia Minor (Turkey), but some of them sailed across the Mediterranean and settled in northern Africa. The descendants of Lud are usually, according to Josephus, connected with various Anatolian peoples, particularly Lydia (The Assyrians called Lydia "Luddu") and their predecessors, the Luwians; a cross-reference to this is Herodotus' assertion (Histories i.) that the Lydians were first so named after their king, Lydus (Λυδός). All of this archaeology is consistent with the biblical account.

5. **Aram** (The Syrians), the Biblical name for Syria, is located north and east of Israel. Aram is the Hebrew word for "Syria." Whenever the word Syria appears in the Old Testament, it is a translation of the word "Aram." The Syrians call themselves Arameans, and their language is called Aramaic. Before the spread of the Greek Empire, Aramaic was the international language and was widely used in Jesus' time. These facts give ample testimony to the accuracy of the biblical account.[132]

In addition, we have seen ample evidence of the Chinese language being codified after the dispersion with ideographs relating directly to the Genesis accounts of the creation, the worldwide flood, and Babel. The chart on the next page shows the extreme amount of agreement between the biblical genealogy and that of the Miautso people in China.

The Miautso Bloodline
The Descent of Man According to the Miautso People of China

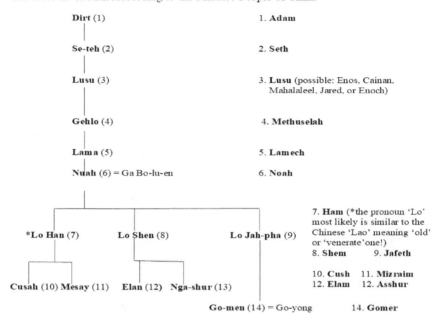

Dirt (1) — 1. Adam

Se-teh (2) — 2. Seth

Lusu (3) — 3. Lusu (possible: Enos, Cainan, Mahalaleel, Jared, or Enoch)

Gehlo (4) — 4. Methuselah

Lama (5) — 5. Lamech

Nuah (6) = Ga Bo-lu-en — 6. Noah

*Lo Han (7)   Lo Shen (8)   Lo Jah-pha (9) — 7. Ham (*the pronoun 'Lo' most likely is similar to the Chinese 'Lao' meaning 'old' or 'venerate' one!)
8. Shem   9. Jafeth

Cusah (10) Mesay (11)   Elan (12) Nga-shur (13) — 10. Cush   11. Mizraim   12. Elam   12. Asshur

Go-men (14) = Go-yong — 14. Gomer

Adam in Miautso was known as "Dirt," which, of course, would refer to his being made from the dust of the ground, as stated in the Bible. Adam's son Seth was known as "Se-the" by the Miautso.

Methuselah, the oldest person in world history according to the Bible, was named "*Gehlo*" by the Miautso. The pronoun "lo" in the word Geh**lo** is close to the Chinese "*lao*," which means "old" or "venerated." **Lamech** in the Bible is called "Lama" by the Chinese. **Noah** was known as Nuah by the Chinese.

In the Bible, the three sons of Noah were **Ham, Shem, and Japheth**, corresponding to the names of Nuah's (Noah) sons, who were "**LO Han, LO Shen, and Lo Japhu.**" The similarities are not only striking but apparent. Ham's son Cush was known as "Cusah." Ham's son Mizraim was called "Mesay." Shem's son Elam in Chinese was known as "Elan," and his son Asshur was called "Nga-<u>shur</u>." Japheth's son Gomer was referred to as "Go-men" by the Chinese.

Thus, we have Chinese writings from thousands of miles away from the Middle East, which are in amazing agreement with the biblical account of the dispersion. At the very least, these writings were copied from the biblical account. But moreover, they are being carried in such a distant history gives good evidence that these were believed to be actual histories. Two sets of American Indian records reflect these biblical accounts as well.

One test of the Bible is to research human records found to be reliable by other attaining works and see if the Bible's accounts match. If not, then the Bible may be in error, which would hurt its case as the infallible "Word of God." The "Table of Nations" in Genesis chapters 10 and 11 is loaded with people and place's names and ripe for just such a test. Historian Bill Cooper wrote of his research on the Table of Nations, "I spent more than 25 years digging into the Table of Nations, looking for a fault, an error or a false statement, or a historical inaccuracy. I found not one."[133] In this section, you have seen an excellent substantiation for the biblical account of Babel and the dispersion as it is found in ancient historical records from all over Asia, Europe, and Africa.

Belshazzar Was Not an Error

Bible skeptics used to claim that the book of Daniel and therefore the Bible erred when it said that **Belshazzar** was the last king of Babylon. But archaeology has proved the Bible right.

The Bible says in Daniel chapter 5 that King Belshazzar and his court were drinking wine and were "praising the gods of gold and silver, bronze, iron, wood, and stone (committing drunkenness and idolatry while enslaving God's people). Then it says, "Immediately the **fingers of a human hand** appeared and wrote on the plaster of the wall of the king's palace, opposite the lampstand. And the king saw the hand as it wrote. Then the king's color changed, and his thoughts alarmed him; his limbs gave way, and his knees knocked together. The king called loudly to bring in the enchanters, the Chaldeans, and the astrologers. The king declared to the wise men of Babylon,

'Whoever reads this writing and shows me its interpretation, shall be clothed with purple and have a chain of gold around his neck and shall be the **third ruler of the kingdom**'"(ESV).

Was this story told in the Bible a legend and mythical, as many used to say, or was it a factual account of what occurred?

Years ago, skeptics of the Bible denied that there ever was a king of Babylon named Belshazzar since no relics or records had been found outside of the Bible which verified his existence. These skeptics were keenly aware and interested in proving the book of Daniel to be in error (and thus not God-inspired) because of the book's otherwise uncanny record of having its predictions of the future fulfilled in history.

Although Daniel lived in the 6th century BC, historians wanted to date the writing of Daniel to the time of the Maccabees four centuries later in the 2nd century BC. This would allow them to say that Daniel's predictions were written after many of the predictions he "foretold" had come to pass, and thus they portrayed the whole of the book as a lie, and Belshazzar just added to their fuel they thought.

The Bible says that the "writing on the wall" episode occurred on the same day the city of Babylon, capital of the nation of Babylonia, fell to the Medo-Persian Empire under King Cyrus the Great.

It was Daniel, according to the Bible, who gave King Belshazzar the interpretation of the writings on the wall (and where we get the saying "the writing is on the wall" for a fatalistic view of something which will occur regardless of whether we want it to or not, it's inevitable). In verses 26 through 30, Daniel reveals to the king that the writing said God was bringing the days of his kingdom to an end, that it would be divided and given to the Medo-Persians and the Bible claims that King Belshazzar was killed that very night.

However, all other known historical records once disagreed. Ancient historians such as Herodotus, Megasthenes, Berossus, and Alexander Polyhistor and many cuneiform documents were united in claiming that the last king of Babylon was Nabonidus, with no mention of Belshazzar.[134]

Up to 1854, the name Belshazzar was found only in the book of Daniel and some other literature which either stated or could be proved to have been quoting from Daniel. The case against the Bible and the book of Daniel looked strong, and it was one of the main evidence sighted by those believers in the "higher criticism" as to the fallibility of the Bible.

But, starting in 1854, a series of discoveries would occur which would prove the Bible to be correct. In 1854 four clay cylinders with identical inscriptions were excavated from Ur (more of these would be found in the 1960s). These were King Nabonidus Cylinders, which contained Nabonidus' prayer to the moon god for "Belshazzar, the eldest son- my offspring."[135] Thus, the existence of Belshazzar was confirmed as Nabonidus' firstborn son and heir to the throne of Babylon.

Then in 1882, a translation of another ancient cuneiform text called the Nabonidus Chronicle tablet was published. In this document, Nabonidus was described as an "absentee king," spending most of his time in Tema, Arabia, some 450 miles away. The king left Belshazzar, which the text calls the "crown prince," to take care of affairs in Babylon during that time. The tablet also explains that Nabonidus was away from Babylon when it fell. It says that two days before Babylon fell, Nabonidus had fled from the Persians when they defeated him at Sippar, so Belshazzar (who skeptics thought didn't exist) was actually the highest-ranking authority in Babylon when it fell.

Next, the Persian verse account, published in 1924, says that when Nabonidus started out on a long journey, he "entrusted the kingship" to "his oldest, the firstborn." So, Belshazzar clearly functioned as king for many years when his father was away.

More ancient cuneiform texts were found in the early 1900s, which also mentioned Belshazzar. One of them, a tablet from Erech, said both Nabonidus and his son were jointly invoked in an oath, suggesting both had royal authority.[136]

Skeptics still quibble that Belshazzar was never officially installed as king, but what is clear from archaeology is that he existed, and he was the ruler in charge (and thus referred to as king) at the time Babylon fell. This situation also makes sense of one piece of trivia from the biblical text. Why get from Daniel the interpretation which he so desired did he offer only the **third position** in the kingdom? Why not the second? He could not do so, since he and his father were coregents! Third place was the highest position available for him to offer!

Now, if Daniel was written hundreds of years after this all occurred, with no other accounts recording the fall of Babylon that the supposed writers of Daniel might have access to, how did they get so many details right about what occurred at the fall of Babylon? How did they know Belshazzar even existed or that he was second in command? No, the fact that Daniel is historically accurate, even down to seemingly insignificant details, shows it was written near the time these things occurred. The book of Daniel was right all along, and archaeology has proved this to be true. In fact, Daniel and the Bible had a better understanding of Belshazzar and his role than most scholars and writings for more than 2000 years. This is not surprising only if the Bible is really God's Word. If it is not, then this is just one more amazing thing in Daniel which scholars have no explanation for.

Daniel and His Three Friends Verified as Historical Figures

One of the most fantastic sets of accounts in the Bible is that of Daniel and his three friends, who were given Babylonian names of Shadrach, Meshach, and Abednego. They were captured together during the Babylonian occupation of Israel and brought as young men to Babylon. The book of Daniel includes the accounts of "Daniel in the lion's den," the "writing on the wall" episode we just related, and his three friends being "thrown into the fiery furnace."

It is fascinating to know that these four men can be verified as historical figures by secular archaeology. An ancient text was found (the Istanbul Prism—IM 7834), dated 595 BC. It listed about 50 of King Nebuchadnezzar's court officials, including:

- Shadrach: the chief of the royal merchants
- Meshach: the overseer of the slave girls of the palace, with three other men
- Abednego: the secretary of the Crown Prince

More specifically, this prism has lists inscribed of Babylonian Court Officials (*meshannim*), Town Officials, District Officials, and more. The Court Officials (the meshannim) are those closest to the king. Twelfth in the list is Mushallim-Marduk, one of the overseers of the slave girls; the fifteenth is, Ardi-Nabu, who was secretary (*sipiru*) to Amel-Marduk, the son of Nebuchadnezzar and Crown Prince; and eighteenth is Hanunu, chief of the royal merchants (*rab tamkari*).

All of these were positions of the greatest trust, and it is interesting to note that Mushallim is the Babylonian form of the Hebrew name Mishael…Ardi-Nabu means "Servant of Nebo," and is the original Babylonian form of the Hebrew Abed-Nebo, which holds the same meaning, but which in this case was corrupted—as we have seen—by Daniel to the meaningless Abednego…And lastly is Hanunu, chief of the royal merchants, which is a direct transposition into Babylonian of Shadrach's Hebrew name, Hananiah. This is extraordinary authentication of the book of Daniel and its faithfulness to the historical record.

Daniel records Mishael's Babylonian name as Meshach. This may be a deliberate contraction of Mushallim-Marduk, which is how his name is inscribed in the Istanbul Prism—i.e., Mesha[Ilim-Nardu]k = Meshak. Such a contraction would, of course, blot out the name of the pagan 'god' Marduk.[137]

Put in context, this prism artifact refers to Daniel's three friends and the events in Daniel 3:2: -…setting up of an image on the Plain of Dura, an area outside of Babylon, probably of the chief god Marduk, and Nebuchadnezzar's insistence that all his subjects, and especially these officials, bow to the image as a show of loyalty to both god and king."[138]

Further, The Nebuchadnezzar Chronicle (BM 21946 in the British Museum) refers to this insurrection or rebellion in 595/594 BC, the calling of western vassal kings (e.g., probably Judah's King Zedekiah, as per Jeremiah 51:59a) to the Plain of Dura, and the punishment of fire to all those, who did not show obedience to the pagan god and to the king. But, in further support of the biblical account, this artifact also includes the insight that the King turned frim "his god" after this affair. Babylonian kings never dwelt overlong in their records on the subject of rebellion. It put their kingship in a bad light. But the Prism, and Daniel 3 between them, tell us that these and many other officials were summoned to Babylon, in particular to the Plain of Dura outside Babylon, to make obeisance to an image which Nebuchadnezzar had set up…But the real point of the summons was that, after the rebellion had been put down, each official would thereby be required to renew his oath of loyalty to the god of Babylon, Marduk, and so to his representative on earth, Nebuchadnezzar, the king.[139]

The book of Daniel also states correctly that the Babylonian punishment for blaspheming the gods of Chaldea consisted of being burned alive… a cuneiform inscription was later found…which designated it [some ruins found between a synagogue in Babylon and the Palace of Nebuchadnezzar] as a place in which blasphemers of the gods were burned. On top of all this…

- Alexander the Great had the book of Daniel read to him circa 332 BC when he considered destroying Jerusalem.[140] This clearly indicates that Daniel was written before that time as opposed to modernist beliefs.
- The prophet Ezekiel was a contemporary of Daniel. Ezekiel came in the second wave during the exile from Judah, circa 597 BC. Ezekiel was written circa 593-573 BC and confirms the existence of Daniel. Ezekiel 14:14 (NIV): "even if these three men—Noah, Daniel and Job—were in it [Jerusalem],

they could save only themselves by their righteousness, declares the Sovereign LORD."

It is clear that this pivotal book in the Old Testament talks of real historical people, and events described in this book, as fantastic as they seem, are independently verified in secular records as real history!

King David Outside of the Bible

It had been charged that the Bible was in error for the wide amount of time spent on the life and reign of the Hebrew King David, whom some skeptics used to say was a fictitious and mythical person who never existed. However, the "Tel Dan" inscription, as well as the "Moabite Stone," have made it clear that he was a real person in Hebrew history, as the Bible describes.

The "Tel Dan inscription" chiseled on a ninth-century BC stone slab (or stela) that furnished the first historical evidence of King David from the Bible. This inscription, or "House of David" inscription as it is sometimes called, was discovered in 1993 at the site of Tel Dan in northern Israel in an excavation directed by Israeli archaeologist Avraham Biran.

The broken and fragmentary inscription commemorates the victory of an Aramean king over his two southern neighbors: the "king of Israel" and the "king of the House of David."

The stela's fragmented inscription, first read and translated by the renowned epigrapher Joseph Naveh, proved that King David from the Bible was a genuine historical figure and not simply the fantastic literary creation of later Biblical writers and editors. Perhaps more important, the stela, set up by one of ancient Israel's fiercest enemies, more than a century after David's death, still recognized David as the founder of the kingdom of Judah. All of this, of course, was right in line with what is printed in the Bible.[141]

Likewise, the previously described Mesha Stele (also called the "Moabite Stone") is a stele (inscribed stone) set up around 840 BC by King Mesha of Moab.

As we told you before, it constitutes the major evidence for the Moabite language and is a "cornerstone of Semitic epigraphy and Palestinian history." The stele, whose story parallels, with some differences, an episode in the Bible's Books of Kings (2 Kings 3:4–8), provides invaluable information on the Moabite language and the political relationship between Moab and Israel at one moment in the 9th century BC. It is the most extensive inscription ever recovered that refers to the kingdom of Israel (referred to as the "House of Omri"—Omri was commander-in-chief of the army of the Northern Kingdom of Israel under Elah, who ruled for two years, 886-885 BC.); it bears the earliest certain extra-biblical reference to the Israelite God Yahweh, and if French scholar André Lemaire's reconstruction of a portion of line 31 is correct, the earliest mention of the "*House of David*" (i.e., the kingdom of Judah).[142]

In addition, the Moabite Stone verifies the Bible's contention that the Moabites worshiped the pagan god Chemosh. It verified the existence and location of several Moabite places noted in scripture, including Attaroth, Mehdeba, Beth-Baal-Meon, Kirithian, Nebo, Jahaz, Beth-Dib-Iathian, Beth-Bamoth, Horonian, and the Arnon riverbed. The stone's description of Moab's defeat of Gad not only verifies the biblical account of these skirmishes but also verifies from a secular record that one of the prophecies of Balaam in Numbers 22-24 came to pass with specificity![143]

Evidence Confirms the Burning of Jerusalem by Babylonians Described In the Bible

The Bible in Jeremiah 39:8, and 52:13, 2 Kings 25:9, and 2 Chronicles 36:18-19 records that the Babylonians invaded Judah and burned the palace as well as all of the houses. Archaeologists excavating the "City of David" section in Jerusalem have discovered evidence that these passages of the Bible are historically accurate.

Researchers at the site in the "Jerusalem Walls National Park" have found many burnt artifacts dating from 2,600 years ago (the exact time of the biblical references), confirming these references in the Bible that describes the burning of Jerusalem by the Babylonians. Jerusalem is thought to have fallen around 587 BC.

These findings, including burnt pottery, wood, grape seeds, and bones all covered in layers of ash, provide further evidence that the Babylonians "burned all the houses of Jerusalem," as described in the five biblical citations alluded to.

The archaeologists from the *Israel Antiquities Authority* discovered the artifacts beneath layers of rock in the eastern part of the "City of David." Amongst them were also dozens of jars used to store grain and fluids. Many of these items bore stamped handles and rosette seals, enabling the researchers to date the artifacts to 2,600 years ago. These jars are also consistent with the fact that Israel was taken after a siege, and thus, the filled jars of grain stored up to try and wait out the siege as the Israelis had done before with Sennacherib.

"These seals are characteristic of the end of the First Temple Period," explained Dr. Joe Uziel with the Israel Antiquities Authority, who led the excavation. "[They] were used for the administrative system that developed towards the end of the Judean dynasty."

The fact that the fire damage to the artifacts can now be dated to 2,600 years ago corroborates accounts in the Bible of the Babylonians burning the city. The reference to this event appears in the Book of Jeremiah, chapter 39. Further in 2 Kings 25:8-9, the Bible states:

"Now on the seventh day of the fifth month, which was the nineteenth year of King Nebuchadnezzar, king of Babylon, Nebuzaradan the captain of the guard, a servant of the king of Babylon, came to Jerusalem. He **burned the house of the Lord, the king's house, and all the houses of Jerusalem; even every great house he burned with fire.**"

These discoveries at the "City of David" dig add to existing evidence, which includes the discovery of Babylonian arrowheads dating from around the same time, that the burning of Jerusalem by the Babylonians was a historical event as well as a biblical one.[144]

Long-living Kings at Kish (Sumer)

Sumerian writings have shown a list of kings also mentioned in the Bible, who supposedly lived from 10,000 to 64,000 years ago, according to Sumerian records with debated interpretations of their mathematics. These Babylonian and other traditions have been embellished over time, a phenomenon we have discussed before.

It was later realized that the Babylonians had two bases for arithmetic calculations, based on either tens or sixties. When the records were retranslated using the system of tens rather than sixties, they totaled to within 200 years of the biblical record showing an impressive amount of agreement with the Hebrew Scriptures. Furthermore, both the biblical and Sumerian lists talk of the same personages and number of kings (It should be noted that the Sumerian accounts were corrected for by other documentation, not the Bible). This shows extra-biblical substantiation for these biblical accounts and their veracity.[145]

The Supposedly Mythological Hittites

The Hittites, according to the Bible, were descendants of Heth (Genesis 10:15). They were a Canaanite tribe dwelling near Hebron in the time of Abraham (Genesis 15:20,21) and subdued in the Israelites' invasion (Exodus 3:8 Joshua 3:10). They were not, however, exterminated in that invasion: Uriah was a Hittite (2 Samuel 11:3); Solomon used their services (1 Kings 10:29 2 Kings 7:6).

These are only a few of the forty references in the Bible of the Hittites. For centuries there was no archaeological evidence for them, and skeptics called them mythological and cited the references in the Bible as proof of biblical errors.

But, in 1906, archaeologist and historian Hugo Winkler found 10,000 of the Hittites clay tablets in a huge library at Boğazkale, Turkey, written in a hitherto unknown Hittite language. These tablets were deciphered in 1924 by the Czech scholar Bedřich Hrozný. These 10,000 tablets tell of Hittite culture and history and attest to their existence. His work uncovered this site as the capital of the Hittite Empire in the fifth and sixth century BC and showed that their culture, at its height, rivaled the mighty Assyrian and the Egyptian cultures. These finds give evidence that this culture and people group existed just as the Bible said they did and verifies the forty biblical references in the biblical accounts.[146]

The Hittite word for "retainers," which means "servants trained in a man's own household," is *hanakim* (Genesis 14:14). This term is used today only here in the Bible. Execration texts of the Egyptians (found on fragments of ceramic pots, which seem to have been used in ritual magical cursing of surrounding peoples) gives us the meaning of this term, and it is correctly used in the Bible record in Genesis 14.[147] This evidence further verifies the existence of the Hittites as shown by Hugo Winkler's work and supports the biblical account of the Hittites.

Goliath's City Found

Archaeologists led by Aren Maeir of the "Martin Department of Land, Israel Studies and Archaeology" at the Bar-Ilan University and an international support group of archaeologists from all over the world have unearthed the gate and fortified wall of Gath, an ancient Philistine city in Israel. The Bible says this was the home of Goliath (1 Samuel 17:24). Later, in 1 Samuel 21:12-13, the Bible tells us that David fled to Gath to escape King Saul. There he faked madness and made marks on the gates of the city.

Other recent discoveries at the site include the earliest decipherable Philistine inscriptions, containing two names similar to the original form of the name "Goliath." There is also geological evidence of an earthquake at this site. An earthquake event at this site is mentioned in the Bible in Amos 1:1.[148] Thus, these finds lend credence to several biblical passages as relating true history.

The Long Day

Dr. Nelson Glueck, President of Hebrew Union College till his death in 1971 and one of the foremost modern Palestinian archaeologists, says, "...absolutely no archaeological discovery has ever been controverted in a biblical reference."

Well, if that is so, what about the references in the Bible to longer than naturalistic days. There was a day when the sun actually moved backward in the sky recorded in the Bible (2 Kings 20:8-11) and the day that the sun stayed up magically while the Israelites did battle (found in Joshua chapter 10). To most, this seems incontrovertible proof of the Bible being in error since our laws of physics dictate that the earth must revolve around the sun and our planet must rotate in such a way without change so as to make such claims of reversing or stopping the passage of time or movement of the sun relative to Earth impossible.

What makes this all seem more indefensible are the multiple "urban legends" surrounding supposed but false proofs of this story. For decades since the sixties, there has been an untrue story floated by both believers and scoffers that there was an investigation by NASA computer scientists which verified the missing times in the Bible from Joshua 10:12-14 as well as 2 Kings 20:10-11. However, research done by an investigative reporter William Willoughby, the religion editor of the Washington, D.C. Evening Star, in 1970 showed that NASA engineers had no knowledge of such a story or investigation and that the methodology supposedly used by the "spacemen" as the NASA engineers are referred to in the story, could not have verified the absence of time in the past.

Further, Willoughby and others found that this "myth" was probably derived from a similar story originally written all the way back to before 1900 by a man named Totten. All of this background would seem to place the stories of lost time, the sun standing still, etc., into the realm of fanciful myths invented by desperate Christians, who wished to believe in the Bible in spite of the naturalistic evidence to the contrary.[149]

However, the Bible is not the only ancient record of extended days. Many cultures (including the Chinese and Egyptians) have records and writings about extended days (The Chinese record says it happened in their "year of the world 2554," which coincides with the biblical time of the long day occurrence). Similarly, and of great note, is the fact that six Indians groups from both North and South America and South Sea Islanders have records of a long night (other side of the world),[150] which would have occurred if God had intervened in nature and physics and performed these miracles.

Most scientists today write off these accounts from around the world as mythical since they do not fit within their worldview of only naturalistic answers being scientific. However, the number, similarity, and coordination of these accounts show amazing evidence that a supernatural or radically unnatural event took place. We discount these accounts at our own peril and risk missing the truth of our existence by choosing a reality for ourselves that does not include God, not because there is not widespread evidence for his existence and his supernaturally intervening in his creation, but because we are locked into a "non-god" worldview which will not allow us to even consider that God could have done what so many cultures and historical manuscripts including the Bible say He did![151]

Accuracy in Cultural Understanding and Use of Writing

In the ancient world, it would be impossible for a writer in the 7th century BC to know the details of life in 2000 BC. So authors in the 7th century BC did not write historical novels with realistic and minute details of geography and correct cultural environments and language of past cultures as we see so often today since there were few libraries and almost no resources from which to do research.[152]

This is why Dr. Kenneth Kitchen concluded that the old idea that the patriarchal stories in the Bible were written either during the divided monarchy or even later and were added to the Bible and not part of the original Genesis manuscripts is a charge completely without merit. The details, linguistics, names, and cultural descriptions are just too "spot on" to be anything else but the writings of contemporary witnesses.[153]

The Historical Evidence for Jesus Christ

One "Urban Myth," which has been pushed by skeptics recently, is that Jesus Christ was a myth, not a real person, and never existed except as a folktale. Nothing could be further from the truth, as Christ is one of the most verified people in history.

Jesus Christ is spoken of throughout the New Testament's twenty-seven books of the Bible. These twenty-seven books were all written within about sixty years of His death and resurrection and thus represent "eyewitness" testimony as to Christ's authenticity. Ten of these letters (later referred to as books) were written by Christ's personal friends. At least thirteen of these books or letters were written by the Apostle Paul (also known as Saul of Tarsus), who was an eyewitness of Christ's ministry as a Jewish teacher and who opposed Christ till his spectacular conversion by Christ on the road to Damascus.

Christ is repeatedly spoken of in Jewish writings of his day with respect to how to deal with him. These writings are recorded in the Jewish Babylonian Talmud. The Jewish historian Josephus repeatedly referred to Christ as a real person, and he always referred to him as a real figure in history, not as a myth. These last two sets of references are remarkable since they came from Jewish sources which were opposed to Christ and who tried to circulate the lie after Christ's death that he had not risen, but instead that his body had been stolen by his disciples. The fact that those in opposition to Christ acknowledge his existence speaks volumes as to the truth of Christ's life and existence.

The Qur'an talks of Jesus as an important teacher in history, and nowhere refers to him as a mythical figure. Mohammed, who was setting up his own religion, supplanting Christ as God's prophet, had every reason to try and discredit the historicity of Christ, but he did not do so since Christ's life is so well verified in history. In fact, the Qur'an mentions Christ 25 times while talking about the Prophet Mohammed only four times. In those passages, it refers to Christ as the "Word of God" and "One who gives life." It also talks of his mother, called "Mariam" in the Qur'an more than it does Mohammed and testifies to her virgin birth and holiness before God.

Additionally, ancient non-religious historical writings also record the life of Christ in a way that indicates that he was a real historical figure. Christ was written about as a real person in the writings of Pliny, the governor of Bithynia, around 112 AD. The Roman historian Tacitus wrote of Christ as a real person in history in 115 AD. The popular Roman writer Suetonius wrote of Christ as a real person around 120 AD. He was written off in the Jewish Talmud, although negatively since they thought him not to be the Messiah, but their writings verify his existence as well as many of the acts attributed to him in the New Testament do. All of these and many more secular sources agree with and verify the existence of Jesus Christ as a real person who walked this earth somewhere between 7 BC and 34 AD.[154]

Most historians assume that there are eight elements about Jesus and His followers that can be viewed as historical facts from both non-biblical and biblical historical data, namely:

- Jesus was baptized by John the Baptist.
- He enlisted (called) disciples.
- He had a controversy at the Temple.
- Jesus was crucified by the Romans near Jerusalem.
- Jesus was a Galilean.
- His activities were confined to Galilee and Judea.
- After his death, His disciples continued on with the ministry.
- Some of His disciples were persecuted.[155]

One fascinating proof of both Christ's life, impact on the lives he touched, and the truth of his resurrection from the grave is in the life stories of his disciples. These men also are not only verified as real people in history by the Bible but also by religious and non-religious texts. Of the twelve disciples of Christ (including Matthias, who replaced Judas after he killed himself), eleven of them died martyr's deaths. This included the legendary story of Peter asking to be crucified upside down when they were going to kill him for his faith since Peter reasoned that he was not worthy to die as Christ did. That detail incidentally is not in the Bible and may or may not be correct history, but it is verified he was martyred, and the story is consistent with Peter's character.[156]

What is unmistakable is how these twelve disciples were so greatly energized after the resurrection and ascension of Christ. These men led the formation of the Christian church and seeded its spreading over the entire world. To date, there are now over one billion Christians all over this planet as a result of their efforts. How could this set of people, who fled on the night of Jesus' arrest and who stayed in the shadows throughout his trial, demonstrating their cowardice and loss of faith, be so bold as to defy Jewish and Roman authorities to talk about and witness to the gospel of Jesus, including his resurrection and ascension even to the point of being put to death if they did not stop witnessing or recant? How did these same sheepish souls, who all fled the night Jesus was arrested, find the new courage literally overnight to testify for him till each one except John was put to death for their beliefs and actions on Christ's behalf?

It is exceedingly difficult today to find a person who will stand up for their principles of what is truth when threatened with death. A criminal will often get off in a case by threatening a witness who will then refuse to testify. A boss will threaten an employee with firing if they do not do as they ask, even though what they ask is perhaps wrong, illegal, or harms others. In most cases, people do what they have to do to keep their jobs, lives, and livelihood. Many Christians in Isis-held territory recently were given the choice of converting to Islam or being killed, and many gave in to the pressure to convert to Islam via such pressures.

How then did these twelve men, who we already know from the Bible to be very average men, not courageous and not bold, suddenly find ultimate courage (ask for death) and act boldly as never before after Christ's death? Jesus' death should have had the opposite effect upon them. It should have taught them that his whole ministry was a lie and that Jesus was either a liar or insane since he professed to be the "Son of God." His death should have prompted them to face this reality and shrink from this Jesus worship and protect themselves from association with a religious cult which was clearly in error if they had seen him executed and buried. It is their witnessing his resurrection from the dead which gave them such boldness and attested to what they saw better than any other evidence could.

Why did **atheist historian Gerd Ludemann** accept the post-mortem appearance (after the resurrection) of Christ as actual history? He did so because on multiple occasions and under various circumstances, different individuals and groups of people experienced appearances of Jesus risen from the dead. This is a fact that is almost universally acknowledged among New Testament scholars for the following reasons:

1. The list of eyewitnesses to Jesus's post-resurrection appearances, which is quoted by Paul in I Corinthians 15:5-7, guarantees that such appearances occurred; and

2. The appearance traditions in the gospels provide multiple, independent attestations of such appearances.

With respect to the first supporting line of evidence, it is universally accepted on the basis of the early date of Paul's tradition, as well as the apostle's personal acquaintance with many of the people listed that the disciples did experience postmortem appearances of Christ. Among the witnesses of the post-resurrection appearances were Peter, the immediate circle of the disciples known as "the Twelve," a gathering of 500 Christian believers (many of whom Paul evidently knew, since he was aware that some had died by the time of his writing), Jesus' younger brother James, and a wider group of apostles. "Finally," says Paul, "as to one untimely born, he appeared also to me" (1 Corinthians 15.8 NASB).

The second supporting line of evidence appeals again to the criterion of multiple attestations. The Gospels independently attest to postmortem appearances of Jesus, even to some of the same appearances found in Paul's list.

Wolfgang Trilling explains, "From the list in 1 Corinthians 15, *the particular reports of the Gospels are now to be interpreted. Here may be of help what we said about Jesus'* miracles. It is impossible to "prove" historically a particular miracle. But the totality of the miracle reports permits no reasonable doubt that Jesus, in fact, performed "miracles." That holds analogously for the appearance reports. It is not possible to secure historically the particular event. But the totality of the appearance reports permits no reasonable doubt that Jesus, in fact, bore witness to himself in such a way." This is supported by Jewish records, as well as in the Bible.

The appearance to Peter is independently attested by Paul and Luke (1 Corinthians 15.5; Luke 24.34), the appearance to the Twelve by Paul, Luke, and John (1 Corinthians 15.5; Luke 24:36-43; John 20.19-20), the appearance to the women disciples by Matthew and John (Matthew 28.9-10; John 20.11-17), and appearances to the disciples in Galilee by Mark, Matthew, and John (Mark 16.7; Matthew 28. 16-17; John 21). Taken sequentially, the appearances follow the pattern of Jerusalem-Galilee-Jerusalem, matching the festival pilgrimages of the disciples as they returned to Galilee following the Passover/Feast of Unleavened Bread and traveled again to Jerusalem two months later for Pentecost.

Lüdemann himself concludes, "It may be taken as historically certain that Peter and the disciples had experiences after Jesus' death in which Jesus appeared to them as the risen Christ." (Remember that Frank Morison's research came to the same conclusion). Thus, we are in basic agreement that following Jesus' crucifixion, various individuals and groups of people experienced appearances of Christ alive from the dead. The real bone of contention will be how these experiences are best to be explained.[157]

Ludemann, a skeptic, proposes that everything that the Bible recounts really was a mass hallucination. This is highly improbable, however, since it would require a level of mass hallucination not clinically observed in psychology.[158]

What on Earth caused these sheepish souls the Bible called Jesus' disciples to become so bold and so courageous? It was their witnessing, along with 500 other Christians, of Jesus' resurrection and ascension. They were given a front-row seat to Jesus' proof of His power over death and his proof of being God! How were they so energized to spread the gospel across the Middle East and the Mediterranean? It was because of what they had witnessed for themselves, which transformed their lives like nothing we experience today.

As I pointed out above, you cannot often get a person to put themselves in jeopardy today when they are threatened even for the truth. How could these eleven men, who were put to death for preaching Jesus, to a man have stuck with their story all the way to being executed if they were perpetuating a lie? As I said before, very few people will die for the truth today or yesterday, but **no one except a madman will die for a lie**. One or two of these guys could have been insane, but not all. The fact that they all to a man accepted death rather than to recant their witness of Jesus' life and divinity is logical proof positive of Jesus' resurrection from the dead, His ascension, and their belief in his godhood!

This, along with the multiple secular citations of Christ's life and exploits, make it clear Christ existed and did much of what the Bible says He did. To deny this is equivalent to denying the Holocaust in World War II, which some totally discredited zealots will try and push on society today as a conspiracy theory.

Christ's Impact on History and Culture

Christ's life, verified in history, is also verified in the impact of his life on our culture. Napoleon Bonaparte talking of Jesus, said, "This man disappeared 1800 years ago, and yet he still holds men's character in a vise!" We have set up our whole calendar for the past

1400 years based on his birth. The biggest and widest celebrated holiday on the planet is that of Christmas, celebrating his birth. Over one billion people across the world celebrate this holiday each year, commemorating Jesus' birth as well as Easter, which commemorates his death and resurrection.

We celebrate other key figures in our history, such as Dr. Martin Luther King's birthday, to commemorate his contributions in the realm of civil rights. We commemorate the birthdays of other great men such as the birthdays of George Washington, who led the victory over the British to form this country and who set many of the precedents for the United States presidency, and Abraham Lincoln, who presided over our Civil War to end slavery and keep the union intact. It is interesting to note, though, how such huge accomplishments can fade in our cultures over time. Washington's and Lincoln's birthdays used to be celebrated as separate holidays but now have been morphed into the one-day celebration of "Presidents' Day" lumped in along with all other past Presidents of the United States. Regardless, no one doubts the historicity of Washington, Lincoln, or Dr. King. Christ's impact is so much wider, not just in America, but in the formation of the entire western culture of the world, that it is simple blasphemy of the truth to even suggest he did not exist.

In comparison to these single-day holidays, which may wane over time, Christmas is not a single-day event but the centerpiece of an entire season, in which most of this world focuses on the ideal of the universal brotherhood of man. The almost one billion people in the world in the Catholicized faiths celebrate a full month of what is called the "advent season" leading up to Christmas to commemorate Christ's birth.

But it is not only his birth that we celebrate for more than a month at Christmas time, but we spend a week celebrating his death and resurrection in the spring. Catholics around the world replay his triumphal entry into Jerusalem at the beginning of the Passover week. They also spend an entire 40 days focusing on Christ's sacrificial death as they see it by practicing a season of "lent" for 40 days prior to Easter. We celebrate "Good Friday" across the world to commemorate his death (Good because Christians believe he was dying for our sins) and extend that celebration to the following Sunday when we celebrate his resurrection from the dead, on Easter Sunday.

The entire tenants, foundations, and guidance for western culture over the past 1700 years have been based on the Christian Bible, the Ten Commandments, and the teachings of Christ. Our legal jurisprudence is all based on the Bible.

In contrast, let's look at how we have treated other great figures in history. Alexander the Great lived from 356 to 323 BC. He conquered much of the known world in his time, ranging from Eastern Europe through the Middle East and well into Asia. After conquering Egypt, he had the city of Alexandria constructed in his name. Not only was his birthday celebrated for hundreds of years in Macedon and Greece, in Alexandria, he was given the ultimate honor of the main street of Alexandria (called the "Canopic Road") being aligned so that the sun comes up shining straight down its path on his birthday of July 20. Further, in the time of his reign, this street, on that same night, would point toward the star Regulus, known as the "King Star."[159]

Five hundred years later, the Roman emperor Septimius Severus will close off access to Alexander's tomb[160] and ended celebration of the birth of this conqueror of the world and a person, who both Macedonians and Egyptians thought to be a God was relegated to just mentions in the history books today. No one thinks of celebrating his birthday anymore.

Vladimir Ilyich Ulyanov, better known as Lenin, was a Russian communist revolutionary, politician, and political theorist. He was the father of the Soviet Union. Not only was his birthday celebrated in Russia for decades, but he authored trains of thoughts we marked as "Leninist." A city was named after him, and he was revered as the father and maker of communism and Russian state culture. In the early twentieth century, his writings were taken as "holy writ" in Russia.

Today, while some in Russia still revere him, the city once named after him is no longer called Leningrad but has reverted to its historic name of St. Petersburg. There is a move afoot today in Russia to remove all statues of Lenin from the public squares.[161]

I could go on, but the point is well made. As a slave was assigned to ride along in the chariot with a conquering general when he paraded triumphantly into ancient Rome to celebrate his conquest, the slave constantly whispered into his ear, "fame is fleeting." Society soon forgets even the greatest of accomplishments and has a "what have you done lately mentality."

Yet, two thousand years later, we have over a billion people and all of the western culture which pays honor to Christ's existence. No other person in human history sees the entire culture so affected by their life, and these facts are a living testament not only to his historical existence but bear incredibly strong evidence that in western culture, he is believed to be the Messiah and the Son of God.

The Exodus

One of the most recent objections to the Bible surfaced in the 1950s. It asks whether the Exodus actually occurred. It is pretty much a consensus among Egyptologists today that there is no archaeological evidence for the Exodus anytime in the Late Bronze Age (circa 1200 BC), and this lack of evidence and consensus among archaeologists that the Bible refers to Rameses II as the Exodus pharaoh has caused even some Bible scholars to start referring to the Exodus as a moral story, and not historical truth in the last few decades.

Archaeologists Charles Ailing, David Rohl, and John Bimson debate this view, however. While it is true that there is no archaeological evidence for the Exodus around 1200 BC, that date may be the problem. Egyptologists and Bible Scholars have traditionally given a date for the Exodus around 1200-1250 BC due to scripture which infers that Rameses may have been the Pharaoh at the time of the Exodus, and archaeology shows the city of Rameses was built during this time, and thus they place the Exodus during the reign of Pharaoh Rameses II.

The aforementioned archaeologists, including Rohl, believe the biblical reference to the city Rameses may, however, be referring to that **area** and not to the city Rameses, nor the time period in which Rameses was built and inserted editorially later by scribes. They point to the fact that hundreds of years before the burial city of Rameses existed, this same area was the site of the ancient Egyptian city called **Avaris**. In the ruins of Avaris, and at the time that this city existed in the same area which will later become Rameses, is evidence of Joseph, his family, the seven-year famine, the Plagues, and the Exodus.

A New Chronology for Egyptian history of the ancient Near East has been developed by English Egyptologist David Rohl and other researchers, beginning with publication of *A Test of Time: The Bible—from Myth to History* in 1995. It contradicts mainstream Egyptology by proposing a major revision of the conventional chronology of ancient Egypt, in particular by re-dating Egyptian kings of the 19th through 25th Dynasties, lowering conventional dates up to 350 years. Rohl asserts that the New Chronology allows him to identify some of the characters in the Old Testament with people whose names appear in archaeological finds.[162]

David Rohl's published works, A Test of Time (1995), Legend (1998), The Lost Testament (2002), and The Lords of Avaris (2007) set forth Rohl's theories for revising the dating of major civilizations of the ancient world. "A Test of Time" proposes a down-dating (bringing closer to the present), by a few centuries, of the Egyptian New Kingdom, thus requiring a major revision of the conventional chronology of ancient Egypt. Rohl asserts that this would permit scholars to identify many of the major events in the Old Testament with events in the archaeological record and identify some of the well-known biblical characters with historical figures who appear in contemporary ancient texts. Lowering the Egyptian dates also dramatically affects the dating of other dependent chronologies, such as that currently employed for the Greek "Heroic Age" of the Late Bronze Age, removing the Greek Dark Age and lowering the dates of the Trojan War to within a couple of generations of a 9th-century-BC Homer and his most famous composition: The Iliad.[163]

The New Chronology places King Solomon at the end of the wealthy Late Bronze Age rather than in the relatively impoverished Early Iron Age. Rohl and other New Chronology researchers contend that this fits better with the Old Testament description of Solomon's wealth, and it clears up inexplicable gaps in dependent European and Mediterranean chronologies.

Furthermore, Rohl shifts the Israelite Sojourn, Exodus, and Conquest from the end of the Late Bronze Age to the latter part of the Middle Bronze Age (from the Egyptian 19th Dynasty to the 13th Dynasty and Hyksos period). Rohl claims that this solves many of the problems associated with the historicity issue of the biblical narratives. Rohl makes use of the archaeological reports from Tell ed-Daba (ancient Avaris) in the Egyptian eastern delta, which show that a large Semitic-speaking population lived there during the 13th Dynasty. These people were culturally similar to the population of Middle-Bronze-Age (MB IIA) Canaan.[164] Rohl identifies these Semites as the people upon whom the biblical tradition of the Israelite Sojourn in Egypt was subsequently based.

Towards the end of the Middle Bronze Age, archaeologists have revealed a series of city destructions that John Bimson and Rohl have argued correspond closely to the cities attacked by the Israelite tribes in the Joshua narrative. Most importantly, the heavily fortified city of Jericho was destroyed and abandoned at this time. Rohl contends that the New Chronology, with the shift of the Exodus and Conquest events to the Middle Bronze Age, removes the principal reason for that widespread academic skepticism of the biblical account.[165]

It should be noted that the "lynchpin" for much of Egyptian Chronology is the writings of the Egyptian Historian Manetho. His works are taken as almost gospel by Egyptologists, but with one great exception. He mentions the Exodus in his writings as referred to by First Century Roman historian Josephus.[166] Also, the Exodus, as confirmed by the Roman historian Cornelius Tacitus wrote that most of his sources were in agreement that there was an Exodus from Egypt led by a man named "Moses,"[167] and Josephus wrote of the Exodus as well.[168]

Rohl's, Ailings, and Bimson's views allow for a lot of discoveries by a host of archaeologists, which show a ruler's house and palace at Avaris, which easily could have been that of Joseph. It was in the land of Goshen, consistent with the biblical account. The mansion had 12 pillars and 12 graves reminiscent of the twelve sons of Jacob and the 12 tribes named after them. Further, the mansion showed Semitic artifacts showing that it was not Egyptians, who inhabited this ruling mansion in Goshen, but people from the Syrian area (of which Canaan was part). The grave of the head of the household was in the shape of a pyramid which only occurred with high rulers (which Joseph had been elevated to). That tomb contained a statue of a light-skinned person and had red hair, which is how the Egyptians depicted the Semitic and had multicolored coat at his feet as Joseph is described to have worn in the Bible! This tomb also was empty, as would be expected if it were Joseph, as his bones were transported back to Canaan in the Exodus as the Bible recorded. Further, the excavations at Avaris showed Goshen in this earlier time was populated by Semitic peoples, which easily could have been the Israelites as they were shepherds![169]

Part of the preparations for the seven years of famine was the regulation of the Nile via a canal referenced on Egyptian artifacts as the "Waterway of Joseph," which verifies Joseph being of this earlier time period. When the famine comes, no one outside of Egypt had food, which means everyone has to come to the Egyptian pharaoh for food, and a dramatic shift in wealth occurs in this time when all the surrounding nations, peoples, and lands came under the command of Egypt. At the same time, the splintered ruling of different provinces of Egypt called "nomes" were turned over to the total rule of Pharaoh, which easily could have occurred because everyone, including the ruling princes of the provinces, had to bend to Pharaoh, who had the only food.[170] All of this is found in archaeology and is in lockstep with what is recorded in the Bible.

This new timeline moves the occupation of Goshen by Israelites to the Middle Kingdom of Egypt. There is evidence here of the same brick construction described in the Bible, as it is shown all through Egyptian history. Also, the Avaris site shows a period of prosperity and growth of the Semitic population followed by a lack of prosperity which corresponds to the Israelites first being welcomed and prospering in Goshen under Joseph and then being enslaved later as the Bible says occurred. There is also archaeological evidence at the end of this period of huge amounts of baby deaths and further burial remains, which show a generation later of only 40 percent males, and 60 percent females survived that generation. This indicates that the 50 percent baby mortality rate recorded in remains at this time were primarily directed at the males, just as the Biblical story was told of how Moses ended up in the river to be found and adopted by the Egyptian Queen to escape Pharaoh's male slave baby execution order. Furthermore, the names of Hebrews have been found recorded in the Egyptian Middle Kingdom writings, and many of these same names are in the Bible, verifying that this all occurred earlier than Egyptologists have agreed that it did.[171]

There is an Egyptian papyrus ("Admonitions of an Egyptian Sage," also called the "Ipuwer Papyrus") which in detail tells of the plagues coming upon Egypt during the earlier Middle Kingdom. It also says that **the gold and treasure of Egypt were given over to the slaves, and they left**, just as the Bible says. According to the Bible, not only did this wealth go with the Israelites, but the Egyptian army was destroyed.[172] Thus losing its wealth, their agriculture, their first-born sons, its army, and its slaves, Egypt would have been impoverished and vulnerable to attack, and this is what is indicated at the end of the Egyptian Middle Kingdom as a period called the dark era when Egypt fell into a period of weakness and impoverishment. This is exactly what would have occurred if the Exodus had happened at this time!

Furthermore, the Avaris site shows a tremendous number of mass graves (due to slavery and plagues) and then abandonment (the Exodus) of this site in Goshen, just as we should find if the biblical account were true.

The archaeology of the Land of Canaan of the Middle Bronze Age shows a conquering and destruction of the city fortresses of Jericho, Hazor, Hebron, Arad, and more, all during the time of Jericho's destruction and thus in complete concert with the biblical account. The cuneiform tablets at Hazor describe King Jabin, and that is exactly who the Bible says Joshua killed at Hazor. The demise of Jericho was dated far before the Late Bronze Age, which is one reason why so many scholars doubt the Exodus account of the Bible. However, the dating of the destruction of Jericho does fit with the Early Bronze Age and all of the other evidence we have for the Exodus. In fact, there is a burn layer in Jericho and fallen walls corresponding to the biblical account. Also of interest are full jars of grain in Jericho showing a short siege before its destruction (one week as the Bible describes) and one wall piece with domiciles in it left standing exactly as the biblical account states (Rahab's domicile was not destroyed, but the rest was).[173]

What is interesting here is that all of this was researched and proposed by *Professor Rohl, who is an agnostic and not a believer*. He is simply following the evidence. If you would like to see a rather fine compilation of the research, the debates, and the biblical and archaeological perspectives on this whole topic of the Exodus, we would invite you to view the documentary *Patterns of Evidence: The Exodus,* which can better than anything else we have seen put all of this subject matter together for the laymen.

There is other anecdotal evidence that supports the truth of the biblical Exodus account. As we detailed in the section on Joseph, Egyptian scholars agree that the Exodus accounts use Egyptian references with names and cultural trappings, which show that the writers were well versed in the culture of the day. We would not expect such cultural accuracy to show in the writings of the Exodus if it were a mythical event added to the Bible centuries later by Jews, who had little knowledge of ancient Egyptian culture.[174]

Until the time of Rameses II in the 13th century BC, it was common in Egyptian writings for the title "Pharaoh" to stand alone with no name added. From Rameses onward, the name of Pharaoh was usually added. Likewise, in Genesis and Exodus in the Bible, there are no pharaoh's names added until the time of the divided monarchy when the pharaohs were identified in the Bible just as they are in Egyptian writings.[175] This all supports the idea of the pharaoh of the Exodus being a ruler before the usually agreed upon Rameses II, as David Rohl and others have suggested.

Many skeptics charge that there is no evidence in Egyptian writings for the Exodus. To understand the omission of the Exodus from Egyptian writings, we need to understand Egyptian culture. The Egyptians were infatuated with the afterlife, and their religious beliefs convinced them that if they were forgotten by the living, they would lose their immortality in the afterlife. This is why they spent enormous efforts to record their names and images on monuments throughout Egypt.

Egyptians despised their enemies. To not even mention the names of their enemies was the ultimate in contempt and disrespect. Thus, Egyptian hieroglyphics have been shown repeatedly to alter and ignore historical events to favor Egyptians and positive history for Egypt. Revisionist history (rewriting or changing history to fit the viewpoint of the historian) is indeed a very old practice and one which has been used by many cultures over man's existence. Today's counter-culture movement in the U.S. is trying to do just that.

For Moses not to name the pharaohs' names would be his way of rejecting their authority over him. Remember, Moses was brought up as an Egyptian in the Egyptian royal court and would naturally think like an Egyptian. Is it any surprise when he omits the names of the pharaohs in the Bible?

Likewise, when the entire nation of Egypt was decimated by a series of plagues; followed by slaves (the lowest of the low in their society) walking away not only with their freedom but also much of the wealth of Egypt; followed by Egypt's powerful military force being destroyed in the Red Sea, it is little wonder that all of the records of the people responsible for this shameful period in the eyes of the Egyptians (the Israelites) would be purged from Egyptian records and monuments. This concept was not lost on the director Cecil B. DeMille in his excellent and classic film portraying the Exodus called "The Ten Commandments." When Moses is cast out of Egypt for killing another Egyptian, who was beating a slave, pharaoh had all records of Moses' name wiped from existence and even forbade the speaking of his name. Such was their concept of stealing a person's life and existence from them.[176]

Another point is the absurdity of the claim that it was a fabricated story that the Jews were slaves in Egypt. If you are going to make up a story about your heritage, you make your ancestors great men, or rich men or rulers, or powerful warriors. Anything but slaves. Especially since they were supposed to be the "favored and chosen people of God." If you were making up a story about their ancestry, it would certainly be any story, but the one told of Israelite slavery in Egypt unless the account was essentially true.

Also, if there was no Exodus, then the Jews based their most important annual festival and religious rite, the Feast of the Passover, on an event that was purely fictitious. Further, the story of Egyptian slavery is unique. It is not the normal story of a nation conquered and taken into exile, but the unique story of Jacob, a Semitic shepherd, his family moving to Egypt in a time of famine and their becoming a significant people group in Goshen, which can be historically verified.[177]

As we have detailed here, contrary to secular consensus, there is excellent evidence for the Exodus!

Tablet "Sinai 375a"

As mentioned in the last section, there is a consensus among most archaeologists that there is no evidence of Hebrews in Egypt. In addition to the wealth of evidence previously discussed, there is **Tablet "Sanai 375a."** The tablet is written with letters formed using Egyptian Hieroglyphics and is Hebrew writing according to one archaeologist's interpretation of the writing on this tablet.

Dr. Douglas Petrovich of Wilfrid Laurier University in Waterloo, Canada, determined that the letters comprise what is probably the original Hebrew alphabet. He has published his findings in his book, "The World's Oldest Alphabet," using the highly respected Carta Publishing House in Jerusalem.

One of the references on this tablet is reported to be about Ahisamach mentioned in Exodus. Exodus 31:6 (NLT) says, "And I have personally appointed Oholiab son of **Ahisamach**, of the tribe of Dan, to be his assistant...." The inscriptions date from the time period the Hebrews were to have been in Egypt, between 1882 and 1446 BC. While other archaeologists admit this is an ancient Semitic tongue (since they admit it has Semitic linguistic markers), they say it has to be something other than Hebrew due to their general rejection of the Exodus account. However, they have no objective evidence to support dismissing this inscription as Hebrew.

More interestingly, Petrovich was able to translate sixteen inscriptions. Those inscriptions included details about the Hebrews in Egypt, including details about Moses and Asenath (Joseph's wife according to Genesis 41:45). These details not only give even more evidence for Hebrews in Egypt during the time the Bible claims, but also gives details making it clear this is more than just any Semitic language, but most likely early Hebrew.

Many archaeologists are very skeptical of Petrovich's work, but in view of the evidence, this skepticism seems more devotion to their own beliefs and commitment to the Hebrew not being in Egypt during the Egyptian Middle Kingdom, rather than any use of scientific or linguistic critiques of Petrovich's work.

What is really disturbing to other linguists is that Petrovich's work seems to support that not only were the Hebrews in Egypt, as the Bible says, but that Hebrew was the first alphabet of humans.[178] This is a controversial idea in contemporary archaeology but is perfectly in line with the Bible. And it is what we would expect to find if the biblical account is the first origin account of this world.

Evidence for Yahweh Worshippers in Canaan in the 15th Century BC

A "Land of worshippers of Yahweh" is the hieroglyphic inscription on the *Egyptian Stoleb Inscription* from the time of the Egyptian pharaoh Amenhotep III (1390-1352 BC), indicates an early date for the Israelites in Canaan.

At the end of the 15th century B.C., the Egyptian Pharaoh Amenhotep III built a temple to honor the god Amun-Ra at Soleb in Nubia (modern-day northern Sudan). Within the temple area are a series of columns on which Amenhotep III listed the territories he claimed to have conquered. Each territory is listed by a relief of a prisoner with their hands tied behind their backs over an oval "name ring" identifying the land of the particular foe. The most interesting from a biblical perspective is a column drum that lists enemies from "the land of the Shasu (nomads) of Yahweh." Given the other name rings nearby, the context would place this land in the Canaanite region. In addition, the prisoner is clearly portrayed as Semitic, rather than African-looking, as other prisoners in the list are portrayed[179]

This evidence testifies against those who would say that the Exodus did not occur till the 13th century BC and thus contradicting the biblical record. This ancient stele gives verification to the biblical account that the Jews were already well established in Canaan (the Promised Land) early in the 14th century BC. This is more substantiation for the Exodus, having occurred well before the modernists and Dame Kathleen Kenyon propose it did. It is part of a mounting set of evidence for the Exodus occurring as the biblical timeline would put it during the fifteenth century BC.

Problems With Traditional Egyptian Chnorology

Many Bible critics use the Egyptian chronology to try and discredit biblical historical accuracy. However, as we have already demonstrated, assuming the reliability of the traditional Egyptian chronology could be a mistake.

In addition, archaeological evidence (by its very nature) is open to interpretation (earthen pots and old bones do not come with labels on them telling how old and what they were). Evidence corroborating biblical events can be difficult to pinpoint due to the fact that there is debate regarding the correct time periods to be searching in, as well as even the specific geographical areas to investigate. For example, Bible scholars debate both the date and the route of the Exodus, as well as the locations of Mt. Sinai and Kadesh Barnea, among others. Despite these difficulties, we do find archaeological evidence to corroborate the biblical narrative of the ancient Israelites, as we have already detailed.

Where Does Traditional Egyptian Chronology Come From?

It should be noted, the Egyptian chronology was developed **before** we had the capability to translate hieroglyphics. Jean-Francois Champollion was the first person to translate hieroglyphics in 1822.[180] Prior to this, Egyptian chronology was pieced together based on the writings of classical authors like Herodotus and Siculus. Modern advances have shown most of these writings to be woefully inaccurate.

Another source for the traditional Egyptian chronology was the *"Aegyptiaca,"* written by **Manetho**, an Egyptian priest in the third century BC. The Greek king of Egypt, Ptolemy II, commissioned Manetho to compile a history of Egypt. The problem is, Manetho's history was never intended to be a chronological account of Egyptian history. Charles Kimball points out in his book, *A Biblical Interpretation of World History*, "Manetho's main goal was to prove to the Greeks that the Egyptians were the world's oldest people..."

Kimball goes on to explain that Manetho was, in fact, competing with two men endeavoring to make the same claim for their nations: Berosus for Mesopotamia and Eratosthenes for the Greeks.[181] Thus, Manetho had an inducement to stretch Egyptian dates as much as possible and possibly beyond the truth.

Manetho organized Egyptian history into the thirty dynasties that are recognized today.[182] But there are big problems with using his work. First, Manetho's original text is gone. All we have are various quotes of his work from the Roman writers Eusebius and Africanus and an excerpt from his writings from Josephus.[183] These two versions don't even agree on names or how years are counted. Here's an example from Kimball's book, "Syncellus, who copied Africanus' list, wrote, 'The twenty-fourth dynasty, Bocchoris of Sais, for six years: in his reign a lamb spoke [a short gap in the manuscript] 990 years.' Meanwhile, Eusebius wrote, "Bocchoris of Sais for 44 years, in his reign, a lamb spoke. Total 44 years.' We are left guessing whether the 24th dynasty lasted for six years, 44 years, or 990."

Kimball also points out that the names and ages that Manetho gave for the 18th and 19th dynasties have been proven wrong at almost every comparison by evidence left by the pharaohs themselves. James H. Breasted, author of *History of Egypt*, says that Manetho's history is "a late, careless and uncritical compilation, which can be proven wrong from the contemporary monuments in the vast majority of cases, where such documents have survived."[184]

I mentioned earlier that Manetho measured time differently. He used "regnal years" like all the other ancients did. For example, "in the 5th year of King So and So." If you add all these reigns consecutively, you end up with quite an inflated timeline due to the addition of a multitude of nonexistent generations. Which, if you'll recall, goes right along with the purpose for which he was commissioned, to prove that the Egyptians were the world's oldest people. In reality, each dynasty was not successive. Some kings shared the throne as co-regents, and many dynasties more than likely overlapped. Kimball quotes renowned Egyptologist Sir Alan Gardiner, "what is proudly advertised as Egyptian history, is merely a collection of rags and tatters." There are more gaps than evidence.

This leads us to another issue with traditional Egyptian chronology. Historians had to come up with a way to align Egyptian regnal years with modern BC dates. So, in 1904 Eduard Meyer came up with a theory called the "Sothic cycle" to reconcile the dates. Traditional Egyptian chronology is based on this theory.

What is the Sothic Cycle Theory?

Dr. Elizabeth Mitchell explains, "Meyer proposed that the Egyptian calendar, having no leap year, fell steadily behind until it corrected itself during the year of the '*rising of Sothis*' [Sothis is a star we call Sirius]. The theory says that the Egyptians knew that 1,460 years were necessary for the calendar to correct itself because the annual sunrise appearance of the star Sirius corresponded to the first day of Egypt's flood season only once every 1,460 years (like a broken watch that is correct twice a day) and that the Egyptians dated important events from this Great Sothic Year."

This would be great if there were actually any evidence that the Egyptians actually reckoned time this way, but there isn't. To add insult to injury, the two non-Egyptian writers who espoused this concept (a Roman named Censorinus and Theon of Alexandria) don't agree on the starting point of the Sothic year. As it turns out, this so-called Sothic year is impossible to pinpoint due to this fact that Dr. Mitchell mentions, "…whenever Egyptian writings mention the rising of Sothis in connection with a regnal year, the pharaoh is unnamed, or the reference is ambiguous."

Does Egyptian Chronology Hold Up to Scrutiny?

The Hebrew chronology in the Bible isn't the only source that Egyptian chronology is inconsistent with. It disagrees with the Assyrian chronology, the history of the Hittite people as they coincide with Assyrian history, carbon dating, and even with itself according to Egyptian records that historians now have the capability to decipher. It was completely misaligned with European histories, and those were brought together by **assuming** the Egyptian chronology to be accurate and introduced large "*dark periods*" with no archaeological evidence for them in European chronology, which may well have never occurred, but which are necessary to support its working with the *assumed* to be true Egyptian chronology.

The popular idea that the Bible is proved incorrect by the standard Egyptian chronology is not only unproven, but there is considerable evidence we have already examined to suggest it is not the Bible that is in error, but instead, it is the currently accepted Egyptian chronology which is in error.[185]

Josephus and Other Extra-Biblical Sources

There are many extra-biblical sources that verify the contents of the Bible. One of these external sources is the first-century Roman historian Flavius Josephus (AD 37/38–97). In his writings, he mentions more than a dozen individuals talked about in the Bible, including Herod the Great, Herod Antipas, Caiaphas, Pontius Pilate, John the Baptist, Jesus called the Christ, James "the brother of Jesus, called Christ," Felix, and Festus.[186]

Other historical sources outside of the Bible corroborate details surrounding:

- Long life spans prior to the Flood. Claims of long lifespans among the ancients have been found in the records of the Egyptians, Babylonians, Greeks, Romans, Indians, and Chinese. Dr. Bryant Wood points out, "The Sumerian King List, for example, lists kings who reigned for long periods of time. Then a great Flood came. Following the Flood, Sumerian kings ruled for much shorter periods of time. This is the same pattern found in the Bible. Men had long life spans before the Flood and shorter life spans after the Flood."[187]
- The confusion of language as we have in the biblical account of the Tower of Babel (Genesis 11:1–9)[188]

- The campaign into Israel by Pharaoh Shishak (1 Kings 14:25–26), as recorded on the walls of the Temple of Amun in Thebes, Egypt.
- Fall of Samaria (2 Kings 17:3–6, 24, 18:9–11) to Sargon II, king of Assyria, as recorded on his palace walls.
- Defeat of Ashdod by Sargon II (Isaiah 20:1), as recorded on his palace walls.
- Campaign of the Assyrian king Sennacherib against Judah (2 Kings 18:13–16), as recorded on the Taylor Prism in the British Museum.
- Siege of Lachish by Sennacherib (2 Kings 18:14, 17), as recorded on the Lachish reliefs.
- Assassination of Sennacherib by his own sons (2 Kings 19:37), as recorded in the annals of his son Esarhaddon.
- Fall of Nineveh as predicted by the prophets Nahum (1:1–3:19) and Zephaniah (2:13–15), as recorded on the Tablet of Nabopolassar in the British Museum.
- Fall of Jerusalem to Nebuchadnezzar, king of Babylon (2 Kings 24:10–14), as recorded in the Babylonian Chronicle Tablets.
- Captivity of Jehoiachin, king of Judah, in Babylon (2 Kings 24:15–16), as recorded on the Babylonian Ration Records.
- Fall of Babylon to the Medes and Persians (Daniel 5:30–31), as recorded on the Cyrus Cylinder in the British Museum.
- Freeing of captives in Babylon by Cyrus the Great (Ezra 1:1–4; 6:3–4), as recorded on the Cyrus Cylinder
- The revolt against Rome led by "Judas of Galilee" [not Judas Iscariot], the founder of the Zealots (Acts 5:37) as recorded by Josephus.[189]
- The prolonged mid-day darkness on the day Jesus died (Mark 15:33), as recorded by the Roman historian Thallus (c. AD 50), a Greek author named Phlegon, Julius Africanus, and Tertullian.[190]

Erastus, Public Official, and Christian Verified

Romans 16:23 (KJV) says, "Gaius mine host, and of the whole church, saluteth you. **Erastus, the chamberlain of the city** saluteth you and Quartus a brother." Second Timothy 4:20 (ESV) says, "**Erastus** remained at Corinth, and I left Trophimus, who was ill, at Miletus."

Both New Testament scriptures talk of a New Testament convert named Erastus, who was a public official. It is of interest that during a 1929 archaeological excavation of the area near a theater in Corinth, a plaza was located that contained a stone inscription bearing the name of Erastus and indicating that he was a public official.

John McRay says the pavement in which this inscription was found dates to before A.D. 50. The letters are seven inches high. The complete inscription reads:

ERASTVS-PRO-AEDILIT[at]E S-P-Stravit In
full: "Erastus pro aedilitate sua pecunia stravit"

The English translation of the inscription is, "Erastus in return for his aedileship (in Latin, magistrates in charge of public buildings, streets, markets, games, etc.) laid [the pavement] at his own expense."[191]

This is only one of a myriad of identifications of biblical characters identified via extra-biblical texts or archaeological discoveries such as this one, verifying the existence, positions, and actions of biblical characters.

Abraham and the Patriarchs Were Not an Insert

It has been charged by some that the stories of Abraham were written during the 7th century BC to "create" history for the nation of Judah. However, analysis of social, domestic, legal, and political culture revealed in archaeology and the book of Genesis shows that the main features of the patriarchal narratives either fit specifically into the first half of the second millennium BC or are consistent with such dating.

For example, the names of the four kings in Genesis 14:1-4 are known names from the period and region—though not the same men as found in archaeology. The practices of adoption and surrogacy illustrated by Abraham are well attested to in second millennium BC documents.

Mari was the capital of the Amorites until 1760 BC. It was situated 199 miles southeast of Haran, where Abraham lived. The work of Daniel Fleming, an expert in Mari texts, concluded that the writings of the Mari texts are consistent with the Bible and show that the biblical narrative of the patriarchs accurately reflected the culture of the times in the early second millennium BC (the time of Abraham). Personal names such as Noah, Abram, Laban, Dan, Jacob, Gad, Levi, and Ishmael appear in the Mari texts showing that such names were common for the period the Bible claims they existed.

A city named Nahur is mentioned in the Mari texts, as well as in Genesis 11:22-25. The city of Haran, also identified as existing in the Mari texts and in other documentation, is talked about in Genesis 11:32-12:4.[192]

Biblical Characters in Archaeology

Archaeology has artifacts verifying that the biblical characters of Pontius Pilate, Caiaphas, King Jeroboam, Adrammelech, Isaiah, Balaam, Daniel, Shadrach Meshach, Abednego, Nebuchadnezzar, King Sargon, King David, King Solomon, the Queen of Sheba, Christ, King Jehoiachin, Pharaoh Shishak, Cyrus the Great, Erastus, King Herod, the twelve disciples of Christ, the Apostle Paul, John the Baptist, and 110 more showing not only they existed, but verifying much of what the Bible says they did.[193]

The Bible Has Been Found Inerrant with Respect to Historical Finds

In conclusion, regarding the Bible's historicity, it is clear that the Bible is not just a history book, but when it does talk of history, it is always 100 percent accurate wherever archaeological evidence has been uncovered pertaining to its accounts. The 100 percent record of the investigations of Dr. Wilson, the finds of Jericho, Nebuchadnezzar, Sargon, Sodom, and Gomorrah, and many more all bear this out.

Renowned biblical archaeologist, Dr. Joseph P. Free, said "Archaeology has confirmed countless passages which have been rejected by critics as unhistorical or contradictory to known facts...Yet archaeological discoveries have shown that these critical charges... are wrong and that the Bible is trustworthy in the very statements which have been set aside (by critics) as untrustworthy...We do not know of any cases where the Bible has been proven wrong."[194]

Jeffery L. Sheler, Religion reporter for U. S. News and World Report, after three decades of reviewing contentions of biblical errors and archaeological reports, said, "In extraordinary ways, modern archaeology is affirming the historical core of the Old and New Testaments, supporting key portions of crucial biblical stories."[195]

Professor Nelson Glueck (world-renowned scholar and archaeologist) stated, "I have excavated for thirty years with a Bible in one hand and a trowel in the other, and in matters of historical perspective I have never found the Bible to be in error... It may be stated categorically that no archaeological discovery has ever controverted a Biblical reference. Scores of archaeological findings have been made which confirm in clear outline or exact detail historical statements in the Bible. And, by the same token, proper evaluation of biblical descriptions has often led to amazing discoveries."[196]

Geology Supports Catastrophism, Not Uniformitarianism

Just as the Bible is not primarily a history book, it also is not primarily a science text. But when it does talk of science, if it is God's writing, then any scientific reference will be 100 percent accurate.

In the realm of geology, the Bible paints a vastly different picture of Earth's history than do secular scientists of today. Conventional science today is built on what is called "**uniformitarianism.**" This concept is often described with the phrase *"the key to the past is the present."* This concept says that everything on this planet has been going along as we see it today for billions of years and that changes to this planet are only very slow and gradual.

The Bible, however, paints a picture that the world, instead of being put together gradually over billions of years, was instead constructed quite rapidly, and its formation was influenced by big events or catastrophes. This worldview leads to the concept of "**catastrophism,**" in which the Bible says that God intervened in this reality at various times and formed our world rapidly in "*big events*" of geologic and cultural history.

When we look at the earth and rock strata, the evidence seems to point more to catastrophism than uniformitarianism. There have been books by Dr. John Morris and others that have made this point, and I will not belabor it. However, a few examples seem appropriate here to show how well geology agrees with the Bible and is in contradiction to secular geology.

The Great Discontinuity

Across the world is a line of discontinuity (change between rock layers) which is called by many the *Great Discontinuity*. It is found below the bottom of sedimentary rock strata layers and borders the boundary between the lowest sedimentary layers and the solid igneous and metamorphic bedrock below. This is exactly the type of evidence the creationist would envision if the worldwide flood of Noah's time occurred.

It shows places all over the world where it appears a great cataclysm occurred, which literally shaved off all rock strata above this discontinuity (line of change). Note that this layer is generally placed below the Precambrian era (the layer where we first see life forms) and reveals an event that secular geologists would have said occurred more than 540 million years ago, but which indicates that all of the sedimentary rock geology above this line was sheared off. The power to shave off literally thousands of feet of rock layers all over the world indicates nothing less than a worldwide flood event.[197]

The Grand Canyon

The Grand Canyon is a literal museum that testifies to the No-ahic flood event. The walls of the canyon contain millions of nautical fossils arranged end to end in the same direction, indicating they were set down by strong water currents with these animals and rock debris suspended in strong currents. The thousands of feet of layers of sedimentary rock show graphically how the Earth was covered by water, and the Grand Canyon itself is a vast sea life graveyard which shows how these creatures were violently taken to their burial by a massive flood.[198]

One large mid-layer of the canyon is what is called the Tapeats Sandstone. This sedimentary layer covers not only the Grand Canyon but extends across North America, into Central America, and across Greenland (pictured to the right in light shading). The vastness of this sedimentary  layer attests to all of this rock being laid down in what could never be characterized as a local flood and could only be interpreted as the result of a worldwide deluge.[199]

Further, there is the myth that the Grand Canyon was somehow cut by the flow of the Colorado River over millions of years. Anyone who visits the Grand Canyon from the South or North rim and looks at Colorado as a minuscule ribbon at the bottom of this huge chasm knows how unsatisfactory this explanation is. Such an explanation violates common sense. Pair that with the fact that Colorado enters the canyon from the east and the top of the canyon is a plateau which is more than a mile above the terrain to the east of the canyon, meaning that Colorado would have had to travel **uphill** more than a mile to begin to cut the canyon. This is clearly impossible.

These facts have led many secular geologists to the conclusion that it was not the Colorado that cut the Grand Canyon over millions of years, but the bursting of a huge inland lake north of the canyon which led to a deluge of water which cut the canyon in just a few days or weeks, at a time that its sedimentary rock was still soft. This is a conclusion that fits well with the biblical account of the flood, but which goes against the uniformitarian worldview of mainline geology![200]

Mt. Saint Helens

In the early 1980s, Mt. St. Helens erupted in Washington State in the United States. Creationists find that this catastrophic event did many things to provide exceptional support to a biblical worldview. One result of this eruption was that the pyroclastic blast (explosion of fire, magma, sedimentary rock, dust, and gases) which came out of this volcano erupted sideways and not upward, literally blowing out a side of the mountain.

This blast formed what is called a mini-Grand Canyon below the eruption and did so in minutes, not hundreds of millions of years. It also laid down hundreds of feet of sedimentary layers of rock strata, and again it did this in just a few days and not over millions of years. This evidence falsifies the assumption that whenever we find multiple layers of sedimentary rock buried in the ground, that it took many millions of years to lay these layers down. Mt. St. Helens demonstrated that such layers, which had been assumed to take hundreds of millions of years, can be laid via catastrophic natural events in a matter of hours.[201]

How Do You Make a Fossil?

The conventional answer to this question literally does not pass the smell test. The conventional answer is that something dies and is gradually covered over a very long period of time by dust and debris. Eventually, it is buried deep enough to be fossilized. Question: "What happens to anything when it dies today?" Answer: "It is almost invariably scavenged and eaten." On land, if an animal dies, coyotes, vultures, and other scavengers make quick work of the free meal, and what is left is eaten by ants, other insects, and microbes. If bone chips or other parts remain after the scavengers, they are broken down by bacteria and the elements. Thus, something dying and slowly being covered over in a uniformitarian way is not how most fossils are made.

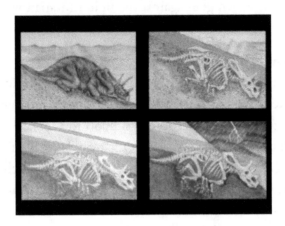

To get a fossil, the best and most logical way is for the animal to be quickly buried. This quick burial prevents scavengers from eating the remains and keeps most insects and bacteria from attacking the corpse. Once buried, the carcass can now be impinged upon by the underground water and minerals underground to start replacing the organic material with rock material, which is what a fossil truly is, rock material in the shape of the animal it took the place of.

Note how this scenario not only is the best way to make a fossil and is undoubtedly how most fossils were made, but this methodology fits perfectly with the worldwide flood scenario and is in conflict with the normal slow processes assumed by evolutionary science.

Fossil Graveyards

To make this point even more clear is the existence of fossil graveyards all over the world. From Karoo, South Africa, to the Gobi Desert, to Bighorn, Wyoming, to Canadian graveyards, and on and on, the world is full of massive fossil graveyards.[202]

Such graveyards fit perfectly within a creationist worldview of large numbers of corpses being washed into underwater valleys in the midst of the torrential flood. This point is underscored by the fact that these "graveyards" are located primarily in valleys adjacent to mountainous and highland areas the animals were trying to get to escape the onrushing floodwaters. However, such graveyards go against the assumption of slow, gradual processes being at work as conventional geology would theorize.

The Death Pose

Also, figure into your thinking the fossil evidence of the "death pose" as pictured at right. It is amazing how many fossils all over the world are found in this position. It was theorized for decades that either this pose was the function of muscle contractions that arched these animals all over the world into this "death pose," or that water burial whipped their necks back and arranged them in this pose after death.[203]

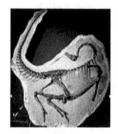

It has now been found that muscle contractions in most of the animals found in this pose would not have caused their necks to crane back as they are found in the rock strata, but instead would have caused them to curl up in the fetal position with their necks tucked into the body, instead of out, as we often find a dead animal's carcass to have done in death on the surface of the Earth.

The better, more scientific answer for these death poses all over the world is that these animals were all caught when buried in mixtures of water and mud, which was overwhelming them and caused their deaths, and we see their last pose in death of craning their necks toward the heavens trying to get their last breaths as they were covered over and suffocated or drowned. Again, this very plausible explanation fits well within the catastrophic worldview of the Bible but is at odds with conventional geology.

Thus, it is clear from the evidence cited that the Bible describes an Earth history that fits well within the geology we find, but that same geology is at odds with evolutionary and uniformitarian assumptions.[204]

Niagara Falls Erosion Rate

Up until the recent past, when the top of Niagara Falls was reinforced with concrete, the water was carving a channel upriver toward Lake Erie at the rate of about 4 to 8 feet per year. Note that while many contemporary geologists will quote a rate of just one to three feet per year, that is a dated calculation made by an English researcher almost 200 years ago and does not conform to records we have of where the falls were during colonial times and where it is today.

The Niagara channel is now about 7 miles long and growing at an average rate of 4 to 8 feet per year means that Niagara Falls is between 4,500 and 8,750 years old.

Noah's Flood could have eroded half of the seven-and-a-half-mile-long Niagara River gorge in a few hours as the floodwaters raced through the soft sediments and drained off the continent. Thus, this is another physical geological feature that fits well within a time frame suggesting the whole Earth was reformed on grand scale about 5000 years ago by a worldwide cataclysm.[205]

Dating the Mississippi River Delta

The Mississippi River is one of the largest Rivers in the world. It is the chief drainage system for the North American Continent, and it transports between 200,000 and 700,000 cubic feet per second of water into the Gulf of Mexico. Before 1900, best estimates are that the Mississippi transported 400 million metric tons of sediment each year down the river into the Gulf of Mexico and deposited these sediments into its growing river delta or into the gulf itself. Erosion rates and the amount of sediment accumulated both in the delta and in the gulf indicate that it is only a few thousand years old.[206]

Further Mississippi River calculations indicate that its delta would have filled the Gulf of Mexico in ten million years. That has not occurred, meaning the Mississippi and probably the North American continent and the Gulf in their present configurations are far less than this age.[207]

Since the Mississippi Delta now fills in only a small part of the Gulf of Mexico, it is obvious that the river has not been flowing into the gulf for many millions of years. At current rates, the Mississippi River delta would reach its current size and form in about 5000 years. *Is that figure only accidental?* The coinciding of both this rate for the formation of the Mississippi River delta, as well as the formation of Niagara Falls, starts to give us an indication that the age of North America is likely the same.

What about the Nile River in Africa?

Using its flow rates and current delta size, we can calculate that the Nile River delta of Egypt also gives a calculation of about 5000 to 6000 years. Likewise, the Po River delta of Italy could have developed in only a few thousand years. This suggests these rivers have been flowing into the oceans only since the major flood that covered the earth a few thousand years ago, as the Bible contends.[208]

Interestingly, there is a "Nilometer" which has been used by Egyptians for about five thousand years to keep a record of the Nile's height for agricultural use. This record is right in line with the biblical record.[209]

What Happened 4300-6000 Years Ago?

The **Sahara Desert** is the largest hot desert in the world, covering 3,600,000 square miles of land. Incidentally, the word Sahara in Arabic means "desert," so you may laugh to find out that when we call it the Sahara Desert, we are saying "desert desert." We have records of where this "great desert," as the Arabians call it, extended to in past millennia, and thus, we know how fast it has been expanding through history. The recorded history and the math working backward from today both say that this greatest of all worlds' deserts started around 5000 years ago and has been expanding across northern Africa since that time.[210]

Further verification that the Sahara was green and watered 5000 years ago is that researchers found markers of ancient rivers buried beneath the sand dunes. Previous research has found evidence of such a river network in marine sediments off the West African coast. Rocks and other materials characteristic of a riverbed had been deposited on the oceanic coast, just as a river delta would push its contents into the sea. Researchers have also discovered a submarine canyon on the continental shelf off the coast of western Africa. Dubbed Cap Timiris Canyon, the underwater corridor also suggested the past existence of a river system in Western Sahara.[211]

Coral is a colony of sea animals that grow in collections together and on top of previous generations of corral. Their growth rates can be calculated to find out how old each colony we find is. According to intensive research and such calculations, the oldest coral colony in the world is about 4270 years old.[212]

We can **date trees** by counting the number of *tree rings* when we cut a cross-section into them or take a core sampling. Now, each ring does not always equate to one year, as some years have a late freeze and a second growing season, but this happens with enough regularity so that we can get a good estimate of a tree's age by counting its rings and adjusting for a small amount of double growing seasons. Using these calculations, the oldest trees in the world, which are still living today, are about 4900 years old.[213]

Our oldest written records by man date back only about five thousand years.[214] What do all of this evidence and facts indicate happened 4300 to 6000 years ago?

This gives us nine geologic clocks which say something dramatic happened to reshape the Earth 4300 to 6000 years ago, and this is only a sampling of such clocks; there are more. These pieces of evidence, along with the more than 270+ flood legends from cultures all over the world, attest to the fact that his world was remade about 5000 years ago, just as the Bible describes by a worldwide cataclysm.

Population Growth

One of the more interesting pieces of evidence that this world was remade some 5000 years ago, as the Bible would suggest, is population growth. If you start with the first two homo sapiens or modern humans according to the evolutionary time scale and give those first two humans a very conservative growth rate for their population of just ½ percent per year (that is only one-quarter the current growth rate of humanity, which is currently around 2 percent per year) in the one million or so years since those first humans evolved, they would have produced 10^{2100} people on the earth today.

That means that all of the continents of the earth would be covered foot to foot with people stacked on top of one another, rising up into space and filling much of the universe. Certainly, there has never been anything approaching that type of population on earth.[215]

Is something wrong with this math, or did something happen between the dawn of man on this planet and today?

If instead you start with eight people as we would have after Noah's flood, and projected the same very conservative ½ percent per year growth rate, today we should have 6 to 7 billion people. The world population today stands at just over seven billion people. Is this only a coincidence, or does this indicate the entire human race "started over," as it was, some 4500+ years ago at the time of Noah as the Bible says we did?[216]

Historical-Do Geology and History Support the Bible?

We have ample evidence that the Bible's historical accounts are verified in archaeology, geology, and in light of other historical writings. We have found enough evidence for this to convince the average open-minded person. But remember that most people are not open-minded, and there are those that no matter how much evidence they are presented with, will resist being convinced because of the high stakes of belief in the Bible. If the Bible is true, then there is a God, and they are responsible to Him. That is a place many people do not wish to go, no matter the wealth of evidence presented.

So far, we have shown that the origin accounts from across the world suggest that most, if not all creation stories, have borrowed elements from an original creation account, which would have to be awfully close to the biblical account. We have now seen that archaeology and geology seem to support the biblical accounts, contrary to widely distributed reports to the contrary. This is the start of an intriguing case for the Bible really being the Word of God, as it has met the first two of our six predictive questions of what we should find if it is God's writing. Finding that the Bible meets the first two of our expectations is interesting, but there is still the possibility that it is purely coincidental, and that both of these sets of evidence agree with our premise and that the Bible, although seeming to be verified, just seems so, and the Bible is, in fact, the written by men, not a god.

Still, these are two large sets of evidence in agreement with our premise and which we predicted to find. Statistical probability says that's two things taken two at a time; the chance of either of these evidence sets being found true before we started was 50-50 (we could have verified them to be true or found them false). Now that we are two for two on our investigated questions, probability says that you multiply the two probabilities together to get the chances of their happening by pure chance. Thus, the probability of finding both of these first two data sets to support the Bible as God's words is ½ X ½= ¼ or 25 percent. Therefore, with the evidence we have seen so far, the mathematical odds are down to just 25 percent that the Bible was constructed purely by chance and the evidence presented is all coincidental, and the Bible is not God-inspired. Conversely, with just two data sets evaluated, there is a 75 percent chance that the Bible is proving to be what it says it is, the "Word of God."

Will the Bible be verified in our future predictions? Let's see.

What about God Writing History in Advance?

If the Bible is the Word of God, and God is the omnipotent being, who knows all, then he should be able to predict the future. This is especially true since most interpretations of scripture say that God is outside of time and can see the future and the past simultaneously.

Thus, let's investigate the Bible to find where it has predicted the future. Then, lets' see what the Bible's track record with regard to such predictions is.

God Writing History in Advance

There are about 2500 prophecies found in the pages of the Bible. About 2000 of those have been fulfilled without error so far. Some of these prophecies were made and came to pass over 3000 years ago, such as the enslavement of Abraham's descendants (Israel) in Egypt. Fifty of these biblical predictions have come true in the last 200 years, such as the reformation of Israel as a nation-state.[217]

The Bible in the Old Testament proposed that any prophet should be tested and found **errorless** with regard to his prophecies. We will apply the same error-free standard to the Bible itself. Also, if these prophecies are from God and not man, then we would expect these prophecies not only to all come true but be far more specific than the very generalized and unclear prognostications of human soothsayers and supposed clairvoyants.

For example, *Nostradamus* is noted by many as one of the most fruitful of future forecasting prophets of all time. Yet, there are two things about his quatrains (prophetic verses of poetry that stand out). The first is that the bulk of his supposed prophecies are written extremely vaguely in poetic and metaphorical verses and could apply to multiple events which recur in history. The second thing about his writings is the vast amount of prophecies that have not come true. If the Bible was inspired by God, and they are his words, then we would expect a far better track record than this and far more specificity with regards to his prophecies. Such specificity would make it clear what he is talking about so as to prove the Bible's authenticity and show these are his words and actions and not that of men.

The late and famous secular prophetess *Jeanne Dixon* (1904-1997) gives us another example of the greater specificity we will be looking for in the Bible if it is from God. Dixon, a famous supposed clairvoyant and seer of the past century, was credited for such things as predicting the assassination of John F. Kennedy. While Dixon in the 1950s did foretell the assassination of a U.S. President, she did not say which one or when.[218]

This is a hallmark of supposed prophets to give vague predictions, which will inevitably occur in some form and then take credit. U.S. history is replete with assassinations of Presidents such as Lincoln and assassination attempts such as Ronald Reagan's. The odds were on her side that this prediction would be fulfilled within her lifetime, and it was. When examining the Bible, we will expect not only far more frequency of correct predictions but far more specificity of those prophecies so that it is clear that it came from someone who absolutely knew what was to come to pass.

Errorless predictions and specificity which defy the laws of probability: These are two high tests that no book written by men could hope to pass. Let's see how the Bible does with these standards.

The Tomb of Cyrus the Great

An inscription on the tomb of the great Persian monarch Cyrus the Great reads:

O man, whoever you are and wherever you come from, for I know that you will come—I am Cyrus, son of Cambyses, founded the Empire of the Persians and was king of the East. Do not grudge me this spot of earth which covers my body.

—Cyrus

The Hebrew prophet Isaiah wrote in Isaiah 44:28 (KJV), **"That saith of Cyrus, He is my shepherd, and shall perform all my pleasure: even saying to Jerusalem, Thou shalt be built; and to the temple, Thy foundation shall be laid."** Archaeological evidence says that Isaiah wrote this very specific prophecy, even including the future person's name somewhere between 150 and 200 years before King Cyrus of Babylon was born![219]

Now, some critics of this striking prophecy, which came to be 100 percent true, claim that either Isaiah was not written when advertised or that this prophecy was later inserted by subsequent scribes copying Isaiah. There is no archaeological or scholarly proof for either of these critical contentions. Their only reason given for this contention is that man could not make so accurate and specific a prophecy. That it is statistically impossible, and thus, it must have been inserted later. They discount out of hand any possibility of God's intervention and say that this is reason enough to say that it was inserted into Isaiah after Cyrus' reign. This is a contention often made in the literature as a criticism of the biblical prophecies, but in all cases like this one, they offer little or no evidence of changed texts, nor any proof of it being inserted. They merely assert that it was humanly impossible for prophecies of this specificity to be made by man, and to that, we agree. Man could not do it!

About 366 Predictions of Christ

There are about 366 predictions of Christ which scholars have identified in the Old Testament foretelling of the coming of the Messiah (Jesus Christ). Some of these supposed predictions are a little symbolic or need interpretation. That goes for the first proposed prediction of Christ, which is in Genesis 3:15 (also known as the proto-evangelism).

In Genesis 3:15 (NIV), the Bible says, **"And I will put enmity between you and the woman, and between your offspring and hers; He will crush your head, and you will strike his heel."** This was God talking to the serpent (Satan after he tempted the woman to sin). Many scholars interpret this verse as being the first prediction of Christ. Taken as they interpret it, this verse means that Christ will be born of a human woman as Christ was and that he would come into this world to crush the serpent (Satan) as the Bible says he did with his life and substitutionary death for us on the cross. It also refers to how Satan will forever be nipping at ours and Christ's heels, tempting us and him. Interestingly, it also makes reference to a fear most women innately have of snakes.

There are, however, many more of the 366 predictions of Christ in the Old Testament, which are far clearer and seem to unmistakably point to Jesus Christ as the Messiah. An example of these is Zechariah 12:10, which predicts that Christ will be born into the **line of King David** and that his **"side will be pierced"** as it was on the cross by the sword of a guard. In Zechariah 9:9, the Old Testament predicts that the Messiah will ride in a procession on a **donkey**, which is how He made his triumphal entry into Jerusalem in the final week of his life. Psalm 69:21 says that the Messiah will be given **gall and vinegar**. This combination of fluids is exactly what is recorded that Christ was offered as he hung on the cross.

Psalm 34:20 (NIV) says that **"He protects all his bones, not one of them will be broken."** Crucifixion was a horrible means of death since it took so long; it was horribly painful and cruel. Those crucified had to raise up on their legs to get their body weight off their diaphragm so that they could breathe. Eventually, they would get so tired that they could no longer raise themselves and suffocate from their inability to raise up. A common practice of the Romans in crucifixion was to break the legs of any prisoner who did not die by a certain time if they needed to move on. The writings of several books verify that Christ's bones were not broken as foretold in the Old Testament since he died before they got around to doing this.

Isaiah 7:13-14 alludes to his being **"born of a virgin."** This is a very specific prediction that can only be pointing to Jesus Christ, as he is the only person in history with multiple sources which claim that is how he was born. Isaiah 55:4-7, 9, and 12 all refer to the Messiah's role as **intercessor** for us. This is the place the Bible says Christ put himself in when he accepted to die for us on the cross for our sins.

Psalm 41:9 clearly refers to **Judas Iscariot** when it tells of a person who will betray the Messiah. Hosea 6:2 predicts that he will **rise on the third day,** as Christ is reported to have done by 500 witnesses, and he, in fact, predicted of himself in the New Testament three times. Micah 5:2 says he will be **born in Bethlehem**, which He was, but as in most biblical prophecies, it is amazingly specific since it says he will be born in **Bethlehem Ephratah**, distinguishing it as the Bethlehem in Judah, just south of Jerusalem, and not the Bethlehem in Galilee which also existed at the time of Christ's birth.

Malachi 3:1 specifically predicts a messenger who will be sent before the Messiah to point people to him. This is a clear prediction of ministry of **John the Baptist**. Isaiah 40:3 tells of John the Baptist's penchant for living like a **wild man in the wilderness,** which is specifically outlined in the New Testament.

Dr. Peter Stoner has done the math on how likely it is that Christ could have fulfilled any amount of these 366 predictions of his life. Now, as we have said before, some of these Old Testament predictions are either unclear to us due to symbolism or debatable whether they actually refer to the Messiah. So, Dr. Stoner just considered eight of the clearest of predictions, multiplying together the probabilities of each one of these eight events occurring in the life of one man.

The chances of his being born in Bethlehem, as foretold in Micah 5:2, was 1 in 280,000. The chances of having a forerunner to Christ, who would proclaim him to be the Messiah, was 1 in 1000. The chances of his riding into Jerusalem on a donkey were 1 out of 100. The chances of his being betrayed by a friend were 1 in 1000. It was foretold in Zechariah 11:12 that He would be sold out for 30 pieces of silver, which Matthew 26:15 confirms. The chances against this amount matching were 1 in 1000. The Old Testament foretells of this same 30 pieces of silver being used to purchase a Potter's field, and that is what is recorded happened with this money in Matthew 27:3-10, and the huge chance against this occurring by chance was 1 in 100,000. Everyone speaks up in their own defense when put on trial, but Jesus did not speak in his own defense as predicted in Isaiah 53:7, with the odds of this being 1 in 1000. The chance of Christ being killed by crucifixion out of all the ways there are to die was 1 in 10,000.

It turns out that the chances of Christ fulfilling just these eight prophecies was 1 out of 10^{28} (one chance out of the number 1 followed by 28 zeroes) for eight prophecies. Such a number is the equivalent of winning the lottery four times in a row, which anyone would understand is, in all practicality, impossible unless it is intentionally arranged by an intelligent force for it to work out this way.

If, however, we calculate for the forty-eight clear predictions for Christ, which are both foretold in the Old Testament and clearly occurred in the New Testament, then the chances of one person fulfilling all of these balloons to 1 out of 10^{157}.[220]

Now, such numbers don't mean much to anyone but mathematicians. So let's put these numbers in perspective. Mathematically, anything which has a probability lower than 1 out of 10^{50} chances is mathematically impossible. **It will not happen!** The chance of Christ not being the Messiah as described in the Bible easily meets this test, and the math testifies to it. But, again, most people do not understand or trust math, so let's make this number even clearer.

The chance of winning the lottery is 1 out of 5,200,000. The chance against Christ fulfilling all 48 clear prophecies is the equivalent of winning the lottery more than 72 times in a row! Such logic will make it clear to most people that Jesus Christ was the person foretold of in the Old Testament as the Messiah since to say otherwise means we believe that someone could accidentally win the lottery 72 times in a row and not believe that the lottery was rigged in some way for them.[221] Thus, we have here a whole list of biblical prophecies, with a degree of specificity which man could not achieve and only which God could.

Of course, there will be those, who will claim that Jesus Christ was a charlatan or lunatic, who was obsessed with painting himself as the Messiah, and they will say that he arranged to have all of these things happen to him to make it all a self-fulfilling prophecy. Now, while it is true that many things described of Christ could have been arranged, there are many he could not have. The probability of these occurrences alone, which he could not control (such as not breaking his bones, born in the line of David, born in Bethlehem, etc.), show that he was the Messiah foretold in Old Testament scripture!

In Psalms chapter 22 (NIV), it says:

> … despised by the people. All who see me mock me; they hurl insults, shaking their heads…they say, "let the Lord rescue him. Let him deliver him"…my bones are out of joint…my mouth is dried up…they pierce my hands and my feet… They divide my clothes among them and cast lots for my garment.

This is an unmistakable and accurate description of the events at Christ's crucifixion.

It is impressive enough that this very accurate description meshes with what is recorded in the gospels as well as other Jewish writings foretold about a thousand years before it occurred. It is even more impressive and testifies to this being a Godly inspired prediction when we recognize the fact that these predictions were written in Psalms by King David 400 years before Persians *invented crucifixion* during the 6th century BC.[222] How did David, or an editor of David's time, so accurately describe a method of execution which will not be invented for more than three centuries without the help of the Creator? Without understanding that God had to inspire this passage, it absolutely boggles the mind how it could have been so accurate in its predictions and descriptions of future events.

The Bible Predicts the Day Christ Would Reveal Himself as the Messiah

Another of the 366 predictions of Christ is a startling one. The Old Testament book of Daniel contains a prophecy that accurately predicts the exact day on which Christ declared himself as the Messiah. The passage, starting at Daniel 9:24, indicates that 483 years would pass from the day that the order was given to rebuild Jerusalem until the day of the declaration of the "Messiah the Prince."

We know from other Old Testament texts that the order to commission the rebuilding of Jerusalem was given on March 14, 445 BC. If we count forward exactly 483 Jewish years (a Jewish year was 360 days long), this equals 173,880 days, and we come to a date of April 6, 32 AD. What happened on that day in history? It was the date on which many believe Jesus arranged to have himself declared the Messiah by riding into Jerusalem on a donkey, just as another Old Testament scripture foretold.[223]

The Messiah's entry into Jerusalem on a donkey had been predicted hundreds of years earlier in Zechariah 9:9. Thus, exactly on the day predicted by Daniel, 173,880 days after the proclamation of Jerusalem be rebuilt, Jesus rode into Jerusalem revealing himself to be the Messiah, in a way no Jew could miss as declaring himself the Messiah! As the people sang the Messianic song signaling their understanding and belief in his declaration, the Jewish religious authorities (also understanding what was implied) told Jesus to stop the worship of himself. Jesus responded, **"I tell you, if these should hold their peace, the very stones would immediately cry out!"**(KJV) as recorded in Luke 19:40.[224]

30+ Prophesies Fulfilled 1948

More than thirty biblical prophecies were fulfilled on April 22, 1948, when Israel was recreated as a nation by partition action of the United Nations. Israeli leaders formally constituted the nation of Israel on May 14, 1948. In Luke chapter 21, Christ not only predicted the destruction of the temple, which came to pass in 70 AD, but he also described the world as it would be in the second coming and the condition of Israel today. This accurate description of the geopolitical situation which Israel is now in is eerily described with uncanny accuracy in this chapter.

Ezekiel chapter 20: 30-43 are among those prophecies of Israel's rebirth for the third time as a nation which is unparalleled in the history of nations. Ezekiel 20 verse 34 (ESV) says, "...I will bring you out from the peoples and **gather you out of the countries where you are scattered**...."

In the first dissolution of the nation-state of Israel, the Israelites left their land and became slaves in the land of Egypt for hundreds of years. Clearly, the text could not be referring to this restoration of Israel since it had already happened at the time of the writing of Ezekiel, and they only had to be gathered from one country, not all over the world.

The second time Israel is erased as a nation-state is with the Babylonian captivity (just after 600 BC). During this time, the nation-state of Israel did not exist, its lands were owned, ruled, and inhabited by the Babylonians and then the Assyrians, which had conquered Israel, and the bulk of the Israelites were captives in the nation-state of Babylon for 70 years. Again, while this re-assemblage of the nation of Israel was miraculous and an indication of God's hand in this second restoration of Israel as a nation-state after being more than three generations in captivity in Babylon, it is not this captivity which is being referred to in Ezekiel, since once again the gathering of the Israelites had to be from only one country, Babylon.

Also, in Amos chapter 9 (KJV), it says, "… though they go into captivity before their enemies, thence will I command the sword,…I will **sift the house of Israel among all nations**…that day will I raise up the tabernacle of David that is fallen…" Note that it says God will "sift" (search and bring) from among *all nations* (the whole world) and bring them back to Israel. That makes this prediction specific to the third re-assemblage of the nation of Israel, which occurred in 1948. Please take note of how much of a "God thing" this is!

How many other nations have been recreated after going into non-existence three times? *The answer is none, zero, not a one!* No other nation has such a history, and this testifies to this nation's special relationship to God. Moreover, what other nation has ever been put back together after being out of existence as a nation for more than eighteen centuries? **Again, the answer is none, zero, not a one!** This looks like a God thing, because it is!

Jeremiah 31 (KJV) says:

> … I will bring again the captivity of my people of Israel, and they shall **build the waste cities, and inhabit them; and they shall plant vineyards, and drink the wine thereof; they shall also make gardens, and eat the fruit of them…**they shall no more be pulled up out of their land which I have given them, saith the Lord thy God.

(Ezekiel 36:35 echoes this same prediction of Israel **reclaiming a garden from the desert!**)

This is an uncanny description of Israel today. Anyone who has visited Israel today will testify to how the Israelites are "reclaiming" their nation from the desert. They have planted so many vineyards, gardens, and fruit groves in Israel that it not only appears as a green oasis as compared to the desert around it, but they have actually lowered the year-round ambient temperature indicating how pervasive this greening of Israel has been, which was so well described in the book of Jeremiah.[225]

Around 1450 BC, at the time of the Exodus, the books of Isaiah, Jeremiah, and Ezekiel all make it clear that there were forest groves in Israel. In King Solomon's days, they had tree planting projects to restore what they had used in the building of the temple and city (Ecclesiastes 2:4-6). The destruction of those forests in earnest began with the destruction of the temple in 70 AD under Titus of Rome. The Romans used vast amounts of wood for crucifixions and construction of war machines. Muslims, who will take over the area after the expulsion of the Jews and after the Romans further deforest the area, will use large amounts of wood to construct Mosques for the next several hundred years. During the Crusades, much of the remaining forests were used for firewood and for building castles and fortifications between 1096 and 1291 AD.[226] Centuries after this, the Turks used the remaining wood in the area for railroad ties and powering steam engines. By the 1900s, there were no trees left in the mountains of Israel and very few in cities such as Jericho.

The prophet Isaiah had foretold as part of the reclaiming of the land of Israel from the desert that her forests would be refreshed and the forests restored in the "End Times" so people would know God had a hand in it!

Isaiah 41:19-20 (NKJV) says:

> *I will plant in the wilderness the cedar and the acacia tree, The myrtle and the oil tree; I will set in the desert the cypress tree and the pine and the box tree together, That they may see and know, and consider and understand together, That the hand of the LORD has done this, and the Holy One of Israel has created it.*

During the twentieth century, over *250 million trees have been planted in Israel*. In a time when the world is experiencing unparalleled deforestation due to the spread of civilization, Israel was the *only nation* in the world to enter the twenty-first century with a net gain of trees compared to the previous century![227]

Another facet of this prophecy is that 55 percent of Israel is located in the Negev desert (which gets only one inch of rain per year) has become the "breadbasket" of the Middle East and also produces 5 percent of the world's flowers, putting Israel third in the world in floral production. This thriving floral industry brings more than two hundred million dollars to its economy each year.

To achieve this feat, Israel has become a world leader in agro-technology, especially in growing plants and flowers in dry, hot climates. Their expertise in the genetic cloning of seeds adapted to dry environments, drip irrigation, and fruit picking robots is so valued by Europe that Israel is frequently selling their technology to the Europeans. Overall, Israel has become the world leader in agricultural research and development. They have even genetically engineered plants to grow using the "brackish water reservoirs" located below the Negev desert! All of this is why the United Nations has declared Israel to be "the most agriculturally efficient land on Earth!"[228]

Water treatment plants were developed in Israel, which recaptures 86 percent of used water for irrigation, making Israel first in the world in water reclamation. Spain comes in second at just 19 percent reclamation of used water. Further, desalination plants were designed and built to convert sea water into fresh water. In 2013 they opened the Sorek Desalination Plant located just south of Tel Aviv, which can produce seven million gallons of fresh water every hour! Still, desalination makes up only 55 percent of their water use since their reclamation systems are so cutting edge, as described before.[229]

This "flowering of Israel" was predicted in scripture. Isaiah 27:6b (KJV) says, **"...Israel shall blossom and bud, and fill the face of the world with fruit."** Until the twentieth century, most scholars would have written off this verse as being only a spiritual prophecy, as they thought it meant only that the savior would come through Israel. Today we see this verse has a very literal interpretation, and it again testifies to how clear and specific biblical prophecy is, as opposed to the supposed mystics of today.

Ezekiel 36:5, 11:15, Ezekiel chapters 40 - 48, and Hosea 2:2 give many more examples of Old Testament predictions of Israel's reformation as a nation in modern times, which have come to pass.

One very interesting prediction to come true of modern Israel was foretold in Zephaniah 3:9 (KJV), where it says, "For then will I turn to the people a **pure language**, that they may all call upon the name of the LORD, to serve him with one consent." This may well be the foretelling of the use of Hebrew as the national language of Israel, which required its reclamation from being a dead language.

Hebrew had been read by anthropologists and some clerics but not used as a conversational language in any nation of the world for about 1800 years. Its being resurrected from the dead and used again as a national conversational language is unparalleled. In fact, the number of languages that have ever come back from the dead like this outside of Hebrew is **none, zero, not a one!** Again, this is God putting his unmistakable hand on what should be recognized as his intervention in the history of man. In doing so, he is also fulfilling his covenant relationship and protection of the Israeli people, as well as demonstrating to the people of Earth that, unlike us, he always keeps his commitments.

Israel Literally Resurrected as Foretold Three Times!

The reconstitution of the Israeli state in 1948 was just the latest biblically foretold re-assemblage of Israel in history. Such a reconstitution, as noted before, has occurred nowhere else on Earth to any other nation on Earth, but it has occurred for Israel not once, but three times!

The original nation-state of Israel was created with the clan and lineage of the forefather of Israel known as Abraham (circa 2000 BC).[230] Around 1875 BC, the nation of Israel moved as a group for the most part to Egypt to flee famine in their land. They will take up residence in the land of Goshen in Northern Egypt first as honored guests and then as slaves. Their total time in Egypt will be about 400 years. Around 1450 BC is the time of the Exodus and 40 years later, the retaking of the lands of Canaan and the first re-assemblage of the nation-state of Israel.[231] The date and accuracy of the Exodus and retaking of the lands of Israel are debated in contemporary archaeological circles today. My extensive article previously in this book on the archaeological proof for the timeline stated supports this dating.

Sometime prior to 586 BC, the prophet Jeremiah will write in Jeremiah 32:36-37:

> *You are saying about this city, 'By the sword, famine and plague it will be handed over to the king of Babylon'; but this is what the LORD, the God of Israel, says: I will surely gather them from all the lands where I banish them in my furious anger and great wrath; I will bring them back to this place and let them live in safety.*

This is the prophet correctly foretelling of the re-assemblage of Israel for the second time in history. Eerily, the Bible makes this prediction super specific by foretelling that the captivity in Babylon before re-assemblage would be for exactly 70 years (Jeremiah 25:9-12 and 29:10), a term which has been confirmed in other archaeological records. As we spelled out in the previous section, no other nation-state on Earth has gone out of existence for long periods of time and been reassembled even once. For Israel, this miracle has occurred three times, and each had been specifically predicted in the Bible for each miraculous occasion.

The people of Israel
Will Never be Completely Destroyed!

In Leviticus 26:44, the Bible said that God would **never allow the people of Israel to be completely destroyed**.

As detailed previously, between 1875 BC and 1450 BC, the Hebrews left their land and lived in Egypt (the last 150 years of which they are oppressed and put into slavery). In slavery, in Egypt, the nation-state of Israel literally did not exist. Such a situation historically has killed off most ethnic groups and assimilated them into the slave owners' or conquerors' culture. In addition, according to Exodus 1:22 and archaeology, the Egyptian Pharaoh tried to eradicate the first-born males of Israel while in slavery.

But the Hebrew race of people survived amazingly as no other group in history has. They will be restored as a nation-state and as a people to their lands around 1450 BC in accordance with the Exodus account.

During ancient times, Queen Athaliah (2 Chronicles 22:10 circa 840 BC) tried to destroy all of the royal heirs from which the Christ child would come. In the fifth century BC, Haman (Esther 3:4-9) plotted genocide against the Jews to eradicate them.

Around 600 BC, ten of the twelve Tribes of Israel were all but wiped out by the Assyrians. And the Babylonians later persecuted and enslaved what was left of the people of Israel. But, instead of assimilating or perishing, some of the people eventually returned to their homeland and recovered their way of life around 536 BC.

The recovery was complete, complete enough that Jerusalem again had been restored as the center of Jewish life and as a nation-state. This later will allow the followers of Jesus to begin a process in Jerusalem by which Christianity later spread throughout the world.

Hearing of Jesus' birth, King Herod tried to kill the baby Jesus by killing all male babies two years of age and under in Bethlehem and the surrounding vicinity. The baby Jesus was saved by God, directing his parents to flee to Egypt.

After the destruction of the Temple in 70 AD and the Roman army coming in force into Israel to put down all rebellion, the nation-state of Israel will be dissolved, and its people will be disbursed throughout the world. They will be apart from their lands with no geographic nation for their ethnic group to call their own for more than 1800 years. Most ethnic groups begin to lose their identity, starting with the second generation living outside their culture in a foreign culture.

An excellent but sad example of this can be seen today in oriental immigrants to the U.S. Research has shown that immigrants from the "Pacific Rim" have such deep cultural devotions to work and achievement that when they come to the U.S. that they most often succeed wherever they are planted, even in some of the worst places in America. Their children, who are taught this deep work and achievement ethic, have been shown to thrive and achieve educationally over and above other American students, even in schools with terrible learning environments such as East St. Louis! This achievement/work ethic, however, sadly fades after the first generation of children produced in the U.S., as the next generation is often softened and inculcated into our indulgent lifestyle in America, and the achievement and production of second-generation Pacific Rim students in America come close to being undiscernible from any other American students. Thus, they are losing a great deal of their cultural heritage and ethos just within two generations of being immersed in another culture![232]

Research shows that by the fifth generation living in a foreign culture, ethnic groups lose their identity. You never hear of people today claiming to be Moabites, or Philistines, or Amorites. Such cultures which surrounded Israel and lived with Israel thousands of years ago have been absorbed into other cultures, but Israel's identity somehow magically has not. Such disbursement as the Jews endured would mean the end of any recognizable ethnic group, as they would be absorbed into the cultures they moved into within centuries.[233]

The Jews were expelled from England in 1290 AD and from Spain in 1492[234]. If you have not yet figured out that there has been an outright push by Satan to do away with God's people throughout history, then you are not paying attention, but the Jews are.

The 1940s saw the hideous execution of Hitler's "final solution" as he and the Nazis tried to rid the world of anyone but what they believed to be the evolutionary superior "Arian Race." In the "holocaust," over six million Jews were killed. Yet despite this latest attempt to rid the world of Judaism, the Jewish people would survive and be reintegrated as a society and nation-state in their former lands in 1948 by partition agreement among the United Nations.[235]

Today, Islamic states have made it their stated goal is to wipe out Israel. **Leviticus 26:44 (NIV) says:** "Yet in spite of this, **when they are in the land of their enemies, I will not reject them** or abhor them so as to destroy them completely, breaking my covenant with them. I am the Lord their God."

Predictions for Tyre

In Ezekiel chapter 26, verses 3-21 of the Bible, some extremely specific predictions are made concerning the ancient Phoenician city of Tyre. These predictions were written by the prophet Ezekiel in 586 BC. The prophecy stated that the city would be destroyed as many nation-states would come against it. The Bible predicted that Tyre would be made base as the **top of flat rock and that fisherman would spread their nets over the site. The towers and walls would be destroyed,** and the debris would be **scraped clean, and Tyre would be left barren** (ESV).

This prediction seemed very unlikely at the time it was made in 586 BC as Tyre, at the time, was an impressive city-state of prominence with imposing defenses. Further, Herodotus in his history gave evidence that Tyre had been in existence for 220 years. But, three years after the prophecy was given, King Nebuchadnezzar (yes, the same one so many Bible scholars of the "higher criticism" for centuries thought did not exist, but did) laid a 13-year siege on the mainland of Tyre. When he finally entered the city, he found that most of the people had moved from the city to an island one-half mile off the coast. There they had fortified a city on this island with walls reaching to the very edge of the sea, making further attack almost impossible at that time.

However, over 200 years later, *Alexander the Great* laid siege to the island city of Tyre. Since he had no fleet, he had his army demolished the old city of Tyre; they then cast the debris into the sea and built a 200-foot causeway out to the island. This allowed Alexander to move his army across the land bridge and destroy the island city. So, the city-state was totally destroyed as scripture predicted (the old city literally stripped bare, specifically as the Bible predicted), but Tyre's history does not end there.

Many subsequent attempts were made to rebuild the city were made, but each time sieges by enemies would destroy the city all over again. Today, both the original city and the island city are bare rocks where fishermen can be observed laying their nets to dry, just as the Bible predicted![236]

God's Curse Upon Sidon

Some twenty miles north of Tyre is the city of **Sidon**. The prophet Ezekiel prophesied in the Bible that due to their immense sinfulness, the city of Sidon would have a miserable and bloody future.

In Ezekiel 28:22-23 (NKJV), it was foretold, **"Behold, I am against you, O Sidon… I will send pestilence upon her, and blood in her streets; the wounded shall be judged in her midst by the sword against her on every side…."**

Through the centuries, Sidon has been one of the bloodiest locations on earth. Soon after the prophecy was given by Ezekiel from God, the city was captured by the Babylonians. Later, over forty thousand died in a rebellion against the Persians. The Greeks captured the city under Alexander the Great in 330 BC. It continued to be the scene of many fierce battles during the Crusades and various Turkish wars.

Today, the city is part of Lebanon and only twenty miles from Beirut. This area is and has been a hotbed for extremist attacks, guerilla fighting, and terrorist attacks for decades, with no end in sight. And just as the Bible foretold, even in this day, the nation-state of Lebanon is surrounded by nations on every side which wishes to do her harm. Thus, this area seems destined to continue its miserable and bloody history as far as we can see, just as the Bible predicted more than two thousand years ago.[237]

The Destruction of Babylon

Mighty Babylon, 196 miles square, was enclosed not only by a moat but also by a double wall more than 300 feet high, each wall portion more than 70 feet thick. It was said by unanimous popular opinion to be indestructible, yet two Bible prophets declared its doom. These prophets further claimed that the ruins would be avoided by travelers, that the city would never again be inhabited, and that its stones would not even be moved for use as building material (Isaiah 13:17-22 and Jeremiah 51:26, 43). Their prophetic descriptions are, in fact, the true and well-documented history of the famous citadel.[238]

In fact, there are more than 100 specific prophecies in the Bible concerning Babylon. Almost all of these one hundred prophecies concerning Babylon have already been fulfilled. Below are just a few examples of these biblical prophecies that involve the neo-Babylonian Empire, which rose to power about 2600 years ago and ruled over a vast empire that included Judah (the southern part of Israel).

The following excerpts are from the second edition of the book "100 Prophecies" by George and Ray Konig:

> "Babylon would rule Judah for 70 years.
> Babylon would be attacked by the Medes.
> Babylon's gates would open for Cyrus.
> Babylon's kingdom would be permanently overthrown.
> Babylon would be reduced to swampland."

You will read details of how these were predicted in the Bible and how they came to pass in history in the following sections.

Babylon Would Rule Judah for 70 years

In Jeremiah 25:11-12, the prophet Jeremiah said that the Jews would suffer 70 years of Babylonian domination. Jeremiah also said Babylon would be punished after 70 years. Both parts of this prophecy started to be fulfilled in 609 BC, which is about 2600 years ago. Babylon captured the last Assyrian king and ruled over a vast part of what had been the Assyrian empire, to which Israel previously had been subjugated. Babylon later asserted its dominance by taking many Jews as captives to Babylon and by destroying Jerusalem and the Temple.

This domination by Babylon ended in 539 BC, when Cyrus, a leader of the Persians and Medes, conquered Babylon and brought an end to its empire. Cyrus later **offered the captive Jews the freedom to return to their homeland** (a completely unheard-of thing to do). This fulfilled the first part of the prophecy of Israel falling into Babylonian hands, and amazingly the period of the Babylonian enslavement of the Hebrews was exactly 70 years as prophesied. The Assyrian (Medo-Persians) conquest of Babylon near the end of the 70-year absence from Israel by the Jews fulfilled the second part.

Here is how the prophet wrote of this around 2700 years ago. Jeremiah 25:11-12 (NIV):

> This whole country (Israel) will become a desolate wasteland, and these nations will serve the king of Babylon seventy years. "But when the seventy years are fulfilled, I will punish the king of Babylon and his nation, the land of the Babylonians, for their guilt," declares the LORD, "and will make it (Babylon) desolate forever.

Again, we marvel at the specificity of this prediction as we recounted earlier how King Belshazzar was killed (punished) the night of the Assyrian invasion of Babylon.

Babylon Would be Attacked by the Medes

In Isaiah 13:17, the prophet said the Medes would attack Babylon. This happened about 150 years after Isaiah is believed to have delivered this prophecy. The Medes joined the Persians and conquered Babylon in about 539 BC. Here is how the prophet delivered this prophecy. Isaiah 13:17 (NIV) says: **"See, I will stir up against them the Medes, who do not care for silver and have no delight in gold."**

Babylon's Gates Would Open for Cyrus

In Isaiah 45:1, the prophet said God would open the gates of Babylon for Cyrus and his attacking army. Despite Babylon's remarkable defenses, which included moats, walls that were more than 70-feet thick and 300-feet high, and 250 watchtowers, Cyrus was able to enter the city and conquer it. Cyrus and his troops diverted the flow of the Euphrates River into a large lake basin. Cyrus then was able to march his army across the dried riverbed which had flowed *under* the walls and into the city.

In Isaiah 45:1 (NIV) it says:

> This is what the Lord says to his anointed, to Cyrus, whose right hand I take hold of to subdue nations before him and to strip kings of their armor, to open doors before him so that gates will not be shut…

This prophecy shows that not only was Babylon conquered, but it was conquered specifically by the unborn Medes King foretold of and **named in the Bible**!

Babylon's Kingdom Would be Overthrown, Permanently

In Isaiah 13:19, the prophet said Babylon would be overthrown permanently. History confirms that when Cyrus conquered Babylon in 539 BC, it never again rose to power as an empire. Before the time of Cyrus, however, Babylon had been defeated by the Assyrian Empire but was able to recover and later conquer the Assyrian Empire. However, like Isaiah prophesied 2700 years ago, the Babylonian Empire never recovered from Cyrus' conquest, just as Sodom and Gomorrah never recovered from God's judgment.

Isaiah 13:19 (NIV) says, **"Babylon, the jewel of kingdoms, the glory of the Babylonians' pride, will be overthrown by God like Sodom and Gomorrah."**

Babylon Would be Reduced to Swampland

In Isaiah 14:23, the prophet said that Babylon, which had been a world power at two different times in history, would be brought to a humble and final end. It would be reduced to swampland. After Cyrus conquered Babylon in 539 BC, the kingdom never again rose to power. The buildings of Babylon fell into a gradual state of ruin during the next several centuries. Archaeologists excavated Babylon during the 1800s. Some parts of the city could not be dug up because they were under a water table that had risen over the years, producing a swamp.[239]

Here is how the prophet stated it in Isaiah 14:23 (NIV): "I will turn her into a place for owls and into **swampland;** I will sweep her with the broom of destruction, declares the Lord Almighty." Note that the Bible even got the swampland part right!

Babylon Will be Desolate Forever

Three thousand years ago, ancient Babylon had magnificent hanging gardens once known as one of the "eight wonders of the ancient world." These gardens were surrounded by outer walls rising more than 200 feet into the air and more than 70 feet thick. The walls had regularly spaced towers more than 300 feet high defending the city. These walls enclosed an area of 196 square miles. The venerable "Great Wall of China" is nowhere near this tall, this thick, nor this well situated with defensive towers.

The ancient historian Herodotus wrote that the fields around Babylon were "so fertile he hesitated to write about them, lest people think him insane." Between 1000 BC and 600 BC, Babylon was unquestionably the strongest nation in the known world. The idea that it would be defeated, that its magnificence would be laid to waste, that the fertility of its lands would be lost, and all of this could never be recaptured was not only unthinkable at the time but is historically and statistically unparalleled.

However, that is exactly what was predicted in Jeremiah 51:58 and 62. In these verses, God, through His prophet, made this prophecy concerning the massive fortress of Babylon and its superb gardens and fertile lands. The Bible says, **"The broad walls of Babylon shall be utterly broken…it shall be desolate forever"** (KJV).

Today, the site of ancient Babylon is a trackless wasteland containing huge mounds of rubble. Nothing grows there. Not even a blade of grass lives in this barren desert that was once so lush. Ancient Babylon lies in total ruin. The area can best be described as *"totally desolate."*[240]

More than 2300 years ago, Alexander the Great decided to rebuild Babylon. If he had succeeded, it would have falsified this prophecy of Babylon being defeated and desolate forever. Alexander decided that this spot of ancient Babylon would be a great spot for the capital of the mighty empire he had conquered. He issued supplies to his soldiers to rebuild Babylon. But, immediately after he announced his decision to rebuild Babylon, Alexander the Great was struck dead, and the rebuilding of Babylon was canceled. Was this just a coincidence? In light of the other almost one hundred fulfilled prophecies on Babylon in the Bible, it would appear not to be.[241]

Daniel Predicts Human History over Two Millennia before it all Happens!

In Daniel chapter 2, the Babylonian King Nebuchadnezzar dreams of a statue made of four different materials, identified as four kingdoms:

1. Head of gold, explicitly identified as King Nebuchadnezzar [v.37-38].
2. Chest and arms of silver. Identified as an "inferior" kingdom to follow Nebuchadnezzar [v.39].
3. Belly and thighs of bronze. A third kingdom which shall rule over all the earth [v.39].
4. Legs of iron with feet of mingled iron and clay Interpreted as a fourth kingdom, strong as iron, but the feet and toes partly of clay and partly of iron show it shall be a divided kingdom [v.41].

Parallel to these interpretations in Daniel chapter 7, Daniel has a vision of four beasts coming up out of the sea and is told that they represent four kingdoms:

1. A beast like a lion with eagle's wings;
2. A beast like a bear, raised up on one side, with three ribs between its teeth;
3. A beast like a leopard with four wings and four heads;
4. The fourth beast with large iron teeth and ten horns.

This is explained as a fourth kingdom, different from all the other kingdoms; it "will devour the whole earth, trampling it down and crushing it"[v.23]. The ten horns are ten kings who will come from this kingdom [V.24]. A further horn (the "little horn") then appears and uproots three of the previous horns: this is explained as a future king.[242]

In Daniel 7, the prophet outlines the rise and fall of kingdoms. These kingdoms battle for world dominion. Potential leaders aspire to earthly greatness. Kings and emperors wage war. The stakes are high; dominion of this world hangs in the balance. Finally, a religious-political superpower arises. This power demands the total allegiance of its subjects.

A **beast** represents a **kingdom** (Daniel 7:17, 23).

Winds represent **strife, war, or conflict** (Jeremiah 49:36, 37).

Water represents **multitudes, peoples, and nations** (Revelation 17:15).

The first beast, a lion, is a fitting symbol of Babylon. The Old Testament prophets called Babylon a lion. A lion with eagle's wings was a prominent symbol on Babylonian coins and on Babylon's walls. The lion, the king of beasts, and an eagle, the chief of birds, aptly describes the powerful rule of Babylon from 605 to 539 BC

The fierceness of the Medo-Persian soldiers is depicted in the bear of verse 5. When the Medes and Persians overthrew Babylon, they also conquered Lydia and Egypt. The three ribs in the bear's mouth represent these three nations, Babylon, Lydia, and Egypt, which Medo-Persia ruled in the Middle East from 539 to 331 BC

The leopard is an appropriate symbol of Alexander the Great's empire, Greece. The Greek king conquered with the swiftness of a leopard flying with eagle's wings. Why does this leopard have four heads? When Alexander died in a drunken stupor at age thirty-three, his four generals, Cassander, Lysimachus, Seleucus, and Ptolemy, divided up the empire. Bible prophecy is incredibly accurate. The Greeks ruled from 331 to 168 BC

The Roman Empire, "as strong as iron," conquered the known world in 168 BC by defeating the Greeks at the Battle of Pydna. Under the Caesars, the mighty Roman Empire ruled from 168 BC to 351 AD.

NOTE: The image of Daniel 2 contains four metals—gold, silver, brass, and iron. There are four beasts in chapter 7, a lion, bear, leopard, and dragon. Just as the four metals represent the four successive world kingdoms beginning with Babylon in Daniel's day and passing to Medo-Persia, Greece, and Rome, so the four beasts represent the same four kingdoms. You might wonder why God uses metals in chapter 2 and beasts in chapter 7. In the symbolism of the metals in Daniel chapter 2, God illustrates that no power on earth can endure. The metals are transitory, but His kingdom, "the rock cut out without hands," is permanent. In the fierceness of the four beasts in Daniel 7, God describes the vicious conflicts of political kingdoms as they vie for world dominance.

In Daniel 2, the iron legs, representing the Roman Empire, ended in ten toes, depicting the divisions of Rome. In Daniel 7, the fourth beast has ten horns, depicting the same ten divisions of Rome. Rome was not conquered by a fifth world power. It was divided and overrun by barbarian tribes (especially the Huns) from the north as it decayed from within from 351 to 476 AD.

Since the little horn rose among the ten horns, it must rise in Western Europe, out of the pagan Roman Empire. If the little horn rose among the ten divisions of Rome, it had to rise after Rome was divided or sometime after 476 AD. In the Bible, eyes are a symbol of wisdom or understanding (Ephesians 1:18). This earthly power, rising in the early centuries AD, had human wisdom or understanding equating to the "eyes of a man, not God." The divisions of Rome were predominantly political powers. This new power is different; therefore, it must not be a political power. It must be a religious power, which Christianity and the papacy will fulfill.

This amazing prophecy predicts that a religious-political system would rise out of the old Roman Empire in the early centuries AD. Based on human wisdom, church councils, and man-made decrees, it would attempt to change the very laws of God (change the times and laws as the Bible says). The Bible predicted that the early church would enter into a period of "apostasy" (1 Timothy 4:1-2 and many other places), a time of falling away from God's teachings.[243]

Thus, Daniel, living in the 6th century BC, will correctly predict the order of four successive world powers in correct chronological order. He will intricately describe these nation-states with attributes that will only be known of them when they come to pass centuries later. His prophecies even predict the coming of western civilization and its detachment from the Bible and God's laws as we are witnessing today.

How did an enslaved man living in exile from his home 2600 years ago foresee all of this so accurately and specifically without divine help?

The Destruction of the Amalekites

The Amalekites attacked the Israelites without apparent provocation as they were traveling during the Exodus (Exodus 17:8). **"When you were weary and worn out, they met you on your journey and attacked all, who were lagging behind"** (Deuteronomy 25:17-18, NIV). They later attacked Israel during the time of the Judges (Judges 3:13) and often raided the Israelites' land after they had planted crops, leaving them with nothing (Judges 6:2-5). God punished the Amalekites by ordering Saul to destroy them (1 Samuel 15:2-3) over 300 years after they had first attacked Israel. During that time, the Amalekites had contact with the Israelites and would have heard about Yahweh. They could have repented and changed their ways, but they continued to raid and plunder other cities up to the time of Saul and David (1 Samuel 30:1-3). The Amalekites that Saul and David warred against were clearly no better than their ancestors, who had first waylaid Israel.

The LORD said to Moses, "Write this on a scroll as something to be remembered and make sure that Joshua hears it because I will completely **blot out the memory of Amalek** from under heaven."

Moses built an altar and called it "The LORD is my Banner." He said, **"Because hands were lifted up against the throne of the LORD. The LORD will be at *war against the Amalekites from generation to generation"*** (Exodus 17:14-16, NIV).

"Blot out the memory of Amalek" refers to the extinction of the descendants of Amalek. Clearly, God was not referring to the world's knowledge that Amalek existed (a frequent skeptic claim as a contradiction in the Bible — that Amalek's memory was extended, not "blotted out" by merely mentioning them in the Bible), else God would not have commanded the Amalekites' defeat to be recorded. He wanted the incidents to be remembered, so that future generations would realize that God, not the Israelites, defeated the Amalekites and avenged their unjust treatment of others.

The Amalekites presumably would have been wiped out by Saul in 1 Samuel 15 if he had followed God's instructions. Saul's army did destroy the city of Amalek, but other raiding parties (nomadic bands) of Amalekites survived. These were defeated by David in 1 Samuel 30 with the exception of a few hundred, who escaped (1 Samuel 30:17). The remnant of the Amalekites was finally destroyed by the Israelites almost 500 years later (1 Chronicles 4:43). Thus, while God did blot out the memory of Amalek by wiping out his descendants, he was at war with them for many generations, exactly as the Bible foretold.[244]

This prophecy took about a thousand years to be fulfilled by four different groups of Hebrews, which would eradicate this people group from existence, fulfilling with eerie specificity that this would be a fight and eradication spanning many generations. This shows a godlike knowledge of the specificity of not only what would happen, how it would happen, and who would make it happen.

Edom Will Become Desolate

The prophet Jeremiah predicted that despite its fertility, and despite the accessibility of its water supply in his day and in all history to that time, the land of Edom (today a part of Jordan) would become a barren, uninhabited wasteland (Jeremiah 49:15-20; Ezekiel 25:12-14) due to the brutalities and aggressions made by the Edomites against Israel. His description accurately foretells the history of that now bleak region.[245]

Many great nations have been the subject of biblical prophecies, including the nation-state of Edom. "Edom was a strong nation located next to the Israelites in Palestine. The Edomites, as descendants of Esau (Edom actually means "Red" as Esau was said in the Bible to be "red all over"), were related to the Israelites but were treacherous and idolatrous, frequently warring with the Israelite nation. Their land was rugged, and their capital city, Petra, had a seemingly impregnable position in the rocks of the mountains."[246]

Edom was a rich trade center, and even today, its ruined palaces at Petra (meaning "Rock"), carved out of solid red rock hills, are imposing and a magnificent testimony to human ingenuity. The nation seemed unconquerable. Yet during the height of their power, the Bible in Obadiah, Ezekiel 35:1-15 and Jeremiah 49:16-22 correctly and specifically predicted its overthrow in the future.

Jeremiah 49:15-17 (NASB95) says:

> For behold, I have made you small among the nations, Despised among men. As for the terror of you, the arrogance of your heart has deceived you, O you, who live in the **clefts of the rock**, who occupy the **height of the hill**. Though you make your nest as high as an eagle's, **I will bring you down from there**," declares the LORD. "**Edom** will become an object of horror; everyone who passes by it will be horrified and will hiss at all its wounds.

The Bible predicted that Edom would be destroyed, and all of its inhabitants would disappear. This was a bold prediction not only because of the strength and prosperity of Edom at the time of the prophecy but due to the size of Edom (about the size of the state of New Jersey.)

The fulfillment of these prophecies seemed long in coming. The history books tell us that Edom did well for perhaps a hundred years after their final warning from God's prophets. Then, during the fifth century (400-499) BC, the "Edomites" were overwhelmed by other Arab groups. In turn, these groups were taken over by the Nabataeans, who started living in the area sometime around 312 BC. Under the Nabataeans, the city of Petra flourished until 106 AD, when the Romans conquered Petra. From that time, it slid into disuse, to the point that Edom was almost uninhabited from the 7th to the 12th century AD. It revived slightly in the 12th century when the crusaders built a castle there called "Sel." Afterward, it was abandoned, and it remained so forgotten that it had to be rediscovered in 1812 by Swiss traveler Johann. L. Burckhardt.

But their land has been desolate now for so long that, as the Bible predicted, they are now a long "forgotten people." Today we find nothing but traces of uninhabited towns in what used to be the great nation-state of Edom. If a prophet came to us today and said that the state of New Jersey would be laid waste and totally uninhabited, we would laugh them down, but this is exactly what has happened to Edom. Edom was inhabited for 1700 years, but their cities, their people, and their even their language have now all disappeared from the face of the Earth. The only things living there now are birds, reptiles, and sparsity of other animals, fulfilling to the greatest degree the biblical prediction that **"this area would be forever uninhabited by humans"** and would be **"overrun by animals and beasts!"**[247]

These prophecies of the Bible have been fulfilled exactly as the Bible foretold! In fact, as we described earlier, they have been fulfilled to an extent which seems impossible to humans and is not in line with the vague predictions of human soothsayers but indicates an inside knowledge of the future, which is "otherworldly!"[248]

The Curse Upon Jericho

Joshua prophesied that Jericho would be rebuilt by one man. He also said that the man's eldest son would die when the reconstruction began and that his youngest son would die when the work reached completion (Joshua 6:26). About five centuries later, this prophecy found its fulfillment in the life and family of a man named *Hiel.* The Bible says in 1 Kings (ESV) 16:34:

> In his days **Hiel of Bethel** built Jericho. He laid its foundation **at the cost of Abiram his firstborn, and set up its gates at the cost of his youngest son Segub**, according to the word of the LORD, which he spoke by Joshua, the son of Nun.

The rebuilding of Jericho during this time frame has been verified from archaeology.[249]

Occultic Priests Bones are Burned

One prophet of God (unnamed, but probably Shemiah) said that a future king of Judah, named Josiah, would take the bones of all the occultic priests (pagan priests of the "high places") of Israel's King Jeroboam and burn them on Jeroboam's altar (1 Kings 13:2 and 2 Kings 23:15-18). This event occurred approximately 300 years after it was foretold.[250]

Biblical Predictions for Today

We have cited several of the more than 2000 instances of biblical predictions which have come true in the past (often distant past), but is there any indication that this biblical pattern of the Bible's forecasts coming true today? There is!

Several verses in the Bible predict four stages of the western world's and America's slide away from God, which is only coming to complete fruition today.

Stage 1—Romans 1:18 says God detests any culture which "**suppresses the truth**." For about 170 years, we have tried to explain all creation without the Creator—denying Him! This is the thrust of evolutionary theory. Romans 1:21-22 added to this idea in telling us the godless "**became futile in their thoughts, and their foolish hearts were darkened. Professing to be wise, they became fools**" **(NKJV).** Indeed, we live in an age where the truth is constantly under attack and "spin," and "reinterpretation" abound. We have so lost our way, such that we actually often wonder if there is any "truth" at all, or if everything is just truth for one and not another, or what is right for one is wrong and not truth for another.

Folks, even though it may be difficult to discern what truth is today (in point of fact, that has always been the case for humans), truth is still out there. Either we were created by God, or we were not, and we are just accidents of nature. The bulk of "educated society" today may have a consensus that we are just cosmic accidents, but truth is independent of our votes or feelings on the subject. We can all vote for our belief that there is no God, but if He exists, that does not change the truth of His existence. A person who has just lost a loved one to death can fervently invent in their mind that their loved one is alive and still with them, but that does not change the truth of their loved one's death.

We have deluded ourselves in the last 170 years into thinking that we can define what reality is and that there is no truth except what we define for ourselves that it is and that this "truth" can be variable from person to person and from day to day. My father has an insight into such thinking. He says that whenever we start thinking we are "brighter" than God, we always get into trouble. That is exactly what has happened with the assault on the truth we have witnessed and continue to witness today.

Note, this suppression of "truth" is a direct assault on the authority of God's word, the Bible. This attack says in no uncertain terms that the Bible is just mythical and contains no transcendental truths, but just the wisdom of bygone ages, irrelevant to us today.

Stage 2—Since 1925, there has been a gradual move to eliminate God from our schools and society and to teach only naturalism to our children. Romans 1:20 addresses this when it tells us that all humanity is *without excuse* when they say there is no God, since the very creation in front of us, trees, a planet made specifically for life, the wonder of birth, the wonders of our intricately designed human bodies and so much more attest to the Creator.

Teachers and researchers teach and evaluate all they see through materialism (the idea that what we can see and experience is all there is), and it's all they see. In doing so, we are ignoring Romans 1:20 and the testimony of nature, which shouts there is a God! In 2 Peter chapter 3 (NIV), it says:

> Above all, you must understand that in the last days **scoffers will come, scoffing and following their own evil desires.** They will say, "*Where is this 'coming' he promised?* Ever since our ancestors died, **everything goes on as it has since the beginning of creation.**" But they deliberately forget that long ago by God's word the heavens came into being and the earth was formed out of water and by water. By these waters also the world of that time was deluged and destroyed. By the same word the present heavens and earth are reserved for fire, being kept for the Day of Judgment and destruction of the ungodly.

Like Romans chapter 1, this verse graphically foretells scoffers of biblical truth. Following their own evil desires, they will attempt to redefine reality and truth to their own liking. They question Christ and his second coming. This verse even foretells of the development of the theory of evolution to replace God since the phrase "**everything goes on as it has since the beginning of the creation**" is a very apt restatement of the uniformitarian (everything is happening today as it has in the past—"the key to the present, is the past") ideas which underlies the theory of evolution. In these final verses,

Peter expounds on how man in this day will seek to forget not only the creation but how man was sanctioned by God for his sin with a worldwide flood. There could not be any more concise description of our modern ideas and times.

It says in Romans 1:25 (NIV), **"They exchanged the truth about God for a lie, and worshiped and served created things rather than the Creator."**

Stage 3 began in this country in the 1960s when we began wholesale the sin of "creation worship." This had become prevalent in Europe sometime before then but accelerated with our turn to "nature as god."

The Bible tells us we were created to worship God, and when we reject that, we substitute nature. Today we seem to value eagle eggs, snail darters, and African lions over aborted human babies. Our culture obsesses in unfounded hysteria over climate change and our effect on nature. You can watch any nature documentary and quickly pick up on our religious reverence for nature, but also our total and intentional ignorance of a Creator.

For these sins of suppressing God's truth and ignoring His words, eliminating God from our culture, and worshipping the creation and not the creator, in **Stage 4,** we have brought the Judgment of God upon ourselves. Scripture says God has *withdrawn our restraint upon our sinful natures.* We can see that clearly in the lawlessness, murder rates, abortion on demand, and our other willful disregard for God's instructions today.

Nothing in all nature makes this point more clearly than our sexuality. We ignore God's prescriptions against homosexuality and even try to ignore that God made us male and female. Our assigned sex as being male or female is coded into every cell of the about sixty trillion cells in our bodies. No amount of cross-dressing, hormone therapy, or surgery can change that. This may be the ultimate rebellion (shaking our fist) at God!

Romans 1:26-27 (NIV) tells us we **"abandoned natural relations with women and were inflamed with lust for one another."**

In 2015, for the first time since depravity of the Roman Empire, homosexuality has been equated with biblical marriage. God, therefore, has given us over to a **"depraved mind"** and **"every kind of wickedness"** as people **"not only continue to do these very things, but also approve of those who practice them."**

Rape, murder, envy, deceit, malice, gossip, arrogance are all on the rise in America today. Just as in Sodom and Gomorrah, anyone standing up against these anti-biblical tenants is persecuted. Such a society will be destroyed either from without or from within by weakening themselves morally and culturally.[251] If God overlooks America's sin today, he will have to apologize to Sodom and Gomorrah. I don't believe he will ever do that!

Some will try and write off these Bible verses as not applying to any particular culture or time but being general comments on how cultures deteriorate. While there may be some validity to this appraisal, the parallels between what the Bible foretells and how our culture has regressed in the past sixty-plus years is striking. How did Peter and Paul get this right 2000 years ago, unless they had inside information from the Creator?

All the Old Testament
False Gods will Disappear from Society

Around 600 BC, Jeremiah 10:11 (NLT) said, **"Say this to those who worship other gods: 'Your so-called gods, who did not make the heavens and earth, will vanish from the earth and from under the heavens.'"**

At the time of this prophecy, there was an immense amount of idol worship, as had been true for more than a thousand years. This prophecy foretold that all of the widely worshipped idols such as Baal, Ashtoreth, Dagon, Marduk, Chemosh, and so many more, which had been worshipped and engrained in ancient societies for more than a millennia would fade away and no longer be worshipped, as is true today.

Sadly, even though this prophecy has come to pass, and all of the false gods of that time are no longer worshipped, man being an innately religious creature, has now replaced them with a plethora of new idols.

It Appears in the Bible, and God Can See the Future!

As previously mentioned, multiple sources count about 2500 prophecies in the entire Bible. Of these, about 2000 have now come true with *amazing specificity*.[252] This in itself sets up the Bible as being unique, since no other supposedly sacred or "*God-given*" text such as the Qur'an, the Book of Mormon, or the Hindu Vedas has such historical prophecies in them by which to check their veracity.

By just assigning the chance of any one of these predictions the high probability of 1 out of 10 chance for each (most like Tyre would have been far more unlikely than this) for the 2000 fulfilled prophecies now recorded, we get the odds against the Bible making all of these predictions and their coming to pass at 1 out of 10^{2000} (one chance out of 1 followed by 2000 zeroes) which far surpasses any chance for all of these things ever coming to pass as predicted by mere chance.[253] This is a clear indication of God's omniscience (all-seeing, all-knowing).

The scriptures cited in this chapter show more than 400 incidences where God foretold historical events before they happened. These are only a sampling of what is in the Bible! There are many others we could relate to, such as the foretelling of the defeat of the Assyrian city of Nineveh. The prophet Nahum predicts the fall of Nineveh in the mid-7th century BC, several decades before the city actually fell in 612 BC. When he prophesied this, the Neo-Assyria Empire was at the height of its power and seemed invincible. He even specifically predicted they would be drunk when attacked and let down their guard, overestimating the safety of their fortresses, as has all been verified via ancient writings and archaeology.[254]

Likewise, we have not detailed the Jeconiah Prophecy, The Almah Prophecy, the prophecies of Balaam, and more than a thousand more specifically fulfilled prophecies in the Bible.

Was this book written by Nostradamus or *God Himself?* It would seem evident that the Bible has now been verified to exhibit three of the six sets of attributes we said it should have if it really was written by God. The chances of these three sets of evidence all occurring by mere chance are calculated as $\frac{1}{2} X \frac{1}{2} X \frac{1}{2} = 1/8$ or only 12.5 percent. This means the chances of the Bible being inspired by God and his existing are up to 87.5 percent. These predictions by themselves are impressive, and they are starting to lay a strong statistical groundwork for the impossibility of all this happening as the Bible predicted without divine help, but there is far more...

What About Protecting His Word?

In the first two centuries after Christ, both the Jews and Romans tried to eradicate members of "the Way" (What Christians were called and called themselves for the first several decades after Christ's death) and their writings. Both the members of the Way and their writings survived and thrived to this day!

Voltaire (circa 1750), a famous philosopher and outspoken atheist, said, "In sixty years there shall be no Bible." That was more than 250 years ago, and the Bible is still the most sold and printed book in the world, as it has been for centuries. There have been many such pronouncements about the demise of Christianity for two thousand years, but they have never come to pass, in spite of great efforts by nations and people groups to get rid of them.

One of my favorite true stories related to this is about Voltaire's house. Fifty years after his death, this famous philosopher, who predicted the demise of Christianity, had his house sold to a *Bible Institute,* and it became a place where Christian Bibles were made, sold, studied, and distributed for many years. I smile at thinking about how neither God (if He exists) nor the people who bought Voltaire's house could miss the sweet irony in all of this. Nor is it lost on me how Voltaire must have turned over in his grave!

Human Word of Mouth

Human "word of mouth" is a notoriously bad way of transmitting and keeping details straight when trying to transmit information of any kind. There are massive amounts of studies by linguists and archaeologists as to how information or stories handed down from generation to generation by word-of-mouth change over time due to the inaccuracies implicit in this form of communication.[255]

One small demonstration of this phenomenon showing the weakness of oral transmission of knowledge is the old two phrase experiment. We have all probably seen a demonstration of this where a person whispers two phrases into the ear of one person on one side of a room, and that person whispers to the person next to them, and then that person passes the phrases on to the person next to them, and so on across the room. In the end, we ask the last person to hear the phrases to repeat what they were told, and it invariably has changed drastically. And this was with only a couple dozen people transmitting two sentences from one to another, in just a few minutes one night.

I did this same experiment one night during a seminar I was teaching. I whispered into the ear of one lady the following phrases. "Jim went to the aquarium and saw much fish and took pictures of them" After these phrases had been passed by word of mouth from person to person across the room (a group of about thirty people), here is how it came out when the last man to have it whispered to him heard it.

"Tim went to the coast and caught many of the biggest fish in history. He has the pictures to prove it, and some of the fish are now in an aquarium!" Again, this substantial amount of inaccuracy of the transmission of these phrases occurred in a room of just thirty people, transmitting these phrases from one to another in just a few minutes. With this example, it is not hard to imagine just how badly the transmission of any creation story or other account by a people group could be changed, mangled, and distorted over centuries of retellings via millions of people. We should expect this in any oral tradition, to see vast amounts of changes and inaccuracies in later "versions" of accounts or stories as compared to the original. In fact, we do find these types of massive changes in the information of all oral histories we can track across the globe, as we demonstrated in chapter one of this book. However, we also find one grand exception to this seemingly infallible rule, the Bible.

To exemplify how accurate the Bible is and how it defies expectations, we look at the rates of distortion for the Bible as compared to other great literary works from history. When we compare the current Bible to its tens of thousands of manuscripts from over the last three thousand years, we find a difference between the current biblical texts and those ancient manuscripts of less than 0.5 percent (most estimates of this rate are 0.2 percent). That is remarkable and a far lower rate of distortion than we would have suspected if it were the work of man.[256]

By comparison, when we compare the earliest and latest copies of Homer's Iliad, we see a 4.9 percent difference or rate of distortion. The Mahabharata (one of the two great Sanskrit epics of ancient India) shows a 10.4 percent distortion rate between current copies and the oldest copies found.[257]

Dead Sea Scrolls

The Dead Sea scrolls give us evidence of God's words being supernaturally protected against such transmission inaccuracies. The Dead Sea scrolls include a collection of old copies of most of the Old Testament. These were found in sealed earthen jars in caves near Qumran, on the Dead Sea, in the 1940s and 1950s. These scrolls are dated via both historical records, as well as carbon dating, as being somewhere around 2000 years old. There are people who champion dates for these copies anywhere between 300 BC and 100 AD. Many scholars believe that they were placed in these caves in 68 AD to protect them when the Jews were overwhelmed by the Roman Tenth Legion in that year.[258]

When we compare the writings on these copies with our Old Testament translations today, we find that the text has been preserved to 99.999 percent accuracy (only a very few spellings, punctuation, and modifier errors, additions, or deletions — none of which change the meaning of the text). We find that there has essentially been no change whatsoever in what these scriptures say or mean today, as compared to these copies from 2000 years ago.[259] How could that be? The printing press will not be invented until the fifteenth century, allowing for the mass production of copies and allowing human transmission and most copying errors of these texts to be erased from the process. Word of mouth transmission and hand copying techniques used prior to the printing press in most works are seen introducing errors in copying, which mount progressively each century.

Some will point out that most of the transmission of these texts over the last two thousand years has been via written copies (which is what these scrolls are). Thus, suggesting that such hand-written copying is infinitely more reliable than word-of-mouth transmission. While it is true that written copying is demonstrably better at retaining original content, it is far from error-proof and still leads to lots of errors seeping into texts.[260] This is seen in any text which we can find copied by hand over centuries with the partial exception of biblical manuscripts. We say partial because there are some real differences between some manuscripts, such as between the Masoretic Text and the Greek Septuagint. However, all of these differences are in minor areas such as in connecting verbs and participles and numbers, but the transmission of the relevant "theology, accounts, stories and lessons" from scripture are 100 percent intact, in a way we find in no other set of manuscripts which have been hand-copied for centuries anywhere in the world.

A great deal of credit for this incredible amount of accuracy of ancient Bible manuscripts is often given to the Hebrew scholars, who first laboriously copied these Old Testament scriptures by hand for centuries, and then the Maccabees and Catholic Monks, which took up this task after 200 AD. While these groups were very hard-working and had very strict rules to try and ensure that each page copied was an exact replica of what they had copied from (the Maccabees would destroy the whole page if a single mistake in copying was made and start over), it has been demonstrated by research that in spite of such labors and rules, that inaccuracies and personal comments invariably find their way into any handwritten copying.[261] The accuracy of transmission we see in these biblical texts from ancient times till today is simply beyond human capability.

The fact that such inaccuracy of transmission *did not happen in the Bible*, as is demonstrated in our analysis of the Dead Sea scrolls compared to the current Bible, shows God's unmistakable fingerprint on history and protection of His Words!

Scrolls from Ein Gedi Israel

Analogous to the finds of the Dead Sea Scrolls is the more recent find of the scrolls at Ein Gedi, Israel, in 1970. These scrolls carbon date from between 210 and 390 BC. When found, these scrolls had been burned, leaving at that time no hope of unraveling them without their crumbling as archaeologists found when they attempted to unravel a portion of them. However, recent technological advancements have allowed experts to "virtually unroll" 3D images of these scrolls using sophisticated software and x-ray scans that pick up ink remnants (this process resembles CT scanning in hospitals). This has allowed experts to now decipher Hebrew characters from these rolled-up and charred scrolls.

What they found amazed them. Emmanuel Tov of Hebrew University co-authored a technical report on the scroll scans. He told the Associated Press that the scrolls were "*100 percent identical*" to the Hebrew book of Leviticus used today for Bible translations. He said, "This is quite amazing for us. In almost 2000 years, this text has not changed!"[262]

Chinese Ideographs

Just as impressive is the evidence for the even more divine protection of God's word over the 1100 years prior to its being edited together and written down by Moses around 1450 BC. It is thought that the biblical accounts were either all carried forward by word of mouth (very inaccurate) or were recorded on stone and other tablets in such lost works as the "Annals of Adam" and the "Annals of Seth" referred to in some texts.

In either case, the amount of change that would be expected in the original biblical accounts from just after the creation and what would eventually be recorded by Moses would be massive in scope.

What we find from analyzing the Chinese language, however, paints a quite different picture. As discussed before, Chinese ideographs and the origin of the written Chinese language date back to about 2500 BC. As shown previously, Chinese ideographs such as the word for "boat" being comprised of the radicals (pictures) for "vessel + eight + mouths or people." This easily shows a reference to the eight people saved from the biblical flood on the ark. The ideograph for the word "tempter" uses the word pictures (radicals) for "devil + trees + cover," which shows a knowledge of the story of Eve being offered the fruit of the tree and she and Adam having to cover their nakedness after their sin. To make the word "garden," the Chinese used the radicals for "dust + breath + two persons+ enclosure," showing they had a clear knowledge of the original creation account of man being formed from the "dust of the ground," of the "breath of life breathed into them"(biblical "nephesh"), and of two persons being the original two people to inhabit the garden. Many have found more than 118 such Chinese ideographs, which show a clear understanding of the first eleven chapters of Genesis embedded in the Chinese language some 1100 years before Moses wrote it all down.

These ideographs show a clear knowledge by the ancient Chinese of the creation account of Adam and Eve, of the Devil, of Noah, the Ark, and the worldwide flood, of the Dispersion after Babel, and even a clear understanding of the theology of the Trinity (God in three persons, Father, Son, and Holy Spirit). When comparing the theology and knowledge of Genesis chapters 1-11 with Chinese ideographs, we see revealed in these Chinese symbols almost exactly what we find in our current biblical texts. It is amazing to find no discernable errors in transmission or changes in theology or content.[263] This in spite of the fact these biblical accounts, found in the Chinese language, had, presumably, been carried by word of mouth for 1100 years (Chinese language in 2500 BC till Moses wrote them down around 1450 BC) and then copied by hand for the next 2900 years till the invention of the Guttenberg printing press. This unprecedented preservation of God's word is more than impressive and more than unlikely. It is a level of preservation impossible for man.

As noted, archaeological finds and historical records verify the accuracy of the Bible.

Bible Manuscripts

The Bible stands alone as the best-preserved literary work of all antiquity. There are thousands of existing "Old Testament" manuscripts throughout the Middle East, Mediterranean and European regions. What is amazing is how most of these thousands of different copies and manuscripts agree phenomenally with each other.

The manuscript evidence for the "New Testament" is also dramatic, with nearly 25,000 ancient manuscripts discovered and archived so far.[264]

Compare the Bible to Other Writings that We Trust as Authentic Every Day

Skeptics love to note that we do not have the original autographs (the original manuscripts written by Saint Luke, Saint Paul, Moses, and all others) and ask how can we know that what we see today is in any way close to what was originally written? Further, they charge that the Bible is full of errors, and its copies are full of errors. Answering these questions is the work of historians, theologians, and linguists investigating the field of "textual criticism." In this field, a scientific examination of ancient manuscripts of a particular work is compared to one another to arrive at a most probable original text.

So what's the big deal with having tens of thousands of ancient copies of the Bible to work from? What is not thought of, except by anthropologists and other historians, is that no other book has anything like this type of wealth of copies to work from, to check against one another, to assure that the original texts and meanings can be verified. In fact, with most ancient writings, which we and ancient cultures thought to be important, there is only the tiniest fraction of this number of copies as compared to the Bible. However, that does not stop us from believing that the copies of those other works, which we have far fewer manuscripts to check and work with, are any less reliable in keeping their original content. But this is a constant attack on the Bible by modern critics.

We continue to find more and more copies of the Bible. What is interesting is that each time we find a new copy today, it usually agrees to an amazing extent with today's Bible and further confirms that the Bible has been conferred to us today reliably.[265]

Let's look at some of the great works of long past philosophers, scientists, and leaders. These works were judged by their own and subsequent cultures to be of such great value that they have been copied and recopied for centuries and read and reread by as many as a hundred generations of people. These books have added greatly to the philosophies of today.

Julius Caesar, the great Roman leader, wrote *"The Gallic Wars."* Today we have only ten ancient manuscripts to work from of this text. Of these copies we have today, the earliest copy (and therefore the one which should be closest in content to the original) was copied a full 1000 years after Julius Caesar wrote his book. Yet, an analysis of these ten manuscripts in existence today shows good agreement (not perfect and not to the level we see in the Bible), leading experts to believe that we have copies that are very close to the original manuscript.[266]

Pliny the Younger (61 AD—c113AD) was a lawyer, author, and magistrate of Ancient Rome (and, yes, for those, who are wondering, there was a "Pliny the Elder."). Pliny the Younger was a witness to the eruption of Mount Vesuvius on August 24, 79 AD. His "*Natural History*" was hailed as essential reading for centuries. Today we only have *seven* manuscripts of his history to work from. The earliest copy, and supposedly the best one, was copied 750 years after Pliny the Younger died! Yet, experts are comfortable with the analysis that what we have printed today is close to his original manuscript.

Herodotus' *History* is considered the founding work of western literature. His histories were written between 450 and 420 BC. His histories serve as a record of the ancient traditions, politics, geography, and clashes of various cultures that were known in Western Asia, Northern Africa, and Greece at that time, including the rise of the Persian Empire. Today we have only *eight* ancient copies of this great manuscript to work from, and the earliest and perhaps best copy was penned 1350 years after the original! (That's a lot of time for errors to creep in.) But his works do not undergo any of the claims of unreliability that the host of biblical manuscripts do.[267]

Plato was a great Greek philosopher who lived between 427 and 348 BC. He is considered an essential figure in the development of philosophy, especially the Western tradition, and he founded the "Academy in Athens," the first institution of higher learning in the western world. Along with his teacher, Socrates, and his most famous student, Aristotle, Plato laid the foundations of western philosophy and science. Of his works, which were considered essential reading by all educated westerners throughout Europe during the Middle Ages, we have only *seven* manuscripts left to look at today. And the earliest and best copy of his works was copied 1300 years after his words were originally recorded. Yet, what we have is thought of as fairly accurate today.[268]

Homer is generally credited with writing the *Iliad* (an ancient Greek poem about the Trojan War) around the eighth century BC. Compared to the Bible, it has the second most original copied manuscripts to work from, totaling 1750 copies of this ancient text.[269] That, of course, pales in comparison to the Bible, which has tens of thousands of manuscripts from which to check and work from. Even so, the *Iliad* is hailed as one of the great works of history, and its contents are not debated, but the Bible with far more than 20,000 more copies is constantly questioned. There seems to be double standard here which shows a bias by secularists against the Bible.

There are nearly 6,000 handwritten copies of the Greek New Testament which were copied by copyists called Scribes and by groups such as the Maccabees, who devoted themselves to copying the Bible as accurately as humanly possible, to the point that if they made a mistake, they would immediately destroy the faulty copy and start over. They took these pains because they believed they were handling the "Words of God." It is currently believed that we will find another thousand historical copies of the Bible in the future in countries that are currently inaccessible for geopolitical reasons.[270]

We also have more than 10,000 copies written in what is referred to as the "Old Latin" (the Latin translation that existed prior to Jerome standardizing the Latin Bible into his "Vulgate" translation). Further, there are somewhere between 5000 and 10,000 manuscripts in existence of biblical copies in other ancient languages.[271]

Also, various lectionaries exist (documents which contain calendrical or devotional readings of Bible verses), as well as over a million citations of scriptures by church leaders (enough to produce and piece together "virtually the entire New Testament many times over").[272]

There are about 140,000 words in the New Testament, with around 400,000 variants (variations in wording or spelling between different manuscripts, not in just one manuscript). This leads some skeptics to claim there are more variations in the New Testament than words, and thus they paint it as unreliable.

However, there are so many variants due to the tremendous number of copies of the Bible (still the most copied, read, and widely published book in the world and in history). The more copies you have, the more variants you will have.

It is most important to note that more than 99 percent of the variants do not change the meaning of the text. They are all misspellings or differences in word order. Also, a large number of the word variants are not viable (don't fit the context). Thus, no one thinks they were part of the original (for instance, spelling errors, or where a late manuscript has an entirely unique reading that none of the other 20,000+ other manuscripts record). Such rare inconsistencies are not in our current published translations.

These rare variations, due to the wealth of copies we have, allow text critics to trace variants back to their earliest occurrence. So, when we get rid of the many variants (which has been done in our best translations), we can be confident that our Bibles convey essentially what the original manuscripts said. Additionally, it should be noted that no essential Christian belief rests upon just one verse, so no essential Christian belief is challenged by any of the variants.[273]

There is a logical disconnect here, which says there is something more than logic at work. Logically due to the great wealth of the copies we have to work with, the Bible should be honored as the most checked, verified, and substantiated work in all history, and yet it is constantly questioned by scholars and ridiculed by others. It appears that all of this questioning of the most verified and revered book in history is a philosophical debate and not one based on the merits of its manuscripts and veracity. The problem for most scholars and philosophers with the Bible is not its historical accuracy but its content and its origin.

If it's the Word of God and His message to us, then all people cannot claim to be their own boss. If the Bible is God's message to us, it means that they were made by a Creator and are responsible to Him, and man has forever been in rebellion of that concept. This seems to be the very obvious answer, that it is not the Bible's credentials which its critics dislike, but its message.

What is so illogical is that modern critics and purveyors of the "higher criticism" declare that the Bible, due to its ancient origin and the problems we have already discussed with human mouth to mouth and hand-copying transmission, does not contain the same meanings as the original texts. However, these same "scholars" are perfectly comfortable citing the works of Plato, Pliny, Homer, or Julius Caesar and proclaiming that these writings truly reflect the writer's original intents.

The Bible not only has tens of thousands more copies than any other ancient work, but we have copies of the New Testament which have been dated within two hundred years of the original manuscripts, which logic tells us should give us far better copies than these other ancient works, and are far closer to the original texts than any of the other great works of men that we have discussed.

Renowned Bible scholar F.F. Bruce declared: **"There is no body of ancient literature in the world which enjoys such a wealth of good textual attestation as the New Testament."** The Bible (and by extension God) says of itself in Matthew 24:35 (NIV), "Heaven and Earth will pass away, but **my words will never pass away."**[274]

More Genesis in Chinese

We have already discussed how the ancient Chinese language reveals a detailed knowledge of Genesis chapters 1-11. Just another example to underscore how the theology and content of the Bible's message have not changed in 4500 years in spite of, presumably, being transmitted for eleven hundred years by word of mouth and then hand-copied by men for the next 2900 years.

In Genesis 2:7 (NKJV), the Bible says, **"...God formed man of the *dust* from the ground and *breathed* into his nostrils the *breath of life*; and man became a *living being.*"** Now compare these words in today's Bible to the radicals first used by the Chinese in 2500 BC to make the word *"create."* Not only is their knowledge of Genesis clear, but note that radicals used for the concept *"create"* are identical to the wording in Genesis 2:7. How is it that no meaning whatsoever could be lost or distorted in this way over the course of 4500 years with the added problems of human transmission?[275]

口 + 土 + 辶 + 丿 = 造
Breath   Dust   Walking   Alive   To Create

It Appears God has Protected His Words!

In spite of whole nations who would eradicate Jews and Christians, and their writings, they have proliferated throughout history. In spite of human and technological limitations, the Bible shows inerrant accuracy to an unbelievably miraculous extent! This is God's unmistakable fingerprint on history and his word!

Therefore, it would appear that the Bible has now passed four of the six tests we proposed for it if it really is the writings of the Creator of everything. With four tests passed, there is still a chance that this is all coincidental, but that chance is getting smaller. At this point, with the evidence already presented, mathematically, the chances of each one of these four premises could have been proved true or false. So each had a ½ or 50 percent chance of being proven right. Therefore, with four premises in a row being proven right, mathematically, we are taking four things four at a time, and thus the chances of these things to all have occurred to be true by chance is ½X½X½X½= 1/16. This means there is only a 1/16 chance or 6.25 percent chance that all of these things we have examined happened purely by chance. Logically that leaves approximately a 94 percent chance that this coordination of these four premises being proved true did not happen by chance but by some coordination. We would suggest that the coordinator of all of this is the God of the Bible, and if so, then the Bible is the writings of God as it purports to be. Let's see if this mounting case for the Bible as God's Word proves out with our last two tests?

Philosophical And Logical Coherence

Does the Whole Book of the Bible Hang Together with a Single Theme and Evidence of a Single Writer (God)?

The Bible is a collection of sixty-six books, written by around forty authors, over a period of about 1500 to 1900 years, in three different original languages and on three different continents. NO human in history could have coordinated its content from start to finish. If God wrote and/or inspired the writing of all of the 66 books of the Bible, then we should find just such a correlation of content and themes, which no human could have instilled in its writing. In addition, if God wrote or inspired the Bible, its text would not only reveal one mind writing and coordinated themes, but its original texts would also be inerrant when compared to historical and scientific findings. This is a very high expectation for any book and one which only the product of a god would be expected to uphold. The question is, what do we find when we examine the Bible and its contents?

Most people in our society today have not read through the whole Bible. Many in our society have no idea about what is in the Bible at all, except for what they have heard second-hand from others. Much of our society believes the Bible to be passé, dated and irrelevant, and thus not worthy of study, much less the guide for our modern lives. Let's encapsulate for you what is in the Bible and let you make a decision for yourself as to whether or not there was a guiding mind behind it all.

The thirty-nine books of the Old Testament tell us of God, His creation, our place in His creation, and the relationship He wished to have with us. He also gave us His laws which showed us how to live and pointed us toward our need for a Messiah. God then gave us a few thousand years to demonstrate to ourselves that we could not keep the ten simple main laws He gave us, known as the "Ten Commandments."

Like any good parent, God knew that while He could lay down rules for his kids, they would have to experience life on their own, make their own mistakes, and find out for themselves that God's way of life and His rules were the best way to live. He also gave us time to find out that we could not "save ourselves" (find our way back to God) by living perfectly (which we cannot do) and working our way up to God's state of perfection.

The twenty-seven books of the New Testament show us God knew that we would discover that we could not live perfectly and that we would find ourselves in need of another way to get ourselves back into a positive relationship with God. The New Testament, along with the Old Testament, makes it clear that God had a plan to "bridge the gap" between sinful men and a Holy God from the beginning of time. The Old Testament points to a Messiah, and the New Testament tells us of a Savior/Messiah who came into the world to give us the "way out." The name used for him by the Old Testament Hebrews was Messiah (although of the thirty-nine uses for the term Messiah or "anointed one" in the Old Testament, only the Psalms 45:7 reference appears specifically pointing toward Christ)[276], and in the New Testament, He is called Jesus Christ, who is described by the Bible as being the Son of God, who took the form of a man, so that He could live the sinless life we could not. He then sacrificed Himself in our place so that He could take onto Himself the judgment we deserve so that it will not fall on us.

In support of this coordination of theme, both John 5:39 and Luke 24:25-27 are direct references where Christ said that the whole of the 39 books of the Old Testament were a testament of Himself!

Let's now focus on how each set of books verify one another and contain the same themes and content.

The King James Version (KJV) of Isaiah 40:11 says, **"He shall feed his flock like a shepherd: he shall gather the lambs with his arm, and carry them in his bosom, and shall gently lead those that are with young."** This is not only an image and prediction of the Messiah but corresponds to how Jesus himself and other gospel writers portrayed his ministry. It is clear from our perspective in hindsight that both the Old and New Testaments were in concert with what the expected Messiah was to be (although the Old Testament Hebrews had difficulty seeing that Christ's was to be a heavenly kingdom, and not the military leader of a kingdom here on earth). The Old Testament in as many as 366 places predicted the Messiah (whom the New Testament reveals is Jesus Christ), and Jesus fulfilled them all!

What is always both sad and fascinating is how the Jews at the time of Christ, and the Jews of today, miss identifying Christ as the Messiah. This gets somewhat easier to understand when you consider the political times of His first coming. At the time of Christ's ministry on earth, the nation of Israel was a conquered territory of Rome. What the people yearned for was not a spiritual savior but a military savior in the form of King David, who would free them from captivity. This illusion was and is partially fed by prophecy of the Messiah being born in the line of David, the ultimate military leader of Israel's history. It is also fed by the fact that man never gives proper credence to his sins and overlooks the need for spiritual salvation in lieu of more tangible creature freedoms and comforts.

Wages of Sin is Death Throughout

In the Old Testament book of Ezekiel 18:4 New International Version (NIV), it says, "For everyone belongs to me, the parent, as well as the child, both alike belong to me. **The one who sins is the one who will die.**" Note how close this is to the New Testament in Romans 6:23 (NIV), where Paul wrote, "**For the wages of sin is death**, but the gift of God is eternal life in Christ Jesus our Lord."

Note that in the bold text of both the Old and New Testaments is the same theme and message. It has not changed since we were kicked out of the garden that the "**wages of sin is death**" (remember that we suffered spiritual death as a result of that sin, also in accordance with this theme). Romans 6:23 is an often-quoted New Testament scripture, but it is a theme that runs all through the Old Testament as frequently the penalty for grievous sins in the Old Testament was death.

See in Romans 6:23 how the "wages of sin is death" message is echoed, but in addition, the second phrase of that verse emphasizes we have the assurance that God has a plan for us to avoid death, and that plan involves and is embodied in Jesus Christ, who is the theme of the New Testament.

God Owns it All

The Bible shows through both testaments that God created everything and owns everything. Both testaments feed into one another on this subject. In the first part of Ezekiel 18:4, it is established that everyone on earth (in fact, in Psalms 50:10-11 and Jeremiah 17:3 it is stated in the Old Testament (OT) that **everything** on the earth, all life, all fields, mountains, and seas) are Gods since He is the Creator. That is a recurrent theme of the Old Testament. Haggai 2:8, Psalm 24:1, Leviticus 25:23, Psalm 104:24, Job 41:11, Genesis 14:19, and so many more places in the OT testify that God owns all of creation!

According to the King James Version (KJV) in Mark 10:6, Jesus himself said, **"But from the beginning of the creation God made them male and female,"** revealing that Christ Himself believed in the creation, and that we did not evolve, but were placed here in this creation. This is what Genesis, the first book of the Bible, teaches, and here Christ states his belief in the truth of that record. Christ agreed that if we are God's creations, then we are His possessions.

Likewise, both 1 Corinthians 10:26 and Psalm 24:1 (NIV) say, **"The earth is the Lord's, and everything in it,"** and in 1 Corinthians 3:23 (NLT) say, **"...and you belong to Christ; and Christ belongs to God."** This is among a list of verses such as Matthew 22:21, John 1:11, 1 Timothy 4:4, and others all say the same thing. That God created it all, so He owns it all. Thus, multiple verses in both testaments echo this biblical truth.

Is He a God of Wrath in the Old Testament, but One of Mercy in the New Testament?

There is a long-held belief that the Bible portrays two different versions of God. A God of wrath in the Old Testament (OT) and a God of mercy in the New Testament (NT). Is the Bible really inconsistent on this pivotal point? If so, it is contradictory since many places in the Bible describes God as unchanging (a concept of God called His "Impassibility.")

Well, to be sure, the OT describes many places where God is wrathful. Examples include Adam and Eve's expulsion from Eden, the Worldwide Flood, Moses against Pharaoh in Egypt, Sodom, and Gomorrah, and so on.

The NT, however, also has ample examples of God's wrath. Ananias and his wife Sapphira were struck dead by God for lying about their giving (Acts 5). The sorcerer Elymas is blinded in Acts 13. Paul was blinded on the road to Damascus, and Christ was crucified on the cross.

In fact, the apostle Paul had an interesting and profound insight that is hidden away in his letter to the Romans. He said in Romans 4:15 (NIV), **"The law brings wrath."**

Theologian James Arlandson says, "I concluded that of the 499 times that God showed wrath in the OT, He shows it against His people 448 times *after the Law of Moses* was thundered down on Mt. Sinai, beginning in Exodus chapter 19. But wrath on His chosen people before the law and covenant in Exodus 19 was shown by God only three times." Abraham potentially could have experienced it twice but did not because God, through His angels, showed him mercy (Genesis. 18:30-32). So actually, it was used only once against Moses, the lawgiver, in Exodus 4:1.

Law and justice are tied to covenant in the OT. Two parties voluntarily enter into an agreement (the Bible describes this as a "blood covenant" in Genesis 15:9-10, not to be broken). The powerful partner (God) promised to keep them safe and bless their agricultural life and resources (Genesis 12:1-2). He also instituted the priesthood to teach them how to keep the law, and He set up the sacrificial system administered by the priests for when the people sinned. This showed them how God takes sin seriously, but it also shows He will forgive. Their laws and their practices were to be a shining light to the pagan world. The righteous party (God) forgave their sins over and over again, for centuries. He sent prophets to warn them of their sin's consequences and remind them of their agreement.

But sometimes, the human party to the covenant (contract) went so far in their bad faith; they broke the law so egregiously for centuries, the aggrieved party (God) finally took action. He judged and punished them, but not in His full wrath and not to destroy them. And after this painful judicial process, painful to God, as well as us, He still forgave and loved them. He was merciful to his chosen lawbreakers. This is the perfect blend of mercy and justice. This is the story of God's wrath in the OT, in a nutshell, and we haven't discussed what kind of lawbreaking they did, acting like the unwholesome (to say the least) nations around them.

An analysis of the OT, as well as the NT, shows Paul's thesis is confirmed: **"The Law of Moses brings wrath."**

The Law was given in the OT times to demonstrate what failure to meet God's law would mean. It also demonstrated His righteousness and holiness, in that God will not countenance sin and rebellion for which there will be stiff penalties and no favoritism. But not only was God's law and His righteousness demonstrated in the OT, but also our need for another way to meet His holy requirement to be with him.[277]

In the OT, he gave us his laws in the form of the Ten Commandments, as well as other laws given to Moses. They were meant to protect us, show us how to live together, how to honor God, and then one thing more. They were to show us what we could not do for ourselves. We could not keep even a list of ten simple laws; thus, we could not earn salvation for ourselves. We would need someone to give us another way to God. That someone will be His Son, Jesus Christ, the Messiah, who is foretold of on more than 300 occasions in the OT, and His coming to earth in human form, dying for us and giving us another way to God. This is the theme of the NT.

Is that all there is to it? God gave us the law, and God showed us He meant to enforce it, so that is why he is portrayed as a vengeful and wrathful God in the OT. But He sent his son to die for us in the NT, the fulfillment of prophecy, thus showing His graceful and forgiving side in the NT?

In truth, these are only partial pictures of both testaments. The OT does have more enforcement of laws and sightings of God's wrath than the NT, but as shown above, there are plenty of examples of God's wrath in the NT, with the ultimate being Christ's death on the cross. God does not change. He does not renege on his promises and contracts (what he calls covenants) as we often do. That is demonstrated throughout the Bible, and by Christ, as the ultimate example for us; Christ fulfilled all requirements of the law.

In the OT, God documents the history of the world, His gracious creation of this wonderful planet, and He gave us life. Initially, we only had one rule to obey (don't eat of just one tree). When we violated that one rule, we were expelled from the garden and deprived of eternal life in penalty for that infraction. He then showed us what it would take for us to earn our way back into his kingdom (the law). He then gave us a few thousand years to prove to ourselves that we could not keep just ten laws any better than we had not kept just the one.

God then gave to us his answer for what he knew we needed, a Savior to bridge the gap between a Holy God and sinful man. This part of the godhead (the Trinity), Jesus Christ, was foretold of in the OT repeatedly and is revealed in detail in the NT. Along the way, though, God is consistent. He reminds us throughout the NT that if we do not take advantage of His free gift of salvation and choose to ignore Christ, then God's wrath, hell, and damnation will be ours (Matthew 25:11 confirms this). His consistent application of justice throughout both testaments should convince us that he will do what he says.

The OT does not show just a wrathful God, but a parent who lets his kids learn for themselves what the consequences of their actions can and will be. In the NT, that same parent, who had planned throughout time to intervene, and did so when it became apparent even to us (His children) that we could not earn salvation for ourselves, and God then put in motion His plan for our salvation (our reconciliation to Him). God is consistent from the beginning to the end of the Bible. His actions, revealed in the Bible, show His consistent attempts and plans to raise up His children and restore them to a relationship with Him. The Bible does not portray two different Gods in the OT and NT, but rather the multiple faces of a Godly parent, balancing His love for His creation with God's innate holy state of being. As we will detail later in this chapter, the people of the OT were saved by the same means as in the NT, by faith. This consistency is a mark of God!

Linguistic and Numerological Clues to the Writer in the Bible

More than a century ago, Dr. Ivan Panin identified many patterns in the Bible, which he touted as proof of **one writer** for the whole Bible. Dr. Panin went on to find many patterns and make some rather controversial claims about their meaning, all of which I do not fully accept. However, his identification of certain patterns repeated in word usage and form throughout the Bible had two interesting results, which I do find credible. First, this data was so convincing to him that he turned from being a lifelong agnostic into a devout Christian. As a result of his analysis, which showed that all 66 books of the Bible gave evidence of one mind writing it, with linguistic and mathematical patterns revealed in each and every book which the 40+ authors of these books could not have contrived to have replicated in each and every writing.

Second, the pattern identification used in Dr. Panin's work has been used by signal corps and military intelligence services across the world for the last century to identify whether messages are in the original form as sent by the sender or have been intercepted by the enemy and changed in some way. This has become common practice in modern warfare and secret communications.

During World War II, the British broke the German "Enigma" code, thought to be unbreakable, by constructing the first working computer. The Americans in that war would repeatedly break Japanese codes, which the Japanese would then replace with a new cipher. The Japanese and Germans did the same to the allies. One thing which these opponents would do to each other would be to intercept communications before they arrived at their destination and "massage" or change the communication subtly so that it would disrupt enemy movements or plans.

It became a common practice of all of these intelligence agencies, such as the American OS (which preceded our current CIA), English MI5, the Russian KGB, and others to use pattern recognition identification of messages to tell whether a message was getting to them as sent by the original sender on their side, or if it had been intercepted and changed in some way by the enemy.[278] These same analysis techniques used by our intelligence services to identify if a message comes from one author and an original author show that the Bible was inspired by one author, even though it was written by more than 40 men, over a period of almost 2000 years.[279]

This evidence gives us intriguing proof of one original author, who inspired the writing of the whole Bible in a way that only a

God could have done. However, there are other commonalities of message in the Bible whose consistency in both the Old and New Testaments also testify to the whole work hanging together as "one mind writing." We will now examine several of those commonalities.

Confession

The Bible has a consistent concept of the need for confession of our sins in both the Old and New Testaments. It is a rather misunderstood concept both inside and outside the church. Yes, it means we are to admit to God, and in some cases man, the sins and trespasses we have committed, but it has a deeper meaning. The biblical concept of confession is agreeing with God that what we did is wrong. If He is God, then he already knows what we did. What He wants from us is an admission of our realization of our guilt and agreement with Him that what we did is wrong and that we will strive not to do it again, which branches into the related concept of repentance. The following verses exemplify this theme of confession throughout the Bible.

First John 1:9 (ESV), "If we **confess our sins,** He is faithful and just to forgive us our sins and to cleanse us from all unrighteousness."

Proverbs 28:13 (ESV), "Whoever conceals his transgressions will not prosper, but he who **confesses and forsakes** them will obtain mercy."

Psalm 32:5 (ESV), "**I acknowledged my sin to you,** and I did not cover my iniquity; I said, 'I will **confess my transgressions to the Lord,**' and you forgave the iniquity of my sin. Selah."

Acts 19:18 (ESV) "Also many of those who were now believers came, **confessing and divulging** their practices."

The verses James 4:7-10, Ezra 10:1-11, and more than twenty other verses in both testaments express this same concept and show "confession" as a consistent theme.

Baptism

It is often thought that baptism (emersion, washing, or sprinkling with water) is only a New Testament concept since it gained wide acceptance after Christ's death with members of "The Way" (what Christians were called in the first century AD). However, there are many examples to show this was not only a New Testament theology.

Exodus 40:12-15 (NIV) says, "Bring Aaron and his sons to the entrance to the tent of meeting and **wash them with water.** Then dress Aaron in the sacred garments, anoint him and consecrate him so he may serve me as a priest. Bring his sons and dress them in tunics. Anoint them just as you anointed their father, so they may serve me as priests. Their anointing will be to a priesthood that will continue throughout their generations."

Leviticus 16:4 (NIV) says, "He is to put on the sacred linen tunic, with linen undergarments next to his body; he is to tie the linen sash around him and put on the linen turban. These are sacred garments, so he must **bathe himself with water** before he puts them on."

Ezekiel 36:25 (NIV) says, "I will **sprinkle clean water on you,** and you will be clean; I will cleanse you from all your impurities and from all your idols.**" Further allusions to baptizing with water can be found in Leviticus chapters 13-15 and 2 Kings Chapter 5.

All of these verses in the Old Testament communicate some of the same concepts of baptism as in the New Testament. This includes washing oneself in water to cleanse of sins or to symbolize that cleansing had occurred. Jesus himself in the New Testament had himself baptized as a symbol of his obedience to God. He was baptized in a river by **John the Baptist,** who practiced this rite for all, who would turn from their sins and commit themselves to God.

The Bible also talks about the separate rite of "Baptism of the Spirit," as the Holy Spirit comes upon the new believer. This phenomenon is foretold in the Old Testament in Joel 2:28-30. It then comes to fruition in the book of Acts and elsewhere in the New Testament.

Baptism is not a uniquely Christian ordinance but is one the Bible shows had been practiced intermittently by the Jews for more than a millennia before Christ came. The NT incarnation of baptism has all of these things attached to it (especially in the Anglican and

Catholic churches) but morphs into a more symbolic ordinance showing what has happened in a person's life when they accept Jesus as Savior in the view of most protestant faiths today

Giving and Tithing

Second Corinthians 9:7 (NT) ESV, "Each one must **give** as he has decided in his heart, not reluctantly or under compulsion, for God loves a cheerful giver."

Malachi 3:10 (OT) ESV, "Bring the full **tithe** into the storehouse, that there may be food in my house. And thereby put me to the test, says the Lord of hosts, if I will not open the windows of heaven for you and pour down for you a blessing until there is no more need."

Luke 6:38 ESV (NT), "**Give**, and it will be given to you. Good measure, pressed down, shaken together, running over, will be put into your lap. For with the measure you use it will be measured back to you."

Proverbs 3:9-10 (OT) ESV **"Honor the Lord with your wealth and with the first fruits of all your produce;** then your barns will be filled with plenty, and your vats will be bursting with wine."

Second Corinthians 9:6-7 (NT) ESV, "The point is this: whoever sows sparingly will also reap sparingly, and whoever sows bountifully will also reap bountifully. Each one must **give** as he has decided in his heart, not reluctantly or under compulsion, for God loves a **cheerful giver.**"

Psalm 4:5 (OT) ESV, **"Offer right sacrifices, and put your trust in the Lord."**

Acts 20:35 (NT) ESV, "In all things I have shown you that by working hard in this way we must help the weak and remember the words of the Lord Jesus, how he himself said, 'It is **more blessed to give** than to receive.'"

These are just a small sample of the dozens of verses in both testaments that show the biblical concepts of giving to others, giving back to God, and tithing (giving back one-tenth of what you have to God). These are consistent themes throughout the Bible, which conveys many purposes beyond just funding the church.

In the Old Testament, there were, in fact, three tithes the Hebrews gave back to God. They gave the Sacred Tithe as described in Numbers 18:21; the tithe of the Feasts described in Deuteronomy 14:22-27; and the Tithe for the Poor taken every three years, as described in Deuteronomy 14:28-29 (thus, over a three-year period a devout Jew would give a tithe of 23⅓ percent of their possessions to God). Most Christian groups today practice only the tithe (10 percent) given to the priesthood like Abraham did in Genesis 14:18-20, which is very akin to the sacred tithe.

Giving teaches us how to help others and gives us hope for others to help us. Giving teaches us how God gives to us when we do not deserve it. Giving involves more than just money. Biblical tithing, as expressed throughout the Bible, involves giving not only our money but giving of our time and our talents. As the Bible describes it, giving and tithing are two ways that God teaches us to have faith, teaches us how to give, how to receive, how to share, disciplines us, and helps us to recognize that nothing is truly ours, but that everything is, in fact, God's. We are only stewards of his creations. We give back to God a small portion on a regular basis in recognition of the fact that as His creations, everything we have is actually His. And we are to do this giving frequently and on a regular basis, to continually remind ourselves of this important concept.

God could have picked more efficient ways to fund the church. He chose our giving back to Him as a way of not only funding His ministry but maturing us. It is in this way in both testaments that God raises up a believer!

The Trinity

The biblical concept of the Holy Trinity (note the word "trinity" is not used in the Bible) says that there is only one God (monotheism), but that God exists in three persons called the Father, the Son, and the Holy Spirit, who are all part of the same God. This concept of three persons in one (as confusing and alien as it is to us) is consistently alluded to throughout the New Testament, but one which even scholars and theologians cannot readily explain since such an existence is outside of our experience, and thus our conception. Some critics will charge that this "Trinity" concept is not shown in the Old Testament, but that is not true.

This concept of the Trinity begins with the very first verses of the Bible. In Genesis 1:1, it says, "In the beginning, God created the Heavens and the earth." The Hebrew word used for God in Genesis 1:1 is "Elohim," which is a plural form of the word "El" (which means God). In the context of Genesis 1:1, there can certainly be no doubt as to who is doing the creating. In the Hebrew language, the "im" ending imputes plurality. Therefore, "Elohim" is the *plural* form of the word "El."

It is interesting to note that *each usage* of this word throughout the Bible is *grammatically incorrect*. It is a plural noun used with singular verbs. According to Genesis 1:1, the Creator of the Universe, **Elohim**, exists as a plural being but is referred to in the singular.

If this were not so, then the word "El" or perhaps Yahweh (translated as "LORD" by Jews since they think it forbidden to say God's name) would have been used. However, the Holy Spirit chose to use the word "Elohim," the plural form of the name of God, in the very first place where the name of God is proclaimed.[280]

Likewise, this plural use occurs in Genesis 1:26, which says, "Then God (plural) said, let us make man in **our** own image, in **our** likeness." It is clear here that God alludes to himself in the plural because God is a plural being. This concept did not originate in the New Testament but at the very start of the Bible. It is further exemplified in the Bible by the picture of man having three parts, a body, a spirit, and a soul, reflecting the three-part personage of the Godhead (some say this is what God means in the Bible is saying we were made in his image.). Current Christian theology has it from John 3:3 that only "born again of the spirit" believers have all three of these parts since the spirit part of us died with Adam's original sin.

Genesis 1:2 then expounds on this plural relationship with an explicit mention of the Holy Spirit. It says, "The earth was formless and void, darkness was over the surface of the deep, and the **Spirit of God** was hovering over the waters. " Here, it is made clear that the Holy Spirit existed, was present, and was part of the Godhead from the creation, and not just another name for God.

This concept is further expounded upon in John chapter 1, where it is stated that the "Word" (the name often used in the Bible for "Jesus the Son") was not only present at the creation but was the action partner of the Godhead, which followed the Father's will, and "spoke" all creation into being.

Genesis 3:22 (NKJ) is another verse in the creation account that clearly refers to God as a plural being. It says, "The LORD God said, 'Behold, the man has become like **one of US**, to know good and evil....'"

The following are verses from the Old Testament which show that this concept of the seeming conflict of monotheism and the Trinity are evident in the Old Testament as well.

Job 33:4 (NIV) says, "The **Spirit of God** has made me; the breath of the **Almighty** gives me life." Likewise, Psalm 104:30 (NIV) says, "When **you** *send* **your Spirit** they are created, and you renew the face of the ground." As well as Isaiah 48:16 (NIV) which says, "...And now the **Sovereign Lord** has sent me, endowed with **His Spirit**."

God the Father is shown in Genesis 17:1, Exodus 24:9-11, and Exodus 6:2-3. All tell of personal encounters with God the Father as it says in Exodus, "God also said to Moses, "I am the Lord. I appeared to Abraham, to Isaac, and to Jacob as God Almighty, but by my name the Lord I did not make myself fully known to them."

The appearance in Genesis chapter 18 is especially significant. Some will contend that it is one of what they claim are a myriad of biblical contradictions. The text says, "the Lord" appeared to Abraham. (A *theophany* is a technical term for such a physical appearance of God.) He appeared to Abraham physically, and **Abraham saw His face, and His feet as well as the rest of Him**. But there are references in the Bible, such as Moses on Mount Sanai, where it is warned that no human may look on God and live. The simple theological answer is that this was the Lord God, but not the personage of God the Father, but God the Son, whom Abraham could look onto without dying, as will be true at His physical appearance as Jesus Christ almost 2000 years later. The fact the translated word lord used here is not Yahweh (not LORD, but "Lord") which translates not God almighty, but is the general term for "lord or master" strengthens the case for this interpretation.

This personal appearance by God the Son makes sense at this time in two ways. The appearance of God himself and not an angel to deliver the news of Abraham having a son in his old age to start the Hebrew line (God's adopted people) underscores the importance of this part of God's plan for us. It is also more than appropriate that the manifestation of God, which will come to earth to save us via this lineage being created through Abraham, is the same person of the Godhead, who appeared to put this plan and lineage into motion, God the Son.[281]

"God the Son" is also mentioned in the Old Testament. "Who hath established all the ends of the earth? What is his name, and what is his **son's** name, if thou canst tell?" (Proverbs 30:4, KJV) Then there are the two famous prophecies of Isaiah, quoted so frequently at Christmas time. "Behold, a (literally 'the') virgin shall conceive, and bear a son, and shall call his name Immanuel (meaning **'God with us'**)" (Isaiah 7:14, KJV). "For unto us a child is born, unto us a **son is given**: . . . and his name shall be called Wonderful, Counsellor, **The mighty God**, **The everlasting Father**, The Prince of Peace" (Isaiah 9:6 KJV). There is also the very explicit reference to someone "like the **son of God**" in the furnace with Meshach, Shadrach, and Abednego in the book of Daniel.

Perhaps the most explicit verse in this connection is found in Psalms chapter 2. "The LORD hath said unto me, **Thou art my Son**" (Psalm 2:7, KJV). Then this Messianic psalm concludes with this exhortation: "Kiss the **Son**, . . . Blessed are all they that put their trust in him" (Psalm 2:12, KJV), which not only tells of the Son of God but foretells of his future status as our Savior, and the way to salvation is to trust in and have faith in Him.

All of these verses from the Old Testament clearly show the concepts of God the Father and Lord, the Spirit of God, and the Son of God. These concepts of the deity are mirrored in the New Testament in John 1:1-3, 18; John 6:46; Matthew 28:19; 2 Corinthians 13:14. The clearest of these is Matthew 28:19 (NIV), which explicitly says, "Therefore go and make disciples of all nations, baptizing them in the name of the **Father and of the Son and of the Holy Spirit...**"

Acts 28:25 (ESV) says, **"The Holy Spirit was right in saying to your fathers…"** affirming the belief that the words of the prophets were guided by the work of the Holy Spirit in Old Testament times and writings. Similarly, Peter, when quoting from the book of Psalms, stated in Acts 4:24-25 that while the words came from the mouth of David, it was the Holy Spirit speaking. In 2 Peter 1:20-21 (ESV), Peter said, **"No prophecy was ever produced by the will of man, but men spoke from God as they were carried along by the 'Holy Spirit.'"** These verses not only affirm the New Testament belief in the actions of the Holy Spirit in the Old Testament but give us insight into this unimaginable to us relationship of God speaking through the Holy Spirit, who is a part of Him.

Now critics contend that in many cases, the terms "God" and "Spirit" are used interchangeably for God. They would claim Genesis 1:2 (KJV) where it says "...the **Spirit of God** moved upon the face of the waters..." is just such a case, and that "Spirit," "Holy Spirit," and "God" were used in the Bible interchangeably. What they are implying is that there are not three personages, but just one called by different names.

But, as seen in both Old and New Testaments, it is clear the Bible defines three distinct personages of God. Thus, while the Bible does on occasion refer interchangeably to God as "God the Father," "LORD," and "Spirit," this does not vitiate the Bible's description of the three personages of God but often exemplifies them. They are all three parts of the same entity.

We have made the case that God the Father, the Son, and the Holy Spirit personages can be seen in the Old Testament. But it is also true that there is more information about the Holy Spirit and God the Son in the New Testament than in the Old Testament books. This is, in fact, makes good sense. Even though all three personages existed as part of God from the beginning, God the Son and the Holy Spirit only became recognizably operative to us in New Testament times and from there forward.

In the New Testament, Christ comes to earth to fulfill God's plan for salvation. His ministry is the focus of the New Testament. It, therefore, should be expected that much more will be said of and about him in the New Testament than in the Old Testament.

Likewise, Christ, just before he ascended, said that the Holy Spirit would then come on to all of us and into all of us. This phenomenon had been described in the Old Testament, such as when the Spirit came upon King Saul when he was crowned and withdrawn later. Part of the "**New Covenant**" in the New Testament is that we will now be "sealed" by the Spirit. The Spirit will live in us and never leave us. This everyday within us, very intimate coexistence with the Spirit within the life of each Christian was a major part of the "New Covenant" in the New Testament. Thus it is not surprising but expected that there is far more about the Holy Spirit in the New Testament than there was in the Old Testament.

Still, it is clear the personages of the Spirit of God and the Son of God are not the sole creations of New Testament Christians, but they are a consistent doctrine of the three personages of God as taught throughout the Bible. From all of this, we judge the Bible to be very consistent with respect to the concept of the Trinity from beginning to end.

Gentiles to be saved from the Start

Some see a dichotomy or conflict in the accounts of the Old and New Testaments in that the Old Testament gives accounts of the Jews as God's chosen people, and then in the New Testament, the goal shifts to saving the gentiles (non-Jewish). The Jews believed they were God's chosen so wholeheartedly that they made jokes such as "God made gentiles because someone had to pay retail." Or closer to home, the apostles themselves bore a prejudice against gentiles as described in Matthew when Peter revealed that Jewish law forbade him from eating with, going into the house of, or in any way associating with a gentile. This was an early form of racism taught not by the Bible but by Jewish culture.

We can verify that this racism, or view of gentiles as possibly subhuman, was a Jewish cultural phenomenon and not a biblical concept by what the Bible says in the Old Testament. Genesis makes it clear that the Bible says we are all of *one blood*, both Jew and gentile, as well as all men and women. This is not only a biblical statement but one which is verified genetically. Genetics has shown that we have only one race of humans, the human race, and what we call races are only different <u>people groups</u> of the same species, which do have minor differences in skin color, stature, and facial features.

Further, it was made clear in Genesis 12:3 (NIV) that it was God's goal to eventually reclaim all of humanity as his when it says, "I will bless those who bless you, and whoever curses you I will curse; and **all peoples on earth will be blessed through you**." Apostle Paul in Galatians 3:8-9 explains how this passage, spoken to Abraham as a promise, was being fulfilled in his ministry to the gentiles.

Thus, the two testaments are not in conflict. God used his special relationship with the Jews not only to give us His laws and our Savior but also His message in the scriptures. But it is apparent from both testaments that it was God's intent from the beginning to offer salvation to "**all peoples of the earth.**" This is alluded to in Romans 11:25 (NT) and is symbolically portrayed and foretold in the OT book of Ruth.

Romans 1:16 makes it clear that Jesus (the Messiah) came first to the Jews (God's chosen people). But, when they rejected Him, as foretold in scripture, the focus of His New Testament ministry shifted to the gentiles.

The Worldwide Flood

In Luke 17:27, the Holman Christian Standard Bible (HCSB) says, **"People went on eating, drinking, marrying and giving in marriage until the day Noah boarded the ark, and the flood came and destroyed them all."** This verse, as well as others, shows Jesus believed in the story of the worldwide flood and the Ark, just as it was recorded in the Old Testament. Indeed, not only are the people, who say there never was a worldwide flood and claiming to be a Christian believer are being very inconsistent, they are, in fact, calling Jesus a liar in light of this text!

What is so fascinating today in this discussion of the flood of Noah's day is how scientists theorize that Mars, a planet with not a drop of liquid water on its surface today, is thought to have once been completely covered with water, and thus conventional scientists are crediting the features we see on Mars today to worldwide flooding. However, when we consider the Earth, which has 70 percent of its surface covered by water (and more than three times that amount of water contained in the earth's mantle[282]), they say that such a worldwide flood could never have occurred on this planet. These two statements not only defy logic but are easily seen as inconsistent by laymen, who have little knowledge of science.

This much is clear, the Old Testament talks of a worldwide flood, and New Testament figures also talk of a worldwide flood, and they voice agreement of this flood and Noah as real history.

Bible Heroes are all Very Flawed!

One of the most logical proofs for the Bible not being mythological, or made up, is shown in what the Bible says about the Jews, the supposed Bible heroes, and early Christians. The Bible does not romanticize them as perfect people but instead shows them to be very flawed. If you are making up a religion, you will not do that. You would make most of your characters and forefathers to be great and almost perfect people, "paragons of virtue," and bigger-than-life role models.

One example of this is King David, perhaps the most revered of all Jewish heroes. The return of a King like David is still looked for by Orthodox Jews, who believe the Messiah has yet to appear. My father, however, saw David for what he often was in the Bible, and it became a stumbling block for him with finding faith for many years until he came to grips with the point of a hero with such "clay feet." My father would often ask how God could call David a "man of His own heart" (as is said in the Bible), in light of all the terrible sinfulness David did?

While King David was a great military leader, he was also an adulterer, a murderer, committed genocide, and was a horribly lax father. My dad lamented for years the incongruity of calling such a sinful man, one whose sins are far worse than most humans in the history of mankind, a "man of God's own heart"?

When you examine the scriptures, however, you find that David's sins were always followed by remorse, a confession to God of his sins and acts of contrition, as well as a turning away from that sin. What is revealed in the Bible about David and about us all is that God is not interested in only using perfect people since there are none on this planet, and there never have been short of Jesus Christ. What God does look for are sinful people who will own up to their sins, repent of them and acknowledge God as their Lord.

If you are the ancient Hebrews, inventing a religion, you will not make the central hero of the entire Old Testament such a deeply flawed individual, but that is what is in the Bible because it appears that was the truth about this real and verified historical man.

Likewise, Abraham, whose life takes up more than half of the book of Genesis, the father of the Jewish people, whose lineage the nation of Israel came from, was frequently a weak individual for most of his life. He did not wait on God as he was told to do. He had sex with his wife's maid so as to get offspring promised to him by God. In his advancing age, he did not have the faith to believe God would provide a child to him and his aging wife. He lied to Pharaoh in Egypt (Genesis chapter 12) about his wife (told him she was only his sister) and almost got her raped. He would not learn from this mistake and did it again later, again putting her in peril by doing this with King Abimelech (Genesis 20). The Bible records many more mistakes by this supposed *hero* of the Bible.

Adam and Eve sinned and got us all thrown out of paradise. One of their sons will commit the first murder on earth, even murdering his own brother!

Noah, a man, described as the only righteous man left before the great flood, will fall into drunkenness after the flood.

The people of Israel, released miraculously from bondage as slaves in Egypt, will distrust and disobey God on multiple occasions throughout their journey. Yet, God will not abandon his commitment to them. They complain even though bread and birds fall from the sky each day for them to eat, their clothes never wear out (forty years not wearing out, a miracle), they are given victory after victory over superior numerical forces, and yet all they do is complain, fall into pagan worship of other fictitious gods, and disobey God's instructions to them frequently.

Moses, God's chosen leader for the Exodus from Egypt, was a murderer. When God appointed him to be His instrument, Moses tried to get out of it every way he could. His actions were not that of a brave hero but of a flawed and normal man. He will eventually sin after many years of service to God by not following God's instructions, which will prevent him from entering the Promised Land.

Elijah, the greatest of the Old Testament prophets, will sin against God by fearing for himself and running from a woman's scorn. He will also, for a time, become self-absorbed and curse his surroundings during a "pity party."

Jonah, another prophet of God's in the Old Testament, when told to go and preach repentance to the sinful city of Nineveh, is afraid for himself and the reaction of the people of Nineveh. He will literally run from God and disobey God to the point of showing that he will in no way follow God's directions. God has to literally kidnap him, rather miraculously, and force Jonah to do his will. After it is all done, though, God forgives the people who do come to repentance in Nineveh, which angers Jonah, who reveals an angry and unforgiving spirit in himself. Still, God used him!

Simon Peter, the leader of Jesus' disciples, is a weak individual, who betrays Jesus not once, but three times the night before Jesus is executed. He was also an impetuous and volatile individual who would, on one occasion, take a sword and lop off the ear of a priests' representative. He would frequently speak without thinking.

John the Baptist was a complete weirdo. He dressed in rough camel's hair (right out of a caveman movie), was wildly unkempt in appearance, and ate wild honey and locusts (grasshoppers). This is the man God gave the high honor of being the "town crier," like Paul Revere, who pointed everyone towards the Savior.

One of Jesus' hand-picked disciples (Judas Iscariot) will sell him out for thirty pieces of silver!

Paul was originally chief prosecutor of Christians, killed Christians, and persecuted the early Christian church.

The Bible uses testimonies of women for God's acts, as in Ruth, also in the ministry of Jesus. This the Bible did in spite of the fact that in their culture, the testimony of women could not be used in court and was considered legally unreliable and useless. If you are inventing a religion, you will get better witnesses than that.

Why give all of these supposed Bible heroes such failings unless it was the truth of their existence, and the Bible is only reporting what actually occurred and who they actually were. This is not a made-up, glorified, and romanticized tale which never happened, but a very real account of the sinful and weak people we see in ourselves each and every day. And it all appears to have been done intentionally, to show us that there are no perfect people and that God is looking for those who will admit that and turn to Him for help. These are the people God chooses to use, and this is a consistent theme throughout the Bible.

The New Testament Believes
in the Words of the Old Testament Prophets

Luke 1:70 (KJV)says of God, **"As he spake by the mouth of his holy prophets, which have been since the world began."** and Romans 1:2 (NIV) says, **"the gospel he (God) promised beforehand through his prophets in the Holy Scriptures."** Both of these verses show that the New Testament writers believed in the authentic writing by God through his prophets in the Old Testament. This belief in the Old Testament writing is echoed as well as Acts 3:21, 2 Peter 2:21, 2 Peter 3:2 revealing a repeated and definite belief that the Old and New Testaments are connected and that the statements in the Old Testaments are still valid with reference to the New Testament.

Now let's look at some quotes by Jesus Christ in the New Testament.

Mark 7:10 (KJV): "For **Moses said,** Honor thy father and thy mother; and, Who so curseth father or mother, let him die the death:"

Matthew 22:32 (KJV): "I am the **God of Abraham, and the God of Isaac, and the God of Jacob?** God is not the God of the dead, but of the living."

Matthew 12:40 (NIV): "For as **Jonah** was three days and three nights in the belly of a huge fish, so the Son of Man will be three days and three nights in the heart of the earth."

Matthew 24:37 (NIV): "As it was in the **days of Noah**, so it will be at the coming of the Son of Man."

Galatians 3:29 (NIV): "If you belong to Christ, then you are **Abraham's seed**, and **heirs according to the promise."**

These are just a sampling of the many comments made by Christ which reflect His treatment of the Old Testament prophets and Old Testament teachings as both truthful and real. Not only Christ, but multiple New Testament writers made statements showing their belief in the Old Testament prophets as real people led by God and that the OT related real history. Christ and the New Testament authors both believed in the reality of the Old Testament prophets, and the reality of the Old Testament accounts as they referred to them no less than 100 times in the context of real history! It is this reality described in the Old Testament that the New Testament authors used as a basis to build their faith upon in the New Testament.

Passover Becomes Communion/Lord's Supper

In the Old Testament account of the Exodus, when the last of the plagues come upon Egypt to force them to let the Israelites go, the firstborn of everyone in Egypt is killed, except for those who place the lamb's blood over their entryway, signaling the "death angel" to "pass over" that house. This story not only leads to one of the most intriguing and climatic parts of this account but gives the historical background for the Jewish practice of Passover, which the Jews would reenact each spring to commemorate this event for the last 3400+ years.

In Exodus chapter 12 (NIV), the Bible describes how they are to commemorate this event:

> The animals you choose must be **year-old males without defect**, and you may take them from the sheep or the goats. Take care of them until the fourteenth day of the month, when all the members of the community of Israel must slaughter them at twilight. Then they are to **take some of the blood and put it on the sides and tops of the doorframes of the houses** where they eat the lambs.

This event, central to the Jewish faith, not only commemorates this Exodus event but perfectly symbolizes the sacrifice of Jesus Christ, which was yet to come. Note that it is a lamb (as Jesus is described many times in the Old and New Testaments) to be sacrificed, and one who is young and "without blemish" (equating to being perfect and without sin), just as Jesus would be when crucified.

This event was also central to the Old Testament system of atonement, where an animal without blemish was offered by each family each year in atonement for their sins. The New Testament book of Hebrews chapter 10 describes Christ's reason for coming to earth and how his coming changes the meaning of the whole sacrificial system of atonement. The unending sacrifices in the Old Testament were necessary since we could never atone for our sins by ourselves, and we needed to be constantly reminded of this.

One very special part of the Jewish Passover meal, also known as the "Seder meal," is the "Afikomen." Early in the Seder meal, one wafer of the unleavened bread (Matzah) is taken from the basket of Matzah (thin and wafer-like bread, with piercings and stripes on it), a piece is broken off, wrapped in cloth, and hidden in the house (just like Christ's body was wrapped in burial cloth and was buried in the earth) by the father or person officiating the meal (this broken-off piece is the *afikomen*). The meal proceeds with several courses. When the third of four cups of wine is drunk, the "cup of redemption" (the Jewish sacrificial system was one of the yearly animal sacrifices to atone for sins. This cup symbolizes a final redemptive act of blood to atone for all sins and will be given to us by the coming Messiah.) It is the signal for the final thing to be eaten at this meal, the *afikomen*.

The kids present at the ceremony search throughout the house to find the hidden piece of unleavened bread. (Unleavened because leaven is associated with sin in this ritual, and thus bread without leaven is "without sin." Again, the symbolism of Christ's sinless life is unmistakable). The child who finds the afikomen is rewarded, and the host breaks off a small piece of the broken piece of bread and passes it around to everyone else to break off a small piece as well. Thus, the last part of the meal to be eaten (just as the last thing which will occur on earth is the second coming of the Messiah) is a piece of pierced and striped bread easily symbolizing Christ, who was pierced and striped from His lashings. The wine is symbolic of His spilled Blood, just as the juice in the communion practices of Christianity symbolizes Christ's shed blood. This final part of the meal is a striking replica of the Christian communion meal, which has been celebrated for the past 2000+ years.

During this whole Passover service, an untouched cup is set aside during the meal. It is set aside for Elijah, the Old Testament prophet expected to come back to earth and identify the coming Messiah. At the end of the meal, the whole family will look to the house's entry door and check to see if Elijah walks in with the Messiah. When he does not show, his cup is left alone, and they all sing a song and a prayer asking God to bring Elijah and the Messiah to them by next year's Passover event.[283] This whole celebration looks toward the coming Messiah, which the New Testament says is Jesus Christ!

Christ came not only to pay the price for our sins in a final and forever way but to do away with this sacrificial system, making his life both the focus of the whole sacrificial system and the climaxing moment of that system.

The Old Testament prophet Jeremiah foretold of this change in the sacrificial system in Jeremiah 31:31-32 (NIV) when he said:

> "The days are coming," declares the Lord, "when I will make a **new covenant** with the people of Israel and with the people of Judah. It will not be like the covenant I made with their ancestors when I took them by the hand to lead them out of Egypt, because they broke my covenant...."

Jesus is quoted as saying the following in the New Testament book of Corinthians 12: 25-26 (NIV):

> In the same way, after supper he took the cup, saying, 'This cup is the **new covenant** in my blood; do this, whenever you drink it, in remembrance of me.' For whenever you eat this bread and drink this cup, you proclaim the Lord's death until he comes.

This was Christ performing the Passover ritual with his twelve disciples in the upper room the night before he would be arrested and eventually crucified. It is clear that, at this moment, Christ transforms the Passover meal, which had been reenacted by the Jews for almost 1500 years in memorial of the death angel "passing them over," and changing it into a commemoration of His sacrifice of

His sinless life for the sins of us all. He makes it clear that the bread symbolizes His body and the wine (or juice) His Blood, which is spilled to substitute for all of us, who have sinned and owe a debt of death for that sin.

Thus, New Testament Christians celebrate the Lord's Supper or Communion, just as Jesus transformed and fulfilled this Old Testament ritual of the Passover. The whole of the Passover celebration was one of remembering the "Passover of the death angel" and looking forward to the coming Messiah. The New Testament identifies Christ as that Messiah. The continuity of this theme, and its execution, is clear from the beginning to the end of the Bible.

The Golden Rule

The Golden Rule of **"loving others as you do yourself"** and thus treating others as you would like to be treated is thought to be only a New Testament (Matthew 7:12) concept, but it's not.

In the Old Testament, Leviticus 19:18 (KJV) says, "And thy hand shall not avenge thee; and thou shalt not be angry with the children of thy people; and **thou shalt love thy neighbor as thyself**; I am the Lord."

This Old Testament quotation is equivalent to and was written at least 1500 years before this same concept is echoed specifically in the New Testament books of Matthew, Mark, Romans, Galatians, and James.

In the book of Exodus, we're given the "*Ten Commandments*," which have been the center of jurisprudence in western civilization for more than a millennia. Central to Old Testament law, and western law, is the idea of "equity." There is a legal concept used in western jurisprudence based on the Bible, which says, "to get equity, you have to give equity." In lawyer-speak, this is the equivalent of "do unto others as you want to be treated," the pure concept of the "*Golden Rule*."[284]

The first four of the Ten Commandments are all about our relationship with God and are articulated in the first part of the Jewish

"*Shema*," which a Jewish male kept tied onto his forehead in a box called the "Tefillin" to keep their relationship with God in front of them, and before their eyes. The scripture from Deuteronomy 6:5 (ESV) kept in the box said in part, **"You shall love the LORD your God with all your heart, with all your soul and with all your might."** These words are a summary of the first four of the Ten Commandments.[285]

The last six commandments all deal with how we are to relate to one another. Further, much of the Old Testament books of Exodus, Leviticus, and Deuteronomy, as well as many other places in the Old Testamen,t gave very particular laws and commandments governing how we are to treat one another. Thus, the Jews were very conscious of an unwritten addition to the Shema, which similarly summarized these last six of the Ten Commandments as stated in Leviticus 19:18 (NIV), saying to **"love your neighbor as yourself."**

Jesus related His belief that these same overarching laws described and undergirded the whole of Old Testament law when He answered a lawyer's question of what was the "greatest commandment" in scripture. Jesus in Matthew 22:35-40 (KJV), "Jesus said unto him, Thou shalt love the Lord thy God with all thy heart, and with all thy soul, and with all thy mind (restating the Shema). This is the first and great commandment. **And the second is like unto it**, **Thou shalt love thy neighbor as thyself. On these two commandments hang all the law and the prophets."**

The Jews in attendance at Jesus' words recognized both of these overarching concepts of Old Testament laws as what they had been taught of Jewish law and the Old Testament scriptures since their births.

In Matthew chapter 7, Christ explains in detail how we are to treat others as ourselves. Then specifically in verse 12 (NLT), He says, ***"Do to others whatever you would like them to do to you. This is the essence of all that is taught in the law and the prophet."*** This explanation underscores the connection between this well-emphasized teaching in the New Testament, which Christ points out, is the essence of the last six of the Ten Commandments, as well as all that was taught by the Old Testament prophets. Indeed, "love your neighbor as yourself" is a theme that runs throughout the Bible.

Definition of Marriage and Prohibition of Homosexuality
Jesus is quoted in Mark 10 (NRSV) saying:

> **But at the beginning of creation God 'made them male and female.' 'For this reason a man will leave his father and mother and be united to his wife, and the two will become one flesh.'** So they are no longer two, but one flesh. Therefore, what God has joined together, let no one separate.

This puts Christ in accord with the Genesis account (specifically Genesis 2:24 and 5:2). There is much misinformation in the media today by people who are either illiterate in terms of the Bible or are simply twisting the truth or lying to push their agenda when they say that Christ never talked to the topic of gay marriage. He clearly defined marriage here as being between a man and a woman, which logically says it is not between two men or two women in Christ's view.

Also, in the New Testament, Paul in 1 Corinthians 6:9 (HCSB) stated, "Don't you know that the unrighteous will not inherit God's kingdom? Do not be deceived: **No sexually immoral people**, idolaters, adulterers, or **anyone practicing homosexuality,**" This is a plain statement of what is said on many occasions in the Old Testament, that all forms of lesbian and homosexual sex are forbidden.

Two verses from the Old Testament book of Leviticus exemplify unity on this point. Leviticus 18:22 (ESV) says, **"You shall not lie with a male as with a woman; it is an abomination."** Then in Leviticus 20:13 (ESV), it says, **"If a man lies with a male as with a woman, both of them have committed an abomination; they shall surely be put to death; their blood is upon them."** We do not follow the ceremonial laws of the OT today found in Leviticus and elsewhere in the OT because Jesus ended the intercessory priesthood of men. However, we still follow many of the moral laws of the Levites.

Other passages forbidding homosexuality from both testaments are Genesis chapter 19; Romans 1:18-32; 1 Timothy 1:8-11; and Jude 7. However, it is important to note that the Bible speaks only of homosexual behavior (which would include lust, which is choosing to fantasize about behavior), not unchosen feelings. God will not judge a Christian guilty for his or her involuntary feelings. Whether we decide to follow or believe in this or not, the Bible in both testaments is very consistent on this theological point.

Further, Deuteronomy 22:5 specifically speaks to the very contemporary issue of transgenderism. This verse makes it clear that it is an "abomination to God" for men or women to cross-dress or try and assume a sexual orientation other than that designed into them at conception.

Now, I will not in this section try to defend this position scientifically or address its cultural ramifications. We will do this in the next chapter. What is clear from the Bible is that it says in both Testaments that God created us male and female, and that was the design for marriage, none other. Across the Bible, homosexual behavior and acting outside of your assigned at birth sex are defined as sinful.

Abraham to Christ

Most good literary works obey the literary rule of having a topic paragraph or chapter, to begin with, to tell the reader what the book is about. This will be followed by subsequent paragraphs or chapters which "flesh out," define, and elaborate about the topics. Most will ultimately end in a concluding paragraph or chapter, called a summary, which recaps what was said.

The Bible, as a total book, shows this type of literary planning. After detailing the historical accounts of the creation, the flood, and the dispersion after Babel, we come to the story of Abraham. The story of this one man takes up fifteen chapters of the book of Genesis, thus signifying the importance of his life. The details on this one life are very unusual for the Bible, also attesting to its importance.

At age 75, Abraham was of age to retire and was a wealthy rancher. At this peculiar time of life, God directed him to leave his home and extended family. To this point, his name in life was Abram (which means "High Father") which seemed satirical at age 75 since he had never had children. The Lord had said to Abram in Genesis 12:1-3 (NIV):

> **Go from your country, your people and your father's household to the land I will show you. "I will make you into a great nation, and I will bless you;** I will make your name great, and you will be a blessing. I will bless those who bless you, and whoever curses you I will curse; **and all peoples on earth will be blessed through you."**

He eventually will be given children. One of these children will start the bloodline of the nation of Israel. Abram's name will be changed to "Abraham" (meaning the "Father of Many") by God, which foretells of the vast groups of people, both Jewish and Arabic, which will all trace their lineage to him.

His life from age seventy-five to over one hundred is a storied one. He will alternately follow God's directions and then compromise or go against them. His is the story of the beginning of not only the people of Israel but of the beginning of the other Arabic peoples who will oppose Israel to this day.

Abraham's "on again, off again" faith in God is a foreshadowing of what will happen to the people of Israel, who will alternately follow God and then fall away from Him and then come back again, only to fall away once more. It is also emblematic of how almost all people struggle with sin, failure, success, and wanting to be better than they are. This pattern is thematic of the whole Old Testament and is carried forward into the New Testament.

Note, however, that the life of Abraham does even more than just foreshadow the tumultuous relationship the nation of Israel will have with God over the next three thousand years. His life points to the conclusion of this whole story in Jesus Christ when in Genesis 12:3 (NIV), God said, **"…and all peoples on earth will be blessed through you."** This reference to Christ is made crystal clear when Genesis chapter 23 it describes how Abraham is tested after he is finally given a son, in his very old age, and was challenged by God to offer up his son as a blood offering to God. Although God stops him at the last moment, this story signifies how deep his faith in God and love for God had grown throughout his life. It also clearly foreshadows what God will do by allowing His son, Jesus Christ, to be sacrificed and killed to atone for our sins. Incidentally, God stops Abraham just short of sacrificing his son and provides a ram to be sacrificed instead. This all symbolizing and foreshadowing that it will not be man's sacrifices, but God's sacrifice which will bridge the gap between God and men (Genesis 22).

Christ was that final blessing to all peoples, not just the people of Israel.

In the New Testament gospel of Matthew chapter 1, it shows an understanding of this overarching story for the whole Bible when it says, **"This is the genealogy of Jesus, the Messiah, the son of David, the son of Abraham: Abraham was the father of Isaac, Isaac the father of Jacob, Jacob the father of Judah and his brothers"** (NIV). In the next fourteen verses, Matthew recounts the major descendants of Abraham, including Joseph and King David among many others, and concludes in verse 16 with **"and Jacob the father of Joseph, the husband of Mary, and Mary was the mother of Jesus who is called the Messiah"** (NIV).

These verses reveal a knowledge of the inextricable tie between Abraham and Jesus Christ. Jesus Christ, whose life and ministry are the whole reason for the New Testament, is shown in both Genesis and Matthew not to be an afterthought by God after man fell from grace. Instead, it shows that the coming of Christ to earth, and his sacrifice, was God's plan from the beginning of creation. This is reaffirmed in Genesis 3:15 (NIV), where God says to the serpent

(Satan), **"And I will put enmity between you and the woman, and between your offspring and hers; he will crush your head, and you will strike his heel."** This verse somewhat cryptically describes how the son of woman will ultimately defeat the serpent (Satan). This verse is called the "*proto-evangelion*" since it shows from the time of the creation that the plan for our salvation was already set in place.

This story of man's sin, intermittent repentance, and coming back to God, only to sin again, shows man's need for a "bridge" for sinful men to reach a Holy and sinless God. This need for a "way back to God" was fulfilled in the life and death of Jesus Christ. This is an essential retelling of the whole Bible, and it is not only contained and foreshadowed in the life of Abraham but played out throughout the rest of the Bible. The stories of Abraham and Christ are not only intertwined but point to the underlying purposes of the whole Bible.

Likewise, the last book in the Bible, Revelation, acts as a concluding chapter to this book, telling us not only how it will all end but how and why several things were done down through the centuries for God's original plans to be fulfilled.

The Bible Claims God is in Control, so, "Why do Bad Things Happen to Good People?"

There is a consistent thread throughout the Bible of God having control over His creation, and yet there are consistent accounts of His people being in troubling situations. This seems contradictory.

Isaiah 41:10 (NIV) says, **"So do not fear, for I am with you; do not be dismayed, for I am your God. I will strengthen you and help you; I will uphold you with my righteous right hand."**

Psalm 46:1 (NIV) **"God is our refuge and strength, an ever-present help in trouble."**

Psalm 22:28 (ESV): **"For kingship belongs to the Lord, and he rules over the nations."**

Psalm 115:3 (ESV): **"Our God is in the heavens; he does all that he pleases."**

Proverbs 16:4 (ESV): **"The Lord has made everything for its purpose, even the wicked for the day of trouble."**

Proverbs 16:9 (ESV): **"The heart of man plans his way, but the Lord establishes his steps."**

Isaiah 45:7 (ESV): **"I form light and create darkness, I make well-being and create calamity, I am the Lord, who does all these things."**

Isaiah 14:24 (ESV): **"The Lord of hosts has sworn: "As I have planned, so shall it be, and as I have purposed, so shall it stand."**

Matthew 19:26 (ESV): **'But Jesus looked at them and said, "With man this is impossible, but with God all things are possible."'**

Luke 12:22-26 (NIV): **"Do not worry about your life, what you will eat; or about your body, what you will wear. Life is more than food, and the body more than clothes. Consider the ravens: They do not sow or reap, they have no storeroom or barn; yet God feeds them. And how much more valuable you are than birds! Who of you by worrying can add a single hour to his life? Since you cannot do this very little thing, why do you worry about the rest?"**

Revelation 1:17 (NIV): **"Then He placed His right hand on me and said: Do not be afraid. I am the First and the Last."**

These and many other verses support a consistent theme in all 66 books of the Bible that we are to trust in God, that He is in control, that He created everything, and nothing is impossible for Him. But then both unbelievers and believers ask, "If God is good and in control, why is there so much trouble in the world?"

The answer is found in the same beginning book of Genesis, in which we find the first proclamations of God's infinite creative power and authority over all. At the beginning on this planet, all was good, and we followed all that God said. Man and woman, however, decided to sin (following temptation by Satan). We said that we desired to be God and decide for ourselves what is good and bad, and to decide for ourselves what to do or not do. In essence, we "showed God the door." We asked God out of the world He gave us and created for us in a perfect condition. We said, "We can take it from here!" In doing, so we unconsciously gave over dominion of this world temporarily to Satan (this is substantiated in 1 John 5:19). Why should we be surprised when things go wrong in a world in which its creator has been asked to step aside and the "father of lies" put in control? In such a case, how can God be held responsible?

You can see for yourselves what a poor job we have done of running the world by ourselves. We are constantly at war, fighting amongst ourselves, killing, lying, cheating, stealing, giving into constant lusts, and more. God, however, did what we would probably have never had the strength to do, nor the wisdom to do.

When we first sinned, He stepped aside (but not out) of His creation and said, "Okay, you want to run things without me; let's see how you do." Genesis tells us that He kicked us out of Eden (a perfect environment) and physically and genetically changed the world so that it is balanced, but as part of the curse instituted the "dog eat dog" planet it is today, matching our sinful state. He intervenes from time to time for His purposes and for His people, but He in many cases does not exert total control since we ignorantly asked Him not to. We continue to do so, feeding our selfish desires and trying to run our lives our way, and not His.

One of the most perplexing aspects of this idea of God in control, but allowing bad to occur even to God's own is expressed in Romans 8:28 (ESV) where it says, **"And we know that for those who love God all things work together for good, for those who are called according to his purpose."** Paradoxically, it is only in the context of "free will" where both good and bad choices can be made, that true love can exist.

It is sometimes difficult for us to see the good in many different tragedies. But the testimonies of many people call attention to their finding truth in these verses.[286]

While my faith and experience have found this to be an operative truth in this troubled world, that God does support us, even in times of trouble, and exerts control when it is within His will and for our good, it may not be yours. However, it is clear from the wealth of scripture and accounts throughout the Bible that this is a well-established theme from one end of the Bible to the other. God gave us free will and with it the consequences that follow our choices and actions. Because God has been asked to step aside, we will not always experience perfect justice in this world.

Repentance

Biblical "repentance" is a somewhat unique concept to the Bible. If asked, the general public will most often define "repentance" as just being sorry for what we have done. The biblical definition for this concept, however, is somewhat different and involves something more. The Bible rather consistently defines repentance as not only being sorry for sins we commit, but so sorry that we commit to turn from that sin and not repeat it.

This concept of repentance runs throughout the Bible, but it is highlighted in four places which show how much of an overarching theme it is.

We have just described some parts of the life of Abraham. In many ways, his is not a story of initially strong faith, but of initially weak faith, which grew with time and experiences. He would often stray from what God wanted. He lied, he did not follow God's directions, he compromised with men, and he often showed a distrust for God's power. Yet, he was chosen as the father of all Israel (God's chosen people on earth). Why?

The one thing Abraham did do consistently after he sinned was to repent. Although he sinned often, in only one case did he commit the same sin twice. In almost all cases, when he sinned, he confessed that sin and turned from it as a commitment to God to not make such a mistake against God again. This, I believe, is why he was honored by God.

The next great example of a repentant spirit in the Bible is King David. Both the Old Testament book of 1 Samuel and Acts 13:22

testify to God's calling King David a "man of His own heart." This in spite of his great sinfulness!

David did many great things, but he was also very sinful. He committed adultery. He also had the husband of the woman David slept with killed. He committed genocide. He was a very poor parent who did not discipline his children well at all. How could this be a "Man of God's own heart?"

The message here is not in what he did but how he came back from these sins. He consistently came to God with repentance whenever he was convicted in his mind of his misdeeds. Unlike Abraham, who with all his sins only repeated one of them once, David never did. He would have a truly repentant spirit, and once he resolved with God to ask for forgiveness and never do that sin again, he never did. These two men also had another attribute in common, which no doubt adds to God's approval of them. They both sought God's leading in what they did. This again denotes an attribute God would want to see in us all.

In the New Testament, "John the Baptist" told people that Christ was coming. He preached a need for repentance and used baptism as a symbol for starting over with a new life in God's spirit. Repentance was, in fact, the core of what John preached to people. He was so obsessed with preaching repentance that he lost sight of all else. He did not keep up a home. He dressed in rags, ate grasshoppers and other insects at hand, and was generally looked on as "nut" by the Jews of his day because of his obsession with repentance and Christ.

His ministry points us to the way to Jesus Christ, which is through repentance. This is a constant theme in almost all books of the New Testament. It was the theme of the ministry of Jesus Christ while on the earth. This concept of repentance was first shown in Genesis, underscored again in the life of King David, and not only runs through the rest of the Old Testament but is a key theme of the New Testament.

Forgiveness and our "Sin Nature"

Forgiveness is a concept that echoes across the whole Bible. Matthew 6:14-15 (New Testament, NIV) says, "For if you **forgive** men when they sin against you, your heavenly Father will also **forgive** you. But if you do not **forgive** men their sins, your Father will not **forgive** your sins."

Isaiah 43:25-26 (Old Testament, NIV) says, "I, even I, am he who **blots out your transgressions**, for my own sake, and **remembers your sins no more**. Review the past for me, let us argue the matter together; state the case for your innocence."

First John 1:9 (New Testament, NIV) says, "If we confess our sins, he is faithful and just and will **forgive** us our sins and purify us from all unrighteousness."

Daniel 9:9 (Old Testament, NIV) says, "The Lord our God is merciful and **forgiving**, even though we have rebelled against him;"

Numbers 14:19-21 (Old Testament, NIV) says, "In accordance with your great love, **forgive** the sin of these people, just as you have **pardoned** them from the time they left Egypt until now." The LORD replied, "I have **forgiven** them, as you asked."

These verses are just a very small sample of this major theme throughout the Bible. Forgiveness is shown to Noah's family, to Abraham multiple times, to King David often, to Jonah, and scores of other people in the Old Testament. Forgiveness is then a major focus of the New Testament, for that is what the Bible says Christ came to earth and died to purchase for us forgiveness.

A lot of people will debate the overriding presence of this concept in the Old Testament because of all the rules and harsh consequences in the Old Testament scriptures. They see all of this, making the Old Testament an "eye for an eye" set of books.

If you read the entire Bible, however, what becomes clear is that the rules for living are given to us in the Old Testament along with harsh consequences both to get us to obey as well as to underscore for us how important obeying God's laws is. But it is also apparent from both Old and New Testament reading that we have a "**sin na-**

ture" in us which was given to us from birth, transferred from our original father in Adam. Even though we often want to do good, this sinful nature won't allow us to always succeed.

Romans 5:12 (KJV): **"Wherefore, as by one man sin entered into the world, and death by sin; and so death passed upon all men, for that all have sinned:"**

Psalms 51:5 (KJV): **"Behold, I was *shapen in iniquity*, and *in sin did my mother conceive me.*"**

Psalms 58:3 (KJV): **"The wicked are estranged from the womb: they go astray as soon as they be born, speaking lies."**

Ephesians 2:3 (KJV): **"Among whom also we all had our conversation in times past in the lusts of our flesh, fulfilling the desires of the flesh and of the mind; and *were by nature the children of wrath*, even as others."**

John 3:5 (ESV) says we are all "**...by our nature children of wrath, like the rest of mankind.**"

These verses all exemplify that this doctrine is consistent in both the Old and New Testaments. This "sin nature," which the Bible teaches that we all have, is teaching in conflict with the popular concept of today by humanists that man is basically good, can control himself, and save himself by good works. Nevertheless, it is a tenant in the Bible, which unifies its message.

It is also why we will forever need forgiveness. The Old Testament recognized this nature, gave us rules to try and control it, but also recognized that we could not. The Old Testament laws actually set up an impossible to attain ideal, which the Jews fruitlessly tried to follow. This ideal inferred that if we kept all the laws, then we would be saved and worthy of God. Our sinful nature described in this same testament guarantees that this way to salvation and God is impossible. Thus, our need for Christ's sacrifice and payment of sins so that we may be forgiven for what we will inevitably do. The harshness of the Old Testament was to point out to very stubborn humanity that they could not do it for themselves. They cannot be good enough to measure up to God's standards, and that another way to God was necessary. That way was and is Jesus Christ (the Messiah), the focus of the New Testament. We would not have known of our need for a savior apart from the law.

It is not that the Old Testament is devoid of forgiveness, and everything is an "eye for eye." The Old Testament is full of the concept of forgiveness and makes it clear of its necessity, as we explored earlier. Adam, Eve, Abraham, Jonah, David, and many, many more Old Testament figures were given forgiveness by God. But God, who created us, knew that we would not turn to His help in Christ until we had proven to ourselves that we could not do it on our own. Much as we have to allow our own kids to learn hard lessons because they want to do it themselves, even though we know they cannot, God allowed us to learn this hard lesson by experience.

The Old Testament, in this way, sets up the New Testament. It shows us several thousand years of our failures to live up to God's standards and how we needed to learn to seek and accept the forgiveness that God had planned for us from the beginning since He knew we could not do it ourselves.

Seek God, and you will find Him

Both the Old and New Testaments have a theme telling the reader that *if you earnestly seek after God, you will find Him!* Jeremiah 29:13 (NIV) says, "**You will seek me and find me when you seek me with all your heart**." This promise is echoed in the Old Testament in Deuteronomy 4:29, as well as thirty-nine other Old Testament verses.

In the New Testament, Luke 11:9-10 (NIV) says:

> So I say to you, ask, and it will be given to you; seek, and you will find; knock, and it will be opened to you. For everyone who asks receives, and he who seeks finds, and to him who knocks it will be opened.

There are seven more scripture sets throughout the New Testament which echoes this same idea that if you seek God, you will find

Him. Moreover, the message from all forty-eight verses throughout the Bible is that not only will you find Him, but that God wants us to find Him and is never far from us.[287]

This idea should come as no surprise, as it dovetails with the central theme of the whole Bible that God has striven to make way for us to have a relationship with Him. It is what we were created for. He knew from the beginning of time that we would sin and separate from Him. But He planned all along to pay the price for our sins, with His son's blood, so that communion between sinful man and a Holy God would again be possible.

Faith and Faithfulness

Faith and faithfulness are themes that run throughout the Bible and are central to its message.

Hebrews 11:1 (New Testament, NIV): "Now **faith** is confidence in what we hope for and assurance about what we do not see.

Psalm 119:30 (Old Testament, NIV): "I have chosen the way of **faithfulness**; I have set my heart on your laws."

These are just two of a bevy of verses from both the Old and New Testaments, which talk about the need for faith and faithfulness by God's followers. The Bible teaches that we cannot save ourselves. Thus God set up a way to Him that we could do. We could show faith in Him and be faithful to Him, and His commands from His instruction manual (the Bible), and He would then accept those with proven faith into His company, His heaven.

Genesis 15:6 says very clearly, *"And he (Abram) believed in the LORD; and He counted it to him for righteousness"* (KJV).

Romans 4:1-5 (NIV) confirms this interpretation that Abraham was saved by faith when it says:

> "What then shall we say that Abraham, our fore-father according to the flesh, discovered in this matter? If, in fact, Abraham was justified by works, he had something to boast about—but not before

> God. What does Scripture say?" Abraham *believed*
> God, and it was credited to him as righteousness.

Now to the one, who works, wages are not credited as a gift but as an obligation. However, to the one, who does not work but trusts God, who justifies the ungodly, their *faith* **is credited as righteousness**.

Such comments were made throughout the Old Testament as Moses, David, Habakkuk, Noah, Ruth, and all the prophets were found to be *"faithful to God."* This is what turns out to be the test God used to impart salvation to His followers in the Old Testament. Not leading a perfect, sinless life since no one can (our sin nature precludes that). All of these examples of salvation for the faithful in the Old Testament books are followed by faithfulness being one of the main themes of Christ's ministry. Thus, it is revealed in the New Testament books that the test for who will be saved has not changed. It is still by faith that we receive Christ's sacrifice of atonement (Romans 3:25).

Why faith? Why an unnatural dependence on God? Why only bestow salvation on the most faithful? Why not the least sinful? [There are persons who never commit to faithfulness, or in any god, who are morally better than most and sin (screw up) less than the rest of us.] Why bestow this ultimate gift of eternal life only for those who demonstrate faith in Jehovah God/Christ?

The inference from the Bible is that it is because God wishes to have around Him in heaven only those who have decided not to be in rebellion with Him. It is not a scorecard of works, of how little we sin or how much good we do. The Bible, instead in all sixty-six books, communicates that God wants the people around Him, who choose to follow him and *choose to depend on Him.* That is what faith is. (Hebrews 11:1 and 6)

What is interesting is how realistic the God of the Bible is about this faith. He knows we are weak and flawed, as He made us. The term "Heroes of the Bible" at times almost makes me laugh. Abraham was found to be faithful to God since he often chose to follow

God's commands, and he got better at that as he aged. However, his story details how he compromised with the world (sin), lied (sin), at times lost his faith (sin), at times did not trust God (sin), and yet it was counted to him by God as being faithful because God forgives us our weaknesses as long as we keep trying to commit to Him! He will forgive us repeatedly, as we sin repeatedly, as long as we keep returning our allegiance to Him.

Likewise, we earlier detailed the failings of Moses, King David, and Jonah. All of these supposed "heroes" in the Old Testament had "clay feet." They were ordinary and very flawed people, with a host of weaknesses as we all have. Yet God counted them as faithful since they had at one time committed to Him, and even though they often failed, they would return to faithfulness to Him.

This is not only true for every Old Testament hero or prophet (with the possible exception of Ruth—note that it was a woman who lived better and more faithfully than most Bible heroes), but this is also true for the supposed heroes of the New Testament.

The Apostle Paul, the most revered leader of first-century Christians and the author of more New Testament books than any other, was first a persecutor of Christians before he was turned to Christ forcefully and almost against his will.

The Apostle Peter, one of the original disciples and the man the Catholics call the first Pope, denied Christ three times the night before Christ's crucifixion. He was rather impulsive and given to rash actions and remarks. Yet because of his faith, Christ counted him as one of his own.

This whole concept is capped off in the New Testament book of Matthew verse 17:20 (NIV) where it says:

> He replied, "Because you have so little faith. Truly I tell you, if you have faith as small as a **mustard seed**, you can say to this mountain, 'Move from here to there,' and it will move. Nothing will be impossible for you.

If you did not know, a mustard seed is an incredibly small seed. It almost looks like a speck of dust.

The God of the Bible communicates in the Bible that He knows our weaknesses, and yet He has set up a way for us to reach Him, which takes into account our failings. This is not only a consistent theme of the Bible and characters in the Bible, but it is a cornerstone of Christ's ministry in the New Testament. In truth, the faithfulness focus has not changed from the first book of Genesis to the last book of Revelation. In the beginning and throughout the Old Testament, we were taught to be faithful to God the Father. In the New Testament, we are taught that salvation comes through faith in Christ, who, as the Bible teaches, is just another form of the Godhead we call the Trinity. Thus, we are still, according to the Bible, whether you are looking at the Old or New Testaments, supposed to exhibit faith in God! This theology does not change!

First and Last Adams

The New Testament verse 1 Corinthians 15:45 (NIV) says, **"So it is written: 'The first man Adam became a living being'; the last Adam, a life-giving spirit."** The Bible presents Adam as the first man and gives the Lord Jesus Christ the curious title of "the last Adam."

The Bible tells us that the first man, Adam, was created by God, in His image and likeness, directly from the dust of the ground. God breathed into Adam's nostrils the breath of life, and he became a living soul (Genesis 1:26–27; 2:7). Thus, the Bible says Adam was not the product of some form of theistic evolution. God did not make him in the image or likeness of an ape, nor from a 'lower hominid' by any lengthy or even abrupt mutational processes. Rather it says God created Adam as an immediate act, **by His word.**

While Adam was made **in the image** of God, Christ is 'the image of the invisible God' (Colossians 1:15, NIV).

The Bible tells us that the last Adam, Jesus Christ, was the One through whom God created all things (John 1:1–3; Colossians 1:15–20; Hebrews 1:2). Thus, according to the Bible, Jesus was pre-existent with God the Father and God the Holy Spirit before Adam lived (John 8:58; Micah 5:2). Nevertheless, in His humanity, He too had a miraculous beginning, when He was incarnated as a human being. His human body was conceived by the Holy Spirit and born of the Virgin Mary (Matthew 1:20–23; Luke 1:26–35).

Adam was created a perfect man, in full possession of all human faculties (probably far beyond our current capabilities), and with a God-consciousness that enabled him to have spiritual communion with God. Initially innocent, sinless, and holy, he was in a right relationship to God, to woman, to himself, and to the natural world around him. But sin would separate him from a Holy God and also separate himself from his previous perfect state of existence.

The last Adam, Jesus, was also a perfect man, one with God (John 10:30; 17:21-22), innocent, sinless, and holy (Hebrews 7:26). Many people somewhat inaccurately refer to Jesus Christ as the "second Adam," a term not found in the Bible. However, Scripture refers to Christ as the 'second *man*' (1 Corinthians 15:47). There have been many men since Adam, but Jesus Christ was only the second man to ever be completely without sin and in a right relationship with God.

According to the Bible, the Gospel of Jesus Christ is the only beacon of real hope for lost humanity. The Bible's integrity is firmly based on the historical truth of both the first and the last Adam.

Adam was the head and progenitor of the human race. Jesus Christ is the head of redeemed humanity (see, for example, Ephesians 5:23). Since Christ died once for all time (Hebrews 7:27; 9:28; 10:10-14), there will never be the need for any further "Adam." Hence, He is the last Adam.

The first Adam gave mortal life with sin and death to all his descendants. The last Adam, Jesus Christ, communicates "life" and "light" to all men and gives eternal life to those who receive Him and believe in His name, giving them 'power to become the sons of God (John 1:1-14).

Adam, representing all mankind, was given dominion over the created world (Genesis 1:26). After being raised from the dead, Jesus

Christ was elevated to God's right hand and given dominion over all things, which were "put under his feet" (1 Corinthians 15:27; Ephesians 1:20-22). The first Adam was lord over a limited domain; the last Adam is Lord of all (Acts 10:36).

Genesis 2:21–23 tells us that God put Adam into a deep sleep, during which time God made Adam's bride, Eve, from Adam's side. A wound in Adam's side produced a bride! Note that once again, theistic evolution is excluded. The text says that God made them male and female at the beginning (Genesis 1:27; 2:7; Matthew 19:4). If Adam and Eve had been sub-human before God breathed life into them, they would already have been male and female, without the need for God to have made them so at this stage.

After the last Adam, Jesus, died upon the cross, suffering the sleep of death for everyone, His side was pierced by a spear thrust (John 19:34 – reminiscent of taking the rib from the first Adam's side). In His death, he paid the penalty for mankind's sins (1 Corinthians 15:1–4). Those who repent and put their faith in Him are united with Christ in a relationship which the Bible likens to that of a bride towards her husband (2 Corinthians 11:2; Ephesians 5:27; Revelation 19:6–8). Thus a wound in the last Adam's side also produced a bride, the true Church! It produced "a glorious bride, not having spot, or wrinkle, or any such thing…holy and without blemish" (Ephesians 5:27).

At the beginning of Adam's life, he underwent a period of testing as to whether or not he would obey God. **"And the LORD God commanded the man, saying, You may surely eat of every tree of the garden, but of the tree of the knowledge of good and evil you shall not eat, for in the day that you eat of it you shall surely die"** (Genesis 2:16–17, ESV).

At the beginning of the last Adam's ministry, Jesus was led by the Holy Spirit into the wilderness to be tempted (or tested—Greek: peirazō) by the devil (Matthew 4:1; Luke 4:1–3).

The first Adam failed the test, and in doing, so involved all humanity in his defeat, dragging the human race down with him. As a result, in Adam, we all stand condemned, spiritually dead, enslaved to sin, and expelled from Paradise (Romans 5:12).

The last Adam, Jesus, was victorious over sin, the flesh, and the devil. As a result, in Christ, believers stand justified and redeemed… liberated from sin, and included in the Paradise of God (Romans 5:18; 1 Corinthians 15:21; Revelation 2:7).

The first Adam disobeyed God. The last Adam was **"obedient unto death, even the death of the cross"** (Philippians 2:8, KJV).

The first Adam experienced the judgment of God, and he ultimately died, and his body turned to dust. Because of his sin, death came upon all men (Romans 3:23).

The last Adam, Jesus Christ, also died, on the cross, to atone for sin (Isaiah 53:5; 1 Peter 3:18; Hebrews 2:9). But He did not stay dead, nor did His body "see corruption" (Acts 2:27; 13:35–37). On the third day, He rose again, thereby overcoming the devil and the power of death for all those who believe in Him (Hebrews 2:14) and bringing resurrection from the dead (1 Corinthians 15:22–23).

Creation was originally "very good" (Genesis 1:31), so the "last enemy," death (1 Corinthians 15:26), was absent. Even the animals were originally all given plants to eat (Genesis 1:30, no carnivore). The actions of the first Adam brought a reign of death and bloodshed upon a once-perfect world, which ever since has been groaning in pain (Romans 8:22). Precisely because of the bloodshed in death by the last Adam, this curse of death and bloodshed will be removed, and creation restored to a sinless, deathless state (Revelation 21:1; 21:4; 22:3).

We are all connected with the first Adam (the natural and legal head of the human race) as depraved and guilty sinners, and so are included in the sentence of death which God pronounced on him. However, all, who are connected with the last Adam, Jesus, through repentance and faith in His redeeming work, are forgiven, and have **"received the free gift of righteousness,"** and so **"have passed from death to life"** (Colossians 1:14; Romans 5:17; 1 John 3:14). Thus, this relationship shows a consistent theme from the first book of the Bible all the way through to the last, and from the first human in the Bible to the last.[288]

Foreshadowing of Christ Throughout the Old Testament

The design of the Ark of the Covenant, The Passover "Seder Meal," Hosea's Marriage, the Hebrew Day of the Atonement, the Hebrew Tabernacle, the Jewish Wedding Ceremony, the position of Chief Priest (first was Aaron), and so many more objects, practices, traditions, and historical accounts were given to the people by God in the Old Testament, and each very specifically pointed toward Christ. These all inextricably tie the Old Testament and the New Testaments together as being inspired by one author, with a coordinated theme.

Jesus as Son of God, Messiah, and Creator is seen Throughout Scripture

One of the attributes of any good book or course of teaching is that it will state its purpose, go on to refine and define its topic, and then restate what it wanted to say or teach. The U.S. armed forces have modeled this type of teaching in its training courses for decades. Their mantra is "tell them what you are going to teach them, teach them, and then tell them what you taught them." This type of triple redundancy repetitiveness is not only good for remembering what was taught, but it is ideal for "fleshing out" what is taught in great detail and making it practical and memorable.

The Bible follows this fine teaching and literary pattern. It tells us early in Genesis that we were made to commune with God, and that God knew our plight of sin separating ourselves from Himself and that He had a plan conceived before creation to bridge that gap in the Messiah/Jesus Christ (Genesis 3:15). From that point on, every book in the Bible reveals and "fleshes out" some attribute of the Messiah/Jesus Christ, who is the focus of the entire book.

The first book of the Bible, **Genesis,** tells us of the Creator. Later in the Bible, we will find Christ was the creative "Word" (John 1), but God sets up in Genesis the human lineage which will eventually be used to bring the Messiah (Christ) to earth, to fulfill God's plan for our salvation.

Later in Genesis, Jesus is the Ram at Abraham's altar. Abraham had taken his son up to the altar to sacrifice him as God had directed. But God graciously provided a nearby ram to substitute for his son, perfectly symbolizing the substitutionary death Jesus will suffer on the cross, not for His own sins, but for ours.

In **Exodus**, He is the Passover Lamb. It is not an accident that the Hebrews were instructed to put lambs' blood over their doorways ahead of the Death Angel's coming as the last curse was put upon Egypt to force Pharaoh to let His people go. That blood covered their sins and let the Death Angel "Passover" them. In the New Testament, Jesus is often referred to as the "Lamb of God," since He will be offered up as the innocent lamb for the slaughter, not for His own sins, but for others.

In **Leviticus**, He is the High Priest. Prior to Jesus coming to earth, our separation from God forced us into many rituals, which could only be accomplished through a "high priest" to go before God for us. This was needed since we were not holy and clean and able to go before God ourselves. This was the Jewish sacrificial system. When Jesus came to earth and died for us, He set Himself up as our intermediary between our sinful selves and a Holy God. After Christ's sacrifice, we no longer needed the Old Testament sacrificial system. Nor do we need a priest to talk to God for us. The reason the curtain was torn from top to bottom in the "Holy of Holies" at the instant of Jesus death on the cross was because a new order had just been put in place, where Jesus is our "high priest" and we can communicate directly to Him and He directly to the Father.

In **Numbers**, He is the Cloud by day and Pillar of Fire by night. God is always with us and available to us if we will only pay attention to and ask for Him. This was perfectly exemplified in Numbers with the visible presence of God with them at all times, both day and night.

In **Deuteronomy**, He is the "City of our Refuge." God is always ready to help us through life and be a refuge for us in times of trouble or challenge. All we need do is ask Him for help, for protection, for guidance, and if we are living within His will, He will provide what we need and be our refuge in His time.

In **Joshua**, He is the Scarlet Thread out Rahab's window. Rahab was a prostitute who helped the Hebrew spies who infiltrated Jericho in their investigation of the "Promised Land. These spies have hunted men who the people of Jericho wished to kill. Rahab helped them escape through a window in the room facing the outside wall of Jericho. She tied together with a *scarlet thread*, which the spies used to climb down out of Jericho to safety.

The symbolism is clear. They were saved by a scarlet thread, just as we all are saved by Jesus' scarlet blood flowing from His body in payment for our sins. Even deeper, this prostitute will be faithful to God and His people, and her sins will be so completely forgiven that she will be allowed to marry a Hebrew and be a part of the lineage of the Messiah/Jesus Christ.

In **Judges**, He is our Judge. God is our judge, but so is Jesus as part of the Trinity. Because of the Messiah's intervention, when God looks at us, He sees not our sins but Jesus' purity. Our only judgment comes from whether or not we have submitted to Jesus as Lord.

In **Ruth**, He is our Kinsman Redeemer. The Jews had a tradition that when a man died, his widow would be wed to his closest relative so that she could be taken care of. In this way, she could be "redeemed," brought back into the family, and cared for.

When Jesus came to earth in the New Testament times, He was 100 percent fully man and 100 percent fully God. That is terrible math, but great theology! He comes in the form of man to reclaim us from our "separated from God sin condition." He experienced all that we experience on Earth and chose to die in our place. He redeems us just as the Jewish Kinsman Redeemer did for Jewish widows.

In **1 and 2 Samuel**, He is our Trusted Prophet. One measure of God, Jesus, and the Holy Spirit as members of the Trinity of God is that they are outside of time and can see the future. Thus, we see demonstrated in these books the omniscience (all-knowing nature) of God. Further, a prophet is not just a seer of the future, but a person, who brings God's Words to His people, just as preachers do today. Jesus in the book of John is defined as the "Word" of God. The Old Testament prophets, as they brought God's words to His people, brought an attribute of the Messiah/Christ to them.

In **Kings and Chronicles**, He is our Reigning King. Multiple places in scripture tell us that the Trinity is everlasting and outside of time. That Christ, as part of the godhead, existed previous to the creation and took an active part in the creation. The Messiah/Christ will change reality with His coming to earth, but the reality of His being King from the beginning of time and till the end does not change and is exemplified and preached in these books.

In **Ezra**, He is our Faithful Scribe. Like Christ, Ezra had many ministries. Ezra was a priest, a scribe, and a great leader. He not only knew God's Word, but he also believed and obeyed it as the Messiah will also exemplify when He comes to earth. Ezra and Christ were concerned for our spiritual future. Remember that Christ is "the Word," and Ezra extolled "the Word" as God's message to us!

In **Nehemiah**, He is the Rebuilder of everything that is broken. Jesus, in His earthly ministry, spent much of His time rebuilding people's lives, bodies, and souls. He made wine when all was gone. He healed the sick. He made the lame walk and the blind to see. He showed us the compassion of the father and how caring for one another should be the norm. This attribute of the Messiah shown all through the New Testament is exemplified in Nehemiah.

In **Esther**, He is Mordecai sitting faithfully at the gate. From Matthew Henry's Concise Commentary, "…Mordecai was not rewarded at the time, but a remembrance was written. Thus, with respect to those, who serve Christ, though their recompense is not till the resurrection of the just, yet an account is kept of their work of faith and labor of love, which God is not unrighteous to forget. The servant of God must be faithful to every trust and watchful for those who employ him. If he appears to be neglected now, he will be remembered hereafter. None of our actions can be forgotten; even our most secret thoughts are written in (God's) lasting registers."

In **Job,** He is our Redeemer that ever lives. Today's cultural mantra is "God is Dead!" But He is not. The message of the New Testament is that He lives and is risen from the dead with a plan for our salvation and the culmination of God's plan for all eternity. Job had everything taken from him, yet he would not curse or blame God. This is because he knew God is ever-present and ever-faithful, as we are to be for Him. Because of Job's faith in an everlasting and faithful redeemer, he was fully restored in this life and the next.

In **Psalms,** He is my Shepherd, I shall not want. In the New Testament, Jesus is described as the "Good Shepherd." He goes with us and guides us as the shepherd of innocent and ignorant sheep. He provides for us in ways we cannot do for ourselves. Jesus told Peter, when asked how to carry on, said, "feed my sheep." This analogy of His care for us stretches from throughout the Old Testament and through the New Testament.

In **Proverbs and Ecclesiastes,** He is our Wisdom. As stated before, Jesus is defined in the New Testament as the "Word." This "Word of God" and wisdom of God is expounded upon in both Proverbs and Ecclesiastes, allowing us to see the Savior before He is born a human.

In the **Song of Solomon,** He is the Beautiful Bridegroom. This great story continued in the New Testament portrays not only the relationship Jesus has with the church but our role to be prepared for in His kingdom. The New Testament story tells of a wedding party that was waiting for the groom to come and the wedding party to begin. The church is often referred to in scripture as Jesus' bride, as He will die for its foundation. When the groom finally shows up, some are ready to go in with him and are part of the wedding feast (the kingdom of God and His presence). Others are not ready (have not surrendered to Jesus by the time of their deaths). These, who are not prepared, are separated from the wedding feast (from God's kingdom) altogether. The symbolism and instruction on Jesus' church and God's kingdom, as well as our responsibility to be ready for His coming, is crystal clear in the New Testament and is referred to in this Old Testament book.

In **Isaiah**, He is the Suffering Prophet. Isaiah has many references in it which can only be talking about the Messiah/Christ, including Isaiah chapters 22 and 53. This book says the Messiah will be a man of "sorrows." This sorrow comes from seeing our plight, how we treat one another, as well as the enormous burden of taking on our sins and dying a substitutionary death for us, which is magically and graphically described in this book about 900 years before it happened.

In **Jeremiah and Lamentations**, He is the Weeping Prophet. Jesus/the Messiah weeps when he sees the evil we do. He wept for Lazarus' relatives when He saw their grief. He wept when He thought of the price to be paid for our sins. He wept when he saw how much the needs of people were. This attribute of the savior, which will be expounded upon in the New Testament, is shown in these two books.

In **Ezekiel**, He is the wonderful Four-Faced Man. In Ezekiel 1 (ESV), it says:

> And from the midst of it there came the likeness of four living creatures. And this was their appearance: They had the likeness of a man. And every one had four faces…As for the likeness of their faces, **each had a human face; and the four of them had the face of a lion on the right side, and the four of them had the face of an ox on the left side, and the four of them had the face of an eagle.**

The face of man shows Christ's appearance as a human man. The face of the lion shows the attribute of the king, which God and Christ are. The face of the "Ox," a beast of burden, shows the Messiah's attributes of humility. The ability to take our burdens on His back, and how He will take our sins upon Himself. And the eagle, throughout the Bible, signifies the soaring, transcendent, powerful divine life of God.

In **Daniel**, He is the fourth man in the midst of the fiery furnace. It says in Daniel that they saw a fourth man in the fiery furnace when God's three men were put into a blazing fire but were not harmed. That fourth figure was described as "like the son of God" because that is exactly who it was. He was there, before His earthly ministry, as a part of the godhead, protecting and comforting His people in the midst of trials.

In **Hosea**, He is my Love that is forever faithful. Hosea is a man of God who marries a harlot named "Gomer" (I agree, that is the worst name for a woman I ever heard). God tells this man of God to marry this prostitute, who will be unfaithful to him, and yet he is to forgive her over and again. This story vividly portrays God's relationship with us. We were created by Him to live with Him according to His laws, but we rebelled and are prostituting ourselves in all manner of evil desires, which are not part of His plans for us. But in spite of this situation, which any normal human would walk away from and throw away such shameful humanity, God will sacrifice His Son for us, and that Son, the Messiah, will tell us not to forgive once or twice, but as often as needed.

In **Joel**, He is the Baptizer of the Holy Spirit. Jesus will have Himself baptized in water, and the spirit will come upon Him at that time as He is baptized in the Spirit of God. The Bible tells us that we are sealed by the Holy Spirit for Jesus' salvation for us. The first introduction to all of these concepts comes to us in the book of Joel.

In **Amos**, He is our "Burden Bearer." Christ came to earth to do things for us we could not do. He led a sinless life, which our fallen natures will not allow us to do. He gave us an example of a sinless existence, which showed us not only how to live, but how far short of God's standards we are. Finally, He took the sin of the world upon Himself and died in our place for our sins. In this, He was and is our burden-bearer!

In **Obadiah**, He is our Savior. Many people, who do not understand either Jewish religion, or Christianity, do not understand what we mean when we say that we are "saved." The Jews themselves missed the meaning of the salvation God intended. Both in Jesus' time and today, they look for a Messiah who will conquer their earthly enemies, as King David did. But God, in His infinite wisdom, designed to bring us a King, who will rule forever, rather than for just the lifespan of a single human hero. Further, this hero will bear our sins and take our sins away so that we are saved from eternal separation from God. This is the superior, and perfect Savior God planned for us in Christ and has brought to us. Obadiah gives us a vision of Christ's unending kingdom and His role as our unending Savior.

In **Jonah**, He is the great foreign missionary that takes the word of God into all the world. The "Great Commission" stated at the end of the New Testament book of Matthew tells us to take the gospel of Jesus Christ to all the world. This concept is seen throughout the Bible and is clearly seen in Jonah, where God directs Jonah to take His words to a foreign land. Along the way, in this book, we also discover that you cannot thwart God's plans by human means. Nor will God allow our human frailties and prejudices to get in the way of His plans.

In **Micah**, He is the Messenger with beautiful feet. Christ came to "fulfill the law," as He put it. He was and is the culmination of God's good news for us, and He came with that glorious message. We also find in Micah such tidbits as the foretelling of Christ being born in Bethlehem (Micah 5:2) and that He will lead as a shepherd does.

In **Nahum**, He is the Avenger. Christ will come to earth to save man. But, if we oppose Him, we will find Him to be an undefeatable enemy and the source of our destruction. The Trinity is the only "God" and, as such, is rightly jealous of that place not only in reality but in our hearts and minds. If men do not give Him his due place as God or otherwise oppose Him, He will avenge himself on them in a mighty way we do not want to experience.

In **Habakkuk**, He is the Watchman that is ever praying for revival. When Christ came to earth, He spent a great deal of time in prayer. Much more than most of us. He did this not only to exemplify to us how to live and commune with God but also to demonstrate our need for communion, advice, and help from the Father. It is promised that if we will pray and ask for the Holy Spirit to intercede for us, that He will communicate for us in ways, we cannot understand and for things we do not even know we need. Christ understood this more than any of us, and the Messiah gave us this picture of a Watchman who knew and prayed for our salvation and revival (recommitment to God).

In **Zephaniah**, He is the Lord Mighty to serve and save. The depth of God's/Christ's graciousness to us is exemplified in this book, as well as throughout the New Testament. This book tells us that the Messiah will come to save us and to serve. We deserve destruction for our sins, but the Messiah will come to restore us rather than to destroy us. He will also, throughout the New Testament, show us that we need to have the attitude of a servant. Christ constantly demonstrated this attitude that we can only get along together and benefit one another if we have an attitude of service and more care for others than for ourselves.

In **Haggai**, He is the Restorer of our lost heritage. We lost our spiritual lives and our fellowship with God in the garden with Adam's original sin. The Messiah (Christ) will come to restore us to right fellowship with God so that we can commune and participate in His kingdom as His children (our lost heritage).

In **Zechariah**, He is our fountain. God is the only fountain for our cleansing from our sins and to cleanse our lands. Only God can fulfill our needs. We were made to commune and live with God. There is a hole in our inner being when we are not united with Him. Only Christ could come and fulfill God's requirement for justice by dying for us and thereby providing for us a cleansing that will never end.

In **Malachi**, He is the Son of righteousness with healing in His wings. In this book, we see the "Son of Righteousness," who can only be the Messiah, Christ, and God Himself since no one else is righteous. We on this planet are all fallen sinners. Christ, as part of the godhead, is not only the only righteous one but the only one who could bring healing to us for our sins.

In **Matthew**, He is the Christ, the Son of the Living God. In this opening book of the New Testament, we find out what Messiah should really be as Christ demonstrates the spiritual kingdom He came to earth to set up.

In **Mark**, He is the miracle worker. Christ's miracles were the "calling card" which separated both He and His disciples after His death and ascension from the "street corner" Messiahs, who proclaimed themselves as the prophets of God. Until the whole Bible is put together about 300 years later, Christ and His disciple's miracles will be an indication of God's support of their ministries. Christ could do miracles because He is the "Lord over all Creation." His disciples could do miracles because they operated in His name and with His authority and power.

In **Luke**, He is the "son of man." For Christ to truly intervene for us and substitute His life for ours, He had to be fully human while still being fully God. As I said before, that is terrible math but great theology! Christ experienced all we did in this mortal existence, including a feeling of separation from God. Yet, He was and is God and thus could truly bridge the gap between us!

In **John**, He is the "door" by which every one of us must enter. Since only Christ could live a sinless life and die in our place for us, it is only through Him that we can approach God. He made Himself the one and only "door to God."

In **Acts**, He is the "shining light" that appears to Saul on the road to Damascus. In the book of Acts, Saul is the Pharisees' chief prosecutor of Christians. Christ, who had ascended, knocks him off his horse, presents Himself as the "Son of God," and converts Saul to being Paul, the Apostle for Christ.

In **Romans**, He is our Justifier. Romans 3:25-26 defines Christ as the one who was given by God to be the only one who can pay for our sins for us. A Holy God cannot stand sin. Through Christ, who is our High Priest and Savior, God only sees His righteousness and not our sin. Theologically, justification is the act of making one just, right, and sinless before God. Only Christ, the Messiah, who paid the price for our sins, can do that.

In **1 Corinthians**, He is our Resurrection. The Resurrection from the grave by Christ is the "Key Central Truth" of Christianity. If it occurred as described in this book and throughout the New Testament, and foretold of in the Old Testament, it is the proof of God's power, Christ's place as our Savior and His power over death, and the substantiation for the Christian religion.

In **2 Corinthians**, He is our "sin-bearer." Again we see Christ described as the part of the Godhead who came to bear our sins.

In **Galatians**, He *redeems* us from the law. When something is lost and found and brought back to us, it is redeemed. That is especially true when it is lost through debt, like being pawned. We redeem it by paying to get it back. Galatians describes how Christ came to earth to redeem what was lost by our sins, our spiritual lives, and our fellowship with God. He bought these lost and incredibly valuable attributes back for us.

In **Ephesians**, He is our "unsearchable riches." In the Old Testament book of Ecclesiastes, King Solomon lamented because he tried everything in the world to make himself happy. He tried woman, riches, power, success and found them all temporary and lacking any permanent fulfillment. Christ came to give us life and fulfillment eternally, a gift of riches that cannot be compared. Paul comments on this immeasurable set of gifts from Christ, specifically in Ephesians 3:8-9.

In **Philippians**, He supplies our every need. Christ not only gives us eternal life and fulfillment but direct access to God through Him and the Holy Spirit. Through that connection, we have access to everything we need, including food, clothing, shelter, and prosperity within God's will and, most of all, communion with God!

In **Colossians**, He is the Fullness of the Godhead bodily. Christ came to earth and accomplished many purposes. Our salvation, our redemption, establishing Himself as our high priest connection to God, but something more. He showed God in bodily form. He revealed to us how God would live and how we should live. Through Christ, we were given an opportunity to "see" God as Christ was both fully God and fully man.

In **1 and 2 Thessalonians**, He is our soon Coming King. The Messiah came to establish God's kingdom on Earth. He promised to return, and we should live in expectation and anticipation of His soon return.

In **1 and 2 Timothy**, He is the Mediator between God and man. As mentioned elsewhere in the New Testament, Christ with His life on earth, His part in the Godhead, and His sacrifice of His earthly life set Himself up as our mediator between sinful men and a Holy God.

In **Titus**, He is our Blessed Hope. The message of all scripture is that we have no hope of eternal life without intercession. There is no life after death without God. Life is not worth living without hope. Loss of all hope is why many commit suicide. Christ, with His sacrifice, gave us "sure and certain hope."

In **Philemon**, He is a friend that sticks closer than a brother. Only our Maker knows us better than ourselves and knows our every thought. The Savior lives inside us when invited to. He is always with us, even when we do not feel His presence.

In **Hebrews**, He is the Blood of the Everlasting Covenant. From God giving Adam and Eve animal skins, to the blood sacrifices of the Old Testament, to the blood over the doorposts which protected the Hebrews from the death angel to the sacrifice of Christ, it was clear that it would require a blood sacrifice to atone for our sins. Christ was the fulfillment of that everlasting covenant.

In **James**, He is the Lord that heals the sick. Christ, throughout the New Testament, healed the sick and showed both His compassion for people, as well as His power over all creation. More than that, though, our ultimate disease is sin, which has separated us from God from Adam's first sin. Christ came as the one way to heal that disease of death all humanity has been under since the curse which expelled us from the Garden of Eden and from God's fellowship.

In **1 and 2 Peter**, He is our Chief Shepherd. In both the Old and New Testaments, the Messiah and Christ are talked of as a shepherd. This is because He leads us to God and to the eternal life God intended for us. It is also a symbol of Christ's humility since, in the Hebrew culture, shepherds were the lowest of the low. Today, their status is only marginally better. Thus, this allusion not only foretells and describes how He will lead us but how we should adopt His humble assumption of the position of servant.

In **1, 2, and 3 John**, it is Jesus who has the tenderness of Love. God is described as both "light" and "love." Surely, there is no greater love than to give up your life for others, as Christ did for us. He also exemplified that love as He led His earthly life, always caring for everyone He met.

In **Jude**, He is the Lord coming with 10,000 saints. This description in the New Testament corresponds to a prophecy by Enoch in the Old Testament, one of the most righteous men described in the Bible. Enoch lived only seven generations after Adam. It signifies that when Christ returns, it will be with a host of angels and saved people (saints).

In **Revelation**, "Lift up your eyes church for your redemption draweth nigh, He is the King of Kings and the Lord of Lords." (paraphrase of Luke 21:28, KJV). Revelation is the concluding book of the Bible. It underscores what will happen as God, through Christ, brings His plan for bringing man back to Him, and restoring His creation to its original perfect state, and restoring His kingdom throughout His creation at the end of time.[289]

There are many continual threads in the Bible that bind it together, but none more so than the concept of the Messiah and Jesus Christ. Messiah not only is a thesis that runs through every book of the Bible, but which is the main purpose for the Bible. God's recognition of our need for a savior, which He foresaw before the creation, and which He had a plan for before we were ever created. His plan to restore us came to fruition in Jesus Christ. In fact, Jesus Christ is quoted as saying exactly this. In Matthew 5:17 (NLT), he said, **"Don't misunderstand why I have come. I did not come to abolish the Law of Moses or the writings of the prophets. No, I came to accomplish their purpose."**

In Revelation, the last book of the Bible, Christ is called the "*alpha and the omega*," the first and last letters in the Greek alphabet, signifying that He was there as the Creator in the beginning and will be there as Lord at the end of time. Similarly, He is the Creator, who spoke the universe into existence in the first chapter of Genesis according to both Genesis and the book of John. Christ is also the central figure in the end times, as the last book of the Bible expounds upon.

All Humans are of One Blood

The Bible describes in Genesis 1:26-27 that God created two people originally, a male and a female and that all future generations came from this original pair of humans. The Bible further underscores this point in Genesis 3:20 (ESV), where it states that Adam called his wife **"Eve, because she was the mother of all living."** The Old Testament teaching is clear that we are all of **one race**, and not multiple races.

Likewise, in the New Testament, the Apostle Paul in Acts 17:26 said, according to the New International Version:

> From *one man he made all the nations*, that they should inhabit the whole earth; and he marked out their appointed times in history and the boundaries of their lands." The King James translation says it

this way. "And hath made of *one blood all nations* of men for to dwell on all the face of the earth, and hath determined the times before appointed, and the bounds of their habitation.

It is clear from these verses that the New Testament also teaches that we are all of one race today and from the beginning of creation.

Thus, we find complete consistency from these two sets of books penned more than 1500 years apart. What will be really interesting is what you will find later in this book that modern genetics and biology support this concept that all men, whatever nationality or skin color, are all the same race.[290] Thus, modern genetics research confirms what the Bible says about human beings and race. And this is not just an inconsequential agreement between what the Old and New Testaments say about man. What is said by the Bible and believed in our souls is that all men really are created equal, as the United States Constitution says. If we are all one race, without one more superior than another, then we are, in fact, all brothers. What kind of difference would that have made throughout our bloody history of humans, had we really believed that, and what kind of difference would that make in the world today if all humans, Jews, Muslims, Anglos, Blacks, Asians, Indians, regardless of country of origin or skin color or creed believed wholeheartedly that we are one race and brothers?

We cannot seem to grasp this point which genetics today confirms, but it is clear throughout the Bible that the Bible understood and teaches this basic truth which we have such trouble grasping today.

The Concept of "Original Sin" in Both Testaments

In 1 Timothy 2:14 (BSB), it says, **"And it was not Adam who was deceived, but the woman being deceived, fell into transgression."** Also, in 1 Corinthians 11:3 (NIV), it says, **"But I am afraid that just as Eve was deceived by the serpent's cunning, your minds may somehow be led astray from your sincere and pure devotion to Christ."** These verses relate not only a belief in the doctrine of original sin, but they also relate a complete belief in the literal telling of the "fall of man," as it is written in the book of Genesis.

This doctrine or theology of "**original sin**" in the Bible is a consistent one throughout its scriptures. In Matthew 15:19 (ESV) in the New Testament said, **"For out of the heart come evil thoughts, murder, adultery, sexual immorality, theft, false witness, slander."** Likewise, in the Old Testament book of Psalm 51:5 (ESV) said, **"Behold, I was brought forth in iniquity, and in sin did my mother conceive me."** These verses both echo the same theme of man is corrupt and sinful from birth. That his core is evil, and he is in need of redemption.

Many New and Old Testament verses repeat this same concept, such as Romans 3:10, Genesis 6:5, Mark 7:20-23, Ephesians 2:3, 1 John 1:10, and Ecclesiastes 7:10, just to name a few. We discussed this idea and theology earlier as man having a "sinful nature."

What is interesting is how at odds this doctrine is from the humanistic philosophies of today. Humanists believe that man at his core is good, not evil, as the Bible describes. Since these positions are diametrically opposed to one another, it makes sense that one of these can be true, but both cannot. Since man's whole history reveals a pattern of greed, lust, corruption, war, conflict, crime, and our current continuation of these ills, it would stand to reason that the better case can be made for the Bible's interpretation for human nature, than that of the modern humanist movement.

Thus, it is clear that both testaments of the Bible agree that we are born with a sinful nature; and evidence from our past and present seem to make a good evidentiary case for the truth of the Bible's depiction of man's fallen nature.[291]

We have Found Many
Coherent Themes Throughout the Bible

What we started with was a question of whether the Bible was logically coherent, as if written by one mind and with a single theme. Many skeptics would say that the Old and New Testaments are separate entities that have very different themes, writing styles, and different levels of historical accuracy. What we have shown in this section is that the Bible believes in and that the two Testaments (which give two covenants, law and grace), rather than being contradictory, go together, forming the primary focus of the need and provision of a savior.

Many question (and we will examine this in the next chapter) the veracity of Old Testament accounts, particularly in Genesis. However, the Bible does not have this problem. The New Testament writers show that they believe in Genesis and the whole Old Testament as real history. The New Testament writers referenced the Old Testament Bible over one hundred times, showing that they believed in its authority and repeatedly restated the Genesis accounts as trustworthy and accurate on sixty occasions. Even Jesus Christ quoted from Genesis sixteen times, revealing His belief in such biblical tenants as marriage being between a man and a woman, Noah and the worldwide flood, Adam, and original sin, and more. Further, *every New Testament author referenced Genesis* showing their universal belief in its authority and inerrancy.[292]

Likewise, there are 2800 cross-references that can be identified between the Old and New Testaments where the New Testament is referring back to the Old Testament, or the Old Testament writers are foretelling and pointing toward the New Testament.[293] We have exemplified only a small sample of these cross-references in this chapter and in previous chapters. The Bible and its authors obviously believed that it was written as one book, with **one mind writing**. The themes we have transmitted in this chapter underscore this, as do the 2800 cross-references. The fact that we can communicate a cogent set of themes of the creation, the fall, the flood, the need for a savior, and Christ's coming all show evidence for the Bible reflecting a single work.

Baptism, Faith, Repentance, Giving, The Golden Rule, Original Sin, Forgiveness, One Blood, Heterosexuality, Communion, Confession, Seeking God; These are but a few of the many topics and places in the Old and New Testaments which shows the same themes and concepts. We have also seen a belief by the New Testament writers that the Old Testament described real events factually, and a belief by the Old Testament writers that they were pointing us to a day when God's plan to build a bridge back for us, back to God, would be fulfilled in Messiah (Jesus Christ), who is the focus of the New Testament. Thus, we would seem to have more than enough evidence that even though the Bible was written by 40+ authors over almost two millennia, it hangs together as being philosophically and logically coherent to the extent of showing one mind writing and directing its writing.

It All Hangs Together

The Old Testament tells us of God's creation, our place in that creation, how we broke our fellowship and injured our relationship with God, and it gives us His laws. It tells of how God gave us thousands of years to teach ourselves that we could not keep even the ten simple laws, which are now the basis of all western civilization. It then reveals how He had a plan for bringing us back to a correct relationship with Him because having created us, He knew our limitations and that we could not do it ourselves.

The New Testament tells the story of the completion of God's plan to restore our proper relationship to Him. It tells us that God knew before the creation that man would destroy our relationship with God, and also, before the creation, He had a plan for bringing us back into fellowship with Him and bridging the gap between a Holy God and sinful man. But He would execute this plan only after we already proved to ourselves we could never accomplish it by ourselves.

That plan for restoring our relationship with God was Jesus Christ, who is the focus not only of the New Testament but the entire Bible. He died to pay the price for restoring our relationship with God and brought this whole story full circle back to Genesis. This central theme is underscored in the Old Testament by the structure of the Tabernacle, the position of Aaron as Chief Priest, the construction of the Ark of the Covenant, the life and marriage of Hosea, Abraham's willingness to sacrifice his son, the Passover Celebration and so many more constructs in the Old Testament all were specifically structured to reflect the coming Messiah, fulfilled in the New Testament.

Jesus verified how all this is tied together with his words in the New Testament book of Luke 24: 19-24 (NIV), when on the road to Emmaus, He told some disciples:

> "About Jesus of Nazareth," they replied. "He was a prophet, powerful in word and deed before God and all the people. The chief priests and our rulers handed him over to be sentenced to death, and they crucified him; but we had hoped that he was the one who was going to redeem Israel. And what is more, it is the third day since all this took place. In addition, some of our women amazed us. They went to the tomb early this morning but didn't find his body. They came and told us that they had seen a vision of angels, who said he was alive. Then some of our companions went to the tomb and found it just as the women had said, but they did not see Jesus."
>
> He said to them, **"How foolish you are, and how slow to believe all that the prophets have spoken! Did not the Messiah have to suffer these things and then enter his glory?"** And beginning with Moses and all the Prophets, he explained to them what was said in all the Scriptures concerning himself.

He came to fulfill what was foretold of Him in the Old Testament.

One Mind Writing

In spite of the Bible being written by about forty authors, over more than 1500 years, in three languages, it reveals a coordinated set of themes and a continued thesis that comes to a positive conclusion at the book's end. All of these things make it appear as if it was *one mind writing* it, and that is what we would have expected to find if God wrote the Bible.

We have now shown that five of the six big questions about what we should find in the world, and in the Bible, "If God wrote the Bible," have been positively verified. This is making a very good logical case for God being the author of the Bible. Statistically, with just the evidence we have seen thus far, there is less than a 4 percent chance that all of this evidence appeared simply by accident. But our investigation is not yet over. We have one more big question to explore, which has a special significance in our modern scientific age...

PRESCIENCE

**If God Wrote the Bible,
the Bible should show Prescience. Does it?**

Prescience is writing in the Bible, which reveals an understanding of science far in advance of our scientific breakthroughs. Now, the Bible is not a science textbook. But, if it is the words of an infallible God, then where it does talk of things referring to science, it should be 100 percent correct and reliable. Further, if God is the Creator of all things, as the Bible describes, then He and thus the Bible should deeply understand the science which underpins all creation.

When we examine the Old Testament, we find that in more than a hundred statements, the Bible reveals an in-depth understanding of scientific knowledge 3000 years before man discovered these things. Likewise, we find dozens of verses that reveal this same seemingly unexplainable understanding of scientific discoveries that man has only recently uncovered, and yet the Bible shows an understanding of them almost 2000 years ago in the New Testament writings.

To explain these scientific nuggets in the Bible, we will relate a host of scientific studies and tell you a number of true stories in this section that will put these scientific truths in perspective. First, let's review a little scientific history to set the stage for our first story. The microscope was invented around 1600 AD. Galileo invented the telescope in 1609.[294] Anton von Leeuwenhoek first observes bacteria under a microscope around 1674.[295] This all shows that

253

during the 17th century, we are getting the apparatus to investigate our universe and the micro-universe which makes up our existence.

What Happens in the 19th century (the 1800s)?

In the 1860s, Louie Pasteur will demonstrate that all life comes from previous life (biogenesis) and invent his pasteurization process by which bacteria in milk and other products can be eradicated, showing that we now have a knowledge of these microscopic life forms and are beginning to understand what they might be doing to us.[296]

By the later part of this century, Robert Koch will organize disease theory into a set of postulates where we can discern whether or not diseases are being transferred via microscopic organisms.[297] All of these discoveries set the stage for the story I will now tell you about a 19th-century doctor who paid attention to these discoveries and put them into practice.

A True Story

Ignaz Philipp Semmelweis (1818-1865) was a Hungarian-Austrian physician. In 1847 he was made head of the "Maternity Department of the Vienna Lying-in Hospital." Incidentally, I always laugh at that hospital's name since I don't know what else you would do in a hospital *but lie down*?

When Semmelweis took over at this hospital, there was a real problem with babies dying in this hospital. The hospital had two wards for delivering babies. They had a doctor's ward where doctors delivered the babies and a midwives' ward where midwives (grandmothers and other experienced women) helped deliver babies.

The statistics on these two wards were somewhat astounding. The doctor's ward had a 25 percent mortality rate. That is, in the year before Semmelweis came in as head, almost 100 of the 400 babies delivered in the doctor's ward died! However, the mortality rate in the midwives' ward was only 1 percent, as just 4 out of 400 babies delivered in their ward in the same year died before they left the hospital. How could this be? It is as counterintuitive as it is astounding!

Semmelweis studied what was going on in both of these units to try and solve this problem. He noted that one difference between the wards was that the doctors were frequently going directly from doing autopsies to delivering babies without washing up before they did so. Indeed, rather than being clothed in the pure white surgical smocks we see today, these doctors prided themselves on being covered in blood and their coming to the delivery room covered in blood from autopsies and previous deliveries. This the doctors saw as a badge of honor to show how much they had done that day. On the other hand, the midwives washed themselves, the babies, and mothers in hot water.

Now the Bible is full of verses instructing the cleansing by water, especially in the books of Exodus, Leviticus, and Numbers, where there are no less than twenty-one verses that give instructions on cleansing oneself with water. In Leviticus 6:27 (NASB95), it says, **"Anyone who touches its flesh will become consecrated; and when any of its blood splashes on a garment, in a holy place you shall wash what was splashed on."** Perhaps the midwives in faith paid attention to these verses.

Semmelweis, with the background of discoveries going on around him in the 18th and 19th centuries, which we described, suspected that something was transmitting diseases to the babies, and it might be microscopic. To try and solve this problem, he required his doctors to wash their hands before they helped deliver babies. Incidentally, this new policy was extremely unpopular among doctors, as any change in a long-standing policy would be in any organization. The doctors neither had the same understanding of microbial action as did Semmelweis nor did they even consider that their actions could be responsible for all these deaths, even though common sense would tell them so. Likewise, their pride was being assaulted by an "outsider," who was trying to tell them how to practice medicine by changing the way they had "always done it."

In the next year, using the new washing procedures, the mortality rate in the doctor's ward went down twenty-fold. It went down to the same 1 percent mortality rate that the midwives had, with only five out of about 400 births in the doctor's ward dying. You would think this result would be met with adulation and praise for Dr. Semmelweis. **Instead, he was fired!** This result is sad, but the results of the next year were even sadder as the doctor's ward's mortality rate the next year after Semmelweis was fired returned to 25 percent, and another 100 babies died as the doctors ceased washing their hands.[298] I want you to remember this story as we see what the Bible says about blood transmission.

Moses Write Numbers 19

It tells us in Numbers chapter 19, which was written by Moses, that **any person touching a carcass must be washed!** If the doctors in Vienna had paid attention to this simple verse from the Bible, then the hundreds of babies which died in the doctor's ward in Vienna for years would not have died.

It also says in Numbers 19 (NIV) that **"and every open container without a lid fastened on it will be unclean."** Note that this scientific insight was written down almost 3000 years before Pasteur, Koch, and others discovered how such an open jar would yield an excellent growth medium for bacteria, much of which is harmful to us. How did Moses know this 3000 years ahead of the rest of humanity?

Break the Pots!

Leviticus 11:32-33 (NASB) says:

> **Also anything on which one of them may fall when they are dead becomes unclean**, including any wooden article, or clothing, or skin, or a sack—any article of which use is made—it shall be put in the water and be unclean until evening, then it becomes clean. **As for any earthenware vessel**

**into which one of them may fall, whatever is in it
becomes unclean and you shall break the vessel.**

So this says if a dead or diseased animal comes in contact with your clothes, skin, or furniture, then wash it, which is good hygiene. But remarkably, the Hebrews were told that if such an unclean dead or diseased thing got into one of their pots, to just break it and throw it away. Would we do that today? Certainly not. If something diseased or spoiled got into one of our pots today, we would simply clean it, sterilize it and reuse it. So is this one of those places not in evidence of God's knowledge of prescience, but instead is evidence of a biblical error or ignorance? As it turns out, it is not an error.

In the time this was written, the technology and the practice of glazing earthen pots were not widely used.[299] This technology and practice will not become common for another 600 years. We glaze all of our pottery today to seal it so that nothing can get into the ceramic or earthenware fabric and take up residence there that we do not wish to be there, such as germs. Since three thousand years ago, they did not so glaze their pots; if diseased, infected, or spoiled food was in a pot, it could easily be absorbed into the clay pots. This spoiled or diseased material could then infect newly placed food put into these pots later, even if they had been thoroughly washed. Thus, with unglazed pots, the only sanitary and safe thing to do was to destroy them and use another. How did Moses and the Hebrews know that?

Don't Eat

The Bible in Leviticus 11 (this is reiterated in Isaiah 66) says not to eat rodents and hares. Our modern medical knowledge tells us that these animals can harbor bubonic plague, rabies, and some of the worst diseases known to man. In terms of what we know today, this is excellent advice for a primitive culture to follow. The question is, how did they ever figure this out? Man has eaten rabbits (hares) throughout history, as we have dogs, and in many cases without harm. How were the connections made without scientific studies on these animals being carriers of diseases?

Numbers tell us not to eat reptiles. Today we find that to be good advice since they often live in stagnant waters, which is an excellent growth medium for all sorts of bacteria and parasites.

We are instructed not to eat cats. While feeding on domesticated cats seems repugnant in our culture today, it has been a common practice over the history of man. But cats feed on rodents, which have been proven to be carriers of many of the worst diseases known to man.[300] The question is, how did the Bible figure this out when people all the way up through the Middle Ages and the "black death" could not figure this out?

We in western cultures have benefited from these hygiene laws for centuries in so many ways. We even benefit from them today. Today many cultures in tropical regions eat fruit bats. It is common in these places to see bats offered at marketplaces for consumption. As it turns out, bats are a major carrier of the Ebola virus, a terrible disease that kills people horribly by making them bleed uncontrollably. The control of Ebola has been the scourge of Africa for decades. It is also believed that COVID-19 came from bats. This very infectious Coronavirus was responsible for the more recent world pandemic. We in western cultures, perhaps because we have followed the Bible, find the eating of bats neither appropriate nor desirable.[301] Bats are specifically forbidden to be eaten in the Bible in Leviticus 11.

The Israelites were instructed not to eat dogs, which has been common practice in many cultures, who find them a delicacy! Dogs, however, can harbor rabies and a host of other diseases, which we now immunize them against. Since, in ancient times, all dogs did not get sick nor spread disease, how was this figured out by Semitic nomads some three thousand years ago?

Numbers include further Mosaic laws about preventing the transfer of diseases from animal to animal. Most of which were not readily known to be true until the last century or two.

Moses Wrote Leviticus 11

In the book of Leviticus, Moses also wrote that the Israelites were allowed to eat from the cattle family, sheep, goats, deer, fowl, and fish *with scales and fins*. How was all this figured out when most other cultures ate everything else on a regular basis is not clear.

Unclean

Leviticus declares that things in the water without scales and fins are unclean, along with cats, dogs, birds of prey, reptiles, hares, and swine. We have already covered some of the scientific reasons now given for not eating reptiles, dogs, and cats. But, what of these other "unclean" animals not to be eaten by man?

Hares (rabbits) frequently feed on rodents and thus would be just as dangerous as eating cats. Birds of prey like the hawk or eagles, or scavengers like the vulture, also would eat rodents, as well as decaying and exposed meat. However, it would be most interesting to determine just how these ancient nomads figured out that swine (pigs) and "things in the water without scales and fins (i.e., crawling water animals like crawfish and clams) were also dangerous to eat.

Swine (pig) diseases are numerous, including carrying typhoid, as well as trichinosis roundworms, which are small parasitic worms you can get from pork that is undercooked. It is particularly difficult to understand how ancient Jews could have discovered that swine transmitted trichinosis? Trichinosis worms are only transmitted when pork is not thoroughly cooked or cured as we do today. Further, the incubation period (time from when you are exposed to a disease to when you first show symptoms) for trichinosis is anywhere between 10 and 50 days.[302]

So we have a disease which is not usually contracted, since in most cases ancient peoples, by the nature of outdoor cooking, did thoroughly cook their pork and ate it with no issues. When they inadvertently did not cook it, and they did infrequently contract trichinosis, it never appeared for about a month or more. Is there any way you connect an illness to something you ate a month ago and had eaten many times in the past with no ill effect?[303]

The Bible prohibited the eating of crawling sea animals, crawfish, clams, and the like. These are found in the mouths of streams and rivers. Question: What was done in rivers and streams throughout history till the last couple hundred years?

Well, people washed their dishes in streams by hanging them on lines (like clotheslines which some people used to use and some still use today to dry clothes), but which allowed the pots and pans and utensils to just dip into the running water, which did much the same thing as our modern dishwashers, and in some cases a fairly good job of cleaning the utensils. This, of course, put a lot of dirt and decaying material into the water.

Women and some men throughout history would wash clothes in streams and rivers by pounding the dirty clothes on rocks as water ran over them or hanging them in water like the dishes. In both cases, more material was put into the running waters. The easiest latrine throughout history has been to go to the bathroom in the local stream or river. Likewise, if people wished to bathe throughout history, most would do so in the local stream or river. The easiest way to get rid of food scraps and other trash without burying it was to throw it in the rivers and have it washed away.[304]

Thus, what have clams and crawling water animals been taking in throughout our history on Earth? They have been sucking in raw sewage! But how did the ancient Israelites figure this out?

How Did Moses Know?

How did Moses and the ancient Israelites know all of this, which is not revealed in most other cultures of the time? Some would say it was only common sense. But, if that were true, why was this knowledge not common with most other cultures and nations? Common sense, as we described, would not have helped with Trichinosis in pigs since it most often did not infect people due to good cooking, and when it did, it would be as much as a month later after eating before the disease would present itself.

It could not be that they somehow guessed at microbial bacteria, since even the doctors we told you about in the 19th century in Vienna, who were going from autopsies to baby births, could not figure that out in a day when microscopes were available, and disease theory and pasteurization were being developed! Even when someone like Dr. Semmelweis suspected this, it was not believed or transferred to others, as was the case in the Vienna Lying-in Hospital, which fired him and killed another hundred babies the next year in willful ignorance.

Many have suggested that the source of the Bible's incredible medical knowledge was the Egyptian culture, the highest culture at the time of the writing of the Old Testament Bible. A culture that the Israelites had just been in contact with for hundreds of years. Well, let's look at what was in Egyptian medical knowledge from the 19th to the 12th centuries BC when the Israelites would have been exposed to this culture.

Records from this time show that Egyptian medical knowledge was as backward as the rest of the world except the Bible. The Egyptians would treat most illnesses by bleeding the patient with leeches. This was a time-honored method used with the fairly logical theory that there was some type of poison or toxin in your body, which we had to get out of you. The only problem was that this method rarely extracted any large amount of the bacteria or other infection which caused the malady. This treatment was used by cultures for thousands of years all the way up to the 19th century in the United States of America!

How did the ancient Egyptians treat cuts and wounds? They recommended placing animal manure on the wound.[305] This is not only the wrong way to treat a wound but is an excellent way to promote an infection!

Also, for some weird reason, the Egyptians decided that dead and often festering mice were an effective remedy for the problem of toothache. The dead mice would be mashed into a paste and applied to the afflicted area in the mouth. For serious toothaches, a whole dead mouse would simply be applied directly to the tooth. Common sense tells us that this treatment would not have worked in curing the aching tooth, but again it had an excellent chance of causing a full-blown infection!

Nope, the Hebrew obviously did not get this incredibly accurate and, ahead of its time, medical knowledge from the Egyptians.[306]

Such Knowledge Not Possible Till 19th Century

The medical knowledge set forth in the Bible by Moses could not be found in the history of man practiced and or discovered until the 19th and 20th centuries AD. For Moses to know all that he put down in the first five books of the Bible, he would have had to have had the equivalent of modern degrees in food chain theory, microbiology, disease theory, and bacterial immunology.[307] Was this true, or did he have help from the manufacturer, designer, and Creator of all life?

The Bible on Sanitation

In Deuteronomy 23:12-13 (NIV), it says:

> Designate a place outside the camp where you can go to relieve yourself. As part of your equipment, have something to dig with, and when you relieve yourself, dig a hole and cover up your excrement.

This seems like just good common-sense advice for good sanitation, which could have been gleaned from centuries of trial and error to get the best practices of sanitation. What is of interest here is that these instructions, like the rest covered in Leviticus, Numbers, and Deuteronomy, show no error based on cultural biases or local customs. No "wives tales" of putting "butter on a burn" instead of ice as was the popular myth when I was a kid. Instead, it invariably gives excellent advice to the Jews on how to live in the safest way and best way possible. How could the Bible invariably give such sound advice, at all times, without error?

Somewhat related to sanitation via latrines outside of camp is the concept of separating out and isolating infected individuals from everyone else, called "quarantine." There are more than a dozen verses in the Bible that prescribe quarantining individuals for a variety of maladies. Several of these are in Leviticus chapters 13, 14, and 15. Leviticus 13:46 (KJV) says, "All the days wherein the plague shall be in him he shall be defiled; he is unclean: he shall **dwell alone; without the camp shall his habitation be.**"

If this biblical knowledge had been applied during the fourteenth century AD in Europe, the devastation of the "Black Death" could have been mitigated. During this time, the sick and dying were kept in the same one-room dwellings as the rest of the family, and they wondered why so many people died? Instead of paying close attention to the Bible, they often blamed all of these deaths on "evil spirits."[308]

The Bible on Biology

As I said before, the Bible is not primarily a science book, but where it does talk about science, if God is its author, it will have to be 100 percent accurate. Let's search the Bible and see if there really is evidence that God is the Creator of all life, in which case, He would intimately understand the workings and construction of His created life forms.

The Bible on Circumcision and Blood Coagulation

The liver starts using vitamin K to produce the blood proteins, thrombin, and prothrombin between the 5th and 7th days after birth, which are vital in the twelve-step process of blood coagulation which allows for coagulation of blood when we have a simple cut in our skin. Without this complex process, we would bleed to death any time we had a small cut anywhere on our bodies, or clots would form randomly and uncontrollably in our bodies and thus killing us by randomly cutting off blood flow. Peak production of prothrombin is reached on the *8th day of life*.

Genesis 17:12 directed Jews to circumcise male babies on the **8th day after birth**. This was a religious rite and custom signifying devotion to God in males, much as baptism does today. However, it is not only a religious rite nor a barbaric one. It turns out this practice is both hygienic and healthful. Scientific medical studies today have shown that this procedure, when done correctly on male humans, can reduce the risk of disease. In fact, the United States Centers for Disease Control (CDC) today endorses its use.

A report from the CDC said, "...the scientific evidence is clear that the benefits outweigh the risks," Circumcision involves the surgical removal of the foreskin covering the tip of the penis. Germs can collect and multiply under the foreskin, creating issues of hygiene which are alleviated when the circumcision procedure is done.

Clinical trials, many done in sub-Saharan Africa, have demonstrated that circumcision reduces HIV infection risk by 50 to 60 percent, the CDC guidelines note. The procedure also reduces by 30 percent the risk of contracting herpes and human papillomavirus (HPV), two pathogens believed to cause cancer of the penis.[309]

The question is, how did the Bible writers know all of this 3500 years ago? Not only is this procedure healthful, but the Bible directed it to be done on the first day in which the baby reached his full ability to coagulate the blood and thus endure the procedure with little risk to the infant. The biblical instructions reveal an eerie knowledge of the blood coagulation system, which man will in no way fathom for another 3500 years.

Incidentally, this highly complex process of blood coagulation could not have occurred by chance in any organism before it bled to death for lack of this highly fine-tuned system, which both rapidly coagulates the blood and forms clots where cuts occur. But it also refrains from forming clots throughout the rest of the body and cuts off the clotting process just when it is positively accomplished so that this process does not run out of control and cut off circulation.

If this process is absent or dysfunctional in some people, abnormal bleeding occurs. Abnormal bleeding can result from disorders of the blood clotting (coagulation) system, platelets, or abnormal blood vessels.

Clotting disorders occur when the body is unable to make sufficient amounts of the proteins that are needed to help the blood clot and thereby stop bleeding. These proteins are called clotting factors (coagulation factors). All clotting factors are made in the liver. The liver requires vitamin K to make some of the clotting factors.[310] How did the Bible have such a keen insight into this 3500 years ago?

Ribs can Regrow!

Perhaps one of the most ridiculed of all biblical claims in the book of Genesis, and repeated in 1 Timothy 2:13, is that woman was formed from one of man's ribs. Now, if there is a God, and He is the Creator, then He could have created woman in many ways. But this way is theologically fulfilling, in that it ties men and woman together as one race genetically, ties these two people together in an intimate way not since repeated, and ties together their lineage and their sin condition.

If you were wondering, men do not have fewer ribs than women. There is no missing rib, which would be the "smoking gun" in this story. However, there are three excellent explanations for this, even if the biblical account is correct. First, God could have simply replaced the rib in Adam, which he took out. Second, as research has now shown, the rib taken from Adam could have regrown naturally. Scientists have now found that under certain conditions, the rib is the one bone of the body which when removed, will naturally grow back! (Some other organs such as the tonsils will spontaneously regrow as well if a portion of this organ is left attached when the tonsil is removed.)[311]

If the membrane covering the ribs, called the "periosteum" (from the Greek meaning "around the bone"), is left intact, then ribs can regrow. You have probably had a personal experience with this membrane, as when you are eating spareribs, this membrane often sticks to your teeth. Regrowth is fostered in the rib cage by a rich blood supply provided by the attached intercostal (meaning "between the ribs").

Dr. David Pennington, the first plastic surgeon in the world to successfully reattach a human ear says, "rib periosteum has a remarkable ability to regenerate bone, perhaps more so than any other bone."[312]

Incidentally, the third possibility in this story is that Adam's rib may not have regrown, and God did not replace it. Even so, Adam's children and subsequent humans would not have a missing rib because of this surgery. Skeptics claim that since men and women have the same amount of ribs as they do today, its evidence that the creation of woman from man via a rib is false. This, of course, is a straw man argument. It is dependent on a disproven 18th -century idea called Lamarckism which said that the behaviors or traits learned or developed by one organism will be transferred to its offspring.[313]

The idea was that a giraffe got a longer neck because its father stretched his neck till it became longer, and this exercised attribute was passed on to the next generation. Or, it says that since Arnold Schwarzenegger was a bodybuilder, his kids will all be born with great strength. Science has shown that such acquired characteristics are not inherited. Thus, this argument falls apart. Even if a rib was ripped from Adam, his offspring would produce within themselves the normal full set of ribs. Their DNA instructions would see to this.

Science today has shown that the account of a woman formed from man's rib is not scientifically impossible.

We are Held Together by God's Power
Colossians 1:16-17 (NIV) says:

> For in him all things were created: things in heaven and on earth, visible and invisible, whether thrones or powers or rulers or authorities; all things have been created through him and for him. He is before all things, and **in him all things hold together.**

If you read the entire chapter that verse came from, it makes it clear that everything created was so created by Christ. He was the instrument God used to create everything. Well, where does science come into this?

The bold words tell us that all things are **held together by His power.** There are two things found in science on the microscopic level which seem to be in concert with these verses.

The first is in the scaffolding structure of every person on earth and every animal and plant. As an adult, we are a collection of over fifty trillion cells, all of which are held together, on top of one another, and in place by molecular pins called "laminins."[314]

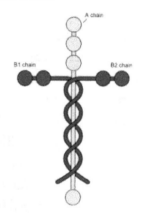

If these "molecular pins" did not exist, you would be just a blob of cells on the floor like a pile of melting Jell-O. We are actually held together by these molecules and their attachments to lattices of collagen. Note that the accompanying picture shows that the shape of one of these molecules is in the shape of a cross. Do you think that it is an accident that the molecules which literally hold us together look so remarkably like the "Cross of Christ?"

On the subatomic level, our atoms are held together by four forces which we can describe as the gravitational, electromagnetic, strong and weak nuclear forces. While we can describe them, *we have no clue how these forces actually work. None whatsoever!*

Similarly, it is now theorized that there is zero-point energy in all of the vacuum of space which could be a sign of Christ's power holding everything together. The notion that God's power holds us together in these forces is every bit as scientific as anything we have come up with because we have come up with absolutely nothing to explain these fundamental forces of nature. It is revealing indeed that the Bible had it right, that there are forces or powers which literally hold us together and which are invisible to the naked eye, as alluded to in Hebrews 11:3.

Does the Bible Hint at Knowledge of DNA?

The King James Version of the Bible translates Psalm 139:16 as follows, **"Thine eyes did see my substance, yet being unperfect; and in thy book all my members were written, which in continuance were fashioned, when as yet there was none of them."**

In truth, you were designed before you were made. You were not just cobbled together by accident in the womb. Your strands of DNA in the nucleus of nearly all of your trillions of cells have a blueprint for how you were to be made, which governs how you grow, function, age, and die. This blueprint is written on *deoxyribonucleic acid (DNA),* which is a string of over three billion nucleotides (chemical computer codes), written in four dimensions, using computer coding far beyond the binary coding we use in our modern computers today.[315]

It is fascinating to me that until as late as 2007, we did not fully realize all this. Until the completion of the ENCODE Project in 2007, it was believed that only about 1.5 percent of the genome was coded to form life's chemicals in rare areas of the genome called genes. These genes coded for proteins, and the rest of our DNA was previously considered useless junk! Only after small sections of our genomes were tested from the supposed "junk DNA" sections (which were considered useless random nucleotides strung together with no purpose) did we get evidence that these portions of the genome which do not directly produce proteins, instead of useless junk, were found to have important functions. This research found that the supposed "junk DNA" regulates cell functions, acts as genetic switches, holds the plans for building cell structures, as well as body structures, and serves as computer check codes for what, when, or whether to do a function.

The resemblance of what we find in non-gene DNA to the "If, then" conditional checks we program into our computer programs is striking, with one large exception. The coding on DNA is far more complex than that used in our most advanced computers. So much so that we have only decoded the 1.5 percent of the genome containing protein-producing genes. The other 98 percent of our genome, most of which have now been proved to be functional, but which we haven't been able to read, as their coding is still too complex for us to decipher![316]

This recent insight that basically the whole genome may be functional puts a real crimp into the evolutionary theory as it pertains to genetics. It made real sense that if our genomes were built by random chance processes, that there could be some parts (the genes, for example) that coded for useful information. But it would be expected from such accidental random construction that the bulk of our DNA would be random useless strings of nucleotides, which had been called "Junk DNA." It was supposed to be in these huge regions of "Junk DNA" that a lot of mutations and variations occurred silently, which were not expressed until they eventually and accidentally coded for something to be expressed in the genome either positively or negatively. This was thought to be the main mechanism in evolution's variation and production of new information, a portion of phenomena that scientists have called "genetic drift."[317]

Since it now has been proven that there is no "Junk DNA," there is no place for the endless, pointless, and non-expressed sorting of nucleotides to occur. Even worse for evolutionary theory is that when we thought the genome was 98 percent junk, it fit right into evolutionary ideas of what our genomes should look like if it had been cobbled together by random chance processes. The fact that we now know that essentially all of our genomes are functional not only makes it look designed but makes the mathematical odds of its being designed by an outside intelligence almost a mathematical certainty.[318] When people ask me what the best evidence is for God's creation we have today is, I usually respond that it is DNA!

Indeed DNA shows that all parts of you, "all of your members," were predesigned and coded for assembly before you were made. You were then fashioned in the womb from these preset instructions. This truth was written in Psalm 139 three thousand years ago. How did the Bible get this close to the truth about how we are made unless its writers had inside information from the Creator?

Biogenesis

According to the Bible, everything reproduces according to its "**kind**." This point was repeated ten times in the first chapter of the first book of the Bible (Genesis). In the simplest interpretation of these verses, the Bible says that "life always comes from life." That is a restatement of the *"Law of Biogenesis"* formulated by the work of Louis Pasteur in the 19th century. On the surface, this is just common-sense science and observation. Cows always produce cows. Chickens always lay eggs, which, if allowed to hatch, reproduce chickens. Every kind reproduces its own kind. We have never throughout the history of man observed a kind which produced another kind of animal, or a seed which produced another kind of plant than the one it came from.[319]

But that is not what men have thought over the centuries. For most of the history of man, cultures have expressed and repeated a concept of *"spontaneous generation."* Spontaneous Generation says that at some point, nonliving material became alive.[320] Today this idea has morphed into the idea that inanimate material (dirt, rocks, water, etc.) became alive via some strange process. This "life from lifelessness" is also called *"abiogenesis."*[321]

For most of man's history, multiple old wives' tales, myths, and fables have been told of how different living things "sprang" into existence from lifeless materials.

For more than a thousand years, stories were circulated that said they knew how to make mice from lifeless materials. The story went that if you collected a lot of trash in the corner of a barn, then out of that pile of trash, a mouse would be produced from nonliving material.

The truth, which came to light with prolonged observation (the basic experimental tool of science), was that mice are not produced from the nonliving trash in the barn. Instead, mice, already alive, already produced as the living offspring of other mice, are attracted to the pile of trash in the corner of barns as they scavenge for food.

Another story said that a frog was produced by just getting some mud, water, and weeds together for a period of time. In truth, of course, it is not the mud and water which produces the frog, but the mud and water attract the frog since this is the environment this amphibian is designed to live in. Since the frog lives there, it will lay eggs in the muddy water, which will yield tadpoles when the eggs hatch. They will develop in the water and eventually develop into a frog, as its DNA is preprogrammed to do.

Another tale said that flies were produced out of decaying dead meat.[322]

A famous set of experiments by the Italian scientist Fransisco Redi demonstrated this was not true in 1668. Redi put some decaying meat into a *closed jar,* and no flies were produced. However, he also set out some meat in an *open jar* (a control group), let it decay for days, and flies and worms (maggots) appeared on the meat, and then flies developed from those maggots.[323]

What we now know through Redis and others scientists' careful observations is that flies are attracted to meat. They not only land on the meat and eat some, but they lay their eggs in the decaying meat. Thus, when they hatch, the larvae which come out of the eggs (maggots) will have food since the maggots will also dine on the decaying meat. After a time, these maggots will then develop into flies. Again, what scientific observation has demonstrated in these three cases, and in all others that we have ever observed, is that **life always comes from life.** It never "pops" into existence from a collection of nonliving materials.

The theory of evolution is based on *abiogenesis.* According to this philosophy, at some point in the far distant past, life came from lifeless material. The problem with this thesis is that it has never been observed. Thus, abiogenesis fails in its lack of observable, repeatable, testable, and falsifiable testing, which is supposed to be the basis of science, not what we can dream up as stories!

Conversely, the Bible affirms its knowledge of this fact of nature that life always comes from life, in spite of the contrary stories so prevalent in the cultures of the time the Bible was written in. So how did the Bible get this right when all other sources up to and including modern times told such stories of life from lifelessness?

Every Animal Created According to Its "Kind." Is that Scientific?

As previously stated, eleven times in the first chapter of Genesis (in Hebrew meaning "Beginning"), it says that every type of animal, insect, fish, plant or insect would reproduce only according to its "kind."[324] This would seem at odds with the current theory of evolution, which states that every life form on earth has developed slowly over many millions of years in small steps via adaptation and modification. In fact, a plain reading of the Bible on this point disagrees with the theory of "macroevolution" (the idea that one species varies and changes until it becomes another species, then another, then another till becoming a completely new body form).

Another way of saying this is macroevolution theorizes that the first simple cell accidentally formed on this planet. Then, over eons of time, from that first cell, life developed into multicellular organisms, then into fish, then amphibians, then reptiles, then mammals, and eventually man.[325] The Biblical account is explicitly at odds with such a theory.

Further, a plain reading of Genesis 1 shows a completely different order for the creation than the proposed order of development via the evolutionary process. Let's look at a few examples of these divergent orders. The Bible says the world was first made of water, then land formed. Evolution says that the Earth first formed as a ball of magma, which cooled to dry land, and water was added later.[326]

The Bible says that life first appeared *on land* on Day 3. Evolution says that life first appeared *in water* in a prebiotic soup.[327] The Bible says the first life on Earth were plants, whereas evolution says it was single-celled organisms. According to Genesis 1, the Earth was formed before the sun and stars. Stellar evolution theory says the sun and stars would have formed before the Earth.[328]

The Bible says that birds and fish were both created on the same day. Evolution says that fish developed many millions of years before birds.[329] The biblical order says that whales were created before reptiles. Evolution, of course, says the reverse.[330] The Bible says that birds were created on Day 5, while insects (creeping things) were made on Day 6. But, of course, evolutionary theory says that insects developed millions of years before birds.[331]

There are many more of these disconnects between the biblical and evolutionary order for creation. Dr. Bill Tierney (then head of the Biology Department at the U.S. Air Force Academy) at a conference I attended in Granby, Colorado, in 1986, presented this information to me and convinced me that you could believe in evolution, or you can believe in biblical creation, but not both. They cannot be compromised together, nor made compatible. And since "evolution" is stated to be a "fact of science," this proves the Bible is in error. Or does it?

Before we proceed, one thing needs to be clarified about the creation model. When the Bible says that everything "reproduces according to its kind," it does not mean the Bible says speciation (the changing of a kind of animal from one species to another which are closely related, like a terrier and a beagle) does not occur, which it clearly does. What it does say is that one **body form or "kind"** cannot vary so much as to become a whole new body form or kind. The biblical concept of "kind" roughly equates to the family or genera level of current scientific taxonomy. It allows, and in fact, demands that a large amount of variation is not only allowed but programmed into each created kind, so they can adapt to new environments.

For example, it would fit into the biblical creation model of kinds for all dog species, wolves, and coyotes we see today to have all developed over time from an original set of generic dogs (the dog kind).[332] This type of variation within the kind was first identified by Edward Blyth in 1835, and some call this microevolution,[333] which the biblical model would allow for. Others simply refer to this as variation and adaptation.

Let's look at what the Bible says, and what data from nature actually says, and see which fits better, the biblical concept of kinds or the evolutionary hypothesis of infinite variations of life forms, one changing into another?

As previously stated, when we look at the rock strata all across the earth, it is covered by sedimentary layers miles deep, with millions of fossils buried in the rock strata. These sedimentary layers are most often arranged in flow layers which suggest they were rapidly deposited by water and fast flowing sediments, which is exactly what you would expect if the Bible were true, and a worldwide flood actually occurred.

When we examine these millions of fossils buried in the sedimentary rock layers, we find current species, variations on current species, and extinct species. But, except for a very few debated examples, we find none of the transitions between kinds of differing body forms.[334]

Shrimp fossils have been found, which secular scientists have dated at 170 million years old, which are exactly like modern shrimp. Fossils of horseshoe crabs, which are supposedly 450 million years old, show almost no variation over time. We have found impressions and fossils of stingrays which are dated 250 million years old but show no discernable difference between these ancient species and modern rays. Dragonfly impressions dated between 150 and 300 million years old show no difference when compared to current species, except some species are larger. These are just a few examples of a wide variety of organisms that some people refer to as "living fossils."[335] What this data shows is **stasis** (no change) over time, not the infinite variation we would expect if every life form on earth had developed via evolution.

Perhaps the most revealing of the "living fossils" is the *Coelacanth*. The Coelacanth is a fish that was thought to be extinct until it was discovered to be alive in the deep-water oceans, first off Madagascar and then a second species of Coelacanth in the waters off Japan.

Before these living examples were found, we had found fossils of Coelacanths, and it had been theorized that it was one of those very rare and debated examples of "transitional forms" between one biological kind and another. It was believed that the fossils found suggested this was a fish developing a primordial lung, as well as strong bottom fins were developing into "proto-legs." This was thought of as a transition between fish and amphibians, just what the evolutionary theory would say we would find if evolution were true.

When we got to examine the actual living Coelacanths in nature, we found they were only normal fish. No primordial lungs, but standard gills. No proto-legs, but just standard fins on the bottom of its body, not attached to its spinal column. So this example not only shows stasis over 450 million years[336] but debunks the idea that it was a transitional form between kinds. This evidence again shows what we would expect from the biblical creation model, not evolution.

Another thing in paleontology that seems to agree with the biblical model and confounds the evolutionary view is what is called the *"Cambrian Explosion."* The Cambrian Explosion is a deep layer (dated by secular dating at about 530 million years ago) of sedimentary rock strata at which the first complex life first appears on this planet. Below this point, there are no complex life fossils. What is stunning is that in this deep layer, we find almost every major body plan (or kind) embedded in it. This *sudden appearance* of almost every type of life form on earth is not what is predicted by the evolutionary paradigm, but it is exactly what we would predict to see if the biblical model is true.[337]

Further, as covered in a previous section, everything we have observed and recorded as far back as man has records agrees that *everything reproduces according to its kind*. It is common sense. A bird lays an egg, and out comes a bird of that species or close to it due to minor variations in the two parents' DNA. We never get a crocodile or a pony coming out of a redbird egg. When a cow has a calf, it reproduces another cow. We never see a wolf, nor a giraffe coming out of a pregnant cow. Everything does seem to reproduce according to its kind! And, as we spelled out in the previous section, this reproducing only according to its kind is perfectly in concert with the "*law of biogenesis,*" which says that life always comes from life. Evolution, on the other hand, says that sometimes in an unknown distant past, life came from nonliving materials (abiogenesis—life from lifelessness).[338] This has never been observed and is not science but unproven philosophy.

Some biologists, when asked about this, will claim that they see evolution happen today by observing bacteria change in very short periods of time. Scientists like to observe bacteria because they reproduce rapidly and frequently. Bacteria can vary and change between one bacterium and another more than in most species since they can actually trade genetic information with another bacteria via strands of DNA called plasmids.[339] But, with all of this rapid variation, even though we do get a lot of speciation and variation, at the end of the day, or the month, or a year, what we still have is just bacteria! **The body form, the kind, has not changed!**

In light of the apparent stasis, and the fact we cannot really see evolution happening today in front of us, evolutionists like the late Stephen Jay Gould of Harvard and Richard Goldschmidt at UC Berkley have theorized that there is very little evolution going on for millions of years (stasis), which is followed by very short periods of rapid evolution between species and kinds. This rapid period of evolution is fostered by unusual periods of solar radiation activity or other even more exotic temporary factors. This would explain why we find so much stasis in the rock layers, but it leads to a ridiculous reality. What it says is that a reptile is exposed to radiation or new bacteria or something, and it lays an egg and produces a badger or wolf in just a generation or two. Goldschmidt's theory was, in fact, called the "*hopeful monster theory.*"[340]

Why would respected members of the secular scientific community propose such ridiculously outlandish ideas? It is because they are honest enough to examine the wealth of fossils we have today and recognize that gradual evolution over millions of years is not what it exemplifies. However, instead of relenting to the logical alternative of the biblical creation account, they try to re-invent evolution to a ridiculous extent, just so they do not have to admit a supernatural force could have been at work here.

Thus, in spite of the consensus that evolution is true, when we look at the data in the fossil record and nature, we find that the scientific data better fits the creation model rather than the evolutionary model. Thus, the creation model is a viable scientific alternative, which has not been disproven by science, and in fact, the theory of everything we see being created according to created kinds is scientifically supportable.

Different Flesh

In the New Testament book of 1 Corinthians, verse 15:39 (KJV), it says, **"All flesh is not the same flesh: but there is one kind of flesh of men, another flesh of beasts, another of fishes, and another of birds."** Eleven times in the first chapter of Genesis, it says that every "kind" of animal created on this planet has a different flesh. Not only does this show a parallel understanding of the design of the flesh of different created creatures by both the Old and New Testament writers, but it also corresponds to our current scientific knowledge, which reveals each kind of animal and humans possess quite different flesh, as produced by their very distinct DNA sequences.[341]

Such keen insight by the Bible into the construction of every organism having a different flesh is fascinating since most flesh seems the same to the naked eye and to our senses. The blood of all animals is red, the fluid in most all plants is clear or greenish. So many animals such as snake meat, assortments of birds, clams, and many other "fleshes" all look like white meat and taste like chicken (so much so that it's a joke for us to say, "It tastes like chicken"). From these broad similarities, how would the biblical authors figure out that each organism has different compositions of flesh if they did not have insight from the Creator?

Symbiotic Relationships of Fig Trees and Wasps—Amazing!

Del Tackett (the author of the "Truth Project"), while in San Antonio in 2017, related a story about how there were hundreds of species of fig wasps and hundreds of varieties of fig trees, which all corresponded and were pollinated only by a certain species of fig wasp and none other.

Of all the symbiotic relationships I had ever heard of, this was one of which I was not aware. Symbiotic relationships are one of the best evidence of God's designs in nature. Thus, I checked it out and found it's quite true! Incidentally, if you do not know about this relationship, you may want to skip this section as you may never eat a fig again!

As it turns out, about 900 species of "fig wasps" have been identified across the world, as well as about 900 species of fig trees. Each species of fig wasp is adapted to and will only burrow into and pollinate one specific species of fig tree. For example, fig wasp #8 will only burrow into and pollinate fig tree species #8, and fig wasp species #465 can identify fig tree type #465 and will only pollinate it and no other.

If that is not complex enough to show that this incredible relationship was designed by a Creator, then the details will impress you even more.

Fig wasp queens are fitted with rear pointing "saw teeth" on the backs of their hind limbs and mandibles. These "backward teeth" allow the queen to reverse in and burrow into the natural hole already designed into every fig. She is also aided in this task by the elongated and flattened shape of her thorax and head, which are *well designed* to help her slip in. In the process, she will often rip off her wings and antennae. This does not, however, deter her from pollinating the fig species once she has embedded herself and laying her eggs within the fig.

The female wasp then proceeds to pollinate the stigmas and lay eggs in the ovules of some of the florets. This she does by inserting her long ovipositor down the inside of the style (this is an intentional act she is predesigned and preprogrammed to accomplish). The florets that have styles longer than the wasp's ovipositor are pollinated, but no eggs are laid in the ovule, and hence these florets set seed. The wasp larvae feed on the endosperm tissue in the galled ovary, but nothing else so as not to interfere with fig or seed functions. Further, larval development correlates strongly with host fig development, encompassing anything from three to twenty weeks.

Once the wasps have reached maturity, they chew their way out from the galls and emerge into the fig cavity within a short period of each other. The wingless males mate with the females before chewing a hole through the fig wall to the exterior to allow the females to escape. These are the male's only two functions in life, as they die soon afterward! The females either actively load up pollen from ripe anthers into special pollen pockets, or in some species, passively become covered with pollen before exiting the fig in search of young receptive figs to complete the cycle.[342]

Now, let's examine how well and intricately designed all of this is. If the wasps did not have rear-facing teeth, they could not burrow into the fig. Without the predesigned opening in the fig, they could not get in. Without flattened and elongated bodies from the start of their creation, they could not accomplish this process. If this occurred by chance evolution, the first several times this was tried, the suicidal wasp would try and deposit her eggs into an unknown area and kill herself in the process as she lost her wings and antennae. Since she did not yet have the preprogramming (instinct) nor plumbing (ovipositor) needed to deposit the pollen into the proper place in the fig, she would die, her eggs might not be laid or hatched, and the tree would not be pollinated. This scenario for evolution does not further either species.

Even if she accidentally had rear-facing teeth on her body for no apparent reason, burrowed backward into the fig, not for her own food, but to lay her eggs for her young, and could somehow differentiate already between the one species of tree out of 900 which she was to pollinate, and she magically and accidentally came already equipped with the long ovipositor with which she will pollinate the fig as well as lay her eggs, this cycle will still fail. This is because, in the early stages of an evolutionary scenario, the males would not be preprogrammed to eat their way out to clear the way for the new queens, which have to have a clean tunnel for them to exit with pollen still on them to deposit elsewhere. Nor would the carefully controlled balance of males and female eggs be produced and laid, which makes this whole process in the fig possible.

I have heard of a lot of incredible symbiotic relationships, such as with the Egyptian Plover and the Nile Crocodile, sharks and feeder shrimp, ants, and the bull's horn acacia tree, and many more (the actual amount of these intricately designed symbiotic relationships is staggering). But nowhere else have I seen such a relationship so finely configured on both sides, not once, but 900 times, revealing the Creator's hand each and every time. We will look at another such symbiosis in the next section.

This myriad set of relationships is a fascinating set of evidence for God's designs in nature and His existence. But it was not the whole story Del Tackett was getting to that night. You see, there was a theological story being revealed in this relationship as well.

God created all of us to bear fruit. But that fruit is almost never for ourselves, but for the benefit of others. Likewise, the fruit on the fig tree is not for the fig tree but for the wasp and her young. We, too, benefit from the fruit of the fig trees (although I don't know after reading this if you will ever eat one again).

I was always bothered by the story in the Bible where Jesus came upon a fig tree (Matthew 21:18-22, and also in Mark 11:12-14) which had no fruit, and He cursed it, and it withered by the next day. This always seemed to me to be a petulant, if not a sinful thing to do. But, if we understand not only His need for food but also the truth that He (the Creator) created everything, including that tree, to produce fruit, it is understandable that He would curse anything which was not functioning as designed. Similarly, even though He designed and created us and loves us, if we do not follow Him and produce fruit in our lives as He designed, we will also be cursed for not fulfilling our destinies, as He designated them.

God gave us many wonderful things with the fig trees and fig wasps, but also with the entire creation. His designs are a living testament to His unique creative powers. But they also are designed to exhibit for us the purposes of His creation. The purposes that all of us are to live for others and live symbiotically. If we or nature fails to fulfill what we are designed for, we doom ourselves.

This is just one of many new threads in a new teaching series by Del Tackett called "*The Engagement Project*." We are excited by this new series and pray for its positive impact on our world.

Did the Bible get the Mustard Seed wrong?

Matthew 13:31-32 says, "The kingdom of heaven is like a **mustard seed**, which a man took and **planted in his field.** Though it is the *smallest of all seeds*, yet when it grows, it is the largest of garden plants and becomes a tree…."

But some point out that today the smallest seed found to date is not the tiny mustard seed but the microscopic vanilla orchid seed. Was Christ wrong when he said the mustard seed was the "smallest of all seeds"?

The simple answer is no due to the context. The story (parable) Jesus was telling was one the agrarian farmers of his day could comprehend. *In truth*, the smallest seed which they planted (which was the focus of His story) at that time and *still today* is the mustard seed. The vanilla orchid seed will not even be perceived until the invention of the microscope. Nor was it indigenous to the Middle East, but to the Americas. And Christ was not there to give a lesson on future botany about a seed invisible to the naked eye, in a hemisphere they did not even know about, but to teach these people about faith.

Further, not the Hebrews nor anyone of their region would have known of the Vanilla Orchid since it is indigenous to Central America and not the Middle East. Thus, the mustard seed was the smallest seed the Hebrews, who Jesus was talking to, could have knowledge of. Finally, the statement of the smallest seed on earth *"sewn" is a truthful one then and today* since new plantings and setting up of orchards of vanilla orchids by the Aztecs in ancient times and today is done by transplanting cuttings of the vine, not by sewing the microscopic vanilla orchid seed.

On the other hand, the background science on this vanilla orchid seed is fascinating proof of a Designer and Creator. Unlike other orchids, the vanilla planifolia vine needs to be pollinated while it's blooming in order to produce vanilla, and it blooms only one day a year. A special variety of minuscule bees and hummingbirds (only found in the Americas) and orchids were made to work together for His purpose, to create something sweet. The Vanilla plant can only be pollinated by a small flea-sized bee called the Mexican Melipona bee, or a very specialized variety of minuscule hummingbirds. The Mexican Melipona bee is the only insect capable of pollinating this orchid. Both the bee and the hummingbird gain sustenance from this plant. Both are preprogrammed to identify the one day of pollination, know how to unfold the flap of the orchid to gain sustenance, and in the process, get themselves covered in the orchid's pollen. They then fly that same day to other orchids, unfold the flap and pollinate them.[343]

This symbiotic relationship looks designed by a Creator since it simply had to have been. There is no rational naturalistic explanation for how such a very specialized, mutually dependent species could have evolved.

To underscore the point of this being an incredibly special God-created symbiotic relationship, we have the story of the Spanish conquistador, Hernan Cortez, who caused the fall of the Aztecs in Mexico. He loved vanilla and brought back vanilla plants from Mexico to Spain. For 300 years, the Spaniards and other Europeans grew the orchid plant from these cuttings, but no vanilla beans were produced since neither the specially designed bees nor the hummingbird existed in Europe to pollinate this very specially designed flower.[344]

Some will argue that Jesus made an erroneous statement in saying the mustard seed was the "smallest of all seeds," showing His fallibility and that of the Bible. Thus suggesting neither to be divine. In truth, He was relating a simple example, which the farmers of the time could relate to, and in close analysis, we find His statement to be factually true, in that the mustard seed was and is today the "smallest seed **sewn** by farmers." Christ's reference to the mustard seed as the "smallest of all seeds" thus does not reveal His ignorance of smaller seeds.

You were Designed and Made for Complex Communication

The New American Standard Bible translation says, **"Who has put wisdom in the innermost being or given understanding to the mind?"** Also, 1 Corinthians 1:9 says, **"God is faithful, through whom you were called into fellowship with His Son, Jesus Christ our Lord."** Psalms 42:1 says, **"As the deer pants for the water brooks, So my soul pants for You, O God."**

Thus, the Bible claims that we were designed with a purpose to commune and communicate with God and others. That purposeful design included that we could communicate using complex language. Now, what do we find when we look at our human body?

Scientists have learned that both hearing and deaf children try to duplicate the language used in their homes. Hearing children frequently babble in the language of their home until they master usage. You might ask how deaf children communicate or show this ability, or even "hear" the language of their home?

They do this by learning to use language with their hands. Hearing children produce sounds, then syllables, then eventually discernable words and phrases using their voices as they mimic what they hear, and then internalize these symbol's use.

Deaf infants can do the same using their hands. Deaf children first learn to make the hand signs of letters and numbers and string these signs together without meaning. However, at the same age, when hearing infants begin to make meaningful words, which usually occurs around their first birthday, deaf infants begin to show the ability to produce meaningful words using hand signs.

Linguistic and child development researchers were shocked by the realization of this discovery. It shows that the human brain comes with a built-in, unified ability to learn human language. This greatly surprised behavioral scientists because they are trained to assume that mankind has come from some apelike creature, who in turn came from a single-celled organism, which in turn is the result of a random combination of molecules. Why would the end result of such accidental creatures be the built-in (preprogrammed) ability to communicate in any complex language?

This assumption of design is perfectly logical for someone who believes in the Bible as God's word. How else could we communicate in ways above all other animals unless we were designed for it? The converse argument that all of our communication skills and equipment is the result of slow evolution is completely devoid of any logical mechanisms by which the nexus of our vocal systems, pre-imprinted communication wiring in the brains, and ability to both think and communicate conceptually could have evolved at all. Much less at the same time, which is key and essential for the complex communication that man has been capable of as far back as our archaeological records have found.

This leads us to another facet of these skills, which are implied by the Bible and logical for God to put into us. This is conceptual thought and self-awareness. These are main differences between us and the rest of the animal kingdom, and it is perfectly logical that God would have instilled these abilities in us since they would mirror Him. As He said, it was His goal for us to be made in "*His Image*." The mechanisms for us to develop these unique attributes by random chance mutations are both unclear and illogical. How else could we do all of these incredibly complex things unless our minds and bodies were "prewired" for communication and complex thoughts?[345]

Definition of Marriage and
Prohibition of Homosexual Behavior

In the last chapter, we made the point that it is a consistent theme throughout the Bible that marriage is only to be between a man and woman and that homosexual behavior is a sin. But the California Medical Association has voted an opinion that homosexuality is genetic and not necessarily a deviant act. The California Psychological Association has made a similar claim and said that conversion therapy to divert gays back to heterosexual behavior is unfruitful. The American Academy of Pediatrics has also voted to say that conversion therapy does not work to divert homosexuals back to heterosexuality.

With all of this expert input, this should make a great case for the Bible being incorrect on this point of homosexual behavior being a sin (unnatural behavior), but is instead a genetic predisposition that is natural. Does God not even know what predispositions He programmed into some of us? It looks like the Bible is in error, and we have finally falsified it! Or have we?

Studies have abounded recently in search of a genetic link to sexual orientation, but none have found such a link so far which do not have huge methodological questions about them, such as a UCLA study done with woefully little data.[346] A recently published study is one of the few designed specifically to look at sexual orientation with modern genetic tools. This study, led by Alan Sanders at Chicago's North Shore University Health System Research Institute, directly compared about 2,000 homosexual and heterosexual men in order to find genetic differences between them. They didn't find much. Their results found no definite link and were inconclusive.[347]

The bottom line of a perusal of the research data is that there has not been established a scientific link between genetics and our sexual orientation other than the natural "plumbing designs," which make us a male or female, and the presence, or not, of Y chromosomes. There has been a huge amount of investigation in this field for more than the last twenty-five years, but to date, no conclusive scientific evidence that "gayness or transgenderism" is anything more than lifestyle choices and not genetic predispositions.

But the public has heard that this is all "settled science." It must be true that some people are preprogrammed by their genes to be gay, doesn't it?

I have two degrees in education and have taught both math and science now for more than thirty-nine years. No phrase makes me bristle more, nor want to have a violent reaction more than someone who claims this or that is "settled science." There is no such thing! Any politician or speaker who claims such a thing is showing their ignorance on the subject and/or trying to claim expertise where they have none with little to back it up. Again, when we look at the data on this topic, nothing is settled!

But what about these medical and psychological associations which have voted to take stands against conversion therapy and for homosexuality being genetically predisposed? First, let's note that most of these endorsements on this topic by recognized medical associations are evaluating the effectiveness of conversion therapy on youngsters, not on the truth or evidence for a genetic link predisposing anyone to homosexuality. Second, please note that a vote by an association can be politically pressured and not reflect the truth of a situation, as appears to be the case here.

Also, note that even though the American Academy of Pediatrics (AAP) has voted that there is a genetic link to homosexual predisposition and that conversion therapy can be harmful and fruitless, there is also a significant subset of that group which said that the data does not support such a statement. They left the AAP and formed the "American College of Pediatricians" (ACP) so that their members did not have to support such an unfounded scientific position.[348] What we have here are examples of "consensus science."

The ultimate bad example of "consensus science" (when experts vote and the majority says something is true regardless of data) occurred about 400 years ago. At that time, almost all scientists and philosophers across the world, as well as all theologians, agreed that the observational data and the Bible showed that the sun revolved around the earth. Further, these "experts" held that the earth was the center of our solar system and perhaps the universe. Two men, Galileo Galilea and Nicholas Copernicus, had data showing the truth was the opposite; that, in fact, the Earth revolves around the sun and that the Earth is not at the center of our solar system.

It did not matter that Galileo and Copernicus were right. They were silenced. Galileo spent the end of his life on house arrest so that he would not spread his "blasphemous ideas."[349] The whole world except these two men and a very few of their associates were in agreement that the Earth is at the center of everything, and this was "settled science." But it wasn't.

Science, when done right, never tells us what will be true forever but tells us what our best evidence and best theories interpreting that data tell us about the universe around us *today*. Tomorrow we may get more data, or someone will come up with a more persuasive interpretation of the data changing our perception of what is really going on or what is true. **In science, it is never settled!**

Thus, what we know from common sense, and science, is that men and women are constructed differently, both physiologically and psychologically. Men produce sperm, and women hold the eggs to be fertilized with a pre-constructed womb to develop a fertilized egg. Genetically, women have about 60 million more nucleotide base pairs (computer codes) in their genomes than males. (My wife loves hearing that, in that, it tells her that she is a "more complex being" than I am.) Sexual reproduction with humans can only occur between the union of two people of the opposite sex.

The Bible recognizes these very basic and real differences between the sexes. It says this is the way God designed us. It says in the Bible, what has been the truth for almost all cultures throughout the history of man that marriage is to between a man and woman for the progress and support of the society. Homosexuality and transgenderism have almost always been marked as deviant behavior.

It is not just the Bible that is oft misquoted on this subject, but plain research on homosexual activities is often misquoted, twisted, or misunderstood, which has muddied the waters. Kinsey reported some 60 years ago that the population of gays in this country was 10 percent. That figure would make them a large subset of our culture and much larger than anyone had thought. We now know from further research that this study was in error.

Kinsey and Masters studied the orientation of prison populations which are around 10 percent homosexual. However, more recent studies have shown the actual homosexual population in the U.S. to be 2.8 percent male homosexuals and 1.4 percent lesbians for an average of 2.1 percent homosexuals as a part of our total population, or something more than 6 million homosexuals in America today (another study puts this number of gays at 3.8 percent and about 9 million gays). Incidentally, these numbers are twice what is reported from Australia, England, and Canada, which all report homosexual orientations of just above 1 percent.[350]

While this is a large number, it is far from every fourth or fifth person in a group perception that Hollywood and TV have been portraying to us for the past 40 years. Indeed it is this intentional misperception fostered by the movie and TV media over the past 40 years of gays being everywhere and acceptable which has led to a *molded attitude* in our culture today. Thus encouraging us to ignore not just biblical statutes but societal norms, social history, science, and common sense.

Homosexual behavior has been abhorred and unlawful in western civilizations for almost 2000 years. The reasons for this are numerous. Part of it refers back to western civilization's dependence on the Bible for its codes of conduct. But there is far more to these gay prohibitions than that. Kinsey's and Master's work with prison populations shows us that while only about 2 percent of Americans are homosexual, that 10 percent of our prison populations are homosexual. This means these people are five times more likely to be incarcerated than the average American. This tendency of people who ignore societal norms to practice homosexuality is also expressed in terms of other deviant and illegal activities in our societies, which we naturally try to eliminate.

The great cultures of the past, such as the Greeks and Romans, did not start out with open homosexuality as their norm. But their cultures degenerated into such open homosexual behaviors as their cultures lost any sense of right and wrong and then stagnated and died or imploded. I am afraid we are playing out that same sad show in western societies today, as has happened so many times through history. Our Supreme Court, in sustaining gay marriage, had to ignore 1700 years of common law in western civilizations. They also ignored the fact that such a right, as Supreme Court Chief Justice John Roberts stated in his dissent, "is a right found nowhere in the constitution." That decision goes against the very soul of our society and marks a plunge into degradation never before seen in our country.

The Russian culture seems vehemently homophobic, as demonstrated by their negative and unwelcome responses to homosexuals coming to the Olympics there. The underpinnings of this anti-homosexual tendency in Russia is a practical one, however, and not biblical, which we should not miss. Russians have for centuries been faced with the challenge of inhabiting a vast land area. To tame and control so much land, they must have a large population. You do not produce more people through homosexual relations, but less. Thus, their stance against homosexuality is merely a practical one, which may lead us back to the reason God set things up as He did in the first place. Marriage was originally set up between a man and a woman so that we could fill and subdue the Earth. Homosexuality subverts that goal.

Further, psychological studies have shown that kids grow up best and with the most normal psyches when they are raised by two loving parents of the opposite sex. (Children from two-parent families are better off emotionally, socially, and economically, according to a review of marriage research released in the article "The Future of Children," a journal published jointly by the non-partisan Brookings Institution and Princeton University's Woodrow Wilson School.) Both sexes, it seems, bring something different to the table in terms of nurturing and development. This is another characteristic of God's natural design, which we are ignoring in western civilization today when we become accepting of gays as natural and single-parent homes as the new normal.

Many would claim that homosexuality is an orientation "built into" a person by their genetic makeup, which we showed earlier is a position with no scientific basis for claiming as yet. Dr. Georgia Purdom and others have debunked this claim as "junk science." These ideas feed into a mindset we see a lot of today, in which humanists espouse that man is essentially good. Thus, if we are doing something bad, whether it be theft, rape, or homosexuality, then we are genetically predisposed to it or have a diseased mind and are not responsible for our actions.

We do not accept such "junk science" in the realm of murder, theft, rape, burglary, or a host of other sins. But there are those in society today who want us to "buy into" this idea for homosexuality in spite of no compelling science for it. The reason for this is clear. This mindset is divorced from the biblical worldview, which says we have a "fallen" mind and that sin rules us. Those who espouse homosexuality as "natural" in no way wish to accept that instead of being intrinsically good, that man is intrinsically bad because of our sinful nature. This is another form of rebellion from the Creator and the authority of God's Word.

Contrary to current propaganda, research in the animal kingdom coincides with what the Bible, as common sense, would tell us. While homosexual relations occur in the animal kingdom, they are rare and are almost never in the form of a homosexual orientation, but an aberration that does not benefit the species.[351] This research underscores the biblical perspective of homosexual relations as not being natural.

Further, Deuteronomy 22:5 specifically speaks to the very contemporary issue of transgenderism. This verse makes it clear that it is an **"abomination to God"** for men or women to cross-dress or try and assume a sexual orientation other than that designed into them at conception. This corresponds with the scientific biological data we have on this issue at this time as well. A man can change his outward appearance to that of a woman, but he still has sixty-trillion cells in his body, which contain a Y-chromosome which says otherwise.[352]

For a youngster, who is confused as to their sexuality to undergo transgender transition, three things must occur. They must take drugs to inhibit the advance of puberty, which also stunts their natural growth and development. They must be given opposite sex hormones for the rest of their lives, which their bodies were not designed for, and which have unbelievably deleterious effects such as susceptibility to cancers, coronary heart disease, thyroid diseases, and more. The final stage of this transition involves surgical mutilation of the body to make it more resemble sex which the DNA in every cell of that person's body says it is not.

One other effect of both the drugs and the surgery is *sterility in all cases.* No womb or eggs are ever formed or inserted into a male transitioning to female, and no functioning testicles in female transitioning to a male. What is really tragic about this whole issue is that with normal counseling and time given to the youth through puberty, 95% of those children who experience "gender confusion" resolve this in favor of their designed gender by the end of puberty if they are allowed to and properly supported.[353]

In conclusion, it would seem that the Bible is not debunked scientifically by its consistent prohibitions of homosexual and transsexual behaviors. It is certainly out of step with our society, as it is on many issues today and unapologetically so. What we have found from research is that there is no credible scientific data to dispute the Bible's claims that we were designed from the very creation to be heterosexual and that any other activities are deviant and mutated from our design.

Seed of Woman

Genesis 3:15 (KJV) says, **"And I will put enmity between thee and the woman, and between thy seed and *her seed*; it shall bruise thy head, and thou shalt bruise his heel."**

This verse is called the "proto-evangelism" in that it is the first verse theologians view as a metaphorical Messianic prophecy (i.e., "the seed of woman shall bruise the serpent's (Satan's) head"). But more to the biological point is that read literally, it says that there is a human seed in women. Biologically this is substantiated in that for human reproduction to occur, the male's semen mixes with a female's egg, each contributing 23 chromosomes of genetic information.

What is fascinating about this is that the ancient view of a woman's womb for more than two millennia was that her womb was nothing more than a glorified incubator. At the time of Moses' writing of Genesis, it was wrongly thought the seed of the human babies was contributed only by the male. That his seed alone was what was being incubated and nurtured in the woman's womb (no fertilization). This view will hold for more than a thousand years as Pythagoras in the 6th century BC will specifically express this same "male seed only" thesis. No doubt there were some misogynistic biases that supported this view. The discovery of the human female ovum and eggs will not occur until the 19th and 20th centuries AD.[354]

If you want to get an awesome set of facts that will astound you, research the process of how a human baby is part of the developmental process, as the baby's hormones direct actions within the mother. This is quite contrary to long-held beliefs that these processes were somehow preprogrammed into the mother.

Dr. Randy Guliuzza (both a medical doctor and an engineer), in his books and presentations, discusses the miracle of the placental barrier. This barrier protects the baby from the mother's immune system but still allows for the baby to be fed and oxygenated through it. Every attribute and detail of the baby is meticulously designed — to the minute functioning of the baby's hemoglobin, which has a far greater affinity for oxygen than does the mother's hemoglobin. Thus, it can literally snatch oxygen away from the mother's red blood cells as they pass each other in the placenta.

Further, the design of the baby's heart is miraculously fitted with a one-way valve, which allows backward blood flow when the baby is in the womb and reverses blood flow direction at birth. This is just one feature of the process, which enables the baby to live in amniotic fluid, yet receive oxygen through the placenta. The precise events at birth required to transform the baby from a life form living in liquid to an air-breathing life form are miraculous indeed and happen in an instant. These complex and sequenced events must be tightly synchronized so that the one-way valve is forever closed by muscles designed solely for this purpose, all the while redirecting blood flow to the lungs as the baby emerges and takes its first breath. Purposeful and planned, this awe-inspiring wonder is taken for granted today.[355]

How did Genesis get all of this right when none of it is discovered by man for over 3300 years?

The First Woman

While we are talking about a woman's seed. Let's talk about the very first woman. In *Genesis 3:20* (ESV), we read, **"And Adam called his wife's name Eve, because she was the mother of all living."** What about the whole thing of Adam and Eve? Were there really two first people created by God, or is that all a myth? Many evolutionists will tell you it's all a myth since they believe man evolved from the apes, and some form of hominid (ape-man or man) has been around for millions of years.

An interesting piece of evidence is in mitochondrial DNA (mtDNA), which shows that all humans (all the so-called races) came from the same primordial woman (this is called the "Eve Syndrome" in modern science). Not from several races, nor from several "Eves." Anthropologists used to suggest that as many as five races of people evolved from five different groups of African apes long ago. But that theory is now on the wane as this evidence from our DNA shows that we all have come from one first woman, just as the Bible said we did.[356]

A morphed picture has been created using a composite of a million young women's pictures morphed (averaged) together so that we see what the average woman across the globe would look like. There are several interesting things about this picture. The first thing that hits me when I look at it is that she is beautiful. That makes sense from a biblical perspective for a couple of reasons. If God made us, then He likely would have made His creations beautiful, or at least appear so to each other. Such appearances are the basis for sexual attraction because if we were to **"multiply and fill the earth"** as God directed in Genesis, then we would need to be attracted to one another.[357]

Second, scientific studies show that the most viable of any set of related species is the least differentiated. In the dog breeds, it is not the collie, or the dachshund, the sheltie, nor the german shepherd, which is most fit, but the "basic mutt" is the healthiest of all dogs. This is true simply because it has not been "inbred" as all of these "pure breeds" were to give them their distinctive characteristics. Such inbreeding limits a species, exaggerating traits they have but also making them lose the ability to exhibit other traits since they are eliminated from their DNA. In humans, the pure breeds are the product of what we would call incest. As we all know, incest does not lead to generally better offspring but often to ones that are tragically deceased.[358]

It appears that God, in His infinite wisdom, attracted us to the average (genetically speaking). That is what we call beautiful, and that is what we aspire to mate with. Not the pure breeds which genetically would be less fit to survive. In this, we see a beautiful marriage between science and God's intentions for us to populate the earth and God's appreciation of beauty, which He programmed into us!

Some people will speculate that this picture, which represents the average of worldwide female DNA, would somehow look like

Eve since it represents the composite of Eve's original DNA. Unfortunately, that is probably not true for a couple of reasons.

This probably does not precisely resemble the original Eve, even though our mitochondrial DNA says we all came from one original woman. Remember, if the Bible is true, then humanity started over with the eight people who survived the flood by means of Noah's Ark. Thus if anyone, the whole world's DNA and this picture might represent the average of what the wives of Noah's sons and Noah's wife looked like.

This, too, is improbable since DNA research shows that as we have offspring, each generation will vary in terms of different alleles (variations within the genes that cause different skin color, hair color, height, etc.) along with mutations that do filter into each generation to the tune of anywhere between two to one hundred mutations of base-pair codes per generation. This research shows that after ten generations, there is very little if any resemblance between parent and the tenth generation great-grandson or great-granddaughter in their line.[359] Thus, even though we are all descended from Noah and Eve, it is unlikely we look like them.

What is instructive in this photo besides her beauty, which probably does resemble Eve and Noah's wife, are her neutral features. She is not white nor black. Eve would have had in her DNA the vast diversity of skin colors, hair colors, sizes, facial features, height, and so many more attributes which have all differentiated since Eve to give us all the people groups and the more than seven billion individuals we see in the world today.

Evidence that We Were Created and Did Not Evolve from Chimps

The Bible says we were specially created by God and that the kinds are fixed so that only humans produce humans; chimpanzees produce chimps and rhinos. This is at odds with the current evolutionary hypothesis, which says that we evolved such that minute changes over long periods of time allowed fish to turn into amphibians, amphibians into reptiles, reptiles into birds, and mammals, and mammals into man.

Current DNA research supports the Bible's account and not evolution's story. It has often been said that chimp DNA is only about 1 percent different from human DNA, which was evidence touted to support the evolutionary thesis. But these results came from flawed experimental procedures with huge false assumptions. Further research in the past decade has shown this not to be true. Current research by Dr. Jeffrey Tompkins shows we are between 15 percent and 30 percent different from chimps in our DNA. The techniques used to say that we were only 1 percent different were highly questionable and did not meet good scientific standards in view of the ENCODE results.

A 15 percent difference between us and chimps means that in a few million years, our DNA had to have changed by about 400-million positive mutations transforming chimp DNA into ours. The current mutation rates within our DNA (measured between 2 and 100 mutations per generation) show that there is no way this could occur in that period of time, even if every mutation were positive. And that calculation assumes that each of the 100 mutations in each generation was positive.[360] In truth, mutations (DNA copying mistakes) are almost never positive; thus, the idea that random mutations could change chimps into humans in even three billion years is impossible!

If evolution were true, then our DNA should be filled mostly with random DNA codes and only a few which truly code for living chemical structures. This, again, seemed to be the case when research published over the last few decades reported that 98 percent of our DNA was what was called "junk DNA," which fit well into the evolutionary narrative. However, the ENCODE research published in 2007 in the journal *Nature* has blown all of that previous thought away. This research verified that at least 80 percent of our DNA is coded with operative information and not useless junk. The researchers further concluded that with more research, they expected to find that essentially 100 percent of the DNA is coded with such useful information.[361] This research is right in line with the biblical narrative of our being specially designed but is at odds with the evolutionary hypothesis.

The DNA in our cells is information coded with four-dimensional chemical codes, more complex than computer codes. Computer scientists will tell you that coded information does not happen by chance, and neither is it communicated by chance, not in computers, nor within organelles within a cell, nor within organs of the body. Our DNA simply screams that it was designed by a Creator far more intelligent than we are!

The First Man

The Bible says, **"Wherefore, as by one man, sin entered into the world, and death by sin; and so, death passed upon all men, for that all have sinned"** (*Romans 5:12, KJV*). We also read in *1 Corinthians 15:45* that Adam was **"the first man."** God did not start by making a race of men. Both of these scriptures agree with the book of Genesis, which says we all came from a first man. Amazingly, just like the *Eve Syndrome* was discovered in female mitochondrial DNA, there is DNA evidence that we came from a single first man, just as the Bible says we did. Human DNA is composed of 46 collections or strands of the DNA molecule called chromosomes. The "Y" chromosome determines male sexuality, among other things. "Y" chromosome analysis shows we all came from *one original man, as the Bible claims!*[362] One thing to be clear within this data is the Y-chromosome data shows we all came from one original male, but genetically that probably was not Adam, but Noah from which this Y-Chromosome data is pointing to.

A morphed picture has been constructed showing what the average of a million young males from across the world looks like. We find the same things in this picture that we did in the female morphed picture. He is very attractive to us. Thus, it appears we are programmed to be attracted to what is the average DNA structure.

His skin color and features are neither black nor white. He is in the middle (average) of all these. Again, this picture probably does not exactly resemble either Adam or Noah, but it does probably show both of their general appearances since their DNA would have contained the genetic potential for all the variety we see in the world today.

Noah's Daughters In-law

There is one additional thing that may have been found in our DNA that corresponds to the biblical account. Analysis of female DNA from all over the world may indicate *three types* or classifications of Mitochondrial DNA. This suggests that the whole human race was produced from three intermediary women after the initial human woman referred to as Eve.

The Bible says that the human race was repopulated, after the worldwide flood, by the offspring of the three sons of Noah. Is it just accidental that the Bible got this genetic anomaly right, which has only been discovered in the last twenty years? This DNA evidence gives unheard-of evidence supporting the biblical account that the **three wives** of Noah's sons restarted the human race![363]

Genetics Agrees with the Bible to an Amazing Extent!

So, what does the most up-to-date DNA evidence show us? Modern mitochondrial DNA evidence tells us that we all came from the first human woman ("Eve Syndrome"). Further analysis of this same mitochondrial DNA shows that there may be three types of mitochondrial DNA, which exactly corresponds to what we would predict if the biblical account were true! Analysis of "Y" chromosome DNA in males all over the world reveals that we all came from a single first man. The differences between human and ape/chimp DNA are so large that it is clear we did not evolve from them. How could the Bible have gotten all this right over three thousand years ago, when we have only discovered this in complex genetic structures in the last few years?

Goat and Sheep DNA and the Bible

DNA testing has shown that all living goats are descended from five original female goats.[364] Normally, according to the evolutionary hypothesis, there should have been one original female, which had the complete set of mutations, variations, and special genetic markers which make the original goat species come about. Why, then, should there be, in both goat and sheep species, three to five original and distinct DNA types? Why multiple original pairs, and not from one original goat or sheep as evolution would have expected? Fortunately, the Bible has the answer!

God instructed Noah to take seven pairs of each type of "clean" animal on board the ark in order to have animals for sacrifice after the flood receded, as well as to repopulate the Earth. These animals may also have been used to provide food after the flood, as the earth was repopulated with plants and animals. Thus, from the biblical account, we would not expect all modern breeds of sheep and goats to be traced back to only one original pair of sheep or goats, but something less than seven pairs.

Possibly, Noah sacrificed two pairs of goats and two or three pairs of sheep after the flood, or two or three lines of each species became extinct between then and now (a very reasonable and expected conjecture). Or one of these original female lines could have been lost due to disease or accident shortly after the flood. All sheep and goats in the world today descended from the remaining animals carry these sets of DNA markers.

Thus, DNA testing of sheep and goats exactly matches what would be expected if the Bible and the worldwide flood actually occurred, and are in fact, literal historical reality. Again, and again we find that the Bible is the only truly accurate source of truth for such ancient historical knowledge.[365]

Does the Bible show its Ignorance and Error in the account of Jacob and the Spotted Sheep in Genesis 29-31?

If you were in Sunday School as a child, you heard the account in Genesis chapters 29 through 31 of Jacob, who came into the camp of Laban and wanted to marry his younger daughter Rachel. Jacob asked for Rachel's hand in marriage from Laban and promised to work for Laban for seven years to have her as his wife. As you might recall, at the end of the seven years of Jacob's service to Laban, a wedding was planned, and Leah, Rachel's older sister, was substituted under veil to marry Jacob. It was their custom (unbeknownst to Jacob) that the older daughter must marry before the younger could.

Jacob, very understandably, was angry and tells Laban he has wronged him. But Laban pacifies him by promising him Rachel as his wife after seven days of the wedding feast being concluded if Jacob will work seven more years for him. At the end of those second set of seven years, Jacob decides to take his wives and children and return to his homeland. But if he does, Laban will lose his daughters, grandchildren, and a son-in-law, who profited him greatly. So, they make this deal for Jacob to stay… Jacob says to Laban…

> Let me go through all your flocks today and remove from them every **speckled or spotted sheep,** every dark-colored lamb and every spotted or speckled goat. They will be my wages. And my honesty will testify for me in the future, whenever you check on the wages you have paid me. Any goat in my possession that is not speckled or spotted, or any lamb that is not dark-colored, will be considered stolen." "Agreed," said Laban. "Let it be as you have said." That same day he removed all the male goats that were streaked or spotted, and all the speckled or spotted female goats (all that had white on them) and all the dark-colored lambs, and he placed them in the care of his sons. Then he put a three-day journey between himself and Jacob, while Jacob continued to tend the rest of Laban's flocks. Jacob, however, took fresh-cut branches from poplar, almond and plane trees and made white stripes on them by peeling

the bark and exposing the white inner wood of the branches. **Then he placed the peeled branches in all the watering troughs, so that they would be directly in front of the flocks when they came to drink.** When the flocks were in heat and came to drink, they mated in front of the branches. **And they bore young that were streaked or speckled or spotted.** Jacob set apart the young of the flock by themselves, but made the rest face the streaked and dark-colored animals that belonged to Laban. Thus, he made separate flocks for himself and did not put them with Laban's animals. **Whenever the stronger females were in heat, Jacob would place the branches in the troughs in front of the animals, so they would mate near the branches,** but if the animals were weak, he would not place them there. So, the weak animals went to Laban and the strong ones to Jacob.

Genesis 30-42 (NIV)

It seems clear in this section that following God's directions, Jacob placed a striped rod in front of strong-bearing mothers to supposedly induce them to produce spotted and speckled offspring. This is often cited by Bible skeptics as a biblical error, which reflects the Lamarckian myth of scaring mothers and thereby affecting their offspring. But Genesis 31 shows this is probably not what was done.

Laban had been treating Jacob badly, making him work 14-years in return for lying to him and changing his wages ten times. In a dream, which Jacob recounts in chapter 31, it tells of Jacob seeing future generations of sheep producing inordinate amounts of speckled and spotted offspring (the product of a double recessive gene set, which is rare).

The main contention against this biblical account is that it is a myth that genetics can be affected by external forces like scaring the mother. However, epigenetics, a fairly new field of study, has shown that such external effects upon genomes do occur. It turns out that ours and the genomes of other living things have built-in "environment checking" sensors, which, if triggered, moves the DNA to reconfigure itself to adapt to the new environment. So even though this particular type of genetic manipulation with a striped rod has been found ineffective over the years, it is not out of the realm of possibility that sheep at that time possessed just such an environmental check in their DNA programming. This would have allowed Jacob to manage the products of the next generation, and God gave him instructions on how to do it.

The account of the dream Jacob had from God makes this unlikely, however. The dream suggests that God foresaw what the future generations of this stock of sheep would be and transmitted that to Jacob. This could only be done by an entity, who could read the genetic code in sheep and see how they would recombine after mating or could alter the genetics within newborns. The foretelling of how genes will recombine upon mating is beyond our capabilities today. The ability to manipulate genes to produce certain characteristics is a field we are only today making our first forays into, with very mixed results.

Thus, assuming the account is true, we are left with four possibilities of what happened here genetically.

1. It could be that Jacob had a random vision and that no god was ever involved, and the striped rods had no effect upon the sheep mothers. This would mean that by pure random chance, the next generations were heavily populated by the rare speckled and spotted variety, which allowed him to get a prosperous flock of his own. The odds are very much against this. His even asking for such a thing as an experienced keeper of flocks would have been completely illogical.

2. It could be, as epigenetics has shown, that the sheep of that time were programmed in their DNA to react to the striped rod, which affected their offspring's appearance. If true, this would show that the "wives' tales" of affecting mothers of

many species by "scaring" them while gestating or before impregnation used to be possible in some species. We are finding today that environmental cues can alter DNA functions and might support this interpretation. However, the fact that this proves not to be operative in sheep genetics today, as well as the reading of chapter 31 that God foresaw the next generation's products, tends to dismiss epigenetic answers here.

3. It could have been that God foresaw the genetic makeup of the next generation already in gestation inside their mother's wombs and how the next generation after that would combine. God then told Jacob what he would need to select to prosper.

4. It is also possible that God did genetic manipulation either within the wombs of the mothers or manipulated the insemination process to produce the rare speckled and spotted offspring. Both of these last two possibilities mesh best with the chapter 31 account, but they are not necessarily naturalistic. They are "God things," which we resist since we are inculcated in our schooling to always look for naturalistic answers.

Well, what if either possibility 3 or 4 are true. Why would God instruct Jacob to place these striped rods in front of the mothers, which would have no effect on them? The answer to that is to show Jacob, who had done this for him. He was following God's instructions when he placed the striped rods; thus, the product of the inordinately speckled and spotted generations which were produced would be unmistakably associated by Jacob with following God's instructions and God's action.

This is very analogous to the blood sacrifices that man was instructed to do all through the Old Testament. These blood sacrifices in no way cleansed or saved their souls but showed they were following God's instructions and were foreshadowing the one blood sacrifice which would be necessary for their deliverance. The blood sacrifice of Jesus Christ.

Thus, this whole section of scripture is not by necessity in error and may point to epigenetic traits we did not know about or an intervention by God which is unrelated to the striped rods. We, too, often in biblical apologetics, try to dismiss all miracles in favor of finding naturalistic answers due to our upbringing in our secular schools. However, it would be good for us to remember that just by creating the universe and ourselves, God performed miracles we cannot duplicate. Thus we need always to allow room for God inserting a miracle or two into our reality as He sees fit!

Physical Laws of Nature

If God does exist, and the Bible is His writing, then it stands to reason that the laws of nature and science will be consistent with what we find in the Bible. The following sections show how the laws of nature and the cosmos are well described and very consistent with the biblical accounts.

Laws of Thermodynamics

First Law of Thermodynamics

A fascinating truth is that the laws of thermodynamics, on which our chemistry and physics are founded, are described in the Bible. Also, the Bible shows that it firmly believes that these are laws of nature. However, these laws run counter to the theory of evolution, and this sets up a real contradiction in many supposedly scientific assumptions about both.

The first law of thermodynamics says that "Matter is neither created nor destroyed by normal chemical means." In simple terms, this means that things don't just pop into or out of existence. If something is formed, it is formed out of substances already in existence, not "out of thin air."[366] What is interesting here is how well the Bible not only identifies this fundamental law of nature but signifies over and over again its belief in the universality of this law of science.

Psalms 148:5-6 (NKJV) says, "**..He commanded and they were** *created.* **He also** *established them forever and ever;* **He has made a decree which** *shall not pass away.*"

Ecclesiastes 1:9-10 (NASB) says it this way, "*What has been is what will be,* **and what has been done is what will be done;** *there is nothing new under the sun.* **Can one say about anything, "Look, this is new"?** *It has already existed in the ages before us.*"

Second Peter 3:4-7 (KJV) says, "**...all things** *continue* **as they were from the beginning of creation.**"

These scriptures, and many others like them in the Bible, not only reveal that the Bible believes in the first law of thermodynamics but fully understood this was a law of nature two thousand years before it was discovered and codified by modern science.

Now, in science, a law is supposed to be a time-tested rule which is in effect for all places and instances in our observed universe. However, this law is said not to have been in effect at the creation of our universe according to modern science, since the "Big Bang theory" violates this first law of thermodynamics. The Big Bang says that in an instant, all of the matter and energy in the entire universe came into being out of nothing! I find it interesting how the Bible understood the first law thousands of years ahead of modern scientists. Further, the Bible also makes statements consistent with the first law, which we observe every day in nature. Contrast that to the theoretical physicists, who speculate about a time, billions of years ago, when they theorize this law may not have ruled the cosmos.

What is of real interest to me is that the Big Bang is mostly a disconnected set of speculations. Science is supposed to be about what we can observe, replicate, and prove experimentally of what we see in nature. Not what we can dream up! What we have always observed in nature is the operation of the first law. That is science, and the Bible agrees with science in this. Why would we think that the Big Bang could violate such a law, which is so universally proved every day?

The Bible Knew of the Second Law as well!

The second law of thermodynamics says that everything goes from a state of order to disorder. The scientific term for this effect is called "*entropy*," which means that everything we see in all the universe is **wearing out** and going from states of greater order to greater disorder.[367] Again, it is interesting to see how the Bible fully understood this law of science thousands of years ago.

Genesis 3:17-19 (KJV) says that because of sin, "**cursed is the ground** ... both thorns and thistles shall it bring forth ... In the sweat of your face you shall eat bread till you return to the ground."

In the New Testament, Romans 8:19-23 (KJV) says, "The creation was subjected to **futility**...because the creation itself also will be delivered from the bondage of **corruption**." The word corruption from Greek means this same concept of entropy or wearing out.

Psalms 102: 25-27 (NKJV) says, "Earth, and the Heavens... **grow old like a garment...**" There could not be a much better description of the effects of entropy and the second law.

Again, it is striking how the Bible could so graphically describe a law of nature not fully understood or codified three thousand years ahead of science. Equally as striking is how the Bible again has more reverence for this law of nature than do scientists of our day.

We all have experienced this law of nature. Our cars wear out over time, as do our clothes, our wristwatches, our bodies, the paint on our house, and yes, everything we know of wears out. This is what we observe, and that is good science, with a wealth of observations to back it up. Thus it is said to be a "law of nature." However, the theory of evolution contradicts this basic and fundamental law of everything we see. While the Bible and the second law say that everything in the entire universe is wearing out, evolution says that instead of becoming more disorderly, matter and all living things are becoming more orderly. This exception because they are being injected with outside energy (usually from the sun). That instead of wearing out and becoming disorderly, things are becoming more complex. That is not what we observe in nature or in our own lives. In this case, again, the Bible is more empirical, more grounded, and committed to scientific observation than man of our modern theoretical scientists!

Physical Laws are Constant

Some theorists will argue that the physical laws of nature may not be immutable (same everywhere and for all time). However, there is almost no data to support this conjecture. The Force of Gravity, the Laws of Thermodynamics, Inertia, the speed of light, these and many other "laws of nature" and therefore our known universe are deemed by modern science to have constancy. The observations we have to date say the universe's physical laws do not change but can be counted on as things that work in the same way throughout the observed universe and do not change over time.

Most conclusions and calculations done in physical, chemical, biological, and astronomical sciences are based upon an assumption of these scientific laws being constants.[368]

This, however, has not always been the case. As recently as a hundred years ago, a prevalent theory for the creation of the universe was what was called the "steady state" theory. It posited that somewhere in space, the laws of physics were different, such that the first law of thermodynamics (which says that matter does not just "pop" into existence out of nothing) did not exist, or was changed such that matter (e.g., hydrogen atoms) were simply popping into existence from nothing.

The current "Big Bang" cosmology does not rely on such an eternal and localized exception for the laws of nature (although it does depend on a very temporary exception).[369]

Job 38:33 says, "Do you know the **laws that govern the heavens**, and can you make them rule the earth?" (Contemporary English Version)

Jeremiah 31:35-36 (NIV) says:

> This is what the LORD says, he who **appoints** the sun to shine by day, who **decrees** the moon and stars to shine by night, who **stirs** up the sea so that its waves roar-- the LORD Almighty is his name: Only if these **decrees** vanish from my sight," declares the LORD, "will Israel ever cease being a nation before me." declares the LORD.

Ecclesiastes 1:9-10 (NIV) says:

> **What has been will be again, what has been done will be done again; there is nothing new under the sun.** Is there anything of which one can say, "Look! This is something new"? **It was here already, long ago; it was here before our time.**

Psalm 119:160 (NIV) says, "All your words are true; all your righteous **laws are eternal**."

Psalm 119:89-90 (ESV) says, **"Forever, O Lord, *your word is firmly fixed in the heavens*. Your faithfulness endures to all generations; you have established the earth, and it stands fast."**

The first five verses in Psalms 148 talk of the heavens (universe), the stars, the sun, the moon, and then says in Psalm 148:6 (KJV), "He has also **established them forever and ever; He has made a decree which will not pass away."**

These verses and dozens more describe a universe where there are unchanging laws that govern its makeup and motions. These verses are meant to tell us about the unchanging nature of God, but they also tell us that a God of that character established rules for his creation that are immutable. They will not change with time and place, and that is what we have observed to be true in this universe. How did the Bible know thousands of years ago that all of the universe was governed by unchanging and immutable laws when we have only decided this to be true in the last century?

The Constancy of Universal Laws

The Bible says in Genesis 1:1 that God created the heavens and the Earth. Also, in the Bible, Jeremiah 33:25 (ESV) says, **"Thus says the Lord: 'If My covenant is not with day and night, and if I have not appointed the ordinances of heaven and earth…."** If God created everything and gave it all ordinances (laws), then the Bible says they must be constant and unwavering. Let's see what we find in the physical laws of the universe we live in.

In nature, we find a **Law of Biogenesis** which states life will always come from life, which is the most verified observation in all of biology[370] and which we have defined in depth in this chapter.

Science teacher Karl Dahlstrom says, "Life requires specific chemistry. Our bodies are powered by chemical reactions and depend on the laws of chemistry operating in a uniform fashion. Even the information that makes up any living being is stored on a long molecule called DNA. Life as we know it would not be possible if the laws of chemistry were different. God created the laws of chemistry in just the right way, so that life would be possible."[371]

The **laws of chemistry** give different properties to the various elements (each made of one type of atom) and compounds (made up of two or more types of atoms that are bonded together) in the universe. For example, when given sufficient activation energy, the lightest element (hydrogen) will react with oxygen to form water. Water itself has some interesting properties, such as the ability to hold an unusually large amount of heat energy. When frozen, water forms crystals with six-sided symmetry (which is why snowflakes are generally six-sided). Contrast this with salt (sodium chloride) crystals, which tend to form cubes. It is the six-fold symmetry of water ice that causes "holes" in its crystal, making it less dense than its own liquid. That's why ice floats in water (whereas essentially, all other solid compounds sink in their own liquid).[372] This property of water, ice floating, is not trivial, for if ice constantly sank, it would make it impossible for seas and freshwater creatures to live in our waters year-round.

The properties of elements and compounds are not arbitrary. In fact, the elements can be logically organized into a periodic table based on their physical properties. Substances in the same column on the table tend to have similar properties. This follows because elements in a vertical column have the same outer electron structures. These outermost electrons determine the physical characteristics of the atom. The periodic table did not happen by chance. Atoms and molecules have their various properties because their electrons are bound by the laws of physics. In other words, chemistry is based on physics. If the properties of atoms were just a bit different, atoms might not even be possible. God designed the laws of physics just right so that the laws of chemistry would come out the way He wanted them to.[373]

There are **laws to planetary motion** which keep the planets orbiting our sun, our Earth in its habitable zone, and keep our very beneficial moon in just the right orbit to support life on Earth. If these laws of physics were not constant, we could not exist for long. Neither could we send rockets to the moon, Mars, nor other planets as our calculations for these expeditions are always based on the immutable laws of motion, physics, and gravitation, which have never been found to vary within our solar system.[374]

Physics describes the behavior of the universe at its most fundamental level. There are many different **laws of physics**. They describe the way the universe operates today. Some laws of physics describe how light propagates, how energy is transported, how gravity operates, how mass moves through space, and many other phenomena. The laws of physics are usually mathematical in nature. Some laws of physics can be described with a concise formula, such as $E=mc^2$. The simple formula $F=ma$ shows how an object with mass (m) will accelerate (a) when a net force (F) is applied to it. It is amazing that every object in the universe consistently obeys these rules.[375]

Notice that the laws of physics are mathematical in nature. They would not be decipherable to us if there were not also **laws of mathematics**. Mathematical laws and principles include the rules of addition, the transitive property, the commutative properties of addition and multiplication, the binomial theorem, and many others. Like the laws of physics, some laws and properties of mathematics can be derived from other mathematical principles. But unlike the laws of physics, the laws of mathematics are abstract; they are not "attached" to any specific part of the universe. It is possible to imagine a universe where the laws of physics are different, but it is difficult to imagine a (consistent) universe where the laws of mathematics are different.

The laws of mathematics are an example of a "transcendent truth." They must be true regardless of what kind of universe God created. This may be because God's nature is logical and mathematical. Thus, any universe He chose to create would necessarily be mathematical in nature. The secular naturalist cannot account for the laws of mathematics. Certainly, he would believe in mathematics and would use mathematics. But he is unable to account for the existence of mathematics within a naturalistic framework since mathematics is not a part of the physical universe. However, the Christian understands that there is a God beyond the universe and that mathematics reflects the thoughts of the Lord. Understanding math is, in a sense, "thinking God's thoughts after Him" (though in a limited, finite way, of course).

Some have supposed that mathematics is a human invention. It is said that if human history had been different, an entirely different form of math would have been constructed, one with alternate laws, theorems, axioms, etc. But such thinking is not consistent. Are we to believe that the universe did not obey mathematical laws before people discovered them? Did the planets orbit differently before Kepler discovered that $p^2=a^3$? Clearly, mathematical laws are something that human beings have discovered, not invented. The only thing that might have been different (had human history taken a different course) is the notation. The way in which we choose to express mathematical truths through symbols or the base system we chose. But these truths exist regardless of how they are expressed. Mathematics could rightly be called the "language of creation."

The laws of nature are uniform. They do not arbitrarily change, and they apply throughout the whole cosmos, as far as we can tell. The laws of nature will apply in the future, just as they have applied in the past; this is one of the most basic assumptions in all of science. Without this assumption, science would be impossible. If the laws of nature suddenly and arbitrarily changed tomorrow, then past experimental results would tell us nothing about the future. Why is it that we can depend on the laws of nature to apply consistently throughout time? The secular scientists cannot justify this important assumption.[376] It appears that the universe and the physical laws which govern all that we can attest to a fine tuner, a Creator, and a designer. This is good evidence for the biblical claim in Jeremiah 33:25 that God did set "the ordinances (laws)" of the universe and all that exists.

Anthropic Principle and Physical Constants

Closely related to the constancy of physical laws are seemingly arbitrary physical constants. These seem to operate everywhere in the known universe. It is well established that our existence in this universe depends on numerous "cosmological constants" whose numerical values must fall within an *incredibly narrow* range of values. If even a single one of these constants or parameters were off, even slightly, life could not exist here. The extreme improbability that so many quantities would align so precisely in our favor, merely by chance, has led some scientists and philosophers to propose instead that it was God who providentially engineered the universe to suit our specific needs. This is called the *Anthropic Principle*, which says the universe appears to have been fine-tuned for our existence.

What follows is just a partial listing of these fundamental constants which allow us to exist.

1. **The Strong Nuclear Force Coupling Constant.** This force holds together the particles in the nucleus of an atom. If the strong

nuclear force were slightly weaker, then multi-proton nuclei could not form because they would just fly apart due to the repulsion from like-charged protons. Hydrogen would be the only element in the universe. In such a case, life becomes impossible.

2. **The Electromagnetic Coupling Constant.** This force binds electrons (a lepton) to protons (a baryon) in an atom. The characteristics of the orbits of electrons about atomic nuclei determine what molecules can be formed as the atoms bind to each other. If the electromagnetic coupling constant were slightly smaller, then few electrons would be held in their orbit about the proton. If, on the other hand, the electromagnetic force were too large, then a proton would not "share" its electrons with other protons in other atoms, and molecules would not form. Either way, the molecules necessary for life could not form.

3. **The Ratio of Protons to Electrons.** Quite improbably, the number of electrons and protons that were created at the beginning of our universe almost exactly equaled each other to better than one part in 10^{37} (1 chance out of a number with 1 followed by 37 zeroes). If this had not balanced out almost exactly, then there would have been a prevalence of either electrons (net negativity) or protons (net positivity), and electromagnetism would have so overwhelmed gravity as a force that the formation of what we see in our universe would not have been possible.

4. **The Ratio of Electron to Proton Mass.** This particular ratio determines the characteristics of the orbit of the electron around the proton. A proton is 1836 times more massive than an electron. If the electron to proton mass were much larger or smaller, then the necessary molecules for life could not form, and life would then be impossible.

5. **The Stability of the Proton.** Each proton contains three quarks. Quarks themselves decay into antiquarks, pions, and positrons. The decay process occurs on an average of only one proton per 1032 years. If that decay rate of the proton were much higher, then lethal doses of radiation would be produced, and the conse-

quences for higher, more complicated organisms (like man) would be catastrophic.

6. **Fine Structure Constants.** These constants relate to each of the four fundamental forces: gravitational, strong nuclear, weak nuclear, and electromagnetic. Fine coupling constants typically yield strict **design** constraints for the universe. Why should this be unless it was planned?

7. **Distance between Stars.** The distance between stars affects the orbits of planets, and even whether they can exist at all. The average distance between stars in our region of the galaxy is about 30 trillion miles. If this distance were smaller, gravitational interaction among stars would destabilize planetary orbits.

This list is by no means complete, and yet it demonstrates why a growing number of astronomers and cosmologists agree on the possibility that the universe was not only divinely created but also divinely designed. American astronomer George Greenstein said, "As we survey all the evidence, the thought insistently arises that some supernatural agency… must be involved. Is it possible that suddenly, without intending to, we have stumbled upon scientific proof of the existence of a Supreme Being? Was it God who stepped in and so providentially crafted the cosmos for our benefit?"

But the physical constants of the universe are not the only factors that seem inexplicably designed for us to exist. There are a considerable number of circumstances demonstrating how our universe, solar system, and planet seem to be very specially designed for life to exist. Here are but a few of the extraordinary features of our cosmos which seem designed for our existence.

1. **Number of stars in the planetary system.** If there is more than one star in the planetary system, then tidal interactions in most cases would so disrupt planetary orbits as to make them unstable, as well as make radiations to planets erratic and unfit for advanced life; if less than one star, then no heat would be produced for advanced life to occur. Fortunately, we live in a single-star system.

2. **The stability of the star.** Our sun is an incredibly stable star. Most stars in the universe are not.

3. **Parent star mass.** If greater, then the luminosity of the star would change too quickly, and the star would burn too rapidly; if lesser, the range of distances appropriate for life would be very narrow. In the latter case, tidal forces would disrupt the rotational period of a planet at "correct for life" distances, for the planet would need to be quite close to the star. Also, ultraviolet radiation would be inadequate for planets to make sugars and oxygen. The mass of our sun is just right to allow us to be far enough from it to be given life-giving radiations, but not so close as to be harmed.

4. **Surface gravity.** If the gravity were stronger on a planet than Earth's, then the atmosphere would retain too much methane and ammonia, and life would be poisoned; if the gravity were weaker, then the planet's atmosphere would lose too much water (as seems to be true on Mars). Again, the size, density, and gravitational strength of our planet are just right.

5. **Distance from parent star.** If the distance were farther, then the planet would be too cool for a stable water cycle; if the distance were shorter, then the planet would be too warm for a stable water cycle. Again, we are in just the right place by some incredible stroke of luck or by divine design.

6. **Axial tilt.** If the axial tilt were greater, then surface temperature differences would be too great, and our poles highly irradiated; if the axial tilt were smaller, then surface temperature differences would be fixed, and we would have no seasons. The axial tilt of our planet is perfect to give us our seasonal rotations, which allow for the cycles of life.

7. **Rotation period.** If the Earth's rotation period were longer, then diurnal temperature differences would be too great; if the rotation period were shorter, then atmospheric wind velocities would be too great. Aren't we lucky they seem just right!

8. **Gravitational interaction with a moon.** If the gravitational interaction with a moon were greater, then the tidal effects on the

oceans, atmosphere, and Earth's rotation period would be too severe (we would live in world like Jupiter where the whole atmosphere is constantly experiencing typhoon and Tsunami conditions); however, if the gravitational interaction with a moon were less, then there would be climatic instabilities, and our deep-sea waters would not be mixed nor oxygenated. Our moon is just the right size, mass, and distance from us to give life-supporting tidal effects, as well as stabilize our axial tilt.

9. **Magnetic fields.** If the magnetic field around our planet were stronger, the electromagnetic storms would be too severe; however, if the magnetic field around a planet were weaker, then there would be inadequate protection from solar radiation, and we would literally "fry." The Earth has a robust magnetic field, which protects us and our atmosphere, allowing life.

10. **Thickness of planetary crust.** If the planetary crust thickness were greater, then there would be too much oxygen transferred from the atmosphere to the crust; however, if the planetary crust thickness was less, then there would be increased volcanic and tectonic activity. We have just the right amount of crustal thickness to allow for atmospheric oxygen retention and to protect us from out of control volcanic and tectonic activity.

11. **Albedo** (ratio of reflected light to total light falling upon a planet). If the albedo of our planet were greater, then runaway ice ages would develop; however, if the albedo were less, then a runaway greenhouse effect would develop (like exists on Venus). Our planet luckily reflects just enough radiations to stay at a life-giving stasis point. Or is it just luck?

12. **Oxygen to nitrogen ratio in the atmosphere.** If this rate were larger, then advanced life functions would proceed too quickly, and spontaneous fires would kill instantly; if this rate were smaller, then advanced life functions would proceed more slowly or not at all. The Earth's oxygen content in our atmosphere is maximized for life.

13. **Carbon dioxide and water vapor levels in the atmosphere.** If these levels were greater, then a runaway greenhouse effect would

ensue, turning Earth into an oven; however, if these levels were less, then the greenhouse effect would be insufficient, and an ice age would develop. The Earth has perfectly balanced amounts of carbon dioxide and water vapor in our atmosphere.

14. **Ozone level in the atmosphere.** If the ozone level were greater, then surface temperatures would be too low; however, if the ozone level were less, then surface temperatures would be too high, and there would be too much radiation at the surface of the planet to support life. We have a very stable and protective level of ozone in our upper atmosphere. (Remember, upper atmosphere ozone is good, low level is bad for breathing).

15. **Atmospheric electric discharge rate.** If the atmospheric electric discharge rate were too high, then there would be too much destruction from fire; if the electric discharge rate were too small, then there would be too little nitrogen fixed in the atmosphere. The Earth thankfully has enough electrical discharge to fix nitrogen in our atmosphere and rainfall, but not so much as to pose a constant threat to life.

These items are just a sampling of more than one hundred finely tuned physical constants and physical attributes of our universe, making it just about mathematically impossible that our universe and our planet were not designed by an intelligent entity. Interestingly, the late Sir Fred Hoyle, an agnostic astronomer, who discovered many of these amazing "coincidences," remarked that "a super-intellect has monkeyed with physics, as well as with chemistry and biology."[377]

First Corinthians 14:40 (ESV), **"But all things should be done decently and *in order*. He remembers his covenant forever, the word that he commanded, for a thousand generations...."**

Romans 1:20 (ESV), **"For his invisible attributes, namely, his eternal power and divine nature, have been clearly perceived, ever since the creation of the world, in the things that have been made. So they are without excuse."**

These verses remind us again of what we have talked about in this section. The God of the Bible is a supremely ordered deity, and there is ample evidence of that order and His designing hand in our universe for all to see.

Earth Science

If God created this world to be inhabited by us, as the Bible says, then that creator must also have an intimate knowledge of this planet, the physical laws which govern it, and the processes which make it habitable. Let's see what we can find in the Bible, which reveals such an understanding of this planet and its ecosystems.

The Water Cycle

The Old Testament book of Ecclesiastes was written by King Solomon almost three thousand years ago. For the most part, it is a rather depressing book in that Solomon expresses how even though he is one of the richest and most powerful men in all history, he does not know what happiness is. But, beyond the moral story of his finding that you cannot "buy happiness," there are some scientific gems embedded in Ecclesiastes. One of those is in Ecclesiastes 1:7 (NIV), where the Bible and Solomon say, **"All streams flow into the sea, yet the sea is never full. To the place the streams come from, there they return again."** This is a marvelously succinct description of the **water cycle**, written in the Bible almost three thousand years before scientists verified this process in nature.

Our current understanding of the water cycle is that water on the earth's surface *evaporate*s into water vapor which rises with heat currents into the atmosphere. There it cools and *condenses* into water droplets forming clouds. These condensed water droplets eventually return to the earth in the form of *precipitation* which waters the ground and provides water for our streams and oceans. Then the cycle starts all over.

How did Solomon, a king of Israel and not a scientist, know of this and other scientific gems which he included in his writings while he was sobbing over how unhappy he was?

The oldest book in the Bible, Job (KJV), adds, **"He binds up the waters in his thick clouds; and the cloud is not torn under them."** Job 37:11 makes it even clearer that water vapor is bound up in clouds.

Psalms 135:7 (NASB95) says, **"He causes the vapors to ascend from the ends of the earth; Who makes lightnings for the rain,...** Jeremiah 10:13 echoes this same knowledge of hydrology which says that clouds are made from evaporated water vapors.

Isaiah 55:10 (NIV) further exemplifies this understanding of hydrology when it says, **"As the rain and the snow come down from heaven, and do not return to it without watering the earth and making it bud and flourish, so that it yields seed for the sower and bread for the eater."**

In fact, the number of scriptures referring to hydrology and showing the depth of the Bible's understanding on this subject are impressive. Job 36:27-28 reveals an understanding of the cycle of evaporation, condensation, and precipitation. Job 26:8, 37:11, and Jeramiah 10:13 makes it clear the Bible understood the formation of clouds came from water vapor. Genesis 16:7 and Psalms 104:19 show an understanding of groundwater coming from springs. Psalms 135:7 again shows an understanding of evaporation. Psalms 104:13 mentions precipitation. Isaiah 55:10 demonstrates a biblical understanding of how precipitation and runoff infiltrate the ground and feeds groundwater. Deuteronomy 32:2 comments on the place of dew and rainwater in the cycle. Isaiah 44:3-4 reveals an understanding of flooding in desert streams. And Ecclesiastes 1:6-7 shows a unique understanding not only of the water cycle but also of cloud movement, the trade winds, and the causal cycles in our atmosphere.

A study of the history of man's thoughts on the water cycle is very revealing here. In the 6th century BC, the Greek Thales Miletus expressed what would be the prevailing idea of water hydrology for more than 2000 years. He theorized that most water on the earth had to come from a huge subterranean freshwater lake. Aristotle, although closer to the truth, echoed this same belief 200 years later that subterranean water was the main source of our surface water. They all believed that rainfall was insufficient to provide for the flow of springs and rivers.

Leonardo da Vinci (one of the most brilliant men of all time) showed this was still the prevalent thinking into the 16th century AD as he pondered in his writings on the underground mechanisms that would lift water into the mountains and provide stream flow (showing they discounted snowmelt as the most significant source). Even in the 17th century AD, Galileo expressed frustration because he could not understand the source of stream flow.

Not until 1674 did Pierre Perrault publish his research on the water cycle was this phenomenon, we all so depend upon, understood by man. He presented a study of the Seine River, beginning at its source, northwest of the city of Dujon. Using numerical estimates, he showed that the river runoff annually amounted to only one-sixth of the volume of water falling over the drainage basin as rain or snow in a year. Thus, he demonstrated that rainfall and snowfall were more than sufficient to water the ground, supply groundwater, and maintain spring and river flows.[378]

Neither King David (who wrote the verse from Psalms 135 correctly describing hydrology) nor the prophets Isaiah and Jeremiah were scientists, and yet their depth of understanding of the complete concept of the water cycle is striking. It is true as some will charge that parts of this hydrologic cycle are self-evident by observing nature. But the whole water cycle was not completely understood until the late 17th century, and yet the Bible contains a very complete understanding of hydrology. Who knew?

Matthew Maury, Virginian Man of the Seas (1806—1873)

He was nicknamed "Pathfinder of the Seas," is often honored as the "Father of Modern Oceanography and Naval Meteorology" and later called "Scientist of the Seas." These honors were given to Matthew Maury due to the publication of his extensive works in his books, especially *The Physical Geography of the Sea* (1855). This was the first far-reaching and comprehensive book on oceanography to be published. Maury made many important new contributions to charting winds and ocean currents, including ocean lanes for passing ships at sea.

In 1825 at age 19, Maury obtained a midshipman's warrant in the United States Navy aboard the frigate USS Brandywine (with the help of then U.S. Congressman Sam Houston). Almost immediately, he began to study the seas and record methods of navigation.

When a leg injury in 1841 left him unfit for sea duty, he retired from the U.S. Navy. Maury devoted his time to the study of navigation, meteorology, winds, and currents. He became Superintendent of the U.S. Naval Observatory and head of the Depot of Charts and Instruments.

Here, Maury studied thousands of ships' logs and charts. He required all ships under the purview of his office to submit records of winds and sea currents recorded during their voyages. He published the *Wind and Current Chart of the North Atlantic*, which showed sailors how to use the ocean's currents and winds to their advantage and drastically reduced the length of ocean voyages. Maury's uniform system of recording oceanographic data was adopted by navies and merchant marines around the world and was used to develop charts for all the major trade routes.[379]

Maury was a devout believer in the God of the Bible and read the Bible daily. In Psalms 8:8, he read that the Bible said there were "**paths of the sea.**" He also read in Ecclesiastes 1:6 that the "**winds have their circuits.**" Most people would read these verses and think them rather poetic, but otherwise not take them literally. Maury, however, took them very literally, as he did all things he read in the Bible. These verses are what propelled him to require all ships using his office to keep records of sea currents and winds during their voyages.

Using the data already available in the Navy Office of Charts and Measurements, as well as the data he had ships collect for his office, he discovered the mid-latitude winds we call the "*trade winds.*"

Sailing ships found this data to be invaluable in helping them make all sorts of transatlantic and transpacific voyages.

He further used this data, submitted it to his office to rediscover and redefine the Gulf Stream. A huge sea current that transports warm water from the Gulf of Mexico to the North Atlantic along the North American east coast.[380] This current had been known at the time of Ben Franklin, who included a drawing of the Gulf Stream in his writings. However, this knowledge had been largely ignored.[381] Maury refined this current's parameters and gave ships data that they could use to either help them cut time off cross Atlantic voyages to Europe or avoid counter currents in part to help cut time on trips across the Atlantic from Europe to the Americas.

The data collected also led him to the discovery of a similar cold-water current transporting cold water from Antarctica north along the west coasts of both South and North America. This current is the main reason that the California cities along the coast, such as San Diego, Los Angeles, and San Francisco, enjoy such moderate climates.

Maury's discoveries cut as much as three weeks off of some trans-oceanic voyages and increased ocean-going safety by keeping ships from predictably dangerous conditions.

A plaque on a Virginia monument to him reads, "He was a genius!"[382] Was he? Or was he just a Christian who firmly and literally believed in the word of God?

Water Deep in the Earth

We will establish later in this book that the Bible claims that the whole earth was formed out of water. There is also Genesis 2:6 (NIV), which says, "…**streams came up from the earth and watered the whole surface of the ground**."

Genesis 7:10-11 (KJV) says, "And it came to pass after seven days, that the waters of the flood were upon the earth. In the six hundredth year of Noah's life, in the second month, the seventeenth day of the month, the same day were **all the fountains of the great deep broken up**, and the windows of heaven were opened."

Does water really spring up from deep inside the earth? Descriptions of huge amounts of water deep underground? One of the major critiques of the biblical worldwide flood account is, "where in the world would all that water come from?" Is the Bible completely off base here, or does it know what it is talking about?

New evidence in 2014 shows more than three times more water than on the earth's surface (in all of the world's oceans, rivers, and lakes) may be hidden 160 to 420 miles underground in the earth's mantle!

A study by Northwestern geophysicist Steve Jacobsen and his co-author, University of New Mexico seismologist Brandon Schmandt, gives evidence that deep inside the earth's mantle, the layer below the crust has hidden within it *massive amounts of water* in the rock. This study found that the water is trapped inside a type of rock called "*ringwoodite.*" It's under tremendous pressure, and it plays a critical role in turning all that rock into magma.

This discovery was made using echo soundings of the deep mantle. Using a network of 2,000 seismometers placed across the entire US, they were able to "listen" to the speed of the waves made by earthquakes as they moved through the varying depths of the Earth's crust. Because water and rock react differently to those waves, they could figure out when the waves were hitting water inside rock pores, as opposed to solid rock.[383]

They also simulated the pressure of being 400 miles below the earth's surface in a lab, so they could test how rock and water would react. And they found that ringwoodite acts a little bit like a sponge at those high pressures: it soaks up water at the molecular level so that more than one percent of its structure is water. In fact, all that water helps explain turning hot rock underground into magma (hot liquid rock). A little-known fact is that every time a volcano erupts, up to 20 percent of the gas ejected is hot water vapor. This gives us a significant source for the water we now see on the earth's surface.

This study comes on the heels of a March 2014 study about a rare diamond that confirmed the existence of water trapped deep below the Earth's crust. Both these studies confirm that a whole lot of water is sitting inside the Earth.[384]

These discoveries are very compatible with the Genesis depiction of the earth having vast storehouses of water buried inside her and the flood account. Another interesting fact is that cool water formed zircons found deep in the earth suggest that this world was formed out of cool water. Not the hot molten formation so often touted by scientists. Zircons are crystals found in the earth that can change color when interacting with temperature or water. Several ancient zircons show early interaction with water, suggesting the early Earth was not magma for 500 million years (what is called a Hadean, or early molten earth) but formed cool. This cool water formation is consistent with the Genesis account.[385]

Also, this data supports that the Bible has it right when it suggests the waters in our oceans came from inside the earth. This is in contradistinction to a once-popular theory for several decades that Earth's water came from cometary collisions with the Earth. But this theory has now been discarded by most due to the differences in "heavy water" (deuterium) found in abundance in comets,[386] and the common water found on the Earth are not the same. Thus, what the Bible says about water on and inside the Earth is consistent with our most recent scientific discoveries. How did biblical authors over three thousand years ago get all this right unless they had help?

Mountains and Valleys in the Deep Ocean

Second Samuel 22:16 (NIV) says in part, **"The valleys of the sea were exposed, and the foundations of the earth laid bare...."** This verse reveals that biblical writers some three thousand years ago knew that there were valleys and mountains in the depths of the seas.

And just to show that this was not some random fluke, where the Bible's flowery language got accidentally close to scientific truth, the Bible showed this same knowledge via another author, who lived 250 years later. Remember that in the Bible is the incredible story of Jonah venturing into the sea in the belly of a huge fish. In part,

Jonah 2:5-6 (KJV) says, "The **waters compassed me about**, even to the soul: the depth closed me round about, the weeds were wrapped about my head. **I went down to the bottoms of the** *mountains*...."

How could the Bible writers know this? At the time of the writing of this scripture, all people could do was explore the shallows of the continental shelves of the oceans. These shelves, which are adjacent to the shores of oceans, are almost universally gradually sloping sand and fine sediment banks. With this sample of the oceans being all those ancient cultures could access, how could they know what was in the deep oceans, which was so much different from what they could observe?

The Oceans Have Springs

In Job 38:16 it asks, "Hast thou entered into the **springs of the sea**? Or hast thou walked in the **recesses of the deep**?"(JPS Tanakh 1917) How did the writer of Job know the oceans have springs? The bulk of these springs were, for the most part, inaccessible to early men. Only with deep water submersibles and diving equipment have we been able to view such springs and vents.[387]

Their existence is also counterintuitive. Earlier cultures could observe that freshwater streams and rivers are often fed by underground springs, but this always produces fresh water. Where salt water could be examined by ancient men, in the Dead Sea and other places, these waters were cut off from fresh water, with the result being the salinization of the water. The common-sense answer was that there could not be springs in the bottom of the oceans since it's the absence of springs that causes such salt water.[388] Further, the assumption of the deep oceans was that it was a vast uninterrupted plane, with no other features such as springs, and possibly with an unknown underground salinized water source.

There are some examples of springs in the shallows of the continental shelves. These could have exemplified for them springs going into the seas, but those could have easily been written off as being a "close shore" phenomena since the larger logic was that seas were produced by a lack of springs. Yet, the Bible knew about what ancient man could not have observed over 3800 years ago. How?

The phrase *"recesses of the deep"* is also intriguing. As pointed out in the previous section, ancient man had no knowledge of how deep our oceans actually get. Everything they saw would have left them with the impression that between landmasses, there was only the gently sloping ocean bottoms, as they experienced near the shore. Thus they had no reason nor evidence to have figured out the great depths of the oceans, which the Bible so expertly attests to. Again this was done far ahead of the time when man could have known this.

Air Has Weight

In Job 28:25 (ASV), it says, **"To make a weight for the wind…"** infers that the writer of Job understood that air has weight. What is novel about this is that the philosophy and science of the time of Job, and for 2000 years thereafter, said that air had no weight. How could you know something which you could not capture had weight? How could you even get this concept when scholars of your time universally believed air did not have weight?

Not until the 17th century will Evangelista Torricelli invent the first barometer, measuring the pressure exerted on a space by the weight of air pressure. In the 1640s, Gasparo Berti had unsuccessfully attempted to make an operational barometer. But in 1643, it will be Torricelli, a student of Gallileo, who constructed a barometer using a tube full of mercury turned upside down into a plate, with mercury in it. It was discovered that the height of the mercury in the tube would vary with the altitude at which the measurement was taken and whether it was a clear or rainy day (rain is typically associated with low air pressure). Interestingly, Torricelli had to construct his first barometer in secret, as he was concerned that his "gossipy and superstitious" neighbors might mistake his experiments as witchcraft and have him arrested![389]

This is another fascinating tidbit where the Bible describes a scientific truth completely at odds with the thinking of its day. Aristotle half suggested that air had weight about 1700 years after the writing of Job, but his conjecture was ignored for almost another 1700 years. Scientists will not demonstrate that air has weight till the 17th century AD work of Torricelli, Berti, and Gallileo.[390] How did the ancient biblical writers continually get these things right?

Four Winds in the Bible? What's That About?

Ezekiel 37:9 (KJV) says:

> Then said he unto me, Prophesy unto the wind, prophesy, son of man, and say to the wind, Thus saith the Lord GOD; Come from the *four winds*, O breath, and breathe upon these slain, that they may live.

Why four winds? There are several views on this answer. There is a culture of the times answer, a scholarly answer based on Jewish theology and culture, and there is a possible scientific answer.

One interpretation is the Four Winds are the power of God in the natural world, basically where "miracles" can occur and where the strength of God is made visible to humans. This interpretation would be backed up by the fact that the Hebrew word translated as "wind" in these passages also connotes the idea of "power." All of these Old Testament verses I will quote could have been translated to the "four powers" just as correctly as the translation of "four winds."

The Prophet Daniel saw a vision by night: **"Behold, the *four winds* (powers) of the sky broke out on the great sea. Four great animals came up from the sea, diverse one from another"** (Daniel 7:2-3, HNV).

The Prophet Zechariah saw four chariots rise up between two mountains and asked an angel what these were. The angel answered: **"These are the *four winds* (powers) of the sky, which go forth from standing before the Lord of all the earth"** (Zechariah 6:5, WEB).

In Ezekiel 37:9, God uses the Four Winds to breathe life into skeletons to create a great army. Again, the interpretation of powers instead of winds may be a better fit for all of these texts.

The Four Winds also carry God's chosen people to their destiny, both in the Old Testament and the New: **"He will send out his angels with a great sound of a trumpet, and they will gather together his chosen ones from the *four winds* (powers), from one end of the sky to the other"** (Matthew 24:31, WEB).

While the scholarly answer is that the "Four Winds" represent north, south, east, and west winds, which are considered favorable in Judaism (as opposed to winds that blow from angles), a more comprehensive answer includes the Four Winds as God's power made manifest on earth.[391]

Modern Science has shown us that we believe that all matter in the universe is made up of atoms. In turn, these atoms are made of subatomic particles held together by what we currently believe to be the four primordial and basic forces of nature, which hold everything together. These four forces described by science are gravitational, electromagnetic, weak nuclear, and strong nuclear forces. These four forces are what hold everything together and make the universe work. Thousands of scientists over the past century, including Einstein, have worked feverishly to try and work out what they call a "unified field theory." This theory would describe how initially, at the Big Bang, there was only one primordial force, which then split into the four basic forces we see today holding everything together. This search for a unifying force for everything is one reason you see particle accelerator research today.[392]

Could it be that the Bible is, in fact, referring in all or most of these verses not to the four winds of the earth but to the equally translatable "four powers" which hold the earth together and make it work? If so, this is another biblical "prescience" insight, made more than three thousand years ahead of our discoveries. If that is true, then it also might be true, as both the Bible books of Hebrews and Colossians states that the original force behind these was one single primordial force, the power of God. Further, the Bible says God/Christ is still today holding these four powers or forces in place and keeps our very existence in place. Could God's power be that "unified force" scientists have been searching for more than a century?

Continental Drift, Plate Tectonics, and Pangea in the Bible!

One of the fascinating things about the Bible is how it is always in concert with all of the many things about our planet, which we have only learned in the past two hundred years. How did the writers of the Bible consistently, and without error, or exception, continually describe or predict the laws of physics, and the structure of the earth, and our universe?

One of those places where the Bible described knowledge of the structure of the earth was its description in the first chapter of Genesis, which says all of the land was gathered into one place.

Genesis 1:9 (NIV) says, **"And God said, 'Let the water under the sky be gathered to one place, and let dry ground appear.' And it was so."**

If all of the waters were gathered into one place, it follows logically that all of the land was gathered together into one supercontinent. A tenant of modern geology is that long ago, all of the lands of the earth were once gathered together in a single supercontinent, which they call "Pangea." How fascinating that the Bible got this one right.

The name "Pangaea/Pangea" is derived from Ancient Greek pan (πᾶν, "all, entire, whole") and Gaia (Γαῖα, "Mother Earth, land"). The concept that the continents once formed a continuous land mass was first substantially supported by Alfred Wegener, a geophysicist and meteorologist, and the originator of the scientific theory of continental drift, in his 1912 publication *The Origin of Continents* (Die Entstehung der Kontinente). He expanded upon his hypothesis in his 1915 book *The Origin of Continents and Oceans* (Die Entstehung der Kontinente und Ozeane), in which he postulated that, before breaking up and drifting to their present locations, all the continents were part of a single supercontinent that he called the "Urkontinent." This had been proposed by others off and on over the previous 200+ years but largely ignored by the scientific community.[393]

Note, the writing of all waters and all land gathered into one place (a supercontinent) was written about 3500 years ago, but we, as a matter of geologic study, only rediscovered this idea and found belief in it as a geological possibility some 400 years ago. Moreover, scientists only seriously considered it might be true for the last several decades.

Connected to the idea of a supercontinent is the concept of continental drift. Continental drift is a theory that explains how continents shift position on the earth's surface. Continental drift is the movement of the earth's continents relative to each other, thus appearing to "drift" across the ocean bed. The speculation that continents might have 'drifted' was first put forward by Abraham Ortelius in 1596.

Others, including 19th-century cartographers, expanded this idea. The concept was independently and more fully developed by Wegener in 1912, but his theory was rejected by some for lack of an impelling mechanism (though this was supplied later by Arthur Holmes). Today the idea of continental drift has been subsumed by the theory of plate tectonics, which explains how the continents move and is now the foundational paradigm of modern geology.[394] Continental drift explained why look-alike animal and plant fossils, and similar rock formations, are found on different continents on opposite sides of the Atlantic.

The Bible says that originally, all of the lands of the earth were gathered in one supercontinent. It subsequently talks of other lands and knowledge of the African, Asian, and European continents. This suggests that the biblical writers knew that this was no longer so, and there were at their time multiple continents.

In fact, the Bible both in Genesis 10:25 (NIV) and 1 Chronicles 1:19 (NIV) says, "Two sons were born to Eber: One was named Peleg **because in his time the *earth was divided*...**" The Bible would either place this division just a few hundred years after the great flood (when Peleg lived) or say that it was ongoing from the time of the flood to this point. The Peleg reference could also indicate that this was the time of the dispersion of people groups by their new languages and tied to the Babel account.

The Bible in Psalm 104:8 (ESV) says, **"The mountains rose, the valleys sank down to the place that you appointed for them."** Most of our ideas of mountain building today are tied to plate tectonic theory. The current ideas are that where the plates come together, there is subduction of one plate (one plate goes under the other), and this forces the other plate to go up, or that they smash into one another, causing an uplifted rift. The Himalayan Mountain range is just one example of what we currently believe formed out of such continental and plate tectonic motions and collisions of landmasses forming an uplift.[395]

So the Bible described 3500 years ago the concepts of the super-continent Pangea, as well as the concept of continental drift, and at least alludes to the effects of plate tectonics. Humans did not have any idea of any of these now fundamental ideas in modern geology until 3100 years later. Again it appears the Bible had inside information!

Sedimentary Layers, Fossils, Continental Shelves, and the Bible
Genesis 8:3 (KJV): **"And the waters returned from off the earth continually: and after the end of the hundred and fifty days the waters were abated."**

If the great flood of Noah's day really did occur, as the Bible says it did, then we would find certain features on the earth. The Bible describes this flood covering all the earth to a depth of 22 feet above the tallest mountains. Such flood torrents would have deposited cross-continental layers of sediments all across the earth and formed vast layers of sedimentary rocks at its conclusion. And in fact, that is what we find as we study the upper crust of the earth. Such a cataclysmic flood as never before seen would also have drowned, scooped up, and strewn across the earth all manner of dead animals and plants, which it would have buried within the sediments all across the earth. Again, that is what we find when we study the upper crust of the earth's surface, layer upon layer of sedimentary rocks, with millions of fossils of dead things buried within them.[396]

Also, if such a huge cataclysm had occurred, in its aftermath, as the waters receded from the continents and back into the oceans, there would have been a huge erosional event. At this time, as much as half the sediments laid down by this huge world covering flood would have been scooped up and redeposited into the oceans. This is a period at the end of the flood event that some geologists call the "Erodazoic Period."[397]

If this huge secondary deposition had occurred, we would be able to find evidence of it on the ocean floors. And when we examine the ocean floors, we find just that. If the continental shelves of every continent were formed by the steady wave actions we see today, then they would be quite different than they currently appear. As far back as man has observed, the tides roll up to our continental beaches, not usually in cyclical tides which run perpendicularly into the beaches, but at angles somewhat skewed to the beaches. If this wave action and that of huge hurricanes and other normal phenomena were the only forces forming our continental shelves, then they would be built up near the beaches and drop off rather drastically fairly close to each beach. Also, the depositional pattern would be vastly different, with deposits stacking up against beaches almost exclusively in wave patterns parallel to the waves' motions.

Further, if this biblical cataclysm occurred, there would have been rapid erosion and water flow of the continents. This would not have allowed for much re-deposition on the continents themselves, but most of the re-deposition would have occurred on the continental margins, out to sea when these turbidity currents were no longer rolling downhill off the land and ran into the deep ocean waters, which would slow them down and cause deposition.

Instead, we find that the continental shelves protrude an average of 50 miles from the continental coasts and, in some cases, much more than that (one shelf extends 600 miles from the coast into the ocean). These continental shelves are relatively flat, generally descending into the ocean only at a down angle of about 0.1° till it reaches the shelf edge between several miles and hundreds of miles out. Beyond this, the angle of descent of the seafloor increases to about 4° in a massive feature called the "Continental Slope." Both the continental shelf, as well as the continental slope, are geologic features made up of sedimentary rock layers showing depositional tracks indicating that they were laid down in water with a direction of flow *away from the continents.*

These huge layers of sedimentary rock surrounding our continents, which thicken as you get away from the coast and measure in depth from some 1500 meters to as deep as 3500 meters of sedimentary layers, comprise these massive sediments surrounding each continent. If the waters of the earth were all drained, these massive *continental slopes* would be the *most impressive geologic features we would see on the planet!*[398]

Today we find similar sedimentary layers forming on a much smaller scale in river deltas. Both the Nile and Mississippi rivers are continually forming larger and larger deltas comprised of sediments that are picked up on the continents and carried by the rivers to the seas, where these currents run into the denser and unmoving ocean waters. This slowing of water allows for the deposition of layer upon layer of sediment. What the continental shelves and continental slopes reveal is this same action of deposits carried off of the continents into the oceans, but on a massively larger scale than even these two huge rivers.[399]

Again, what we find when we examine the continent's margins, is exactly what we would expect to find if the Bible is telling the truth, and a huge flood once covered all of the earth. The continental shelves, as we find them today, could not have been formed by the wave and natural interactions with the sea and continents we see today. But their composition fits perfectly with the biblical account of the withdrawing of the waters from the continents after the flood.

As it says in Psalm 104:6-8 (AMP):

> You covered it (the Earth) with the deep as with a garment; The waters were standing above the mountains. **At Your rebuke they fled, at the sound of your thunder they hurried away. The mountains rose; the valleys sank down to the place which you established for them. You set a boundary that they may not pass over, so that they will not return to cover the earth.**

If the Bible does not know what it is talking about, it is unscientific and mythical; how is it then that evidence of sedimentary rock layers all across the planet, the fossils buried within them, and the continental margins all so graphically fit just what we should find if the Bible is telling the truth?

Astronomy and Astrophysics in the Bible

It is intriguing how much is in the Bible which impinges on the scientific realms of astronomy and astrophysics. Since the bulk of what we have discovered about the cosmos and physics has come about in the last four hundred years (most in fact in the last century), it would be great evidence of the Creator of it all if we can show knowledge of our universe, galaxy, solar system, and space far ahead of man's relatively recent discoveries in the Bible. Let's look at what the Bible says on these subjects.

The Earth Hangs in Space!

The book of Job is considered by many scholars to be the oldest book in the Bible. The writing style, the mention of none of the Jewish religious structures of the priesthood or their traditions or celebrations, plus frequent mentions of ice (close to an ice age) all lead some scholars to say it was written around 1800 BC or earlier. This means that in Job 26:7 (NIV), where it says, **"He spreads out the northern skies over empty space; he suspends the earth over nothing,"** the Bible reveals an understanding of the Earth hanging in space with nothing holding it up. Not only is this an understanding of our place in the cosmos some 3400 years before Galileo and Copernicus, but it is a correct scientific claim in direct opposition to the beliefs of the great cultures and stories of that day.

Hindu culture at that time held the Earth rested on the back of a giant "celestial turtle" as it walked through the cosmos.[400] Mediterranean cultures about this time developed the myth that the Earth was held up in space by a giant person named "Atlas."[401] If you quizzed a hundred cultures about where the Earth was relative to the cosmos, you got almost that many answers. But only the Bible had the correct answer 3800 years ago, that we have verified today not only through telescopic observations but by venturing into space ourselves. How did Job know this 3800 years ago?

How did the Bible Know
the Earth is Round or Had a Circular Orbit?

In Isaiah 40:22 (NIV), it says, "He sits enthroned above the **circle** of the earth, and its people are like grasshoppers. He **stretches out the heavens like a canopy, and spreads them out like a tent to live in**." which reveals two ancient understandings of our cosmos which are hard to reckon with. There is also a debate among linguists and theologians as to what this might be referring to.

First, it says in most translations today that God sits above the "*circle* of the earth." Some Hebraists say this verse is translated more accurately to the "*round* of the earth." In both cases, this would be knowledge thousands of years ahead of its time. How could this be? Also, Proverbs 8:27 reference to establishing a horizon refers to a circular or round Earth.

In this case, there is a partial naturalistic answer. Since the Earth casts a shadow on the moon during a lunar eclipse, it could have been determined by some ancient scholars that the world must be round due to the circular nature of those shadows. This seems easy and reasonable today with what we know of celestial mechanics. However, in the time of this writing, almost four thousand years ago, most of the world did not understand that the Earth hung in empty space, nor that it revolved around the sun, nor that the moon revolved about the Earth. To understand that the circular shadow that they observed going across the moon during eclipses was the shape of the Earth would require an understanding of the makeup of our solar system, a knowledge which will not occur for almost 3000 years after these books of the Old Testament are written. This logical deduction of the Earth being a sphere could also have been gleaned from the old Ptolemaic solar system model, but that was unknown to these writers as well.

Even when this knowledge of the Earth revolving around the sun was proposed, it was dismissed by scientists and theologians alike for a hundred years, as they preferred to keep the Ptolemaic theory of the Earth being the unmoving center of the universe and the sun and moon revolving about it.[402] Indeed, this is an easy sensory mistake to make from our perspective on the ground. How then did the Bible get it right about three thousand years ago, when the whole world, even 2600 years later, would still have it wrong?

The second thing to note in Isaiah 40:22 (NIV) is the Bible's description of **"He stretches out the heavens like a canopy, and spreads them out like a tent to live in."** This makes it clear, as do several other Bible verses that there is a fabric to space, and at its creation, it was spread out like a scroll or tent canopy. In fact, Job 9:8, Genesis 1:5-8, and a total of seventeen different verses in the Bible written by seven different authors in seven different books of the Bible over a span of about 1300 years all say that the universe was spread out in a way that some might say is consistent with modern scientific theories and observations.[403]

These verses are very reminiscent of the modern theories of "inflation" and an expanding universe in astrophysics. But inflation theory was not even conceived of by man until the early 1980s. We did not get theoretical equations (1915) and telescopic observations which caused us to believe the universe might be expanding as the Bible says until the 1920s. We did not get observational and experimental confirmation that universal expansion was accelerating until 1998.[404] Likewise, modern ideas of space being composed of "ether" or filled with "zero-point energy" will not be discussed for thousands of years past Isaiah's writing.

On the topic of the "circle of the Earth," other Hebraists point out that the Hebrew word for ball (dûr) was not used here, as it is used for "ball" in Isaiah 22:18 and elsewhere in the Bible. The Hebrew word used in Isaiah 40:22 was instead chûg (which many interpret as *circle*), and it is used with that meaning in the context of other Bible verses such as Job 22:14 and Proverbs 8:27.

This is a highly interpretative exercise since we are dealing with Hebrew, which was a "dead language" for 1800 years. Thus many times, it is only through context that we derive some word meanings. It is interesting that many other Hebrew words use the Hebrew verb stem of "chûgag" to form verbs for "feast," "celebrate," or dancing," which all show action.

Using this view of the use of this word, it seems possible that the "circular" reference here could be to the motion of the earth since many other uses of this chûg as a verb stem could refer to "*choreography* of the earth." Thus, it is possible that instead of making reference to the round shape of the Earth (which is still possible), that this verse instead alludes to the perfectly choreographed way the Earth resides in our solar system in an almost perfectly circular orbit, which it must for life to exist here.[405] This understanding of the Earth's orbit being an almost perfect circle about the sun did not fit into either the "solid sky" idea of the universe proposed by the Egyptians, nor could it be derived with the Ptolemaic ideas, which will come later. So how would Isaiah get such knowledge of our true place in the solar system?

Whether the correct reference is to the *spherical shape of the Earth*, or its *orbit* is immaterial, as either refers to knowledge unknown at the time of Isaiah's writing, as does knowledge of the "fabric" of space being "stretched out." So the Bible was knowledgeable of these parts of astrophysics at least 2900 years ahead of man's discoveries. Thus, the question not only becomes how did the Bible get these right thousands of years ahead of time, but how did seven different authors over 1300 years get this consistently right when the rest of humanity had no clue of these truths of astrophysics?

Does the Bible Inaccurately Describe the Sky as Solid?

Critics of the Bible often charge that the Bible references an ancient view of the heavens and cosmos rather than a scientific one, revealing that it was not written by the Creator. Ancient peoples often thought that the sky was a solid dome with stars embedded in this dome. This dispute centers on the Hebrew word "*raqia*," which is often translated as "firmament" or "vault," both of which infers a firm surface. Alternative translations of raqia are "expanse" or "spread out thinness."

Thus, Genesis 1:6-8 (ESB) says either:

> Then God said, "Let there be an *expanse* (or firmament) in the midst of the waters, and let it separate the waters from the waters." God made the *expanse* (or firmament) and separated the waters which were below the *expanse* (or firmament) from the waters which were above the *expanse* (or firmament); and it was so and God called the *expanse* (or firmament) heaven....'

The "expanse" translation seems to make more sense. But which interpretation is what was really intended by Moses in the original texts of the Bible?

The translation of *raqia* as "firmament" came from the Septuagint, a Greek translation of the Hebrew Scriptures made in the third century BC by Jewish scholars at the request of the Egyptian pharaoh. They translated raqia to the Greek word "stereoma," which connotes a solid structure. These scholars may have been influenced by the Egyptian view of cosmology which proposed that the heavens being a stone vault. This makes sense in light of this translation was done in Egypt, and they were the most advanced civilization of the day.

But the Hebrew word raqia is best translated purely in Hebrew as "spread out thinness, stamping or stretching into thinness." This same word is often used in the Old Testament in reference to the hammering out of metals into thin sheets.

So in the use of this word in Genesis chapter 1, does it make more sense that the author was intending to get across the solidness of the heavens or the thinness and expansiveness of them. This stretched out thinness concept is consistent with the usage of this word "shamayim" used in Psalm 104:2 and Isaiah 40:22, which speak of the stretching out of the heavens. Then in Acts 1:8, God explicitly calls the expanse heaven, which equates the use of raqia with the word shamayin. It thus seems that the better translation for *raqia is expanse* rather than firmament.

Thus, it would seem that Moses originally intended for "raqia" in Genesis 1 to be interpreted as *expanse* and not firmament. This falsifies the charge that the Bible wrongly described the heavens as a solid vault or surface.[406] It also shows that the Bible did not have a flawed view of the heavens but an inspired one. It shows that the Bible's author some 3500 years ago understood that space was, in fact, an imperfect vacuum, and the Bible shows this understanding more than 3400 hundred years before man would discover this.

The Bible Understood the
Rotation of the Earth and Our Solar System

Luke 17:34-35 (HCSB) says, **"I tell you, on that night two will be in one bed: One will be taken and the other will be left. Two women will be grinding grain together: One will be taken and the other left."**

At the time of its writing, skeptics could have complained about these verses as ridiculous since it depicts that there is both light and dark on the Earth at the same time.

These Bible verses indicate a knowledge by the biblical writer that on one side of the Earth, it can be night, while on the other side, it will be light. How could the Bible know this? How could Luke, who lived two thousand years ago, without knowledge of celestial mechanics, or the spherical shape of the Earth, and only the knowledge of a person, who had never traveled far from home and never experienced the effects of time zones or "jet lag" ever figure this out?

Job 38:12 also verifies this understanding of the Earth as a sphere and the mechanics of our solar system, which has the sun shining upon one half of the Earth while the other half is in darkness.

The Bible Says Everything Was Made from Water

The Bible in Genesis chapter 1 (NIV) says:

> In the beginning God created the heavens and the earth. Now the earth was formless and empty, darkness was over the **surface of the *deep*, and the Spirit of God was hovering over the *waters*...** And God said, "Let there be a vault between the **waters** to separate ***water from water***." So God made the vault and **separated the *water* under the vault from the *water*** above it. And it was so. God called the vault "sky."

Note that the only matter mentioned in the first eight verses is *water*, which infers that the Bible claims that the first matter made in all the universe was water. This biblical concept is verified in the writings of the Apostle Peter, who said in 2 Peter 3:5 (ESV), "For they deliberately overlook this fact, that the heavens existed long ago, and the earth was **formed out of water and through water** by the word of God."

On the surface, this is a ridiculous claim which could falsify the Bible. The current, most popular origin concepts in science today are the Big Bang Theory and the Nebular Hypothesis for the formation of our solar system. Both of these say that the original matter of the universe and this solar system was largely hydrogen gas, not water.[407]

It should be noted that these two theories of origins are far from scientifically proven. The Big Bang Theory does not match several observations we have made of the universe, including the winding, flatness, and horizon problems, among many others[408] requiring unproven concepts of "inflation," "dark matter," and "dark energy" added to the Big Bang cosmology to try and rescue it from how this theory does not square with observations we have made in astronomy.[409]

Likewise, the Nebular Hypothesis, which says that our solar system, as well as many solar systems, were formed naturalistically by the collection of hydrogen and other gases and dust of many other elements as they swirled and fell together gravitationally to form the sun and our planets, is far from proven. Although it is the most popular solar system origin theory today, it should be noted that there are many, many other theories of how our solar system formed. Interestingly, a problem with all of these theories is that none of them (including the Nebular Hypothesis) that seem to work for the formation of the inner "rocky" planets gives an adequate explanation for the formation of the outer gas giants and ice worlds. Likewise, none of the theories which seem to explain the outer planets gives a believable scientific explanation for the formation of the inner planets. Specifically, the Nebular Hypothesis does not explain the retrograde motions of some planets and moons within the system.[410]

Another problem with all of these theories, the Big Bang included, is that none of what we see in the universe should have coalesced together naturalistically. The force of the vapor pressure of hydrogen gas is forty times greater than the gravitational attractive force of hydrogen molecules to each other. This means that hydrogen gas *will not coalesce together* as all of these secular origin theories presuppose but will repel each other, disallowing the formation of stars, planets, and solar systems. Further, computer models of swirling dust in space show that it will form random "dust bunnies" at times, but those are readily broken up by the force of collisions between them and will never form as much as boulders, asteroids, planets, or anything else.[411]

Astrophysicist Dr. Russell Humphreys took the biblical verses cited in Genesis 1 and 2 Peter 3:5 as a starting point and said, "What If everything in the universe really was formed out of water?"

Using this as a starting premise, he examined the magnetic field of the sun. Water on the molecular level is slightly magnetic. If the sun was made out of water and it is as young as the Bible would suggest, then the calculation of our sun assuming its particles were made out of and molecularly aligned like water would produce a star with a magnetic field very close to what our sun's magnetic field is measured at today. If, however, you follow the Nebular Hypothesis that our sun was formed out of a collection primarily of hydrogen gas, then it would have a remnant magnetic field twenty times more powerful than what we measure today.[412]

Our unmanned Mariner 10 and Messenger spacecrafts, when they got to Mercury found something that neither the Nebular Hypothesis nor the Big Bang Theory predicted. They found that Mercury has a remnant magnetic field. Both of these secular theories of origins expected Mercury not to have a remnant magnetic field. Mercury should have such a small mass and be so old that is should be cold and dead, but it is not.

These data points led Dr. Humphreys to make predictions in 1984 of what we would find when we got spacecraft near enough to analyze Uranus and Neptune in the Creation Research Society Quarterly, a peer-reviewed creationist scientific journal. If these huge outer planets were made from an original substance of water, and assuming that they were only as old as the Bible suggests, then he predicted how strong the magnetic fields of both these planets should now be if the Bible were telling the absolute truth about our origins.[413]

Sure enough, when NASA's Voyager II spacecraft flew by both gas giants in 1986 and 1989, respectively, the strength of both Uranus' and Neptune's magnetic fields were almost exactly what Dr. Humphrey's predictions of their strength would be, based on his biblical creation model.[414]

Further, in 2008, when Messenger flew past Mercury and captured a magnetic field measurement, and Humphreys compared it with what Mariner 10 had measured 34 years earlier, this data corresponded with and validated the decaying slope generated by his creation model. Amazingly, Mercury's magnetic field strength had diminished since 1974, right in line with the predicted value of the creation magnetic field model. If Mercury's magnetic field is supposed to have lasted for billions of years, then it should be very stable over vast time periods. But as Messenger's data showed, researchers can measure its decay within a person's lifetime.[415]

Taking all of this scientific data in, it looks as if there is a well-reasoned argument that this solar system was made out of water as the Bible said it was! When a scientific hypothesis or theory becomes predictive of what we will find in nature, it is a big step in proving the validity of that theory. In this case, the evidence shows that the Bible, rather than being in error on this point, has pointed us towards new science.

Every Star is Different from All Others

In the book of **1 Corinthians 15:41** of the Bible, Apostle Paul said, "There is a splendor of the sun, another of the moon, and another of the stars; for **one star differs from another star in splendor**." (Holman Christian Standard Bible). So the Bible says that each and every star in the universe is unique and differs from all other stars. That would seem to differ from the fact that astronomers classify stars into several categories, which would mean many stars are similar. For example, 75 percent of stars are classified by astronomers as "Red Dwarfs."

Red Dwarfs all give off a redder hue of light than our sun, which is a yellow dwarf. They are also smaller and burn cooler than yellow dwarfs. There are many other classes of stars, including red giants, blue giants, and more. Red Dwarfs also, as a rule, are very unstable and are continually ejecting floods of particles that would destroy life.[416]

Recent observations, however, say that the Bible may, in fact, know what it is talking about. When we look at the size, color, spectrum emitted, total and types of radiations emitted, temperature, chemical composition, stability, density, gravitational attraction, and more, we find that no one star is exactly like another. This is true even for stars that fall within one of the large categories called "main sequence." Red dwarfs, which make up the bulk of all-stars, still show variations within this type such that no two stars are exactly alike.[417]

With respect to our own sun, it is classified as a "Main Sequence G2 Yellow Dwarf." That would seem to tell us it is a specific type of star of which there are some others just like it. However, that is not exactly the case. Main Sequence only means that it can be categorized within the star type "yellow dwarf." However, yellow dwarfs only make up about 5 percent of all stars observed. Also, when we compare our star to other yellow dwarfs, we can observe, we can find no other yellow dwarf with exactly the same combination of variables mentioned above. It does not emit lethal doses of radiation periodically as most other yellow dwarfs do. To be specific, our sun is incredibly stable (far more than most other stars) and gives us exactly the types of radiation necessary to support life on this planet.[418] **Note that in the scripture it not only says that every star is different and has its own glory but makes the same statement for our sun individually**. This speaks to what we have found, that not only is there no one star just like another, but our star was specially made for us.

The Bible knew all of this over three thousand years before modern astronomy discovered these things. How did these ancient humans, without telescopes, having no understanding of what stars are, seeing thousands of stars in the heavens, most of which look like identical points of light, know that each was different from another, as we are discovering today?

Number of Stars in the Universe are Innumerable!

While we are talking about stars, let's talk about how many there are. The Bible in Jeremiah 33:22 (Christian Standard Bible) states, "Even as **the stars of heaven cannot be counted**, and the sand of the sea cannot be measured, so too I will make innumerable the descendants of my servant David and the Levites, who minister to me."

When God promised Abraham that he would have innumerable descendants, He drew a striking comparison: "Look now toward heaven, and tell the stars, **if thou be able to number them**: and He said unto him, So shall thy seed be" (Genesis 15:5, KJV).

The total number of individual stars visible in both the northern and the southern celestial hemispheres is about 6,000. Thus, on a clear night, one can see at most about 3,000 stars at the same time. Ancient writings tell us that men of Jeremiah's time (about 600 BC) believed they had counted all of the stars in their heavens and numbered them at just over 3000. It makes great sense they would think so, as so many shepherds, ranchers, travelers, and nomadic peoples would spend many nights in the open under the stars, with great views due to no city lighting of today. It was natural that many would count the stars on a clear night, and via their eyewitness experience, believe that all stars could be counted. This was, they thought, a settled fact! Is that all there is?

With the invention of telescopes, very many previously unknown stars were discovered. Galileo (circa 1609), using his homemade telescope, saw a ten-fold increase in the number of visible stars, up to 30,000. Today, the local Milky Way galaxy (of which our sun is a part) has been found to contain about 200,000 million stars.[419] By the time we start counting all of the stars, in all of the galaxies that we continually discover, the number of stars is truly innumerable. How did the Bible get this right in two places, by two different authors more than 2200 years before man had any way of telling this, nor any inkling that it could be true?

How did the Bible Know about Atoms, Molecules, and Cells?

In Hebrews 11:3 (NIV), the Bible says, "By faith we understand that the **universe was formed** at **God's command**, so that **what is seen was not made out of what was visible**." This same concept is stated as well in Colossians 1:16-17. This says that all creation is made of invisible elements. Science in the last century has discovered that all matter is made of atoms, subatomic particles within those atoms, and molecules which are collections of atoms, and life is always composed of living cells. All of these elements discovered in the last two hundred years are so small as to be invisible to the naked eye, as described in the Bible.

In addition, research has shown that the vacuum of space is not empty but contains energy and fabric, which has been experimentally demonstrated to act like a fluid. If this was what the Bible was referring to rather than tiny particles, then it really would be creation of everything from something which truly is invisible to us even today and discovered only very recently![420]

Now, Democritus, a Greek philosopher, who lived between the 5th and 4th century's BC, argued that all of existence was made up of tiny indivisible atoms (he got the idea from his mentor, Leucippus), but his ideas were ignored for thousands of years by other philosophers, who believed in the *four elements of wind, fire, water, and earth* being the substances which made up all existence, although some threw in a fifth element of the ether for good measure as to what all the heavens were made of.[421]

How could the writers of the Bible have known this? How could they have selected invisible elements as the correct answer when it went counter to the prevailing "science" and philosophy of the period in which it was written?

At the time of the writing of the Bible, science and philosophy of that period thought that everything in the world and in all creation was made of one of four basic elements: wind, fire, earth, and water. Note, these are all things they could see. In this environment, with this teaching being prevalent, how could the Bible correctly record that all matter was composed of incredibly small or invisible elements? It likely could not have unless the biblical writers had inside information from the Creator of all matter!

The Earth was Formed and Created to be Inhabited

Written about 2700 years ago, the Old Testament scripture of Isaiah 45:18 (NIV) says:

> For this is what the Lord says—he who created the heavens, he is God; he who fashioned and made the earth, he founded it; he did not create it to be empty, but **formed it to be inhabited**—he says: 'I am the Lord, and there is no other.

This is an interesting and provocative statement, which goes counter to modern thoughts of the Earth, our solar system, our galaxy, and, in fact, the entire universe being formed by random chance and happy accidents. Which is the truth?

When we explore the attributes of the Earth, which make life possible, we get a look at a large set of circumstances that defy logic if we try to say that it all happened by chance. The Earth has about 70 percent of its surface covered with liquid water, which is a necessity for the types of life we know of. It is a terrestrial planet with tectonic plates and an active molten interior that recycles itself, which is another habitability requirement for carbon cycle life. It has a moderate rate of rotation, making our days not too hot and our nights not too cold.[422]

The Earth is just the right size and mass and with an adequately strong magnetic field, all of which allows it to retain an atmosphere that not only sustains both oxygen-breathing animal life but carbon dioxide breathing plants. It is supposed that the absence of these traits allowed Mars' atmosphere to be stripped away from it or perhaps lost by freezing.[423]

The abundance of inert nitrogen, oxygen, and carbon dioxide as opposed to large amounts of methane found in the gas giants such as Jupiter and Saturn are also a must. But the Earth is not so big or massive as to give us the crushing gravity of Jupiter or Saturn. Thus from these standpoints, it is exactly right! Our mix of 21 percent oxygen is optimal to allow for breathing by ourselves and other organisms on Earth, but it also is small enough so that we do not have the problems of a purer oxygen atmosphere, which would cause massive fires.[424]

The aforementioned magnetic field surrounding the earth not only helps us to retain our atmosphere but it both screens and absorbs a range of moderate and hard radiations which would be harmful or lethal to life. Ozone and water vapor in our upper atmosphere screens us from ultraviolet and infrared radiations, which would be harmful. Our sufficiently heavy atmosphere also acts as the last line of defense from meteors, asteroids, and comets which may fall into the Earth. Via friction, Earth's atmosphere burns up all but the largest of such missiles, thus protecting the Earth's surface and life.[425]

The Earth orbits the sun in what is called the "circumstellar habitable zone" (others call it the "Goldilocks Zone" = "just right"). We are far enough from the sun so that we do not fry and close enough so that we do not freeze. We have a nearly circular orbit which again keeps us within this zone and does not allow us to stray too close or too far from the sun.

Many planets do not have such a nearly circular orbit. Pluto, for example, has a highly elliptical orbit which at times has it inside the orbit of Neptune. If we were just 5 percent closer to the sun than the average 93 million miles we are from the sun, we would fry, and life would not be possible as we know it. If the Earth were just 10 percent further away from the sun than we are, this would be a frozen planet which would negate most life processes.

Also, if we were much, much closer to the sun than we are, our planet would fall into a condition of "tidal lock," as our moon is with the Earth and as Mercury is with the sun. This means that the Earth would cease to rotate as it does, and one side of the Earth would forever face the sun and be scorched at temperatures above that at which our cooking ovens bake, while the other side would forever be in night and frozen. Both conditions would negate the possibility of life as we know it.[426]

The outer half of our solar system is populated by the gas giants Jupiter, Saturn, Uranus, and Neptune, which happily act as a ring of protection for the Earth as they sweep the outer solar system of most debris such as comets and wayward asteroids and they experience most of the collisions which could end life on Earth. This protection was well observed in 1994 when the Shoemaker-Levy comet slammed into Jupiter after first being ripped apart by its gravity.[427]

The Earth has a moon the perfect size and composition for a number of effects vital to life. Our moon is much larger in respect to the size of our planet than most other bodies in our solar system. This allows the moon to stabilize the tilt of the earth at about 23.5°, which allows us to have the consistent seasons for which the life cycles of Earth's plants and animals depend on and are calibrated for. This large moon creates the tides we see in our oceans, which mixes the ocean waters while keeping them oxygenated and preventing stagnation, even to the depths of the oceans.[428]

The moon is also the perfect size and distance from us to allow for the occurrence and viewing of solar eclipses. This was either designed or an unbelievably extraordinary coincidence. Without this amazing accident (or design) of the moon being 400 times smaller than the sun but at the same time 400 times closer to us than the sun, solar eclipses would be impossible. When the moon passes between us and the sun, it completely blots out the full body of the sun but allows us an opportunity to see the sun's corona (its atmosphere) and examine it, which cannot be ordinarily done due to the sun's brilliance. There is no other set of bodies in this solar system that allow for such observations.[429] The large number of craters on the moon also testify to the fact that it has endured many meteor, asteroid, and comet hits that otherwise could have impacted the Earth.[430]

Our sun has been said to be just a very ordinary star and not special in the least, but nothing could be further from the truth. Our sun is categorized by astronomers as a "G2 main-sequence yellow dwarf," which is larger than 90 percent of all stars. Smaller red dwarfs constitute 75 percent of all observed stars. These stars are incredibly unstable and would destroy any type of life via their frequent large bursts of radiation. Also, if we were circling one of these stars, it would give off the wrong type of radiations to serve life, and we would have to be so close to the star to get sufficient heat to have liquid water that we would both subject ourselves to its frequent flares killing life and cause us to fall into tidal lock and stopping our world's rotation. Thankfully, we do not revolve around this most numerous type of star, a red dwarf.

But simply orbiting a yellow dwarf is not what has made life possible on Earth all by itself. Many Yellow dwarfs are paired in binary star systems (two stars in the center of a solar system), which creates an extremely unstable set of radiation sources for life support. Further, most yellow dwarfs observed, while not as unstable as red dwarfs, are *still far too unstable to support life*. Their frequent solar flares and ejections of lethal radiations would doom life. **Our sun is incredibly stable as stars go.** While it has occasional flares and mass ejections, they are far less frequent and severe than almost all yellow dwarfs observed to date, and our sun *emits just the right mix* of spectral and infrared radiations to fuel life on Earth. Again, we either got unbelievably lucky, or this star was designed to support life![431]

Our place in our galaxy is also an incredibly special one. We reside in a spiral galaxy we call the "Milky Way." Our solar system's position is more than halfway out from the center of the galaxy in a position between spiral arms. Astronomers have described this position as being within what they call the "galactic halo zone" or the "galactic habitable zone." We are located far away from the radiation-soaked center of our galaxy, with numerous radiation generating supernovae, and which we also believe contains a massive black hole. The spiral arms are only somewhat better; since stars and debris are so tightly packed in these, the likelihood of collisions with debris such as dust clouds, as well as being subjected to radiations from supernovae, goes way up. Thus, our position away from the center of the galaxy and between spiral arms puts us into another "Goldilocks Zone." This placement perfectly positions our solar system to support Earth's fragile life systems.[432]

Further, this position away from the galactic center and between spiral arms puts us into a position to observe the rest of our galaxy and universe in ways that would not be possible if we were deep within a spiral arm or the galactic center. This is another blessed circumstance like our moon, being in just the right place and the right size to allow us to observe the sun's corona. In this case, our position within the galaxy not only supports life but *maximizes our ability to observe the cosmos.*[433] Again, is this just a fortunate accident, or is this an intentional placement by the Creator not only to protect life but also to make it possible for His creations (us) to see all that He has created?

Indeed, the universe itself seems to be "fine-tuned" for life to exist, as we detailed in a previous section. If the entire universe all occurred by chance, why should it be accidentally fine-tuned with exactly the physical constants necessary to support life?

And the list of happy accidents goes on. In all, it is estimated that our planet, solar system, galaxy, and universe have a total of more than 200 attributes that if any one of them did not exist, then life could not be here. Dr. Guillermo Gonzalez, who has a PhD in astronomy and co-wrote the book "Privileged Planet," has put the odds at our Earth existing as it does and where it does at one chance out of 1,000,000,000,000,000.[434]

When Dr. Gonzalez estimated that ridiculously low chance of us being here and alive by chance, he did so a couple of decades ago when astronomers thought the universe was full of Earth-like planets in habitable zones all over the universe. Decades later, the Hubble and Kepler telescopes have found more than 5000 exoplanets, none of which meet most, let alone all of these attributes which the Earth does to support life.[435] Unlike the prevailing wisdom of a few decades ago, that the Earth is just an average planet, circling a very average star, in a galaxy with nothing special about it, such thinking is now observationally proved to be completely wrong!

Our current information shows that the *Earth is a very special place* and that Dr. Gonzalez's incredibly low estimates of this planet being anything but designed for life are being strengthened each and every day. Indeed, it appears the Bible knew exactly what it was talking about when it said this planet "**was formed to be inhabited**."

The Sun Moves!

For centuries, skeptics have claimed that the Bible is in error since a reading of Psalm 19 can be interpreted to suggest that the Earth is the center of our solar system, and the sun revolves around it. This is what the Ptolemaic view of our universe said for about 1700 years, and most believed it and thought the Bible agreed with them. Of course, we know today that, in fact, the Earth revolves around the sun.

Psalms 19: 1-6 (NIV) says:

> The heavens declare the glory of God; the skies proclaim the work of his hands. Day after day they pour forth speech; night after night they reveal knowledge.... **In the heavens God has pitched a tent** (universe?) **for the sun. It is like a bridegroom coming out of his chamber** (galaxy/universe?)**, like a champion rejoicing to run his course. It rises at one end of the heavens and makes its circuit to the other;** nothing is deprived of its warmth." (This last phrase implies another side to the Earth, and it is not being flat.)

The last two verses (along with Psalms 104:5 and others) are the ones that the skeptics jumped on to say that the sun revolved around the Earth to warm it all. We now know, of course, that this warming of all the Earth is accomplished by the Earth revolving around the sun while rotating on its axis to allow for the surface of the Earth to be equally warmed. So, was the Bible wrong when it said the sun has a circuit or a course?

The old apologetic for this was that the circuit described is just what we observed from Earth, so God was describing what we saw in the sky and experienced, making no comment on what was actually occurring. Today modern science has given us what may be an even deeper meaning to these verses.

Astronomy has revealed to us that our solar system, with the sun at its center, is revolving (moving through space) around the center of our Milky Way Galaxy at a speed of around 500,000 miles per hour relative to the galactic center. This "circuit" will take over 200 million years for the sun and our solar system to complete.[436] Thus, the question comes whether these verses are really a problem for the Bible or a revelation of an understanding of the cosmos thousands of years ahead of man?

Now, what about verses in the Bible which describe the Earth not moving? Wouldn't these contradict this interpretation of the Bible saying the Earth moves and put the Bible in error? The verses in question, such as Psalms 104:5, were leveled against Galileo at his trial since he was advocating for the Earth not being at the center of the universe as the Ptolemaic system did. However, such verses have been theologically interpreted as saying that it was the Jews (referred to as the Earth) were not moving (not evangelizing). Such interpretations would say that these verses were figurative and did not refer to the Earth or our solar system.

Further, an equivalent translation for moved used in Psalms 104:5 where it says in some translations that the Earth will not be moved is "removed" (this, in fact, is a predominate translation of the Hebrew as shown in its inclusion in the King James translation). If inserted, the verse says that the Earth will not be removed (giving it permanence in its orbit and place in the solar system). Such an interpretation turns this whole discussion from a verse that might have contradicted the Bible to one which shows prescience understanding by the Bible thousands of years ahead of man's discoveries.

Gravity in Space

Job 38:31-33 (ASV) says:

> Canst thou **bind the cluster of the Pleiades**, or **loose the bands of Orion**? Canst thou lead forth the Mazzaroth (the Zodiac of constellations) in their season? Or canst thou guide the Bear with her train? Knowest thou the **ordinances of the heavens**? Canst thou establish the dominion thereof in the earth?

These verses, according to many scholars, indicate that either Job or his adviser understood that gravity is an operational force of nature in the skies.

Now, to many of us, this seems a stretch to say that, but let me explain something you may not know. Most constellations (groups of stars) and other star clusters (asterisms) in the sky are made up of stars many thousands of light-years apart from one another and are not connected by their own gravity. They only look to be next to one another from our two-dimensional view of them from the Earth, but they are not.

Of all the identified star groups visible to the naked eye, the Pleiades (Job 38:31) star group (also known as the "Seven Sisters") is one of a very few star groups actually close enough to each other physically (not just as they appear in the sky to the naked eye) and it is now known, they are a gravitationally bound star group traveling in the same direction. Most other star groups visible to the naked eye are unbound, with the possible exception of the Hyades and just a very few other groups visible to the Hebrews in biblical times.[437] Without telescopes and modern apparatus, it was *impossible* for Job to know that these stars were gravitationally linked, and yet the Bible called this star group out of the hundreds of star groups across the sky, inferring they were linked. The odds against citing this truth by accident are mathematically impossible.

Recently some critics of this interpretation of this scripture have claimed that the Pleiades are not gravitationally bound. They say this since Doppler readings of these stars' velocities indicate to them that their relative velocities are such that in 250-million years, these stars will fly apart from one another and not be gravitationally bound; thus, they are not bound. To that criticism, we make two notes. First, via parallax measurements, we can verify that the Pleiades are now sufficiently close to one another in space that their gravitational fields do affect one another. This was also true 4000 years ago when Job was written. If these stars become unbound in 250 million years does not negate the fact they are all gravitationally intertwined (bound) at present. Further, the work of Halton Arp and other astronomers has shown that supposed Doppler measurements of red and blue shifts in some cases may not give us indication of relative velocities but instead something completely different. Thus, there is a question of whether these stars ever will be unbound.

To make it clearer that there is insider information going on here is how the writer added the second clause of this verse, "**or loose the bands of Orion**." This indicates knowledge that the stars in Orion's belt are actually three-star systems that are **not** gravitationally bound but which are flying apart from one another in space in three separate directions (they are "loosed from one another").

Again, there are astronomers who debate that the constellation Orion is truly unbound. They say this whole verse is only poetic license showing God's power. They first agree that while the stars in Orion are so far apart from one another that they are not gravitationally bound as the Pleiades are, but they define them as bound since these stars happen to travel in the same direction and thus are "dimensionally bound." This is just bad semantics on boundedness. Further, these skeptics have noted a group of stars at the core of the Orion, which are invisible to the naked eye which are gravitationally bound since they are so close together. Having a very few invisible to the eye stars bound in the midst of a visible constellation of stars that are gravitationally unbound does not invalidate this scripture nor its indication of God's knowledge of His creation.

Further, this verse refers to other star clusters in the sky and makes a note of their movements being governed by the "**ordinances of the heavens**." This comment comes more than 3500 years before Sir Isaac Newton formulated the laws of motion, which describe the Laws (ordinances) of the heavens which govern star's motions. This verse shows that Job had correct astronomical information far ahead of his time![438]

Radio Waves in the Bible?

In Job 38:7 (NIV), it says, "…while the **morning stars sang together** and all the angels shouted for joy?" Most people over the centuries have assigned this verse as being very poetic, but not in any way true or scientific. However, the last 75 years had shown that this verse may contain some very deep scientific meaning revealed in Job more than 3700 years before man discovered it.

In astronomy today, there are several types of telescopes, including optical, infrared, millimeter-wave, and other radio telescopes. Radio telescopes are dishes that focus themselves on small portions of the sky in search of radio waves from the cosmos. Huge arrays of these telescopes have been constructed to listen to the universe. They were the main components in the SETI (Search for Extraterrestrial Intelligence) project, which went on for decades in search of radio signals from space, which might give us evidence of intelligent life on another planet.

These massive arrays of radio telescopes have never picked up evidence of intelligent transmissions, but many other transmissions have been found. Quasars are objects in space that give off an incredible amount of radio waves and other types of radiation, not given off by stars at this intensity. But it is not only quasars that give off radio waves. Pulsars, in particular, emit pulses of radio waves in audible frequencies. The Crab Nebula pulsar gives off radio waves to a very regular beat! It has been found that stars themselves give off radio waves as one of the spectrums of natural stellar radiation.[439] So when the Bible says that the "stars sang together," it can now be seen not just as poetic, but a very possible knowledge of the radio wave emissions of stars thousands of years before man discovered them!

Further on this point is what also seems to be the rather poetic verse of Job 38:35 (ESV), says, "Can you send **lightnings** that they may go, and say to you, Here we are?" This appears to be a scientifically ludicrous statement that "lightnings" (electricity or fiber-optic light pulses) can be sent and then manifest themselves in speech.

But did you know that all electromagnetic radiation, from radio waves to x-rays, travels at the speed of light? This is why light and electricity enable us to have seemingly instantaneous wireless communication with someone on the other side of the Earth. The fact that light could be sent and then manifest itself in speech wasn't discovered by science until 1864, more than 3,600 years after Job was written. It was then that the "British scientist James Clerk Maxwell suggested that electricity and light waves were two forms of the same thing." Heinrich Hertz will experimentally prove Maxwell's concepts in the 1880s, which is why we today refer to the unit of frequency of a radio wave (one cycle per second) as a *"hertz."*[440]

Light can be Divided

Sir Isaac Newton studied light and discovered that white light is made of seven colors, which can be "parted" and then recombined.[441] Science confirmed this four centuries ago, while God in the Bible declared it four millennia ago!

Job 38:24 (KJV): *By what way is the light **parted**, which scattereth the east wind (power) upon the earth?*

Now, some theologians interpret this verse as figuratively referring to "the light" as the light of God and God's prominence, which they say in this verse "scatters" (disperses and pushes aside) the eastern mysticisms and religions. Thus, this verse may have nothing to do with physical light, or does it?

On top of the discoveries of Newton showing that light can be "parted" (divided into component parts), scattering of light is another concept not understood in ancient times. Certainly, when the sun comes up in the eastern sky at any point on the Earth, its rays are scattered, giving us the brilliant sunrises we love to watch. The scattering of light is a phenomenon resulting from interactions with dust in the atmosphere, differing levels of our atmosphere, water vapor, and more. None of this was understood in biblical times, and yet there is this verse here that seems to have a very modern understanding of physical light.

How did the Bible know something about the nature of light, which was not discovered by man for about 3500 years after Job wrote it into the Bible? "Parting" light is not even a natural concept to those of ancient times. Some will argue that this verse simply makes a theological or poetic comment. But the wording used is precise enough, and the scientific truth so specific that it is difficult to buy such a claim. Also, note that the word "wind" in this verse could have alternately translated as power, further strengthening this interpretation.

Light Moves

Job 38: 19-20 says, *"Where is the **way** to the dwelling of light? And as for darkness, where is the place thereof, That thou shouldest take it to the bound thereof, And that thou shouldest discern the **paths** to the house thereof?* (American Standard Translation) The literal meaning for the Hebrew word used, which is translated here as "way," actually means "traveled path or road."

These verses give a heavy reference to the fact that light moves. That was not known in biblical times, and it is contrary to what was taught prior to just a few hundred years ago. It was supposed for thousands of years that light simply instantaneously existed everywhere it was. There was no concept of it being in motion. For most of man's history, light was seen as a disturbance in the air, whereas air was viewed as one of the four primordial substances of all matter.

Now, Democritus, a Greek philosopher, who lived between the 5th and 4th century's BC, argued that all of existence was made up of tiny indivisible atoms (this could have included light), but his ideas were ignored for thousands of years by other philosophers, who believed in the four elements of wind, fire water and earth being the substances which made up all existence. Thus, scientists have been speculating as to the true nature of light for thousands of years.

There was no way to test light's movement in those times since moving at 186,000 miles per second is so fast that only in more recent times could the movement be discerned.

In the 17th century, Sir Isaac Newton suggested that light might be made of tiny particles which moved in a straight line. Christian Huygens proposed that light traveled as a wave. Scientists now believe that light is a form of radiant energy and that it travels in electromagnetic waves at the speed of light (denoted as "c" = about 186,000 miles per second) in a straight line, as Newton proposed just a little more than three hundred years ago. It takes about eight minutes for light to travel at this speed on its path from our Sun to the Earth. Thus, scientists now believe there really is a "path" or "way" of light, just as the Bible says.[442]

So how did the Bible know this 3800 years ago? It is absolutely amazing that the closer we look at each specific word used in the Bible, the more we cannot but stand in awe of its intricate detail, flawless accuracy, purposeful design, relevance across time, and perfect harmony of content.[443] Only God Himself could orchestrate the writing of such a book over more than 1500 years of time by 40 or more authors!

Prescience from the Very First Verse

The first verse of the Bible (NIV) says, "In the **beginning** God created **the heavens** and the **earth**." It is usually missed by the casual reader, but in this first sentence of the Bible are four prescience claims which modern science is supporting.

"In the beginning…" tells us the Bible claims that there was a **beginning to the universe**. All current scientific theories support this conclusion, including the "Big Bang" cosmology. In fact, everything in our existence has a beginning and an end. We are born and die.

We get a new car and begin to own it. We get married, and a single becomes a married person. This claim seems common sense to us, but in truth, it is not that easy an assumption that the universe had a beginning. This refers not only to the concept of a beginning but the creation of the dimension of **time**. Before the beginning, there was nothing, no matter, no space, no time. Thus, these first three words of the Bible signal the beginning of time and space.

Remember back to our perusal of many of the creation stories from cultures all over the world. Many said that everything had a beginning as the Bible does, but others did not. Some, such as the Gaia and Hindu philosophies, propose that the Earth and the Universe are eternal. Others would posit that there was something here before the beginning, from which a god or matter formed. This is another form of the eternal matter argument. How did the Bible get this simple statement right when there were other competing beliefs to choose from that did not include a beginning but assumed eternal existence? Did the Bible have inside information of how it was all made?

Many scientists up to sixty years ago believed in an eternal universe. Up until then, the leading concept of where matter came from was called the "steady-state theory." This theory says that somewhere in the universe, there is a place where the first law of thermodynamics does not apply.[444] The first law says matter does not just pop into existence. Our current physics is based on this assumption, and yet the prevailing theory in science until the 1960s was that there was some grand exemption to this law. At that time, critics would have said that this scientific belief was in contradiction to the Bible, which not only says that everything had a beginning but also, in multiple places, confirms the Bible's devotion to the first law of thermodynamics being universal (without exception).

In Genesis 1:1 (NIV), it also says that **"...God created the heavens..."** this means that the *fabric of space was created*. Other verses go on to say that God spread out the heavens like unfurling a scroll or a rolled carpet. Both of these descriptions are consistent with modern astronomy. Our observations of the universe not only believe that matter came from nothing in the beginning (the leading theory which includes this is the "Big Bang"), but these theories also include that the fabric of space itself. These theories say that space is more than just emptiness but has a fabric that is not yet well understood but is theorized to have some type of "zero-point" energy within it.

Space was both created and flung out from a central point of creation. Modern astronomy supposes that what they observe is the universe proceeding from a condensed state of initial creation.[445] How did the Bible get this right? How did it know that everything was created in one area of space and stretched out from there to the far reaches we see today? All those other exotic stories from other cultures do not get this right when they say the universe was eternal, or existed in two forms, or was already filled from the beginning. But the Bible does. How can the Bible be so special?

One point to belabor is the idea the Bible describes God **"stretching out the heavens."** This concept is eerily similar to what modern astronomy has theorized about, which is a rapid expansion in the initial stages of the universe. The Bible in Psalms 104:2; Isaiah 40:22; Isaiah 42:5; Job 9:8; and Job 37:18 all say that the Creator at the beginning **"stretched out the heavens"**. Indeed, Isaiah 42:5 says, "Thus saith God the Lord, he that created the heavens and **spread them abroad**…" (Geneva Bible). The timing of this stretching or spreading of the heavens just after they were created completely parallels the secularly theorized "inflation period," which rapidly expanded all of our universe from an exceedingly small region to an immense size.

This theorized expansion does so in a way not possible via the normal physical laws of space and time. Astronomers and physicists cannot explain the cause of inflation. However, this inflation period is a crucial "add on" fix to the "Big Bang Theory" of the universe's formation.[446] The Bible not only describes a period analogous to inflation but gives insight into the fact that it was caused by an actor and power (God) outside of our universe, which explains how this often-theorized impossibility of nature could have occurred.

It was further found first by Edwin Hubble in the 1920s and later confirmed by experiments in 1998 that the universe appears to be constantly expanding.[447] All of the noted verses in the Bible describe an expansion, but these are mentioned nowhere else in other creation stories from around the world. Again, how did the Bible get this one right? Was it divine help?

Astronomer Dr. Hugh Ross has done an examination of the more than 300 creation myths, stories, and accounts from across the world and its varied cultures. This examination revealed to him that only the Judeo-Christian Bible had within its description an account consistent with what we think we know about the universe in modern astronomy. The result of this investigation is what led Dr. Ross, who had before this been an atheist and a skeptic, to investigate Christianity and become a believer.

Finally, this first verse of the Bible (NIV) says, **"…God created the heavens and the earth."** This says that all *matter* in the entire universe was created in the beginning. Again, this claim by the Bible agrees with current theories of universal origins. This claim also vastly differs from the claims of most other creation stories, which claim matter already existed, is eternal, or matter is made after the beginning by a god or force. Modern astronomy constantly tells us that we live in a very ordinary solar system, in no special place in the universe. We are told that we are insignificant, which is contrary to the incredibly special creation described in the Bible.

But, when we examine the Doppler shifts of differing galaxies about our universe, we find that they appear to line up in a series of concentric rings encircling our present place in the cosmos. This could indicate not only that the universe was rolled out like a scroll (as the Bible says) from a central point, but this "quantization of redshift data" shows that our solar system appears to be within 100,000 light-years of the *center of the universe* (also consistent with the biblical account). (It should be noted that this redshift data is quite controversial. Analysis by astronomer Halton Arp suggests that our present interpretation of redshift may be completely flawed. If his analysis proves out, it will not only invalidate this quantized redshift data but also invalidate the measurements of distances to all galaxies we see in the universe and seriously put into question our current expanding universe cosmologies.)[448]

An even stronger set of data for the Earth occupying a uniquely special place in the universe has been provided by measurements of the "cosmic microwave background" radiation (CMB). This very low-level background radiation, seemingly coming to us from deep space, is supposedly the leftovers or "echo" of the Big Bang. This data is at odds with the Big Bang cosmology in two ways. It is far more homogeneous (constant in temperature) than the Big Bang would have predicted via inflation. Yet it has hot and cool regions which seem aligned with our solar system and are symmetric to our solar system!

This data seems to show that the CMB is aligned with the plane of our Earth and our sun and with the ecliptic (plane of our solar system)![449] Contrary to what we have been told by modern astronomy, these two pieces of data would suggest that we are not insignificant, and in fact, our solar system and our planet are located in what might be the most special place in the entire universe! If true, this would be amazingly consistent with how the Bible characterizes this planet and ourselves as special creations.

This data is not only consistent with what the Bible says but leads to two sets of theories proposed by astronomers. These theories show how it is possible for us to have experienced only a few thousand years of existence on this planet and in this solar system, while the rest of the universe has experienced billions of years of time. All of this evidence we are now finding in the cosmos supports what is written in the Bible.

Thus, the Bible states in its first verse that matter, energy, the fabric of space, and time were all created in the beginning together and that the universe is not eternal. These are verified tenants of our scientific observations of our universe today. Again, we ask the question, "How did the Bible get all of this right?" How did the Bible know this when the steady-state theorists of just sixty years ago had not figured this one out? How did the Bible know about stretching of the universe 3400 years before modern cosmologists imagined the same? How could the Bible predict that we live in a seemingly expanding universe when no other scientists nor cultures would describe it as such until the 1920s? These things only make sense if the Bible had inside information from the Creator of all things Himself!

Mathematics in the Bible

More than 4000 years ago, the Mesopotamian states of Sumer, Akkad, and Assyria, together with Ancient Egypt and the Ebla, began using arithmetic, algebra, and geometry for purposes of taxation, commerce, trade and also in the field of astronomy and to formulate calendars and record time. So it is not surprising that there are places with math and mathematical calculations in the Bible. What is surprising is when the math we find in the Bible shows knowledge we have only discovered for ourselves very recently. Here are two examples of higher math principles and calculations found in the Bible.

The Molten Sea and Pi?

Some Bible skeptics charge that the Bible shows a lack of knowledge of mathematics and therefore could not have been penned by an infallible God. First Kings 7:23 says King Solomon made a molten sea (a circular fountain) at God's direction. 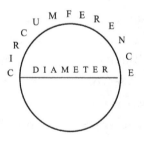 According to 2 Chronicles 4:2, Solomon made it 10 cubits in diameter and 30 cubits in circumference. For those not great at math, this is no problem, but for the mathematician, this could be.

The problem comes from your middle school geometry and math courses. You may remember that C= π x D or circumference equals Pi times diameter. Pi is a geometric constant approximated at about 3.14. (NASA, who has to be extremely accurate with their calculations aiming at distant planets, uses Pi correct to two hundred decimal places). If you multiply 10 cubits (the diameter of this fountain) by 3.14, you should get about 31.4 cubits, not 30 as the Bible says. Did God fail math too?

The problem here is not in God's math, nor in the accuracy of the biblical account, but probably in the accuracy of the cubit measurement in ancient times. The cubit was a measure from the average man's elbow to the end of his hand and fingers. In full-grown men, this can vary from 16 to 22 inches and varies even more with youths. On average, this unit of the cubit is taken to be about 18 inches.

With such an inaccurate measurement tool as your forearm, the actual diameter could have been as little as 9.55 cubits (which rounds to and is approximately 10) and gives a circumference of just 30 cubits around. Or the diameter could have been closer to an actual 10 cubits across, and when measured around came close to 31.4 cubits, but when you take into account the inaccuracies of this measuring system, you find that *only the ten's digit* is **mathematically significant**.

To this, we mean that when using such an approximated measuring instrument, we can only be assured of approximated answers. This gets us into the study of *significant digits*, a mathematical concept only defined and explored in the 17th century AD up to today.[450]

In the nineteen fifties and sixties, before handheld calculators, it was a frequent help for mathematicians and engineers to use an instrument called a *slide rule*, which could quickly estimate large and complicated calculations. The limitation with this handy little device was that it only gave approximated answers for large calculations and the amount of uncertainty in the numbers given limited the certainty of the answer. In the calculation of the molten sea, it would have been understood that the inaccuracy of the measuring tool meant that only a rounded answer for the diameter and circumference measurements could be trusted to one significant digit (the tens digit). This means that even if we were multiplying 10 cubits times 3.14 and the mathematical answer is 31.4, we can only rely on it really being around 30 cubits in circumference due to the inaccuracies in our measurements.

This whole field of significant digits was used regularly in the 1950s, 1960s, and early 1970s due to the use of the slide rule. NASA engineers frequently used them to check inflight calculations. But since the use of calculators and computers replaced the now obsolete slide rule, we no longer consider significant digit accuracy as much since more exact and complicated calculations are easily done. Only when there is uncertainty in the accuracy of measurements does this uncertainty factor again enter the picture, as it does in this biblical narrative.

Incidentally, if the "handbreadth" widths of the sides of the molten sea were subtracted from the 10-cubit diameter specified, then you get a diameter of 9.555 cubits for the inside diameter of the fountain excluding the width of the sides, which when multiplied by Pi gives you a circumference of exactly 30 cubits. Thus, if the biblical reference of a circumference was intended to give the circumference of the inside rim of the fountain and not the outside, then the circumference given is mathematically accurate. This explanation works as well and again says the Bible could do its math!

Thus, we find that in the case of Solomon's Molten Sea, the figures quoted in the Bible may or may not be inaccurate, but may well reveal knowledge of significant digits, a field of math which man will not discover for more than 2500 years after the writings in Kings and Chronicles. What the Bible could be showing here is not inaccuracy or error but an understanding of mathematics thousands of years ahead of man. This further attests to this text being God-inspired!

Supertankers in the Bible?

The Bible in Genesis 6:15 (NIV) says, **"This is how you are to build it: The ark is to be three hundred cubits long, fifty cubits wide and thirty cubits high."**

The cubit was not a perfectly accurate measure, as discussed in the last section. It was the length from a person's elbow to tip of his index finger, and different people's forearms and hands will be different sizes and lengths. In ancient times there were both short and long measures for a cubit. The short cubit was anywhere between 16 and 19 inches in length. The "long cubit" could be around 20 to 22 inches in length.[451] Using the short cubit at 18 inches, this verse would describe the ark as being 450 feet long, 75 feet wide, and 45 feet high at a minimum. Using the long cubit, the ark would have been more than 600 feet long. Either way, this would have made the Ark of Noah longer and wider than a football field and would have filled a modern football stadium to give us an idea of its size. The long cubit measurements would give us an ark a little smaller than the size of our modern oil tankers with which we transport oil and other products.

Regardless of which cubit was used, the comparative ratios of the sides are interesting. The biblical dimensions of 300 cubits length to 50 cubits in length give a 6 to 1 length to width ratio. This is the exact ratio used for constructing modern supertankers, which is a ratio derived from computer simulations for the dimensions which give maximum stability on rough seas.[452]

In 1609, a ship was built at Hoom, Holland using the proportions of the Ark as described in the Bible. This ratio for shipbuilding revolutionized ship designs to the point that by 1900 every large ship on the high seas tended toward the proportions of Ark.[453] If you disbelieve the Bible, how did a person like Noah or any ancient writer, who was not a boat builder by profession, come up with the *perfect idealized proportions* for building a ship of this size? If you do not believe the Bible is God's word, how did it come up with the exact proportional ratios derived from computer simulations[454] for this size ship? The Bible described this three thousand years before ships this size were routinely constructed and before computers were even invented?

To see a full-scale example of this miraculous engineering from 4500 years ago, go to the *Ark Encounter* exhibit 40 miles south of Cincinnati, Ohio, in Northern Kentucky. There *Answers in Genesis* has constructed a full-size Noah's Ark using only wood, wooden pegs, pitch, and the presumed technology of Noah's day. This 520-foot long, three-story high ark is a testament to the accuracy of God's directions to us in the Bible and the authority with which it speaks. Its perfect seaworthy dimensions testify to God's scientific insights thousands of years before man's discoveries. There is also a full-size Ark replica afloat in Holland.

What about the Flood?

What about the flood? Doesn't the contention that a worldwide flood covered the earth falsify the Bible and show that it could not be from God? After all, there is a broad consensus across the world that no such worldwide flood occurred and that this is a myth![455]

Well, you already know how I have shown that consensus science can be very flawed. Just because a lot of people believe it does not make it so. There was almost universal consensus across the world for more than two thousand years that a great way to treat most illnesses was to draw blood out of a person and get the poison out. It had some logic, was universally accepted, but it was just flat wrong![456]

We have already demonstrated in chapter 3 how the Great Discontinuity, sedimentary rock layers with millions of fossils buried within, the Tapeats Sandstone, Mount St. Helens, fossil graveyards, and much other geologic evidence are consistent with a huge hydrologic event on this planet in the past.

The more than 270 cultures with flood legends from across the world hold that sometime in the past, a huge flood occurred, which is recorded by them. The wide distribution of these stories from across the world suggests it was a worldwide event. Some modernists, however, claim that most of these recordings in histories and myths refer to a large flood in the Middle East more than four thousand years ago around the "Black Sea."[457]

There are some problems with this modernist answer, however. First, the broad scope of the flood stories from around the world shows that it was not a local event but truly a worldwide cataclysm. Second, you cannot get a local flood from a plain reading of the Bible. The Bible says that the flood **"covered the whole Earth"** and that it covered the "mountains to a depth of 15 cubits" (about 22 feet). If it were just a local event, why build a huge boat? Why not just move away from the flood location? Modernists try to "read" a local flood event into the Bible, but it simply does not read that way, and in doing so, they have to contort the Bible's words completely out of any semblance of normal meaning.

As shown in this chapter, we now have geologic proof that not only is 70 percent of the earth covered with water to an average depth of more than a mile, but that there is a store of more than three times that amount of water bound up in the earth's mantle. The claim that it is physically impossible for such a flood to occur on Earth is patently false. The Bible also infers that prior to the flood and the tectonic events which may have accompanied or followed the flood (which the Bible says raised the mountains to their present heights), the pre-flood Earth was much flatter with no extremely tall mountains. This would make such a worldwide flood even more plausible. For scientists to contend as they do today that Mars, a planet with no liquid water on its surface today, was once completely covered with water, as are shown by its landforms; and then to turn around and contend that our planet, with such a wealth of water, could not have experienced a global flood is laughable!

In the last section, we saw that the ratio of the dimensions on which the Ark was to be built was perfectly maximized for a large vessel to handle heavy seas, as would have been the case of a violent worldwide flood.

Another contention by skeptics is that the Ark story is fictitious because you could never have gotten all of the ten million+ species of land animals[458] onto the Ark. This fallacious contention is based on the false assumption that you would need to house millions of species and that **"two of every kind"** means two of every species. But as we have demonstrated earlier in this book, the Bible does not say this. The Bible says that two of every unclean **kind** (and seven pairs of each clean kind) were put on board. Thus, there only had to be two from the dog kind. You would not have to have all species of dog kinds, so you need not have two bulldogs, two wolves, two coyotes, two German Shepherds, two terriers, two Labradors, two collies, and on and on. This would have also been true for each and every animal **kind** on the plane. Therefore, if the Bible were telling the truth, you would not need to put ten million species on the Ark, but probably about 4000 or fewer kinds (perhaps 16,000 total animals), the average size being about the size of a small sheep.

With the size of the Ark dimensions given in the Bible, it has been shown that this would fill only about 37 percent of the Ark, leaving ample space for food and human living space on the Ark.[459] The really tricky problems for the practicality of the Ark is not how you fit all the animals into it, but how do you handle the problems of feeding, clearing the waste and air circulation for so many animals in an ancient wooden craft of this size?

There are, however, good answers to these questions as well. John Woodmorappe (that is a pen name) has done a study on the technical feasibility of the Ark. His findings are published in his book, *"Noah's ark: A Feasibility Study"* (1996, Institute for Creation Research publishers). In his book, he shows "…all of the solutions to the putative (supposed) problems with the Ark account…are based on a solid study of low-tech animal-keeping techniques, low-tech husbandry, etc. Moreover, far from being fantastic, speculative, or even theoretical, the techniques and solutions (cited) in this book have been *applied* by various uneducated, pre-industrial peoples throughout history. Much of the contents…discusses and documents this central fact."

You can read the book, or you can go to the previously mentioned "Ark Encounter" exhibit in Northern Kentucky, which shows the ingenious ways that ancient man could have solved the complex problems of waste disposal, feeding, and air circulation for so many animals.

Famous atheist and teacher of evolution, Bill Nye ("The Science Guy" as he bills himself, even though he possesses no doctorate in any science) used an effective "sound bite attack" on the Ark in his debate with creationist Ken Ham in 2014. Nye famously said the Ark could not have been seaworthy in heavy seas since the sinking of the large wooden ship Wyoming (1909, the largest wooden ship built in modern times) supposedly showed the Ark story was impossible! In doing so, he was repeating an often-heard critique of the Ark design as unseaworthy.[460]

What Nye and others fail to mention are the specifics of Wyoming. Unlike the Ark, Wyoming had six large masts, which stressed the hull and gave the ship major stability issues. Before sinking, Wyoming remained afloat for 14 years. This design of Wyoming was cheaply produced in that time period, and like other ships of this period, served for periods of only 10-15 years, which this largest design accomplished. The Ark would only have stayed afloat for a little more than five months. It should also be noted the Wyoming-type ships usually only had a single-layer hull with a poor strap and strake design.

Mechanical engineer Tim Lovett has spent years researching the Ark account. His research led to the design of the Ark built in Northern Kentucky. His research showed that if the design of the Ark included a "bowfin" (wooden sail) and a "skeg" (fixed rudder in front) underwater in the stern, this would have kept the Ark turned into the winds and the waves preventing consistent structural stresses and giving the boat the ultimate angle on which to take on huge waves. These were features all used by the ancient Greeks in ship designs.

Lovett found that if the Ark were built with three keel beams instead of one, with layered strakes (overlapping planking used by ancient Romans and Greeks), being pitched (waterproofed inside and out), used interlocking joints (called mortise and tenon) as well as self-sealing wooden pegs; these would have kept the ship watertight and structurally sound. Further, the layered strakes (multiple hulls used by the Chinese as early as the 1400's AD) could have worn away when debris or stresses hit it in this torrential flood, and the Ark itself would have remained intact and seaworthy.[461] Thus, it appears ancient men could have built a seaworthy huge wooden ship, and all of these designs features are not precluded by the instructions in the biblical account. This is verified as a fact in archaeology by the existence of a huge wooden warship 130 meters in length constructed by the Egyptians during the 3rd century BC.[462]

Thus, we find that a worldwide flood is far from impossible and, instead, is geologically supportable. That ancient writings from across the world agree that it occurred. We find the Bible had a plan for the Ark, which is not only feasible for the technology for the time but is architecturally sufficient for the task. This all shows that instead of the Ark and the flood account being a falsification of the Bible, we instead find that this event is one with a great amount of substantiation in geology and historical writings, as well as in practical science and engineering.

On a side note, it would behoove churches and church schools not to include artwork of cute "kiddy arks" with animals hanging out the top on children's room walls (nurseries may or may not be alright). Also, books detailing the flood to kids also should be screened for these Ark caricatures. Such images are engraved in the minds of impressionable young minds and embed in them the "story-like" ridiculousness of the Ark as just a kid's fairy tale. It makes it far more difficult in later years to emphasize this was real history and perfectly possible. We need to show them realistic models of the Ark from a young age to make this reality come alive for them.

The Seven-Day Week and Proper Work Hours

One of the most interesting proofs of Bible teachings predating not only all other religions but all other cultures is the idea of the seven-day week. Other calendar units can be traced to astronomy or nature. Our months are roughly equivalent to the lunar cycle, upon which many early calendars were based. Our year is equivalent to one revolution of the Earth around our sun. But, the seven-day week, used almost universally by cultures across the Earth, has no such natural guide which man could pick up on to emulate it. The fact that this seemingly arbitrary number has been followed almost universally across the world gives good evidence that all such cultures were following the model for a week first set down in the Bible.

Another interesting thing about the seven-day week is how this seemingly arbitrary number of days is maximized for man's use.

In 1929, the Russians experimented with a "continuous work week" where someone in a family unit was working every day of the week. For example, dad might be off on red day (one day out of seven), mom on blue day, and kids separately on yellow or other days. This continuous work week separated family members from each other on days off and made family bonding and socialization difficult. This was the social experiment being carried out to maximize the individual's productivity and not that of the family, whose value was minimized. This experiment did not lead to better productivity and was very unpopular, so it was scrapped the next year.[463]

Similarly, the Russians in the early twentieth century, along with the Chinese and Europeans, have experimented with all measures of work weeks. They have tried the fortnight or ten-day work week with nine days of labor and one day off.[464] They experimented with a 12-day week. Also, 8-day (ancient Romans), 5-day, 6-day, and 13-day weeks (ancient Aztecs) have been tried.[465]

In this country, we have and are still experimenting with four-day work weeks with expanded ten and twelve-hour shifts on those days. Recently in Europe, there has been a lot of experimentation with three- or four-day workweeks with only 30-hours of work. In

Scandinavia, there are ongoing experiments with five days of work and two off, with only 6-hour workdays, giving only a 30-hour workweek.[466] There have even been experiments with seven-day work weeks with no day of rest.[467]

So, how have all of these varied work weeks panned out when evaluated for the most efficiency and productivity as well as giving the worker rejuvenating rest. The answer overwhelmingly is that the traditional and biblical seven-day week with six days of work and one day of rest seems to yield the most productivity and best efficiency.[468]

The Bible on the subject of work further says in Psalms 127:2 (NASB), **"It is vain for you to rise up early, To retire late, To eat the bread of painful labors; For He gives to His beloved even in his sleep."** This is only one of many biblical verses cautioning against overwork. If you read through scripture, it also says sloth and laziness are sinful. What you get from reading the Bible is a concept that **"we should all work, but not to overwork,"** because overwork is both unproductive past a certain point and unhealthy. What is amazing is how these words written down thousands of years ago are now verified by current medical research. Current research says:

- Working more than 10 hours a day is associated with a 60 percent jump in risk of cardiovascular issues;
- 10 percent of those working 50 to 60 hours report relationship problems; the rate increases to 30 percent for those working more than 60 hours;
- Working more than 40 hours a week is associated with increased alcohol and tobacco consumption, as well as unhealthy weight gain in men and depression in women;
- Little productive work occurs after 50 hours per week;
- In companies with normal overtime, only 23 percent of workers had absentee rates above 9 percent. In companies with high overtime, 54 percent of workers had absentee rates above 9 percent;

- Individuals working 11 hours or more of overtime have an increased depression risk;
- Injury rates increase as work hours increase. Those who work 60 hours per week have a 23 percent higher injury hazard rate;
- In companies with an 8.7 percent overtime rate, researchers found no fatigue-related problems. When the overtime rate was 12.4 percent, however, fatigue-related problems were minor. By the time the overtime rate hit 15.4 percent, fatigue-related problems were severe;
- In manufacturing industries, a 10 percent increase in overtime yields a 2.4 percent decrease in productivity;
- In white-collar jobs, productivity declines by as much as 25 percent when workers put in 60 hours or more.

Many of the problems identified above tie to stress, which connects to hormonal imbalances. Specifically, stress raises cortisol, which can disrupt sleep, appetite, blood pressure, immune system function, memory/cognition, mood, and more.[469]

How did the Bible know that the six-day on, one off work week would be the most efficient and healthful for us? How also did it know the very limits to our work, which modern research is only finding today? It appears once again as if the Bible had inside information from the manufacturer of us all!

Medical Science and Health in the Bible

If God made us, then He is the "manufacturer of all life" and knows more about our workings than we do. Please always remember two things about modern medical science. Doctors call their work with people a "practice" because they are continually learning about human life and other life on this planet. We neither designed nor created this life; its immense complexity means that at this time, we have only a rudimentary understanding of all life systems and how they interact.

It also should be a sobering thought that the death rate today is still 100 percent. We will all die. We might delay it a while with medicine, exercise, and good living, but we are not the Creator. Nor do we actually control our life processes. The following sections show an amazing amount of biblical knowledge of medicine and what is healthful for us, which reveals the Bible knew things about our bodies far before we ever did. If the Bible were written by God, we would expect this.

The Bible Predicts what Medical Science Has Yet to Understand

The Bible in 1 Corinthians 1:27-29 (Berean Study Bible) says:

> **But God chose the foolish things of the world to shame the wise; God chose the weak things of the world to shame the strong.** God chose the lowly things of this world and the despised things—and the things that are not—to nullify the things that are, so that no one may boast before him.

The truth of these verses can be seen when we look at the incredible abilities of people with what is called "savant syndrome." Such people usually must live with caregivers because they have developmental disorders and are either handicapped or totally incapable of living in open society. Yet, they possess extraordinary abilities far beyond those of supposedly "normal" individuals.

One savant cannot count, but he can instantly sum the total of the registration numbers on all of the boxcars of a train speeding by!

A four-year-old blind savant heard a Mozart sonata and went to a piano and played the entire sonata without a mistake. He then went on tour and could play any of 5000 piano pieces by memory!

A pair of savant twins could instantly total the number of letters when shown a printed page.

Two brothers, who could not add the simplest of numbers, could instantly tell which day of the week any date in the past or 40,000 years in the future would fall!

One savant could listen to long passages in any language and repeat them flawlessly without understanding a single word of what he was saying![470]

Such incredible and unexplainable abilities were predicted by the Bible. Even more, the Lord went one step further and explained why He placed these abilities within our supposedly handicapped savants. He did so to remind us of how limited we are. Modern man is perhaps the most arrogantly proud generation of humans ever to walk the earth. We think we own ourselves and our possessions, understand all of creation and contemplate an existence without God. However, God has left us evidence of what we cannot understand and shows us the folly of such arrogance.

A Drink a Day can be Good for You!

Wine was a common beverage and part of the daily fare in Palestine during Old Testament times (Judges 19:19, 2 Chronicles 11:11). Jesus also partook of wine (Matthew 11:19, Luke 5:38-39, Luke 7:34). The Bible tells us wine was a gift from God to gladden men's hearts in Genesis 27:28 and Psalms 104:14-15. Wine was used at weddings and celebrations (John 2:1-3). Wine was used in worship (Exodus 29:40, Leviticus 23:13, Numbers 15:5). Wine was used in trade and for payment of debts (2 Chronicles 2:10, Ezekiel 27:18, Amos 2:8). And interestingly, wine was used as a *medicine* in both the Old and New Testaments (2 Samuel 16:2, Proverbs 31:6, Mark 15:23, Luke 10:34, 1 Timothy 5:23).

First Timothy 5:23 (NIV) says, **"Stop drinking only water, and use a *little* wine because of your stomach and your frequent illnesses."**

Contrary to uninformed secular opinion, the Bible says that there are good medicinal uses for alcohol when *taken in moderation*. On balance, the Bible strongly lectures against getting drunk and the dangers of strong drink on oneself.

Comments from the esteemed Mayo clinic on drinking read almost exactly like the Bible. The Mayo Clinic's webpage on healthy living says, "When it comes to alcohol, the *key is moderation*... (It has been found that) Moderate alcohol consumption may provide some health benefits, such as:

- Reduce your risk of developing and dying from heart disease
- Possibly reduce your risk of ischemic stroke (when the arteries to your brain become narrowed or blocked, causing severely reduced blood flow)
- Possibly reduce your risk of diabetes

(On the other hand)… while moderate alcohol use may offer some health benefits, heavy drinking—including binge drinking—has no health benefits. Excessive drinking can increase your risk of serious health problems, including:

- Certain cancers, including breast cancer and cancers of the mouth, throat, and esophagus
- Pancreatitis
- Sudden death if you already have cardiovascular disease
- Heart muscle damage (alcoholic cardiomyopathy) leading to heart failure
- Stroke
- High blood pressure
- Liver disease
- Suicide
- Accidental serious injury or death
- Brain damage and other problems in an unborn child[471]

Thus, current medical research verifies what the Bible has said for three thousand years. Both say that alcohol taken in moderation can be good for you, but as with most anything, drinking to excess can be dangerous for you. How did the Bible get that right so precisely?

Effect of Emotions on Health

King Solomon, noted for his historic wisdom, wrote or edited the biblical book of Proverbs. King Solomon in Proverbs 16:24 (ASV) said, **"Pleasant words are as a honeycomb, Sweet to the soul, and health to the bones."** and Proverbs 17:22 (ASV) says, **"A cheerful heart is a good medicine; but a broken spirit drieth up the bones."**

Today, modern medical studies are finding ties between emotions and body health all the time.[472] An example of this are studies that show how a positive disposition leading to regular comments and attitudes from people such as "Look on the sunny side of life" can actually help!

An article from the New York Times on this subject from March 17, 2017, said, "Researchers are finding that thoughts like these, the hallmarks of people sometimes called "cockeyed optimists," can do far more than raise one's spirits. They may actually improve health and extend life.

There is no longer any doubt that what happens in the brain influences what happens in the body. When facing a health crisis, actively cultivating positive emotions can boost the immune system and counter depression. Studies have shown an indisputable link between having a positive outlook and health benefits like lower blood pressure, less heart disease, better weight control, and healthier blood sugar levels."[473]

But those scientific studies were not available 2900 years ago when Solomon penned these words. How did he know these things? This question is especially important when you realize that the stresses of survival, marriages, kids, weather, seeking, tending, and growing food, dealing with oppressive government, dealing with the inequities and unfairness of existence meant that almost no one in Solomon's time was exempt from tremendous stresses, as are we. How in this environment could you even discern between the health of the stressed and the unstressed, since almost no one was not extremely stressed?

Going to Church is Good for Your Health!

Twenty medical studies done in the last century show that if a person attends church on an even semi-regular basis (once a month or more), that they will live longer and healthier lives![474]

Proverbs 3:1-2, 7-8 (KJV) promises this! It says there in Proverbs:

> My son, forget not my law; **But let thy heart keep my commandments: For length of days, and years of life, And peace, will they add to thee.** Be not wise in thine own eyes; Fear Jehovah, and depart from evil: It will be **health** to thy navel, And marrow to thy bones.

How did the Bible get such keen medical insight two thousand years before these studies were done? The following section reveals a host of examples of how faith and our health are inextricably linked.

Why are Cool Mist Vaporizers So Healthful?

When you got sick as a child, your mother would often use a "cool mist vaporizer" to help you breathe and clear congestion as you recuperate. The moisture in the vapors given off by this apparatus breaks up and loosens built-up mucus in our lungs and sinuses. You probably do the same today when you are sick, and you should thank your mother for what she did for you then and for teaching you what to do for yourself today!

Genesis chapter 2 gives us insight as to why these vaporizers work so well for us. In Genesis 2:6 (KJV), the Bible says, **"but there went up a mist from the earth, and watered the whole face of the ground."** This says that the original environment we were designed for in Eden was one that had a continually humid environ and thus when we turn on a vaporizer, we are putting ourselves into the environment we were designed for, and that in itself is helpful and healthful for us.

Do you know how George Washington died?

The story of George Washington's death is a very instructive one since it has a tie to a remarkably simple biblical tenant, which will become clear. The following timeline of the events leading to his death is as they were recorded in the memoirs of Colonel Lear, a family friend of Washington.

Thursday, December 12, 1799

Washington is out and about in a snowstorm. He is exposed to snow and thirty-degree weather.

Friday, December 13, 1799

The next day, Washington feels ill. The descriptions of Colonel Lear and his physician make it clear he developed both a tracheal and upper respiratory infection.

Before calling in a doctor, Washington believed he could use a neighbor's help. Washington was a believer in the thousands of years old practice of bleeding a person so that the poisons in their system could be purged. Thus, he called on a neighborhood bloodletter who drew 12 to 14 ounces of blood out of the former President of the United States.

Incidentally, he did this in defiance of his wife Martha's wishes. Martha Washington did not believe in bloodletting and tried to talk him out of it. There may be another moral story here about listening to your wife or women know best, but I don't have the guts nor wisdom to touch either one. Suffice it to say, if he had listened to Martha, he might have lived many years longer.

Saturday, December 14, 1799

The next morning Washington feels worse, and his doctor is called. The doctor arrives at 11 a.m. and drew a basin of blood.

Washington did not show any improvement over the next few hours, so the doctor drew another basin of blood in the early afternoon. Not surprisingly, Washington got worse, and the doctor, now somewhat desperate, drew another 32 ounces of blood at 4 p.m.

Again, not surprisingly, Washington deteriorated over the course of the evening, and he died at 11 p.m. George Washington was literally bled to death![475]

The Bible in Leviticus 17:11 (KJV) says, "**The life of the flesh is in the blood.**" If Washington had paid literal attention to this scripture or to his wife, he might have lived several more years!

All Humans are of One Blood

While on the subject of blood, let's explore the writings in both the Old and New Testaments of the Bible, which say that there is only one blood and that all humans comprise just one human race. A plain reading of Genesis 1:26-27, Genesis 3:20, and Acts 17:26 makes it clear that the Bible teaches that we were created as one race and continue today as one race of people.

That would seem to be a statement that could be tested in the field of genetics. The history of race as a term and concept is very mixed. Many cultures in ancient times ignored physical attributes, and if you were reared in and contributed to society, that society dealt with you and looked at you as a full member. Other cultures, such as the Greeks and Romans, favored physical strength, beauty, and familial traits over self-defined weakness, ugliness, or non-familial traits. These, of course, were early forms of racism and biases.

European medieval models of race generally mixed Classical ideas with the notion that humanity as a whole was descended from Shem, Ham, and Japheth, the three sons of Noah from the Bible, producing distinct Semitic (Asiatic), Hamitic (African), and Japhetic (Indo-European) peoples. This theory dates back to the Bible.

Some early cultures even recognized, without evolutionary theories, or a lot of science, that these traits in people could be very much affected environmentally. This was exemplified in the 14th century AD, when the Islamic sociologist Ibn Khaldun, a proponent of the environmental shaping of a race, dispelled the Babylonian Talmud's account of peoples and their characteristics as a myth. He wrote that black skin was due to the hot climate of sub-Saharan Africa and not due to the descendants of Ham being cursed.[476] Such Arabic writings were generally not accessible to many Europeans at this time.

Johann Friedrich Blumenbach (1752–1840) divided the human species into five races in 1779, later founded on crania research (description of human skulls), and called them (1793/1795): the Caucasian race; the Mongoloid race; the Malay race; the Negroid race; the American race (Indians).

These five groupings, together with two other additional groupings called the Australoid race (added in the 1940s) and the Capoid race (early 1960s), making a total of seven groupings in all, are today known as the traditional racial classifications or the historical definitions of race.[477]

An original five races were theorized early in the 20th century (the "Out of Africa Theory") as being the five original races that came out of five separately evolved ape groups in Africa. This gave us a modern concept of races being completely different species of humans and perhaps even different classes of organisms. Such concepts were underscored by evolutionary concepts of that time, which stressed that such species (races) must be constantly evolving and changing and introduced a supposedly scientific underpinning for racism.

If we were of multiple races, and one race was superior to all others, such as Darwinian evolution would suppose, and such as Hitler theorized, then the teachings of the Bible would be disproven.

What we have learned today via observations and investigations has overturned much of what we used to think about races, which today are more correctly referred to as people groups. Fortunately, it has also removed a supposed scientific excuse for racism.

The science of genetics research has today shown us some fascinating things about humans. The difference in DNA codes between any two humans (even those of different skin colors or supposed races) is only about 0.1 percent. Further, the number of DNA codes for traits distinguishing between people groups (such as blacks and Indians) make up less than 0.01 percent of those DNA codes.[478] Thus, from a biblical and a scientific standpoint, we should stop using the term race to describe different people groups. It is unhelpful, inaccurate, and can be misused rather easily to proclaim things about people groups that are simply not true.

Thus, current scientific evidence shows that the human race is not composed of somewhere between four and seven sub-races as has been theorized and publicized in the past, but that we are all part of a *single human race*. This, not coincidentally, backs up and verifies what has been taught in the Bible for over three thousand years! How did the Bible know this when we did not until advanced genetic research showed it to us only in the last few years?

Living Right is Good for Your Health!

Multiple scriptures give a promise from God that righteous living and following His commands will be rewarded with good health and longer lives!

In Deuteronomy 4:40 (ESV), **"Therefore you shall keep his statutes and his commandments, which I command you today, that it may go well with you and with your children after you, and *that you may prolong your days* in the land that the Lord your God is giving you for all time."**

Proverbs 9:10-11 (ESV) says, **"The fear of the Lord is the beginning of wisdom, and the knowledge of the Holy One is insight. *For by me your days will be multiplied, and years will be added to your life.*"**

Proverbs 3:1-2 (ESV) says, **"My son, do not forget my teaching, but let your heart keep my commandments, for *length of days and years of life and peace they will add to you.*"**

These are just three of a number of such verses which promise good health and long life for following God's commands. The question is, do we find this link to righteous living and good health in scientific studies?

Regular churchgoing is not just good for the soul, scientists say. It's good for the body, too.

Experts who examined an apparent link between a religious lifestyle and health found those who attended church were more likely to take good care of themselves. A 30-year study of 2,600 people suggested those who attended services regularly tended to smoke and drink less, take physical exercise, and maintain stable marriages—all factors in a long and healthy life.

"Our analyses indicate that attendees did not all start off with such good behaviors," said Dr. William Strawbridge of the Human Population Laboratory in Berkeley, California, which carried out the study. "To some extent, their good health behavior occurred in conjunction with their (church) attendance."

The scientists said churchgoers had lower blood pressure, experienced less depression and anxiety, and had stronger immune systems than non-churchgoers, and had less trouble keeping their weight down. Experts have speculated the health benefits of public worship might be partially due to the social support and friendship derived from frequent attendance at religious services.

But Dr. Strawbridge's study instead suggests that overall, churchgoers simply have better and more abstemious lifestyles. It also proved for the first time that churches, synagogues, mosques, or Buddhist monasteries helped create good health behavior, rather than simply attracting people who already took better care of themselves.[479]

People who go to church more often have lower blood pressure than those who are less church-going, according to a 2013 study from Norway. The same was found when analyzing heart patient data of 41,000 patients between 2006 and 2008 in Norway.

People who reported going to church at least three times a month had blood pressure that was, on average, one-to-two points lower than those who didn't go to church. Those who went to church between one and three times a month saw about a 1-point reduction in blood pressure, and those who went once a month or less had about a half-point benefit. This relationship between church-going and lower blood pressure was also found in previous United States studies in all but one study.[480]

Attending a place of worship, whether it be a church, synagogue, or mosque, can have a positive long-term effect on mental health in people over 50, research suggests.

A study by Erasmus MC and the London School of Economics examined 9,000 Europeans over the age of 50 over a four-year period. LSE epidemiologist Dr. Mauricio Avendano said the only activity linked to "sustained happiness" was going to a place of worship. "The church appears to play a very important social role in keeping depression at bay, and also as a coping mechanism during periods of illness in later life.[481]

A Clinical Study released in November 2006 shows a statistical link shown between elderly people, who go to church regularly, who do not develop respiratory problems as fast or as often as non-churchgoers![482]

Some observational studies suggest that people, who have regular spiritual practices, tend to live longer.[483]

Another study points to a possible mechanism: interleukin IL-6. Increased levels of IL-6 are associated with an increased incidence of disease. A research study involving 1700 older adults showed that those who attended church were half as likely to have elevated levels of IL-6.[484]

Spiritual commitment tends to enhance recovery from illness and surgery. For example, a study of heart transplant patients showed that those, who participated in religious activities, and said their beliefs were important, complied better with follow-up treatment, had improved physical functioning at the 12-month follow-up visit, had higher levels of self-esteem, and had less anxiety and fewer health worries.[485]

Different studies suggest that 60 percent to 90 percent of all patient visits to primary care offices are related to stress. Relaxation techniques, as shown in prayer and meditation, have been found particularly useful for patients with chronic pain, high blood pressure, headaches, and irritable bowel syndrome.

A study from the University of California at Berkeley in 2002 says, "...attending religious services may aid the body in addition to helping the spirit." Researchers in California have found new evidence that weekly attendance at religious services is linked to a longer, healthier life.

In this study, researchers from the Human Population Laboratories of the Public Health Institute and the California Department of Health Services, and from the University of California, Berkeley, found that people who attended religious services once a week had significantly lower risks of death compared with those, who attended less frequently or never. This was true even after adjusting for age, health behaviors, and other risk factors. The study was published in the International Journal of Psychiatry in Medicine.

"We found this difference even after adjusting for factors such as social connections and health behaviors, including smoking and exercising," said Doug Oman, lead author of the study and a lecturer at UC Berkeley's School of Public Health. "The fact that the risk of death by several different causes is lower for those, who attend religious services every week, suggests that we should look to some psychological factor for answers. Maybe frequent attendees experience a greater sense of inner peace, perhaps because they can draw upon religious coping practices to help them deal with stressful events."[486]

In all, we find more than twenty studies that confirm a link between church-going and better health. Thus, there is a great amount of empirical scientific evidence which supports what the Bible says on this subject. Again, it is interesting that all of these medical studies cited occurred in the last three decades, and it begs the question of how the Bible writers knew this three thousand years ago?

Prayer, Does it Work?

The Bible says, **"Confess your faults to one another, and pray for one another, that ye may be healed. The effectual fervent prayer of a righteous man availeth much!"** in James 5:16 (KJV).

This is only one of a host of scriptures, both in the Old and New Testaments, which says that prayer can positively affect our health, change the circumstances in our lives, and physically change nature. Thus, the Bible believes that prayer can positively affect our health. What does scientific research of today tell us?

Cardiology and Prayer

To test the effect of prayer on patients, cardiologist Dr. Randolph Byrd conducted a double-blind study of prayer with heart patients.

This study was conducted between August 1982 and May 1983 in San Francisco, California.

Scientific double-blind studies have what are called study and control groups. The group to be studied will be given the treatment or drug to be tested. The control group will not be treated or given the study drug so as to compare those given the treatment with those who received nothing. Heart patients in this study were not told whether they were in the prayer group or the non-prayer group.

In this study, a computer randomly assigned 393 patients from the Cardiology Care Unit at San Francisco General Hospital to either a prayer group or a non-prayer group. Fifty-seven patients declined to participate in the study.

There was no statistical difference between the health of the study group patients and the control group upon admittance to the hospital. That is, as a group, these patients were equally sick.

Prayer group patients were assigned to three to seven intercessors (people to pray for them) with active Christian lives. Intercessors were not allowed contact with the patients. They could not go and see them, call them on the phone, nor write to them. The prayer intercessors were only given the patient's first names and general condition.

These prayer intercessors were asked to pray daily for *"rapid recovery and the prevention of complications and death."*

Ten months later, the prayer group was **five times less likely to need antibiotics** than the non-prayer control group. The prayer group was **2.5 times less likely to suffer congestive heart failure.** They were 6 percent less likely to need intubation and 5 percent less likely to need diuretics, develop pneumonia or suffer cardiac arrest.

Now, I do not want to bore you with instruction on mathematical "null hypothesis" tests, group size effects, and more, so to make this simple, in large studies, differences of 10 percent are usually deemed clinically important and significant enough to pursue and believe the treatment was effective to some extent. If a study shows as much as 50 percent effectiveness, then the doctors have a party. Such results not only mean their treatment works to a great extent and their results are far beyond the realm of chance variation, but they rarely ever see such good results!

In this study, the prayer group patients were 500 percent less likely to need antibiotics than the non-prayer group. That is striking. Further, the prayer group patients were 250 percent less likely to experience congestive heart failure, which again is way beyond statistical norms, and generally shows an incredibly positive effect for the study.

This study was cited by some critics as having poor **"prayer controls"** and the same death incidence. The same death incidence means that approximately the same number of patients died (a small percentage) in both groups.

The "prayer control" criticism, however, is an interesting one. When you conduct a "double-blind" clinical study, you take great care to see to it that the study group (in this case, the "prayer group") gets the treatment you are studying and nothing else. You also take great care to see that the control group does not get the treatment you are studying (in this case, "prayer"), nor any other competing treatment.

Critics of this study noted that the doctors conducting this study did not thoroughly research the spiritual lives, families, and backgrounds of the patients in the two groups. Thus, it was possible that even though the patients in the non-prayer groups had no one from the study assigned to pray for them, that someone else or a group of people in these patients lives could have been praying for them, and the study doctors would not have known it, thus tainting the study results according to some critics.[487]

An Even Better Heart Study

Dr. William Harris, an agnostic (didn't believe in God), took note of the extraordinary results of Dr. Byrd's study. He decided to do an analogous study in 1999 at Saint Luke's Hospital's critical care unit in Kansas City, Missouri. He was joined reluctantly in this study by fellow cardiologist Dr. James O'Keefe, who did not see any reason to include prayer in a scientific study.

This was a much larger 990 patient study of heart patients. This time, however, there were strong "prayer controls." That means the control group, which was not prayed for, had gone through extensive questioning and background investigation to see to it that no one on the outside they could identify was praying for them.

The first names of patients in the study group were given to the Christian intercessors group and asked to pray "for a speedy recovery with no complications" for four weeks. Patients in the study did not know they were being prayed for, and the intercessors were not allowed to contact them in any way, just as in the previous San Francisco study.

After following the patient's progress for one year, this study concluded that the prayer group patients did 11 percent better than the control group, which was not prayed for. That is, they had 11 percent fewer heart attacks, strokes, and complications than the control group, which in this size study is considered statistical evidence of a positive effect for the prayer treatment or "clinically important," as researchers would say.[488]

A Miracle or Simply Chance?

Dr. Elizabeth Targ, a psychiatrist at the Pacific College of Medicine in San Francisco, has also tested prayer on critically ill AIDS patients.

All 20 patients in the study got pretty much the same medical treatment, but only half of them were prayed for by what the study called "spiritual healers." Ultimately, all ten of the prayed-for patients lived, while four who had not been prayed for died.

In a larger follow-up study, Targ found that the people who received prayer and *"remote healing"* (one clinical name for prayer as a treatment) had six times fewer hospitalizations, and those hospitalizations were significantly shorter than the people who received no prayer or *"distance healing"* (another clinical euphemism for prayer).[489]

The Impact of Religion on Health

But prayer is more than just repetition and physiological responses, says Harold Koenig, MD, associate professor of medicine and psychiatry at Duke. Traditional religious beliefs have a variety of effects on personal health, says Koenig, senior author of the *Handbook of Religion and Health*, which documents nearly 1,200 studies done on the effects of prayer on health.

These studies show that religious people tend to live healthier lives. "They're less likely to smoke, to drink, to drink and drive," he says. In fact, people who pray tend to get sick less often, as separate studies conducted at Duke, Dartmouth, and Yale University show. Some statistics from these studies:

- Hospitalized people who never attended church have an average stay of three times longer than people who attended regularly.
- Heart patients were 14 times more likely to die following surgery if they did not participate in a religion.
- Elderly people who never or rarely attended church had a stroke rate double that of people who attended regularly.
- In Israel, religious people had a 40 percent lower death rate from cardiovascular disease and cancer.

Also, says Koenig, "People who are more religious, tend to become depressed less often. And when they *do* become depressed, they recover more quickly from depression. That has consequences for their physical health and the quality of their lives."[490]

O'Laoire Study

A 1997 study by Dr. Sean O'Laoire, measured the effects on the agents performing daily prayers and reported benefits not only for the beneficiaries but also for the agents (those praying for the sick). Further, the benefit levels correlated with the belief levels of agents and beneficiaries in some cases. The study measured anxiety and depression. This study used beneficiary names, as well as photographs.

This study had 496 volunteers: those who prayed (agents, n = 90) and those who were prayed for (subjects, n = 406).

Agents were randomly assigned to either a directed or non-directed prayer group; photos and names of subjects were used as a focus. Subjects were randomly assigned to three groups: those prayed for by non-directed agents, a control group, and those prayed for by directed agents. Prayer was offered for 15 minutes daily for 12 weeks. Each subject was prayed for by three agents.

Subjects improved significantly on all 11 measures of health observed. Agents (those who prayed for them) improved significantly on 10 measures. A significant positive correlation was found between the amount of prayer the agents did and their scores on the five objective tests. Agents had significantly better scores than did subjects on all objective measures. Subjects' views of the locus of God's action showed significance in three objective measures. Improvement on four objective measures was significantly related to subjects' belief in the power of prayer for others.[491]

The Sicher Study

In 1998, Dr. Fred Sicher and his research team performed a small scale double-blind, randomized study of 40 patients with advanced AIDS. The patients were in category C-3 with CD4 cell counts below 200, and each had at least one case of AIDS-defining illness. The patients were randomly assigned to receive *"distant intercessory healing"* (also called remote healing or intercessory prayer) or none at all. The intercession took place by people in different parts of the United States who never had any contact with the patients. Both patients and physicians were blind to who received or did not receive prayer intercession.

Six months later, the prayer group had significantly fewer AIDS illnesses, less frequent doctor visits, and fewer days in the hospital. However, CD4 counts and scores on other physiological tests had no significant variation between the two groups of patients.[492]

Retroactive Intercessory Prayer

A 2001 study by Dr. Leonard Leibovici used records of 3,393 patients who had developed blood infections at the Rabin Medical Center between 1990 and 1996 to study *retroactive* intercessory prayer. To compound the alleged miraculous power of prayer itself, the prayers were performed *after* the patients had already left the hospital. All 3,393 patients were those in the hospital between 1990 and 1996, and the prayers were conducted in 2000.

Two of the outcomes, length of stay in the hospital and duration of fever, were found to be significantly improved in the intervention group, implying that prayer can even change events *in the past*. Also, the "mortality rate (death rate) was lower in the intervention (prayer) group, but the difference between the groups was not significant." Leibovici concluded that "Remote, retroactive intercessory prayer was associated with a shorter stay in hospital and a shorter duration of fever in patients with a bloodstream infection."[493]

More Prayer

Among the 1200 studies cited are studies that show prayer lowers blood pressure and metabolic rate. Almost 80 percent of these studies showed a statistical linkage. Most clinicians credit this effect to the ability of prayer to relieve and alleviate stress since the same effect has been shown with meditation. Essentially medicine would attribute this effect to getting people into a relaxed state or having a calming effect.[494]

Of these 1200 studies on prayer and healing is a sampling of the 191 studies which have been done specifically on prayer and healing, or as many researchers call it, *"remote healing"* or *"distance healing."* Of those, 124 (66 percent) showed a statistical link between prayer and healing. Of the fifty studies judged by peer review scientists to be excellently designed and executed studies, 38 of those studies (76 percent) showed a statistically significant effect by remote healing (prayer).[495]

The Rebuttal Studies

In spite of the fact that over 1200 studies on religion and prayer effects on health have shown an overwhelming connection between prayer and improved health, there have been a few of these studies which debate this conclusion. The most famous of these studies are two studies which often are pointed to by skeptics. These studies skeptics say show there is scientific evidence that "prayer doesn't work." These newer studies published in 2005 and 2006 concluded there was no link between prayer and general patient recoveries.

Since these studies vary so drastically from the vast consensus of studies in the field, it behooves us to analyze these two studies. These studies include the so-called "*Templeton Foundation studies*" and those of Dr. Herbert Benson. These studies found no statistical link between prayer and healing, which differs widely from what most of the studies in the field concluded. What is the difference here?

When we analyze the studies' prayer groups, we find a significant difference between most previous studies. As would happen in the last decade, these studies were more "politically correct" in their outlook than before. These studies, instead of using exclusively Christian intercessors with active prayer lives (as had been done in most previous studies), they used a mixture of catholic monks and ecumenical prayer groups.

Now. Let's analyze what these studies meant by "*ecumenical prayer groups.*" In addition to Catholic monks, they used Jews, Bahia Faith, Wickens, Buddhists, Hindus, Mormons, and many other groups which practice non-Christian faiths, whereas most other studies used solely evangelical Christian prayer groups...[496]

This leads us to a very somber scripture and even more somber conclusion. John 3:3 (ESV) in part says, "**... unless someone is born again, he cannot see the kingdom of God.**" These studies, rather than disproving prayer, tell us what kind of prayer works. In spite of the politically incorrect implications of this conclusion, these studies say that non-Christian prayers do not work in many cases!

This, in fact, makes great sense. If God is the God of the whole Bible and originated the Christian Faith, then it is His church on earth today. If you are going to pray to Satan (as the Wickens do) or to other gods (which, according to the Bible, do not exist) as the Hindus, Buddhists, and many others do, then God will not respond to your prayers. From a Christian point of view and a point of view of a believer in the Bible, these 2005-2006 studies should not have shown a link between these types of prayer and healing, and that is exactly what happened. Rather than these studies disproving the effects of prayer, they define what kind of prayer works.

Two Fascinating Tidbits in the Bible

There are two scriptures in the Bible that tantalize us with both hints of prescience knowledge, as well prophecies of future events. They have to do with the Bible, possibly envisioning the invention of television, airplanes, and the internet.

Did the Bible Know TV was Coming?

Matthew 24:30 (NIV) says:

> Then will appear the sign of the Son of Man in heaven. And then all the peoples of the earth will mourn when they see the Son of Man coming on the clouds of heaven, with power and great glory.

Some skeptics say this is one of those contradictions or errors in the Bible, since physically, if Christ comes back and first appears in the Middle East (as scripture says He will), He will not be physically seen elsewhere till He appears in the clouds there. Such an interpretation also begs the question of why Christ would make multiple entrances for each region.

(SPOILER ALERT!) In terms of our natural sense of logic, this sets up the ultimate Santa Claus killer for kids. When kids are young, they believe in the magical plump elf, who will bring them presents. They do not comprehend the physical impossibility of a man or any naturalistic being able to visit all of the billions of homes in the world in just one 24-hour night-time period. When they get old enough to comprehend the fantasy of this is when many of them fall from belief in Santa.

The traditional answer for this is that God can be many places at one time, and so He may appear around the world all at the same time, which to some is unsatisfactory. However, this answer is completely consistent with the biblical concept of God being everywhere at the same time (omnipresence), being able to read all of our minds at the same time, and knowing all that is going on in all of His creation (omniscience).

However, this verse could have a very special meaning in today's modern society, which the biblical writer Matthew, living 2000 years ago, could have in no way foreseen. If Christ appeared in the clouds over Israel or wherever He chose to appear today, what would happen? This event would be instantly shown on television and transmitted across the world via satellites. **Revelation 9:10-11,** cited in the next section, will support this interpretation that the Bible envisioned a time of TV and satellite communications. Did the Bible envision such an event in a time when such technology would exist? It is an intriguing question.

Did the Bible Know about the Internet, Airplanes, Computers, and Smartphones?

The Old Testament book of Daniel contains a lot of end-time prophecies. In Daniel 12:4 (ASV), it says, **"...the end of time; *many will go back and forth, and knowledge will increase.*"**

This verse, written almost three thousand years ago, is a very apt description of our times. We as a species roam to and fro across this world by air and by sea with unprecedented speed, frequency, and ease. Certainly, no one three thousand years ago could have envisioned how we travel by airplane across the world and by rockets to outer space and the moon.

To underscore this vision of world travel is Revelation 11:9-10 (ASV), which says, "And from among the **peoples and tribes and**

tongues and nations do *men* look upon their dead bodies **three days and a half**, and suffer not their dead bodies to be laid in a tomb. And **they that dwell on the earth rejoice over them, and make merry; and they shall send gifts one to another;** because these two prophets tormented them that dwell on the earth."

The sending of gifts across the world in 3.5 days will not be possible till this modern air flight era, and the viewing of these two bodies across the world will not be possible till the advent of worldwide communications with satellite communications, TV, computers, the internet, and smartphones.

Likewise, the amount of knowledge in the world is exploding. Buckminster Fuller created the "Knowledge Doubling Curve." He noticed that until 1900, human knowledge doubled approximately every century. By the end of World War II, knowledge was doubling every 25 years. Today things are not as simple, as different types of knowledge have different rates of growth. For example, nanotechnology knowledge is doubling every two years, and clinical knowledge is every 18 months. But on average, human knowledge is doubling every 13 months. According to IBM, the build-out of the "internet of things" will lead to the doubling of knowledge every 12 hours.[497]

Truly the amount of information that people are confronted with today is staggering. And as the data above shows, it is increasing exponentially. It has been estimated that the world produced five exabytes (that's one quintillion bytes) of information in the year 2002. That is equivalent to the amount of information produced by man from the beginning of time till the year two thousand. Certainly, this qualifies as a literal explosion of information.[498]

Did the Bible's author see all of this coming? Certainly, Daniel, in captivity in Babylon more than 2500 years ago, could not have seen all this coming without supernatural insight, yet somehow the Bible got this exactly right. How? This is not just prescience. This is one of those 2000 specific prophecies in the Bible which has been fulfilled!

Is there Prescience in the Bible?

We have shown more than sixty examples of science knowledge described in the Bible far ahead of what should have been known for the time. Some researchers say that there are more than 200 such verses or places in the Bible that show such "prescience." Who gave the Bible writers such modern scientific insights?

Former NASA administrator and renowned physicist/cosmologist Robert Jastrow put it this way: "For the scientist, who has lived by his faith in the power of reason, the story ends like a bad dream. He has scaled the mountain of ignorance; he is about to conquer the highest peak; as he pulls himself over the final rock, he is greeted by a band of theologians, who have been sitting there for centuries."[499]

The funny thing about this quote is that Jastrow was an agnostic, not a believer. And yet, his experiences with science and faith have demonstrated to him over and again that the Creator has imbued Christians and the Bible with other worldly knowledge that he and his colleagues have been chasing all their lives.

In an interview with *Christianity Today*, Jastrow said, "Astronomers now find they have painted themselves into a corner because they have proven, by their own methods, that the world began abruptly in an act of creation to which you can trace the seeds of every star, every planet, every living thing in this cosmos and on the earth. And they have found that all this happened as a product of forces they cannot hope to discover. That there are what I or anyone would call supernatural forces at work is now, I think, a scientifically proven fact.[500]

In Conclusion:
No Reason to Compromise!

One contention against the Bible, which we only covered in passing, was the charge that the Bible is full of errors, contradictions and has been proved wrong by science and historical inaccuracies. I believe we have disproved the last two indictments that the Bible has been in any way found to be historically or scientifically inaccurate. But did you notice examples of the contentions of the Bible being in error or contradictory were included in chapters 3, 6, and 7? We showed that Quirinius as governor at the time of Christ's birth and Belshazzar as King in Babylon were possible, and showed the existence of King Sargon, King Nebuchadnezzar, King David, Jesus, the Exodus, Sodom and Gomorrah, the Moabites, and the Hittites. All of these had been questioned as never existing and cited for years as proof of biblical errors. However, they have now been shown to be historically supported, as reported in the Bible.

We also included the "Four Winds in the Bible" and "Sky is Solid" sections to show you how charges of the Bible making incorrect, non-factual, and scientifically wrong statements can be explained by translational issues. We examined the "Mustard Seed" and "600,000 Men" accounts to show how contextual as well as translational issues show the Bible was not incorrect but substantiated by facts.

In all, including sections on the "Molten Sea," "Dispelling the Documentary Hypothesis for the Pentateuch," "Domesticated Camels," "Jacob and Sheep Genetics," and "Writing in Moses Day" sections and others, we examined twenty contentions of the Bible being in error or contradictory, and found all of them to be false claims by skeptics, and the Bible was in each case vindicated.

I had intended to include an extra chapter examining such charges of the skeptics, but I found after a year's research that while there was always a positive response to such claims which supported the Bible, that the claims were so numerous that I could have more than doubled the length of this book and still only have started to address many of them. Further, if I did address many of them, there would always be someone saying, "Well, what about this?" There was just no way you could ever be exhaustive since the skeptics have been working for 2000 years to try and disprove the Bible and compiled a lengthy list of supposed errors. In truth, there does appear, such as in the case of "Sky is Solid" question, that minor copyist and translational errors may have crept in over the centuries to some of our translations. But as in this case, these can be readily discerned and clarified with diligent research in the Bible's favor.

What I can attest to is that after much research, the twenty-one examples included in this book fairly represent how the charges of the Bible being in error or contradictory fall away when closely examined, and in all cases, it appears the original manuscripts of the Bible were free from such errors or contradictions as our thesis for God writing the Bible would expect to be the case.

Conclusions. We have seen ample evidence that:

1. The Bible contains the **original creation account,** and its elements are copied in other culture's creation accounts
2. **Geology and history support the Bible**;
3. The bible has revealed **history in advance** on hundreds of occasions;
4. God has **protected His Word** for more than 4000 years;
5. The **Bible hangs together** with one theme and one writer (God); and
6. The Bible is full of **prescience!**

Using simple probabilities of each of these six propositions either being verified as true or could not be verified started with each question having a simple probability of 50 percent. Statistically, to get six things taken together at the same time, each with a 50-50 chance of occurrence, means that there is only 1 chance out of 64 or less than a 1.6 percent chance of that all of these questions proved positive for the Bible occurred by accident.

On top of these six sets of evidence giving an excellent circumstantial case for the Bible being God's Words. This evidence also gives us something else. The fact that the Bible shows logical coherence, as one mind writing it, shows that the person, entity, or group which wrote the Bible must: have been able to coordinate that cohesion over two millennia (30 times the life span of any man); have been able to protect the meaning of the original manuscripts for thousands of years, which is outside of any man's abilities; have had perfect knowledge of science thousands of years ahead of men, and knowledge of the creation when there were no other human observers; have foreknowledge of historical events before they happen, which is outside the abilities of any normal human; and had perfect knowledge of human history. What do you call such an entity with all of these attributes is God. Along the way to proving that the Bible is God's Word, we have also made an excellent circumstantial case for the God of the Bible being real and existent!

Further, the coordination of all of the 366 prophecies of the Messiah in the Old Testament coming to fruition in Jesus Christ not only supports the thesis of Christ being the theme of the whole Bible but using Dr. Peter Stoner's statistical analysis, it is clear that it is a mathematical certainty that Christ was the Messiah spoken of in the Old Testament. This does not prove God, nor that the Bible is God's Word, but it gives excellent support for the thesis of both of these. It does say that the chances of all of these things, which we said we would find if God wrote the Bible, proving to be true, makes the chances of that all being coincidental extremely low. Thus, the chances that God did write the Bible are actually extremely high.

The question is whether we will believe the evidence and let it bolster our faith, create faith in us where there was none, or walk away from our Creator?

This book was written to help both believers and nonbelievers to be able to weigh the evidence which most cannot take the time to wade their way through, or do not possess the resources to do so, and allow them to make an informed decision about their faith. We give evidence to churches to show that they can trust in the inerrancy of the Bible. Further, this book acts to bolster the faith of the believer and give them assurance that their faith is on sturdy ground. That is important in a day when it seems everyone is attacking the Christian faith as irrelevant, as scientifically disproven, as bigoted, and ignorant.

Perhaps even more important, though, this book gives a rational defense for the Bible and testifies to unbelievers that those who believe are not ignorant and that faith in the Bible and the God who inspired it is something they may need to consider for themselves. This is important for believers as the Bible instructed us always to be ready with a *defense* of our beliefs.

The positive answers to the six questions posed in this book go a long way to substantiate that the Bible is the inerrant word of the one and only God of Creation! Now, it will not prove God, but it makes a particularly good circumstantial case for His existence, His role as Creator, and our faith in His Son Jesus Christ. But there is still a component of faith. You must still decide for yourself whether to believe in God or not.

All we have done here is show that science and historical records have not disproven the Bible, but in fact, supports it in many ways. With that truth, there is no reason for churches, pastors, or other believers to feel that they have to compromise their faith. We can stand on the principles of God's Word, which include belief that homosexuality and abortion are morally wrong, that marriage is only to be between a man and a woman, that divorce should not be an acceptable norm and so many other topics which the Bible espouses that are controversial in our day and thought to be passé. Also, believers need not ever feel that they must accept such unbiblical tenants as atheistic evolution or a compromise that God created us using evolution because that is neither what the Bible says nor is it what good science says.

The evidence in this book attests to the fact that God's truth has been the same since the creation. It affirms that He is the same yesterday, today, and tomorrow and can be depended on for our lives and our futures.

For the unbelievers, this book can be highly evangelical. There is a myth being circulated that faith in God is equivalent to being unscientific. It suggests that any faith is blind faith without reasoning or evidence behind it. The Bible, however, asks us to have a faith that is far from blind. It makes its case for faith based on sound reasons of logic and gives practical evidence that its precepts give us a way of life with which our societies and peoples can best live together. And finally, it is the only religious book, which can be checked and found to be both historically and scientifically accurate to the point of being totally inerrant. Thus, the assertion that it takes blind faith to believe in God is, in fact, untrue!

The Bible, its teachings, its history, and the factual substantiation of its historical accounts and successes of its precepts in the multiple lives and societies described in the Bible attest to this being a faith tested through time and found reasonable, workable, and practical. Belief in God and Jesus Christ, rather than being a blind faith, is found then to be the most reasonably logical decision we can make in light of the evidence both within the Bible and the historical and scientific evidence which supports the Bible's authenticity.

This logical context for belief has become particularly necessary today, as society has grown more and more skeptical of the Bible's inerrancy. It has been suggested by some that no true scientists have faith in anything, but a limited form of science, which rejects any place for God or any nonmaterial answers for how anything in this universe occurred. This last myth is a lie, which is disproven by the history of science and by the large number of distinguished scientists of today, who are believers.

Indeed, most of the absolute giants of science in the western world were men of deep faith and steadfast believers in the God of the Bible. This belief did not limit their science but pushed them forward to explore God's world. It gave them the expectation that God's world would be discernable, an expectation that a materialistic universe without God would have no expectation whatsoever of fulfilling. However, as Galileo and Einstein have famously commented. It is the amazing characteristic of our universe that it is comprehendible to man. Galileo, Newton, and Einstein were all in awe of the fact, as Galileo stated it, they were constantly amazed to find how "God wrote the universe using mathematics!" It was the attitude of Galileo, Kepler, Copernicus, Newton, Faraday, Bacon, Kelvin, and thousands of others that their science was not inhibited by faith, but guided and pushed forward by their faith to think "God's thoughts after Him!"[501]

Such testimonies are not ancient history in science, as many would have you believe. The late **Dr. Wernher Von Braun** was a German scientist who came to the United States after World War II and led the army of engineers who designed the rockets, which literally took us out of this world. He was the principal designer of the Saturn V rocket, which took us to the moon. Von Braun can easily be advanced as possibly the greatest scientist/inventor of the twentieth century, and yet he was a creationist (believed God created us just as described in the Bible), and, who testified that he regularly depended on God's order in the universe, in chemistry and physics to allow for his great accomplishments. This giant of science was not impeded by his beliefs, and his science was not thwarted by his belief. Instead, he said repeatedly that they aided him. He was a deep believer in God, and he saw no problem allowing his faith and his belief in God into his pursuit of scientific discoveries.[502]

Dr. Raymond Damadian is a medical doctor who holds a deep Christian belief in God and has always allowed his beliefs in God to affect and lead him in his investigations in medical science. Dr. Damadian is the inventor of the *Magnetic Resonance Imaging (MRI) scanner*. Dr. Damadian's invention has put him at the front of the list of scientists and inventors of our modern day, and yet he rejects the current definition of science being only that which we can observe in nature. Instead, he always allows for what God has not shown us as yet. Sadly, in spite of his monumental achievement, he was denied a Noble Prize in Medicine apparently because of his fundamentalist religious beliefs.[503] This was a sad day in the scientific community when some very unscientific bias and bigotry reared its ugly head.

Likewise, **Dr. John C. Sanford** not only sees faith in God as central to his understanding of science but actually credits science with leading him to God! If you do not know of Dr. Sanford, he is professor emeritus at Cornell University and recognized as one of the leading plant geneticists on the planet today. He was the inventor of the "biolistic gene gun," which has been used for decades to inject material into cells and cellular nuclei as well as take genetic material out of cells and nuclei. He holds more than twenty-five patents in the field of plant genetics and has started two successful biotech companies, which use his patents to further scientific research and enable other companies to profit from his discoveries. Dr. Sanford and thousands of other scientists today do not see their faith as blind or in any way hindering their pursuit of science.

Dr. Sanford reached his belief in God in a quite different way than the previous two men. Dr. Sanford, unlike Damadian and Von Braun, was an unbeliever for most of his life. But as he delved more and more into his field of genetics, it became vividly apparent to him that there was a designer behind the genetic information he was constantly dealing with. Contrary to popular propaganda, it was not science that made a believer turn from his faith when he "saw the light." Instead, it was science, which revealed God to one of the foremost scientists and inventors of our day. In fact, Dr. Sanford now relates that he only has a deeper understanding of genetics and made breakthroughs in the field of "genetic history" since he was led to belief in God through his study of DNA's complexity.

Letting God be a part of his reality and his science has not limited him but has, as he testifies, opened up whole new fields of investigation and a whole new range of answers which "naturalistic only" investigations never allowed. Like Damadian, he has paid the price for his late-in-life belief in God. Once noted almost universally as one of the leading plant geneticists of our time, he is now ridiculed in the scientific community for daring to tell what his scientific research has revealed to him, that all life on earth appears designed by an intelligent Creator![504]

As the science heroes described before, these last three contemporary leaders in the sciences see faith in God as an integral part of their investigation of our universe. Further, they are constantly impressed by how God has left *His signature in His creations*. However, these are only recognized when we allow for the possibility of God and actually look for evidence of His presence and His unmistakable marks in the designs of nature.

Both the Bible and this book have already given us good reason to believe that God exists through what we have seen and read. But, on top of all that, there are, in fact, two theorems in the realm of logic that tell us that a belief in God goes beyond the Bible itself. The first of these is what is called "Pascal's Wager."

Pascal's Wager

Pascal's Wager is an argument in apologetic philosophy devised by the great 17th-century French philosopher, mathematician, and physicist Blaise Pascal (1623 — 1662). It posits that humans bet with their lives that God either exists or does not.

Pascal argued that a rational person should live as though God exists and seek to believe in God. If God does actually exist, such a person will have only a finite loss (some pleasures, luxury, etc.), whereas they stand to receive infinite gains (as represented by eternity in heaven) and avoid infinite losses (eternity in hell).

Pascal's Wager was based on the idea of the Christian God, though similar arguments have occurred in other religious traditions over the centuries. The original wager was set out in section 233 of Pascal's posthumously published *Pensées* ("Thoughts"). These previously unpublished notes were assembled to form an incomplete treatise on Christian apologetics. The gist of the Wager is that, according to Pascal, one cannot come to the knowledge of God's existence through reason alone (there is a faith component since you can neither prove nor disprove God). Thus, the wise thing to do is to live your life as if God does exist because such a life has everything to gain and nothing to lose. If we live as though God exists, and He does indeed exist, we have gained heaven and eternal life as well as a positive existence while on earth.

If He doesn't exist, we have lost nothing, since if God does not exist, then at the end of life, we will simply cease to exist and never know the difference. If, on the other hand, we live as though God does not exist, and we find after death He really does exist, we will have gained hell and punishment and have lost heaven and bliss. If one weighs the options, clearly, the rational choice to live as if God exists is the better of the possible choices, neither of which can be naturalistically proved. Pascal even suggested that some may not, at the time, have the ability to believe in God. In such a case, one should live as if he had faith anyway. Perhaps living as if one had faith may lead one to actually coming to faith.[505]

Unmoved First Mover

Another logical proof of God's existence comes in the form of the ancient logical theorem of the *"Unmoved First Mover."* Although there have been many derivations of this logical theorem over the centuries, the original is credited to the ancient Greek philosopher Aristotle (384-322 BC).[506]

In his Metaphysics VII, 1072, Aristotle describes that what we see everywhere is that for every movement, change, or motion, there is a cause or mover. And behind that cause or mover was something that caused it to move or act. And behind that, another causer or mover and on and on and on, till you regress backward till you get to the prime mover or first mover of everything in the universe, who was not moved by anything else.[507]

This idea intersects with what we call today the "*Law of Cause and Effect*." If a leaf falls from a tree, it is because sap and chlorophyll had been withdrawn from its veins and the wind separated it. For a seed to grow, it must be grown, watered, and warmed. For a rock to move, it must be kicked, shoveled, an earthquake occurred, or something else caused it to move (it does not move itself). In short, every action we see in our universe has a cause, and that cause will have a subsequent effect.

Aristotle argues, in Book 8 of his Physics and Book 12 of his Metaphysics, what he believes the attributes of the *first mover* must have been. He said, **"that there must be an immortal, unchanging being, ultimately responsible for all wholeness and orderliness in the sensible world."** In other words, if you work your way back to the beginning, there had to be first force, or being which started it all, and caused everything else throughout history and what we see today to come into being and move forward. His descriptions of this "*unmoved first mover*" are eloquently and uniquely equivalent to our concepts of the Judeo-Christian God. Thus, his belief in a god was not due to blind faith but proved to him by the laws of logic.[508]

Ours is Not a Blind Faith!

A logical belief in God, not blind faith, is most important to today's modern society. You cannot tell a person without faith in God: that the creation did not happen as the Bible says it did; that man did not fall from grace by sin as the Bible says he did; that the corruption and decay we see in the world today is not the result of man's fall as the Bible says; that the worldwide Flood never occurred as the Bible says it did; that the "Big Fish" story never happened as the Bible recounts it; that all other miracles in the Bible did not occur, as described, including those of Jesus; but then, after discounting the whole Bible as mythical, then ask them to believe in the saving power of Jesus and that He is God!

No sane person would believe that! I would not believe it! It is this kind of compromised theology that has not only led to sharp declines in people attending churches and being baptized in the last decade but also fostered the exodus of youth from the church that we are now experiencing. We have to turn this around, and the start of that process is a return to Genesis and basic biblical beliefs. We either **believe the Bible from the very first verse,** or we should not believe it at all!

The Ten Commandments are not the *ten suggestions*, even though both our society and many Christian denominations have treated them as such for the past fifty years. Compromising our faith for the ways of the world and Satan is not winning us new converts, as we had mistakenly hoped, but has spearheaded the current "Loss of Faith Crisis" we are experiencing. This may be the advent of the "Great Apostasy" (a biblically predicted "falling away" of people of faith from the church and God to a world of unbelief in the end times via the "reformed dispensational view").[509]

The six sets of evidence in this book make belief in God defensible for the believer, arm them for the attacks from society and unbelievers, and allow them a firm foundation on which to stand against persecution that will invariably occur if believers stand up for all of the basic tenants of the Christian faith.

For the church, what we are talking about is the **"Authority of God's Word!"** Either the Bible has authority as it comes from the one God and our Creator, and every word should be believed, or it is not from God and is only the writings of men and should be taken as having no more authority than any other writing of men. And perhaps even less so since it was written so long ago and is now passé since its supposed wisdom cannot relate to the issues of modern life. The evidence in this book shows that it is very likely that the Bible is "God's Word" and should be believed and followed as His instructions to His creations! Indeed, it was written by God to be our "instruction manual" for living a fulfilling life.

These pieces of evidence will also make belief in God a rational choice for the unbelievers, who had been mistakenly told that the Bible is full of errors and has been disproven by science. We pray you found it all useful.

For churches and unbelievers alike, the material in this book can be the key to reaching generations X, Y, Z, and millennials, as well as the rest of today's society, with the good news of the gospel. For many today, it will only be after they are shown that science affirms the Bible and has a logical basis for its credibility as actual history that they will then listen to its words as those of their Creator. Only then will they see Christ as their potential Savior with His good news message of forgiveness He has for all of us!

The Bible in 2 Peter 1:19-21 says of itself:

> We also have the prophetic message as something **completely reliable**, and you will do well to pay attention to it, as to a light shining in a dark place, until the day dawns and the morning star rises in your hearts. Above all, you must understand that **no prophecy of Scripture came about by the prophet's own interpretation of things. For prophecy never had its origin in the human will, but prophets, though human, spoke from God as they were carried along by the Holy Spirit.**

The Bible espouses that it is the **inerrant Word of God**, and the research presented in this book gives us an excellent circumstantial case for believing that its claims are true!

Epilogue

What do we do with this information?

I hope and pray you found the evidence in this book both useful and persuasive in your journey to decide who and what we are and what reality we live in. If you found all of this persuasive, you may want to know what the Bible tells us about how to put your faith in Christ, have a relationship with Him, and be saved.

Romans 3:23 (NIV) begins to describe for us our condition. It says, **"for all have sinned and fall short of the glory of God."** This is an easy scripture to see the truth in. We all screw up from time to time. No human is perfect, and we prove it all the time. Also, before we can be saved, we must see our condition for what it is. Just like an alcoholic cannot be helped until they reach rock bottom, own up to having a problem, and asks for help, we, too, must come to that same realization about our sin condition.

Romans 6:23 (KJV) expands on our plight as humans. It says, **"For the wages of sin is death, but the gift of God is eternal life through Christ Jesus our Lord."** God, being perfect, cannot countenance sin; thus, we cannot come into His presence as sinners. We must depart from Him; we must die. Further, in His plan to shape heaven full of perfect people, who can live together in peace, there is no room for people devoted to sin, as we so often are.

The good news is that there is a way out of our sin condition, but we cannot do it. It is beyond our capabilities to perfect ourselves, and God knew that. He sent Jesus to live a sinless life. To show us how to live and recognize that it was a standard we could not achieve (and cannot still), and God knew that from the very creation as indicated in Genesis 3:15. He had always planned to bridge the gap between our very fallible selves and a perfect God, and Christ's sacrifice for us on the cross is that bridge.

Romans 10:9-10 (NIV) tells us one requirement for our salvation when it says:

> **If you declare with your mouth, "Jesus is Lord," and believe in your heart that God raised him from the dead, you will be saved. For it is with your heart that you believe and are justified, and it is with your mouth that you profess your faith and are saved.**

You cannot be a "closet Christian!" You must tell the world and others that you believe in God, have committed your life to Him, and mean it. But, simply stating it in public is not even enough; you must mean it in your being. This is why many evangelical church services will end in an invitation to walk up, join the church, and publicly state to everyone in attendance that you have committed your life to God and confess that Jesus is Lord. A prayer to Him of your need for Him and your commitment to Him, along with a public testimony of that commitment, is all that is required to receive Christ's free gift to you of salvation from your own sins.

So our condition is one of being sinners and thereby separated from our Creator. But God knew our plight and has set up a way back into fellowship with Him through Christ's sacrifice on the cross. Now, a little more on our commitment to Him.

John 3:16 (NIV) tells us, "**For God so loved the world that he gave his one and only Son, that whoever *believes* in him shall not perish but have eternal life.**" This verse underscores what level our commitment to Him has to be. If the Bible is true, and we have given you much evidence that it is, then there are demons and Satan who have met God and seen God face to face, and yet they are not saved by this knowledge. Thus, the belief described in this verse must refer to more than just knowing God exists, but committing to Him as our Creator, God and Lord. Satan, in his rebellion, fails this test.

Luke 3:13 gives us a further clarification of what our commitment to Him must be when it tells us, "**I tell you, no! But unless you repent, you too will all perish.**"(NIV) Again, our commitment to Him must be much more than a surface declaration of His existence, nor can it be a fraudulent declaration to other people, which you do not deeply mean. It must be a commitment to Him and to His way of living. Now, the word "repent" as used here is not well understood in our culture today. It means more than just being sorry for our sins and then going out and doing the same thing minutes later. It means we are so sorry for our sins that we turn from them and do them no more.

Now, this does not mean we will live perfectly sinless for the rest of our lives. But it does mean we commit to God that as He shows us errors and sins we have committed, that we will own up to them, confess them to Him, and vow one at a time to turn from them and do those no more. This is a lifelong process that we commit to and which we slip and fall from occasionally. But as we stumble (sin), we pick ourselves up and recommit to Him when we do. This is the **sanctification** process described in the Bible, where we are separating ourselves for God's service and trying to follow Him.

Matthew 7:21-22 (KJV) gives us even more information on the depth of our commitment to Him. It says, "Not everyone that saith unto me, Lord, Lord, shall enter into the kingdom of heaven; **but he that doeth the will of my Father which is in heaven**…Many will say to me in that day, Lord, Lord, have we not prophesied in thy name?" Again, to be saved and part of God's community, we cannot have just a superficial or fraudulent commitment as we so often see people put on different faces for different audiences. Our actions must reveal that commitment, or our lack of action is evidence that we have no commitment to Him at all.

Now, some will miss-read this to say that our works save us, but the Bible makes it clear this is not so. It says in Ephesian 2:8-9

(KJV), "For by grace are ye **saved through faith**; and that not of yourselves: it is the **gift of God:** *Not of works*, lest any man should boast." Our actions reveal our commitment to Him, but they do not save us. As this book has revealed, the requirement for salvation has not changed since the creation. It is **faith in God that saves** and as complete a level of commitment to Him as we can muster is all that is asked and all that is accepted.

I hope you have come to that level of need for Him today so that you pray just such a prayer of deep commitment to living a Christ-like life in light of His example! The Bible tells us that God is ready to respond to us, save us, and seal us for eternity whenever we call on Him and commit our lives to Him!

ENDNOTES

1. www.religioustolerance.org/ev_denom2.htm

2. "The Discovery of Genesis", C. H. Kang, Ethel Nelson, Concordia Publishing House (August 1, 1979), p.15

3. Nelson, Ethel R. Richard E. Broadberry, Ginger Tong Chock, 1997, "God's Promise to the Chinese", Read Books Publisher, Dunlop. TN.

4. Jan Walls and Yvonne Walls (translators and editors), 1984, Classical Chinese Myths: Hong Kong, Joint Publishing Company, p. 135. (BL1825.C48 1984)

5. http://dickinsg.intrasun.tcnj.edu/diaspora/beckymyth.html

6. www.*wikipedia.org*/wiki/Maya_mythology

7. Hesiod, *Works and Days* **and** *Theogony* **and** *The Shield of Herakles,* **translated by Richmond Lattimore. Ann Arbor, University of Michigan Press, 1959.**

8. Stephanie Dalley (ed.). *Myths from Mesopotamia: Creation, the Flood, Gilgamesh, and Others*. Oxford University Press, Revised (February 15, 2009)

9. https://www.christiancourier.com/articles/667-enuma-elish-a-babylonian-creation-account

10. Newman, R. "Authenticating your Collections," Caring for Your Collections, Abrams, New York, 1992, pp. 172-180.

11. Arnold & Beyer (eds.), 'Readings from the ancient Near East: primary sources for Old Testament study', p. 13 (2002).

12. http://history-world.org/sumerian_culture.htm

13. Modern Archaeology and Genesis, Acts and Facts, ICR, Vol. 45, Number 1, January 2016, p. 16.

14. David Leeming (2005). "Islamic Mythology". The Oxford Companion to World Mythology. Oxford University Press. pp. 207–211.

15. "Have You Considered", Bruce Malone and Julie Von Vett, Self-Published in China, 2017, August 11 entry.

16. Answers Magazine, Vol. 11, #4, Oct—Dec. 2016, Answers in Genesis, Hebron, KY, p. 46.

17. Answers Magazine, Vol. 11, #4, Oct.—Dec. 2016, Answers in Genesis, Hebron, KY, p. 46.

18. https://en.wikipedia.org/wiki/Maidu

19. Beckman, T. Maidu and other origin stories from central California, pages.hmc.edu, 1998.

20. Cooper, G., Coyote in Navajo religion and Cosmology, The Canadian Journal of Native Studies, 7(2), 1987, pp. 181-193

21. "Have You Considered", Bruce Malone and Julie Von Vett, Self-Published in China, 2017, October 13 entry.

22. Answers Magazine, Vol. 11, #4, Oct.—Dec. 2016, Answers in Genesis, Hebron, KY, p. 46.

23. Answers Magazine, Vol. 11, #4, Oct.—Dec. 2016, Answers in Genesis, Hebron, KY, p. 46.

24. Answers Magazine, Vol. 11, #4, Oct.—Dec. 2016, Answers in Genesis, Hebron, KY, p. 47.

25. http://www.crystalinks.com/azteccreation.html - myth 2

26. Answers Magazine, Vol. 11, #4, Oct.—Dec. 2016, Answers in Genesis, Hebron, KY, p. 47.

27. "Have You Considered", Bruce Malone and Julie Von Vett, Self-Published in China, 2017, August 11 entry.

28. Answers Magazine, Vol. 11, #4, Oct.—Dec. 2016, Answers in Genesis, Hebron, KY, p. 47.

29. Answers Magazine, Vol. 11, #4, Oct.—Dec. 2016, Answers in Genesis, Hebron, KY, p. 47.

30. "Have You Considered", Bruce Malone and Julie Von Vett, Self-Published in China, 2017, August 11 entry.

31. Answers Magazine, Vol. 11, #4, Oct.—Dec. 2016, Answers in Genesis, Hebron, KY, p. 47.

32. http://query.nytimes.com/gst/abstract.html?res=F50613F-D3A5F13738DDDA90994D0405B838DF1D3

33. Cooper, B. 2012, Authenticity of the book of Genesis, Portsmouth, UK. Creation Science Movement, pp. 392-393.

34. Kang, C.H., Nelson, Ethel R., The Discovery of Genesis, Concordia Publishing House, 1979, p. XII.

35. Kang, C.H., Nelson, Ethel R., The Discovery of Genesis, Concordia Publishing House, 1979, p. 3.

36. Kang, C.H., Nelson, Ethel R., The Discovery of Genesis, Concordia Publishing House, 1979, p. 4.

37. http://en.wikipedia.org/wiki/Walam_Olum

38. http://abob.libs.uga.edu/bobk/walamc.html

39. The Red Record, David McCutchen, Avery Pub. Group, 1993.

40. Brantley, Garry. 1995. Digging for Answers. Montgomery, AL: Apologetics Press.; Kitchen, Kenneth. 1966. Ancient Orient and Old Testament. London: Tyndale Press.; Pfeiffer, Charles. 1966. The Biblical World. Grand Rapids, MI: Baker.

41. Kleiss, Richrd & Tina, A Closer Look at the Evidence, Search for the Truth Ministry; (February 21, 2005) November 17 entry

42. Jackson, Wayne, Biblical Studies in the Light of Archaeology, Apologetics Press (June 1, 1982) pp. 61-63.

43. Thompson, Bert, "A Study Course in Christian Evidences", Apologetics Press (1992), p. 115.

44. Ramsey, W. M., The Bearing of Recent Discovery, Forgotten Books (December 3, 2017), p. 85

45. Morison, Frank, "Who Moved the Stone?", Zondervan, 1987.

46. https://en.wikipedia.org/wiki/Lee_Strobel

47. from McDowell's own ministry website at https://www.josh.org/about-us/joshs-bio/)

48. Quotes from his website http://www.andrekole.org/

49. Bartz, Paul A., "Letting God Create Your Day", Volume 3, Bible-Science Association (1992) page 261

50. http://www.biblearchaeology.org/post/2009/01/Jericho-Does-the-Evidence-Disprove-or-Prove-the-Bible.aspx

51. Chavalas, Mark W. (2003), **Mesopotamia and the Bible**, Continuum International Publishing Group.

52. Davis, C. 2007, Dating the Old Testament, New York: RI Communications, p. 93

53. Chavalas, Mark W. (2003), **Mesopotamia and the Bible**, Continuum International Publishing Group.

54. National Geographic Magazine, May 2014, p. 5.

55. Korfmann, Manfred (1973). The Sling as a weapon. Scientific American, October 229(4), pp. 35-42.

56. Lawrence, Paul (2011). Book of Moses Revisited, WIPF and STOCK Publishers (Eugene, Oregon), p. 122.

57. Hoffmeier, James K., Israel in Egypt – the Evidence for the Authenticity of the Exodus Tradition, OUP, (Oxford/New York), 1996, pp. 83-116.

58. Kitchens, K. A., On the Reliability of the Old Testament, Eerdmans Publishing Co. (Grand Rapids and Cambridge), 1993, pp. 344-345.

59. Kitchens, K. A., On the Reliability of the Old Testament, Eerdmans Publishing Co. (Grand Rapids and Cambridge), 1993, p. 351.

60. Evidence for the Bible, Anderson and Edwards, 2014, DayOne Publications, Leominster, England, p. 15.

61. Ancient Israel in the Sinai – The evidence for the Authenticity of the Wilderness Tradition, James K. Hoffmeier, OUP (Oxford/New York), 2005 p. 155.

62. Evidence for the Bible, Anderson and Edwards, 2014, DayOne Publications, Leominster, England, p. 21.

63. The Miracles of Exodus, Colin J. Humphreys, Continuum, London, 2003, p. 108.

64. Evidence for the Bible, Anderson and Edwards, 2014, DayOne Publications, Leominster, England, p. 21)

65. https://en.wikipedia.org/wiki/Documentary_hypothesis#cite_note-FOOTNOTEVan_Seters2015viii-4

66. Van Seters, John (2015). The Pentateuch: A Social-Science Commentary. Bloomsbury T&T Clark, p. viii.

67. Viviano, Pauline A. (1999). "Source Criticism". In Haynes, Stephen R.; McKenzie, Steven L. To Each Its Own Meaning: An Introduction to Biblical Criticisms and Their Application. Westminster John Knox. P. 38.

68. https://en.wikipedia.org/wiki/Documentary_hypothesis#cite_note-FOOTNOTE-Carr2014434-6

69. https://en.wikipedia.org/wiki/Documentary_hypothesis

70. Ibid

71. Excerpted from https://answersingenesis.org/bible-characters/moses/documentary-hypothesis-moses-genesis-jedp/

72. https://answersingenesis.org/bible-characters/moses/documentary-hypothesis-moses-genesis-jedp/

73. Excerpted from https://answersingenesis.org/bible-characters/moses/documentary-hypothesis-moses-genesis-jedp/

74. https://answersingenesis.org/bible-characters/moses/documentary-hypothesis-moses-genesis-jedp/

75. Archer, Gleason; A Survey of Old Testament Introduction, Moody Publishers; Revised ed.(Oct. 1, 2007), p. 109–113.

76. Excerpted from https://answersingenesis.org/bible-characters/moses/documentary-hypothesis-moses-genesis-jedp/

77. "Revised Works of Josephus," Chapter 10: The Assyrian army pursued and defeated by Abram—Birth of Ishmael—Circumcision instituted, 1912–1910 B.C., taken from: The Online Bible, by Larry Pierce.

78. https://answersingenesis.org/bible-characters/moses/documentary-hypothesis-moses-genesis-jedp/

79. Bulletin of the American Schools of Oriental Research, (334), 2000, Barkley, Lundberg, Zuckerman, 'The Amulets of Ketef Hinnom: A New Edition and Evaluation' pp. 41-70.

80. http://www.bible-history.com/archaeology/assyria/hammurabi-stele.html

81. http://www.bible-history.com/archaeology/assyria/black-obelisk.html

82. http://www.bible-history.com/empires/pilate.html

83. Bible Archaeology Review, BAR 18:05, Sep/Oct 1992.

84. http://www.kchanson.com/ancdocs/westsem/caiaphas.html

86. http://www.bible-history.com/empires/megiddo_seal.html

87. Lost Treasures of the Bible, Clyde E. Fant & Mitchell G. Reddish, Eerdman's Publishing Co. [Grand Rapids & Cambridge] 2008, pp. 152-154.

88. Evidence for the Bible, Clive Anderson and Brian Edwards, DayOne Publications, [Leominster, England] 2014, p. 62.

89. Lost Treasures of the Bible, Clyde E. Fant & Mitchell G. Reddish, Eerdman's Publishing Co. [Grand Rapids & Cambridge] 2008, pp. 148-151.

90. The Annals of Sennacherib, Daniel Luckenbill, Oriental Institute Publications, Chicago, 1924, pp. 23-27.

91. Jerusalem in Bible and Archaeology, The First Temple Period, Andrew G. Vaugh and Ann E. Killebrew Editors, Society of Biblical Literature, Symposium Series, Atlanta, 2003, p. 219.

92. Evidence for the Bible, Clive Anderson and Brian Edwards, DayOne Publications, [Leominster, England] 2014, p.65.

93. Ibid, p.66.

94. Biblical Archaeology Review, Biblical Archaeology Society, (Washington, D.C.) Sept. /Oct. 2008.

95. Ancient Near eastern Texts, ed. James B. Pritchard, Princeton University Press, (Princeton), 1950, p. 321.

96. Biblical Archaeology Review, Biblical Archaeology Society, (Washington, D.C.) Sept/Oct 2013.

97. Evidence for the Bible, Clive Anderson and Brian Edwards, DayOne Publications, [Leominster, England] 2014, p.66.

98. Evidence for the Bible, Anderson and Edwards, 2014, DayOne Publications, Leominster, England, p. 4.

99. www.en.wikipedia.org/wiki/Biblical_narratives_and_the_Quran

100. The Qur'an

101. Rollston, Chris A. (2010). Writing and Literacy in the World of Ancient Israel: Epigraphic Evidence from the Iron Age. Society of Biblical Lit. pp. 53-54.

102. André Lemaire "'House of David' Restored in Moabite Inscription" Biblical Archaeology Review 20:03 (May/June 1994).

103. Albright, "The Moabite Stone remains a corner-stone of Semitic epigraphy and Palestinian history", The Jewish Quarterly Review. University of Pennsylvania Press. 35 (3):1945, p. 250.

104. Rollston, p. 54.

105. [FLEMING, DANIEL E. (1998-01-01). "MARI AND THE POSSIBILITIES OF BIBLICAL MEMORY". Revue d'Assyriologie et d'archéologie orientale. 92 (1): pp. 41–78.

106. Gottwald, Norman Karol (2001-01-01). The Politics of Ancient Israel. Westminster John Knox Press.

107. Bible and Spade, 1999 - 12 (3), pp. 67-80.

108. http://www.icr.org/article/have-sodom-gomorrah-been-discovered/

109. http://www.icr.org/article/have-sodom-gomorrah-been-discovered/

110. Evidence for the Bible, Anderson and Edwards, 2014, DayOne Publications, Leominster, England, p. 5.

111. http://www.answersingenesis.org/articles/nab/does-archaeology-support-the-bible

112. http://www.answersingenesis.org/articles/nab/does-archaeology-support-the-bible

113. George, A. 2011, A stele of Nebuchadnezzar II (Tower of Babel stele), Cuneiform Royal Inscriptions and Released Texts in the Shoyen Collection. George, Andrew, Ed. Bethesda, MD; CDL Press, pp. 153-169.

114. http://creation.com/the-sixteen-grandsons-of-noah

115. Association for the Study of Jewish Languages, Volume 3, 1983, p. 89.

116. Goldenberg, David M., The Curse of Ham: Race and Slavery in Early Judaism, Christianity, and Islam, 2005, p. 18.

117. http://www.isaiah18.com/Cush.html

118. Walker, Tas; "Aboriginal Australians' DNA Link to India", Creation Magazine, 2013, 35(3)9.

119. "Have You Considered", Bruce Malone and Julie Von Vett, Self-Published in China, 2017, August 12 entry.

120. https://en.wikipedia.org/wiki/Japheth

121. The Genesis Record, A scientific and devotional commentary on the book of beginnings, Henry M. Morris, Baker Book House, Grand Rapids, 1976, pp. 247-249.

122. http://www.moscow-city.ru/download/source/zima_Guide_engl.pdf/Engl_13.pdf

123. http://biblehub.com/topical/m/mizraim.htm

124. 'Book of Sothis App. IV', in ref. 1, p. 239, also Ussher, J, The Annals of the World, 1658, sections 1657–1762 am.

125. https://creation.com/ancient-egypt-confirms-genesis

126. Watson, T., Mummy DNA unravels ancient Egyptians ancestry, Nature 546 (7656):17, May 2017.

127. Creation Magazine, vol. 40, No. 1, 2018, p. 8.

128. http://en.wikipedia.org/wiki/Sons_of_Noah

129. Cooper, Bill, After the Flood, New Wine Press, Chichester, England, 1995, pp. 172, 203.

130. Cooper, Bill, After the Flood, New Wine Press, Chichester, England, 1995, pp. 170, 203.

131. Custance, A.C., Noah's Three Sons, Vol.1, 'The Doorway Papers', Zondervan, Michigan, 1975, pp. 92, 117.

132. Strawn, Brent A.,"Shem". In Freedman, David Noel; Myers, Allen C. Eerdmans Dictionary of the Bible. Amsterdam University Press, p. 1205.

133. Cooper, B. 2013. The Authenticity of the Book of Genesis. Portsmouth, UK, Creation Science Movement, pp. 25-27.

134. wikipedis.org/wiki/Porphery

135. livius .org/na-nd/nabonidus/cylinder.ur.html

136. "Belshazzar", Creation Magazine, Volume 37, No. 3, 2015, pp. 12-15.

137. Cooper, Bill. The Authenticity of the Book of Daniel. UK: Creation Science Movement, 2012, pp.25-27.

138. Cooper, Bill. The Authenticity of the Book of Daniel. UK: Creation Science Movement, 2012, p. 25

139. Cooper, Bill. The Authenticity of the Book of Daniel. UK: Creation Science Movement, 2012, p. 29.

140. Cooper, Bill. The Authenticity of the Book of Daniel. UK: Creation Science Movement, 2012, pp. 30-31.

141. http://www.biblicalarchaeology.org/daily/biblical-artifacts/artifacts-and-the-bible/the-tel-dan-inscription-the-first-historical-evidence-of-the-king-david-bible-story

142. Andre Lemaire "'House of David' Restored in Moabite Inscription" Biblical Archaeology Review 20:03 (May/June 1994)

143. Johnson, James J. S.,"Moabite King's Boast Corroborates Genesis", Acts & Facts Mag., Vol. 48, No. 7, July, 2019, p. 21.

144. http://www.iflscience.com/editors-blog/new-evidence-confirms-the-burning-of-jerusalem-by-babylonians-described-in-the-bible/

145. https://answersingenesis.org/bible-history/the-antediluvian-patriarchs-and-the-sumerian-king-list/

146. https://en.wikipedia.org/wiki/Hugo_Winckler

147. Muhlestein, Kerrry and Robert K. Ritner; "Execration", The Mechanics of Ancient Egyptian Magical Practice, Chicago, 1993.

148. https://www.rt.com/news/311581-entrance-gath-biblical-city/

149. http://www.reasons.org/articles/joshua-s-long-day-and-the-nasa-computers-is-the-story-true

150. http://www.geocentricity.com/astronomy_of_bible/jld/index.html

151. "The Bible has the Answer", by Henry Morris, Baker Book House, Grand Rapids, Michigan, 1971, pages 71-72.

152. Evidence for the Bible, Clive Anderson and Brian Edwards, DayOne Pub., [Leominster, England] 2014, p. 7.

153. Evidence for the Bible, Clive Anderson and Brian Edwards, DayOne Publications, [Leominster, England] 2014, p. 6.

154. "A Study Course in Christian Evidences", Bert Thompson, Ph.D., Apologetics Press ,Montgomery, Alabama, 1998, pp. 140-141.

155. Prophet and Teacher: An Introduction to the Historical Jesus by William R. Herzog (4 Jul 2005) pp. 1–6. / Authenticating the Activities of Jesus, by Bruce Chilton and Craig A. Evans, Brill, 2002 pp. 3–7.

156. http://channel.nationalgeographic.com/killing-jesus/articles/how-did-the-apostles-die/

157. The Resurrection of Jesus, trans. John Bowden (Minneapolis: Fortress Press, 1994), pp. 45-207.

158. A.M. Mccrloo, Delusion and Mass Delusion: Nervous and Mental Disease Monographs, No. 79, (New York: Smith Ely Jelliffe Trust, 1949), p. 71.

159. http://www.dailymail.co.uk/sciencetech/article-2218469/Ancient-city-Alexandria-built-align-sun-day-Alexander-Greats-birth.html

160. Kosmetatou, Elizabeth (1998). "The Aftermath: The Burial of Alexander the Great". Greece.org. Archived from the original on 27 August 2004. Retrieved 16 December 2011.

161. "All monuments of Lenin to be removed from Russian cities". RT. 20 November 2012. Archived from the original on 17 November 2015.

162. Rohl, David (1995). A Test of Time: The Bible - from Myth to History. London: Century. ISBN 0-7126-5913-7. Published in the U.S. as Rohl, David (1995). Pharaohs and Kings: A Biblical Quest. New York: Crown Publishers. ISBN 0-517-70315-7.

163. Rohl, David (2002). The Lost Testament: From Eden to Exile - The Five-Thousand-Year history of the People of the Bible. London: Century. ISBN 0-7126-6993-0.

164. Rohl A Test of Time, Chapter 14, pp. 299-325.

165. Dever, William G. (1990) [1989]. "2. The Israelite Settlement in Canaan. New Archeological Models". Recent Archeological Discoveries and Biblical Research. USA: University of Washington Press. p. 47.

166. Flavius Josephus, Against Apion, Book 1, Chapter 14–16.

167. Tacitus, Histories, Book 5, pp. 3–5.

168. Flavius Josephus, The Antiquities of the Jews, Book 2, Chapter 15ff.

169. http://www.biblearchaeology.org/post/2016/01/28/The-Sons-of-Jacob-New-Evidence-for-the-Presence-of-the-Israelites-in-Egypt.aspx

170. http://kgov.com/evidence-for-the-exodus

171. David Rohl's Revised Egyptian Chronology: A View From Palestine, biblearchae-ology.org/post/2007/05/23/David-Rohls-Revised-Egyptian-Chronology-A-View-From-Palestine.aspx, 6 January, 2015

172. Notes on 'The Admonitions of an Egyptian Sage,'" Journal of Egyptian Archae-ology, 1964, pp. 24-36.

173. Mahoney, Timothy P.,'& Steven Law, Patterns of Evidence: Exodus: A Filmmaker's Journey, Thinking Man Media, Minneapolis, MN 2015.

174. Lawrence, Paul, The Book of Moses Revisited, WIPF and Stock Publishers [Eu-gene, Oregon] 2011, p. 122.

175. Evidence for the Bible, Clive Anderson and Brian Edwards, DayOne Publications [Leonminster, England] 2014, p. 11.

176. "Have You Considered", Julie Von Vett, Bruce Malone, printed in China for Search for the Truth Ministries, 3725 E. Monroe Rd., Midland, MI48642, July 26 entry.

177. Evidence for the Bible, Clive Anderson and Brian Edwards, DayOne Pub., [Leon-minster, England] 2014, p. 20.

178. http://www.dailymail.co.uk/sciencetech/article-4009258/Is-Hebrew-world-s-al-phabet-Israelites-Egypt-turned-hieroglyphs-letters-3-800-years-ago.html

179. Ancient Israel in the Sinai – The evidence for the Authenticity of the Wilderness Tradition, James K. Hoffmeier, OUP (Oxford/New York), 2005 pp. 240-243)

180. Bianchi, Robert Steven (2001). "Champollion Jean-François". In Redford, Don-ald B. The Oxford Encyclopedia of Ancient Egypt, Volume 1. Oxford University Press. pp. 260–261.

181. A Biblical Interpretation of World History by Charles Kimball: Appendix I-Problems with Egyptian Chronology available at http://xenohistorian.faithweb.com/worldhis/index.html

182. D. Rohl, Pharaohs and Kings: A Biblical Quest (New York: Crown Publishers, 1995), p. 24. Dynasties are grouped in sets called Old Kingdom, Middle Kingdom, and New Kingdom.

183. A. Gardiner, Egypt of the Pharaohs (Oxford: Oxford University Press, 1961), p. 46, quoted in D. Mackey's thesis. Manetho is quoted by Josephus, Eusebius, Africanus, and Syncellus.

184. A Biblical Interpretation of World History by Charles Kimball: Appendix I- Prob-lems with Egyptian Chronology, RoseDog Books, 2008.

185. Article by Tiffany Denham at http://thecreationclub.com/does-egyptian-chronology-prove-the-bible-is-historically-inaccurate-part-1-problems-with-traditional-egyptian-chronology/

186. Flavius Josephus, The Antiquities of the Jews, Book 18, Chapter 5, p. 2.

187. "Is There Any Confirmation of Biblical Events From Written Sources Outside the Bible?" http://christiananswers.net/q-abr/abr-a009.html

188. Walter C. Kaiser, The Old Testament Documents, IVP Academic, (2001), pp. 79–80.

189. Flavius Josephus, The Wars of the Jews, Book 2, Chapter 8:118.

190. Gary Habermas, The Historical Jesus (1999), College Press Publishing Company, Inc., pp. 196–197.

191. McRay, John, Archaeology and the New Testament, Baker Academic, 2008, p. 331.

192. The Future of Biblical Archaeology, ed. James K. Hoffmeier and Allan Millard, Eerdmans Publishing Co., Grand Rapids and Cambridge, 2004, pp. 203-205.

193. wikipedia.org/wiki/List_of_biblical_figures_identified_in_extra-biblical_sources

194. Free, Dr. Joseph P., Archaeology and Bible History (Wheaton, IL: Scripture Press, 1969), p. 1.

195. Sheler, Jeffery L., "Is the Bible True?", Readers Digest, June, 2000.

196. http://www.answersingenesis.org/articles/nab/does-archaeology-support-the-bible

197. Peters, S.E. and Gaines, R.R., Formation of the 'Great Unconformity' as a trigger for the Cambrian explosion, Nature 484:363, 2012.

198. Morris, J.D., Cumming, K.B. and Ham, K.A., in press. The grandest of canyons. In: Grand Canyon—Monument to Catastrophe, S.A. Austin (ed.), Institute for Creation Research, San Diego, chapter 1, p. 1.

199. D.V. Ager, The Nature of the Stratigraphical Record (John Wiley, New York), 1973.

200. https://answersingenesis.org/geology/grand-canyon-facts/what-carved-grand-canyon/

201. Rowley, P. D., M. A. Kuntz, and N. S. MacLeod. 1981. Pyroclastic-flow deposits. In P. W. Lipman and D. R. Mullineaux, eds. The 1980 Eruptions of Mount St. Helens, Washington. U.S. Geological Survey Professional Paper 1250, pp. 489-512.

202. https://answersingenesis.org/fossils/fossil-record/the-worlds-a-graveyard/

203. http://www.redorbit.com/news/science/970213/the_opisthotonic_posture_of_vertebrate_skeletons_postmortem_contraction_or_death/

204. https://www.newscientist.com/article/dn21207-watery-secret-of-the-dinosaur-death-pose/ - Brian Switek. Watery secret of the dinosaur death pose. 23 November 2011.

205. www.earthage.org/youngearthev/niagara_falls_and_the_young_earth.htm

206. Mehlert, A. W. "Another Look at the Agea and History of the Mississippi River." pp. 121-123. Creation Research Society Quarterly, December 1988.

207. Huse, Scott, Collapse of Evolution, Baker Books, 1997, p. 68.

208. Bianchi, Thomas S., Deltas and Humans, Oxford University Press, 2016, p. 106.

209. http://www.messagetoeagle.com/5000-year-old-tradition-of-nilometer-water-measurement-device-from-pharaonic-times/

210. https://www.livescience.com/28493-when-sahara-desert-formed.html

211. William R. Boos, Robert L. Korty. Regional energy budget control of the intertropical convergence zone and application to mid-Holocene rainfall. Nature Geoscience, 2016; 9 (12): 892 DOI

212. https://www.llnl.gov/news/deep-sea-corals-may-be-oldest-living-marine-organism

213. Morris, Henry M., Scientific Creationism, Maser Books, El Cajon, California, 1984, p.193.

214. Daniels, Peter T. and Bright (ed.), "The Study of Writing Systems", Oxford University Press. 1996, p.3.

215. Morris, H. M. , Scientific Creationism, Master Books, El Cajon, CA, 1984, pp.167-169.

216. Morris, H. M. , Scientific Creationism, Master Books, El Cajon, CA, 1984, pp.167-169.

217. Hunt, David, How Close Are We?, Harvest House Publishers, 1993, pp. 27, 29.

218. http://articles.latimes.com/1997-01-26/news/mn-22407_1_phenomenal-jeane-dixon

219. http://www.bibleresearch.org/articles/a2pws.htm

220. Stoner, Peter W., Science Speaks (Chicago: Moody Press, 1958), chapters 3 and 4.

221. www.beleivers.org.au/radio034.htm

222. https://www.britannica.com/topic/crucifixion-capital-punishment

223. Missler, Chuck, Hidden Treasures in the Biblical Text, Koinonia House, 2000, p. 17.

224. Kleiss, Richard & Tina, A Closer Look at the Evidence, Search for the Truth Ministries, 2005, December 22 entry.

225. http://www.kkl-jnf.org/forestry-and-ecology/afforestation-in-israel/turning-the-desert-green/

226. www.history.com/topics/middle-ages/crusades

227. Kleiss, Richard & Tina, 'A Closer Look at Prophecy", Search for the Truth Ministries, 2019, Feb. 4 entry.

228. Eisen, Sara, Busines is Blooming for Israel's Flowers, www.israel21c.org

229. Reagan, David R., Ph.D., Israel in Bible Prophecy: Past, Present and Future, 2017, pp. 133-141.

230. http://www.slate.com/articles/news_and_politics/explainer/2003/04/where_was_abraham_born.html

231. http://www.bible.ca/archeology/bible-archeology-exodus-route-goshen.htm

232. Gossier, C. School officials seek ways to close gap: Forum focuses on achievement disparities. The Advocate (Stamford, CT), (2006, September 8).

233. Benjamin B. DeVan and Thomas W. Smythe, "The Character of Jesus Defended," Christian Apologetics Journal 5, no. 2, [Southern Evangelical Seminary, Electronic Copyright], 2006, p. 120.

234. Wikipedia and Holmes, Tara, "Readmission of Jews to Britain in 1656", BBC website, June 24, 2011.

235. http://www.history.ucsb.edu/projects/holocaust/Research/Proseminar/tomerkleinman.htm

236. Kennedy, D. James, "Why I Believe", Thomas Nelson Inc., Nashville, TN, 2005, pp. 18-22.

237. Grady, Lee, "Science and the Bible", pp. 118-119 and Kleiss, Richard & Tina, "A Closer Look at the Evidence", Search for the Truth, 2018, Jan. 3 entry.

238. http://www.ucg.org/beyond-today/a-prophecy-about-babylon-confirms-the-accuracy-of-the-bible

239. http://coldcasechristianity.com/2018/from-reliable-to-divine-fulfilled-prophecy-in-the-old-testament/

240. Kennedy, D. James, 2005, "Why I Believe", Thomas Nelson Inc., Nashville, TN, pp. 23-27.

241. Von Vett, Julie & Malone, Bruce, "Have You Considered", 2017, Search for the Truth Ministries, Sept. 30 entry.

242. https://en.wikipedia.org/wiki/Four_kingdoms_of_Daniel

243. http://www.itiswritten.com/unsealing-daniels-mysteries-lesson-7-kingdoms-in-collision and https://bible.org/seriespage/chapter-7-daniel E2%80%99s-vision-future-world-history

244. https://www.rationalchristianity.net/amalekites.html

245. http://www.bibletools.org/index.cfm/fuseaction/Topical.show/RTD/CGG/ID/11009/Edom-as-Desolate-Wilderness.htm

246. Morris, Henry; Science and the Bible, Moody Publishers, 1986, p. 120.

247. Von Vett, Julie; Malone, Bruce, "Have You Considered", Search for the Truth Ministries, 2017, Feb. 26 entry.

248. http://www.clarifyingchristianity.com/fulfill.shtml

249. How Was the Curse on Jericho Fulfilled? Theodore F. Wright, The Biblical World, Vol. 23, No. 4 (Apr., 1904), pp. 263-266.

250. "Authentic, Inspired, Inerrant and True", By Dr. Danielle West-Stellick, Author-House, 2011, pp. 54-55.

251. Von Vett, Julie; Malone, Bruce, "Have You Considered", Search for the Truth Ministries, 2017, July 31 entry.

252. http://www.thewhyman.jesusanswers.com/custom3.html

253. https://www.gospeloutreach.net/bible4.html

254. Stronach, David, & Lumsden, Stephen, 1992, UC Berkeley's Excavations at Nineveh. Biblical Archaeologist 55, pp. 227–233

255. DeFleur, Melvin L., and Larsen, Otto N., The Flow of Information: An Experiment in Mass Communication, Transaction Books, New Brunswick and Oxford, 1958, p. XX.

256. https://bible.org/article/how-accurate-bible)

257. https://prezi.com/cgtf8raylsqt/copy-of-the-book-why-believe-the-bible

258. http://www.bl.uk/onlinegallery/sacredtexts/deadseascrolls.html

259. Archer, Gleason. A Survey of Old Testament Introduction. Chicago: Moody Press, 1985, p. 25.

260. Hendrix, Eddie (1976), "What About Those Copyist Errors?" Firm Foundation, 93[14]:5, April 6)

261. Wallace, Daniel B., ed. Revisiting the Corruption of the New Testament Text: Manuscript, Patristic, and Apocryphal Evidence. Grand Rapids, MI: Kregel, 2011, p. 40.

262. Estrin. D. Scanning software deciphers ancient biblical scroll. Associated Press. Posted on big-story.ap.org, September 21, 2016.

263. Kang, C. H., Nelson, Ethel R., "Discovery of Genesis in Chinese", Concordia Publishing, 1979.

264. www.allaboutthejourney.org/bible-manuscripts.htm

265. http://www.godandscience.org/apologetics/bibleorg.html

266. http://www.godandscience.org/apologetics/bibleorg.html

267. Kantzer, Kenneth, Christianity Stands True, College Press Pub., 1994, p. 31.

268. http://www.godandscience.org/apologetics/bibleorg.html

269. Homer in Print: the transmission and reception of Homer's works; the University of Chicago Library, lib.uchicago.edu.

270. https://blogs.thegospelcoalition.org/justintaylor/2012/03/21/an-interview-with-daniel-b-wallace-on-the-new-testament-manuscripts/

271. G. Bates and L. Costner, "How Accurate are the Copies of the Bible?", CMI Prayer News, July 2017, p. 1.

272. https://blogs.thegospelcoalition.org/justintaylor/2012/03/21/an-interview-with-daniel-b-wallace-on-the-new-testament-manuscripts/)

273. G. Bates and L. Costner, "How Accurate are the Copies of the Bible?" CMI Prayer News, July 2017, p. 2.

274. F.F. Bruce, The Books and the Parchments: How We Got Our English Bible, Fleming H. Revell Co., 1950, p. 178.

275. The Discovery of Genesis", C. H. Kang and Ethel Nelson, Concordia Publishing, 1979, p. 13.

276. www.kingjamesbibledictionary.com/Dictionary/Messiah

277. James M. Arlandson. "The Wrath of God in the New Testament: Never against His New Covenant People." Bible.org. 2014.

278. https://www.nsa.gov/Portals/70/documents/news-features/declassified-documents/cryptologic-quarterly/trafficanalysis.pdf and https://en.wikipedia.org/wiki/Signals_intelligence

279. Missler, Chuck, Cosmic Codes – Hidden messages from the edge of eternity, Koinonia House, 1999, pp. 93-96 summarize Panin's work.

280. Missler, Chuck & Eastman, Mark, "The Creator Beyond Time and Space", Word for Today, 1995.

281. Comfort, Ray, The Evidences Bible, Bridge-Logos, Gainsville, Florida, 2011, p. 29.

282. https://www.newscientist.com/article/dn25723-massive-ocean-discovered-towards-earths-core/

283. http://www.crivoice.org/seder.html

284. https://www.fjc.gov/history/courts/jurisdiction-equity

285. http://www.jewfaq.org/shemaref.htm

286. https://www.christian-faith.com/true-stories-testimonies-of-jesus-christ/

287. https://god.net/god/bible-topics/god-and-you/promises-to-those-who-seek-god/

288. Entire section excerpted from http://creation.com/first-adamlast-adam with permission from Creation Ministries International (CMI) and the author Russell Grigg

289. The overall themes in this section taken from the lyrics from "Name above all Names" by don Moen found at http://web1.calbaptist.edu/uploadedFiles/cbu/spiritual-life/In%20Genesis.pdf?n=25

290. http://sitn.hms.harvard.edu/flash/2017/science-genetics-reshaping-race-debate-21st-century/

291. http://www.openbible.info/topics/human_nature

292. www.smh.com.au/comment/even-among-christians-there-is-strong-support -for-same-sex-marriage-20150604-ghh2vp.htm

293. www.creation.com/how-did-we-get-our-bible

294. King, Henry C., The history of the telescope, Harold Spencer Jones Publisher Courier Dover Publications, 2003, pp. 25-27.

295. Bardell, David (May 2004). "The Invention of the Microscope". Bios. 75 (2): pp. 78–84.

296. Ullmann, Agnes (2007). "Pasteur–Koch: Distinctive Ways of Thinking about Infectious Diseases". Microbe. 2 (8): pp. 383–387.

297. Ullmann, Agnes (2007). "Pasteur–Koch: Distinctive Ways of Thinking about Infectious Diseases". Microbe. 2 (8): pp. 383–387.

298. http://en.wikipedia.org/wiki/Ignaz_Semmelweis

299. http://skywalker.cochise.edu/wellerr/students/glaze2/project.htm

300. https://www.cdc.gov/rodents/diseases/direct.html

301. Guinea Ebola Outbreak: Bat Eating Banned to Curb Outbreak, March 25, 2014, BBC News retrieved from www.bbc,com/world-africa-26735118

302. https://www.cdc.gov/parasites/trichinellosis/health_professionals/index.html

303. www.health.ny.gov/diseases/communicable/trichinosis/fact_sheet.htm

304. https://en.wikipedia.org/wiki/History_of_water_supply_and_sanitation

305. https://www.medicaldaily.com/use-poop-medical-treatments-throughout-history-400497

306. www.reshafim.org.il/ad/egypt/timelines/topics/medicine.htm

307. None of These Diseases: The Bible's Health Secrets for the 21st Century, McMillan, S. I., Revell Pub.; 3 edition (March 1, 2000)

308. Jeffery, Grant R., The Signature of God, Nashville, Word Pub., 1998.

309. http://www.webmd.com/parenting/baby/news/20141202/cdc-endorses-circumcision-for-health-reasons)

310. http://www.merckmanuals.com/home/blood-disorders/bleeding-due-to-clotting-disorders/overview-of-blood-clotting-disorders

311. Wieland, Carl C., "Adam and that Missing Rib", Creation 21(4), 1999, pp. 46-47.

312. Wieland, Carl C., Inteview with Dr. David Pennington, Creation 22(3), 2000, pp. 17-19.

313. http://necsi.edu/projects/evolution/lamarck/webelieve/lamarck_webelieve.html

314. Timpl R, Rohde H, Robey PG, Rennard SI, Foidart JM, Martin GR (October 1979). "Laminin--a glycoprotein from basement membranes". The Journal of Biological Chemistry. 254 (19): 9933–97.

315. https://en.wikibooks.org/wiki/An_Introduction_to_Molecular_Biology/DNA_the_unit_of_life

316. https://www.scientificamerican.com/article/dna-at-60-still-much-to-learn/ and http://sitn.hms.harvard.edu/flash/2012/issue127a/

317. https://www.eurekalert.org/pub_releases/2003-11/iu-anh111703.php

318. http://www.ideacenter.org/contentmgr/showdetails.php/id/1437

319. https://biotech.law.lsu.edu/cphl/history/articles/pasteur.htm

320. Ball, Philip (2016). "Man Made: A History of Synthetic Life". Distillations. 2 (1): 15–23. Retrieved 22 March 2018.

321. Bernal, J. D. (1967) [Reprinted work by A. I. Oparin originally published 1924; Moscow: The Moscow Worker]. The Origin of Life. The Weidenfeld and Nicolson Natural History. Translation of Oparin by Ann Synge. London: Weidenfeld & Nicolson.

322. https://en.wikipedia.org/wiki/Spontaneous_generation

323. https://en.wikipedia.org/wiki/Francesco_Redi

324. Hamilton, Victor P (1990). The Book of Genesis: chapter 1. Eerdmans.

325. Futuyma, Douglas (1998). Evolutionary Biology. Sinauer Associates. p. 25.

326. https://www.britannica.com/science/Hadean-Eon

327. Bada, J. L. (2002). "Origin of Life: Some Like It Hot, But Not the First Biomolecules". Science. 296 (5575): 1982–1983.

328. Montmerle, Thierry; Augereau, Jean-Charles; Chaussidon, Marc; et al. (2006). "Solar System Formation and Early Evolution: the First 100 Million Years". Earth, Moon, and Planets. Springer. 98 (1–4): 39–95.

329. https://en.wikipedia.org/wiki/Evolution_of_fish

330. https://www.smithsonianmag.com/science-nature/how-did-whales-evolve-73276956/

331. "Landmark study on the evolution of insects". Sciencedaily.com. November 6, 2014.

332. https://answersingenesis.org/creation-science/baraminology/what-are-kinds-in-genesis/

333. Dobzhansky, Theodosius (1959). "Blyth, Darwin, and natural selection". The American Naturalist. 93 (870): 204–206.

334. https://creation.com/abandoned-transitional-forms

335. Living fossils: a powerful argument for creation—Don Batten interviews Dr Carl Werner, author of Living Fossils (Evolution: the Grand Experiment vol. 2), Creation 33(2):20–23, 2011.

336. Butler, Carolyn (March 2011). "Living Fossil Fish". National Geographic: 86–93.

337. Carroll, R.L., "Towards a new evolutionary synthesis," Trends in Ecology and Evolution, Vol. 15(1):27-32 (2000).

338. Peretó, Juli (2005). "Controversies on the origin of life" (PDF). International Microbiology. Barcelona: Spanish Society for Microbiology. 8 (1): 23–31.

339. https://www.ncbi.nlm.nih.gov/pmc/articles/PMC4961956/

340. Gould, Stephen J. (1987). "Is a New and General Theory of Evolution Emerging?", Self-Organizing Systems: 113–130.

341. https://www.smithsonianmag.com/science-nature/what-does-it-mean-be-species-genetics-changing-answer-180963380/

342. http://www.figweb.org/Interaction/How_do_fig_wasps_pollinate/

343. https://mexicanvanilla.com/pages/history-of-vanilla

344. Von Vett, Julie, Malone, Bruce, "Have You Considered", Search for the Truth, 2017, March 17 entry.

345. Kleiss, Richard & Tina, A Closer Look at the Evidence, Search for the Truth, 2005, November 22 entry

346. http://www.newsweek.com/being-gay-your-dna-scientists-keep-trying-find-genetic-basis-sexual-741084

347. https://www.nature.com/articles/s41598-017-15736-4

348. https://www.psychologytoday.com/us/blog/political-minds/201705/the-american-college-pediatricians-is-anti-lgbt-group

349. https://en.wikipedia.org/wiki/Galileo_affair

350. https://carm.org/percent-population-homosexual

351. Levay, Simon (1996). Queer Science: The Use and Abuse of Research into Homosexuality. Cambridge, Massachusetts: MIT Press. p. 207.

352. https://www.theatlantic.com/science/archive/2015/10/no-scientists-have-not-found-the-gay-gene/410059/

353. https://www.acpeds.org/the-college-speaks/position-statements/gender-dysphoria-in-children

354. Lopata, Alex (April 2009). "History of the Egg in Embryology". Journal of Mammalian Ova Research. 26 (1): 2–9.

355. Guliuzza, Randy, Communique Newsletter, San Antonio Bible Based Science Association, Nov., 2004, p. 2.

356. http://www.mhrc.net/mitochondrialEve.htm

357. Bayer, C. J., Maternal Impressions, Literary Licensing, LLC Mar – 2014.

358. https://peninsulahumanesociety.org/adopt/mixed-breeds/

359. http://genetics.thetech.org/ask-a-geneticist/how-far-back-can-ancestry-test-go)

360. https://www.icr.org/article/separate-studies-converge-human-chimp-dna

361. https://www.theguardian.com/science/2012/ sep/05/genes-genome-junk-dna-encode

362. https://www.livescience.com/38613-genetic-adam-and-eve-uncovered.html

363. Torroni, A., et al., Harvesting the fruit of the human mtDNA tree, TRENDS in Genetics 22(6):339–345, 2006.

364. Al-Araimi NA, Gaafar OM, Costa V, Neira AL, Al-Atiyat RM, Beja-Pereira A (2017) Genetic origin of goat populations in Oman revealed by mitochondrial DNA analysis. PLoS ONE 12(12): e0190235. https://doi.org/10.1371/journal.pone.0190235). Also, DNA research has shown that all living sheep are descended from three or four original females. (Guo J, Du L.-X, Ma Y.-H, Guan W.-J, Li H.-B, Zhao Q.-J, Li X, Rao S.-Q. 2005. A novel maternal lineage revealed in sheep (Ovis aries). Anim Genet 36:331–6.

365. B. Bower, Science News, October 14, 2006 & https://mathildasanthropologyblog.wordpress.com /2008/06/14/the-domestication-of-the-goat-another-first-from-neolithic-turkey/

366. https://en.wikipedia.org/wiki/First_law_of_thermodynamics#CITEREFMandl1988

367. Atkins, P.W., de Paula, J. (2006). Atkins' Physical Chemistry, eighth edition, W.H. Freeman, New York, p. 78.

368. Trefil, James, Reading the Mind of God (New York: Anchor Books, 1989), p. 1.

369. Kragh, Helge (1999). Cosmology and Controversy: The Historical Development of Two Theories of the Universe. Princeton University Press.

370. https://biotech.law.lsu.edu/cphl/history/articles/pasteur.htm

371. Dahlstrom, Karl, The DNA of Scripture, World Pub. Co., Nashville, Tennessee, 2015, p. 23.

372. Ibid

373. https://answersingenesis.org/is-god-real/god-natural-law/

374. https://earthobservatory.nasa.gov/Features/OrbitsHistory/page2.php

375. Dahlstrom, Karl, The DNA of Scripture, World Pub. Co., Nashville, Tennessee, 2015, p. 24.

376. https://answersingenesis.org/is-god-real/god-natural-law/

377. http://www.thehensonhome.org/anthropic_principle.htm

378. Creation Magazine, Vol. 38 #2, 2016 CMI, pp. 18-19.

379. https://en.wikipedia.org/wiki/Matthew_Fontaine_Maury)

380. http://www.bible.ca/tracks/matthew-fontaine-maury-pathfinder-of-sea-ps8.htm

381. Tuchman, Barbara W. The First Salute: A View of the American Revolution New York: Ballantine Books, 1988. pp.221–222.

382. http://www.bible.ca/tracks/matthew-fontaine-maury-pathfinder-of-sea-ps8.htm

383. https://www.livescience.com/46292-hidden-ocean-locked-in-earth-mantle.htm

384. http://www.sciencemag.org/content/344/6189/1265

385. Carley, Tamara L., et.al., Iceland is not a magmatic analog for the Hadean: Evidence from the zircon record. Earth and Planetary Science Letters, 2014; 405: 85 DOI.

386. https://phys.org/news/2014-02-earth.html#jCp

387. www.amnh.org/explore/resource-collections/earth-inside-and-out/mapping-hot-springs-on-the-deep-ocean-floor/

388. http://www.gw.org/Springs.htm

389. http://barometerfair.com/history_of_the_barometer.html

390. Loria G, Vassura G. Opere di Evangelista Torricelli [Works of Evangelista Torricelli]. Faenza, Italy: G. Montanari, 1919, vol. III, p. 186.

391. http://www.quora.com/What-are-the-four-winds-in-the-Bible

392. https://www.britannica.com/science/unified-field-theory

393. https://en.wikipedia.org/wiki/Pangaea

394. https://en.wikipedia.org/wiki/Continental_drift

395. Steven M. Stanley (2004). "Mountain building". Earth system history (2nd ed.). Macmillan. p. 207. Robert J. Twiss; Eldridge M. Moores (1992). "Plate tectonic models of orogenic core zones". Structural Geology (2nd ed.). Macmillan. p. 493.

396. J. P. Davidson, W. E. Reed, and P. M. Davis, "The Rise and Fall of Mountain Ranges," in Exploring Earth: An Introduction to Physical Geology (Upper Saddle River, New Jersey: Prentice Hall, 1997), pp. 242–247.

397. Barrick, W.D. & Sigler, R., Noah's Flood and Its Geological Implications, Ed. T. Mortenson and T.H. Ury, Green Forest, Ark., Master books, 2008, pp. 251-281.

398. "Continental Margins: Their Rapid Formation during the Flood Runoff", Creation Magazine, Vol. 39, No. 4, 2017, Creation Ministries International, pp. 41-44.

399. https://www.cs.unc.edu/~plaisted/ce/flood.html

400. https://en.wikipedia.org/wiki/World_Turtle

401. https://en.wikipedia.org/wiki/Atlas_(mythology)

402. Gingerich, Owen (2004). The Book Nobody Read. London: William Heinemann, p. 248.

403. http://www.creationists.org/God-streched-out-the-universe-bible-verses.html

404. https://en.wikipedia.org/wiki/Metric_expansion_of_space

405. "Circle of the Earth", James S. Johnson, "Acts & Facts", ICR, Vol. 48, No. 5, p.21.

406. Demolishing Supposed Bible Contradictions, vol. 1, ed. Ken Ham, Green Forest, AR, Master Books, 2010, pp. 30-32.

407. http://www.columbia.edu/~vjd1/origins.htm

408. https://phys.org/news/2010-07-universe-big.html

409. https://www.physicsoftheuniverse.com/topics_bigbang_accelerating.html

410. http://lasp.colorado.edu/~bagenal/1010/SESSIONS/11.Formation.html

411. https://answersingenesis.org/astronomy/solar-system/origin-of-the-solar-system/

412. Humphreys, D.R. "The creation of planetary magnetic fields," Creation Research Society Quarterly, 25 (December 1984), pp. 140-149.

413. Ibid, Humphreys, pp. 140-149.

414. Dessler, A.J. "Does Uranus have a magnetic field?" Nature, 316 (16 January 1986), 174-175. Rossbacher, L. "Voyager II encounters Uranus," Episodes, 9 (March 1986), 17-21. Kerr, R.A. "The Neptune system in Voyager's afterglow," Science, 245 (29 September 1989), 1450-1451. Humphreys, D.R. "Good news from Neptune: The Voyager II Magnetic Measurements," Creation Research Society Quarterly (1990).

415. Humphreys, D. R. 2008. Mercury's magnetic field is young! Journal of Creation. 22 (3), pp. 8-9.

416. https://phys.org/news/2013-07-red-dwarf-stars-planetary.html

417. DeYoung, Donald B, Astronomy and the Bible: Questions and Answers, 2nd Edition (Grand Rapids, Michigan: Baker Books, 2000), p. 176.

418. White, O. R., L. Wallace, W. Livingston, and M. S. Giampapa. 2007. Sun-as-a-star spectrum variations 1974-2006. Astrophysical Journal. 657:1137-1149.

419. https://answersingenesis.org/astronomy/stars/counting-the-stars/

420. G. V. Konyukhov and A. A. Koroteev, "Study of generation and collection of monodisperse droplets flow in microgravity and vacuum," Journal Aerospace Engineering, Vol. 20, p. 124 (2007).

421. https://the-history-of-the-atom.wikispaces.com/Democritus

422. The Privileged Planet, Guillermo Gonzalez, Jay Richards, Regnery Publishing, Washington, D.C., 2004, pp. 48-62.

423. Earth's Magnetic Field provides vital Protection, www.esa.int, March 2012.

424. The Privileged Planet, Guillermo Gonzalez and Jay Richards, Regnery Publishing, Washington, D.C., 2004, p. 64.

425. "How Good is our Neighborhood", Mark Harwood, Creation Magazine, Vol. 39, No. 1, 2017, pp. 24-25.

426. The Privileged Planet, Guillermo Gonzalez and Jay Richards, Regnery, Washington, D.C., 2004, pp. 127-128.

427. "How Good is our Neighborhood", Mark Harwood, Creation Magazine, Vol. 39, No. 1, 2017, pp. 24-25.

428. The Privileged Planet, Guillermo Gonzalez and Jay Richards, Regnery Publishing, Washington, D.C., 2004, p. 4.

429. The Privileged Planet, Guillermo Gonzalez and Jay Richards, Regnery Publishing, Washington, D.C., 2004, p.10.

430. "How Good is our Neighborhood", Mark Harwood, Creation Magazine, Vol. 39, No. 1, 2017, pp. 24-25.

431. Sarfati, J. The Sun: Our Special Star, Creation Magazine, Vol. 22, No. 1, December, 1999, pp. 27 – 31.

432. The Privileged Planet, Guillermo Gonzalez and Jay Richards, Regnery Publishing, Washington, D.C., 2004, p. 152.

433. Ibid, pp. 144-151.

434. The Privileged Planet, Guillermo Gonzalez and Jay Richards, Regnery, Washington, D.C., 2004, pp. 293-310.

435. "How Good is our Neighborhood", Mark Harwood, Creation Magazine, Vol. 39, No. 1, 2017, pp. 25-26.

436. https://www.scientificamerican.com/article/how-fast-is-the-earth-mov/

437. https://yeshuaarmy.wordpress.com/2012/06/27/nasa-stars-and-science-in-the-book-of-job-reveal-your-hebrew-bible-is-accurate/

438. http://coldcasechristianity.com/2013/is-the-astronomy-in-the-book-of-job-scientifically-consistent/

439. http://thespiritscience.net/2015/06/15/nasa-discovers-planets-and-stars-give-off-music-this-is-what-it-sounds-like/

440. Nahin, P.J. (1992). "Maxwell's grand unification". Spectrum, IEEE. 29 (3), p. 45.

441. Ede, A., Cormack, L. B., A History of Science in Society: From the scientific revolution to the present, University of Toronto Press, 2012. Newton, I., Opticks, William Innys (ed.), 1730 (1704).

442. Thompson, Bert, A Study Course in Christian Evidences, Apologetics Press, 1992, p. 132.

443. Kleiss, Richard & Tina, A Closer Look at the Evidence, Search for the Truth, 2005, December 18 entry.

444. https://www.britannica.com/topic/steady-state-theory

445. https://www.cfa.harvard.edu/seuforum/faq.htm

446. "First Second of the Big Bang". How The Universe Works 3. 2014. Discovery Science.

447. Hubble, E.P., The 200-inch telescope and some problems it may solve, Publications of the Astronomical Society of the Pacific 59:153–167, 1947.

448. Anonymous, Quantized redshifts: what's going on here? Sky and Telescope 84(2):28–29, August, 1992. and Guthrie, B.N.G. and Napier, W.M., Evidence for redshift periodicity in nearby galaxies, Monthly Notices of the Royal Astronomical Society 253:533–544, 1991.

449. Huterer, D., "why is the Solar System cosmically aligned?", 2007, Astronomy Mag., 35(12), pp. 38-43.

450. Kenney, J. F. and Keeping, E. S. "Significant Figures." §1.5 in Mathematics of Statistics, Pt. 1, 3rd ed. Princeton, NJ: Van Nostrand, 1962, pp. 8-9.

451. https://www.hindawi.com/journals/janthro/2014/489757/

452. https://preachrr.wordpress.com/2010/08/18/noah%E2%80%99s-ship-building-wisdom/

453. According to "Lloyd's Register of Shipping" in the World Almanac, 1900.

454. http://www.icr.org/article/survival-noahs-ark/

455. https://en.wikipedia.org/wiki/Genesis_flood_narrative#cite_note-39

456. Seigworth, Gilbert R. (1980). "Bloodletting Over the Centuries". Red Gold, the Epic Study of Blood. PBS.

457. Wilford, John Noble (17 December 1996). "Geologists Link Black Sea Deluge To Farming's Rise". The New York Times.

458. https://www.calacademy.org/explore-science/how-many-species-on-earth

459. www.christiananswers.net/q-eden/edn-c013.html

460. Chaffey, Tim, "How could Noah's ark Survive the Storm?", Answers Magazine, July-August 2018, vol. 13, No. 4, pp. 54-55.

461. Chaffey, Tim, "How could Noah's ark Survive the Storm?", Answers Magazine, July-August 2018, vol. 13, No. 4, pp. 58-60.

462. Pierce, L., "The Large Ships of Antiquity", Creation 23(3), pp. 46-48,2000, also creation.com/large-ships

463. http://www.4angelspublications.com/articles/The_Soviet_Experiment.pdf

464. http://www.slate.com/articles/life/culturebox/2014/05/abolish_the_week_the_case_against_dividing_time_into_seven_day_periods.html

465. https://www.reddit.com/r/NoStupidQuestions/comments/2abkt3/is_the_7_day_week_universal/

466. https://www.huffingtonpost.com/2014/06/05/sweden-work-hours_n_5446579.html

467. http://joel.is/experimenting-with-a-7-day-work-week/

468. https://open.buffer.com/7-day-work-week-experiment-wisdom-day-rest/

469. https://www.cdc.gov/niosh/docs/2004-143/pdfs/2004-143.pdf

470. Helping Children Understand Genesis and the Dinosaurs, Living Word Pub., 1992, pp. 11-13 and Kleiss, Richard & Tina, "A Closer Look at the Evidence", Search for the Truth Ministry, 2005, October 16 entry.

471. https://www.mayoclinic.org/healthy-lifestyle/nutrition-and-healthy-eating/in-depth/alcohol/art-20044551

472. https://www.everydayhealth.com/emotional-health/connecting-dots.aspx

473. https://www.nytimes.com/2017/03/27/well/live/positive-thinking-may-improve-health-and-extend-life.html

474. www.universityofcalifornia.edu/news/article/4132

475. earlyamerica.com/review/2005_winter_spring/washingtons_death.htm (memoirs of Colonel Lear)

476. El Hamel, Chouki (2002). "'Race', slavery and Islam in Maghribi Mediterranean thought: the question of the Haratin in Morocco". The Journal of North African Studies. 7 (3): 29–52 [39–42]

477. https://en.wikipedia.org/wiki/Historical_race_concepts

478. https://en.wikipedia.org/wiki/Human_Genetic_Diversity:_Lewontin%27s_Fallacy

479. http://www.dailymail.co.uk/health/article-23308/Why-going-church-healthy.html

480. http://www.livescience.com/36053-church-goers-blood-pressure.html

481. http://www.independent.co.uk/life-style/health-and-families/health-news/going-to-church-has-a-positive-longterm-effect-on-mental-health-for-elderly-10445364.html

482. http://www.thecrimson.com/article/2006/10/23/churchgoing-correlated-with-better-health-a/

483. Strawbridge WJ, Cohen RD, Shema SJ, Kaplan GA. Frequent attendance at religious services and mortality over 28 years. Am J Public Health. 1997;87:957–961.

484. http://www.ncbi.nlm.nih.gov/pmc/articles/PMC1305900/

485. Harris RC, Dew MA, Lee A, Amaya M, Buches L, Reetz D, Coleman C. The role of religion in heart-transplant recipients' long-term health and well-being. Journal of Religion and Health. 1995;34(1):17–32.

486. http://www.berkeley.edu/news/media/releases/2002/03/26_faith.html

487. From the Cardiology Division, Medical Service, San Francisco General Medical Center, and the Department of Medicine, University of California,San Francisco and https://www.godandscience.org/apologetics/smj.pdf

488. http://www.ncbi.nlm.nih.gov/pubmed/10547166

489. http://abcnews.go.com/2020/story?id=132674

490. http://www.godsaidmansaid.com/printtopic.asp?ItemId=705

491. O'Laoire S (November 1997). "An experimental study of the effects of distant, intercessory prayer on self-esteem, anxiety, and depression". Alternative Therapies in Health and Medicine, Vol. 3 Issue 6, pp. 38–53.

492. Sicher, F; Targ, E; Moore D, 2nd; Smith, HS (December 1998). "A randomized double-blind study of the effect of distant healing in a population with advanced AIDS. Report of a small scale study". The Western journal of medicine. 169 (6): 356–63.

493. Leibovici L (2001). "Effects of remote, retroactive intercessory prayer on outcomes in patients with bloodstream infection: randomised controlled trial". BMJ. 323 (7327): 1450–1.

494. http://www.webmd.com/balance/features/can-prayer-heal?page=3

495. google – Daniel Benor MD 2001 191 distance healing.

496. http://www.nytimes.com/2006/03/31/health/31pray.html?pagewanted=all&_r=0)

497. http://www.industrytap.com/knowledge-doubling-every-12-months-soon-to-be-every-12-hours/3950

498. Linda Tischler, Google's Secret Weapon, Fast Company 100, (2005) p. 54.

499. Robert Jastrow, God and the Astronomers, chapter 6, "The Religion of Science" (New York: Reader's Library, Inc., 1992), p. 107.

500. A Scientist Caught Between Two Faiths: Interview With Robert Jastrow," Christianity Today, August 6, 1982.

501. https://todayinsci.com/QuotationsCategories/M_Cat/Mathematician-Quotations.htm

502. https://www.icr.org/article/wernher-von-braun-father-space-flight

503. https://creation.com/super-scientist-slams-societys-spiritual-sickness

504. http://creationwiki.org/John_Sanford

505. https://www.gotquestions.org/Pascals-wager.html

506. https://en.wikipedia.org/wiki/Aristotle

507. Aristotle, Metaphysics XII, 1072a.

508. Sachs, Joe. "Aristotle: Metaphysics". Internet Encyclopedia of Philosophy.

509. http://www.whitehorsemedia.com/articles/?d=134#.VZhiA8J0wW4

ABOUT THE AUTHOR

Scott Lane is a retired schoolteacher who spent 33 years teaching math and science on the secondary level in Texas public schools. He has earned four teaching certifications. He has both bachelors and master's degrees in education from Texas A&M University. He has spent over 35 years in the study of creation science and biblical apologetics. He has been conferred further certifications in the fields of biblical apologetics and creation science by the **International Association for Creation** (IAC).

He is married to his wife Brenda with three grown children and nine grandchildren. They all live in the San Antonio, Texas area. He is a deacon at Cibolo Valley Baptist Church.

He has been the President of the **San Antonio Bible Based Science Association** (SABBSA) for most of the last twenty years. This ministry has a weekly radio shows called **"Believing the Bible"** which delves into topics of biblical apologetics and creation science heard in twelve U.S. markets and 120 countries. Mr. Lane is one of the hosts of this program. A link to podcasts of this program, as well as a wealth of Mr. Lane's video seminars (including one covering the topics in this book), are available on SABBSA's website at **www. sabbsa.org** , as well as a host of other resources.

CPSIA information can be obtained
at www.ICGtesting.com
Printed in the USA
LVHW011343060322
712502LV00003B/3